江苏大学国家级一流专业"英语"专业建设成果
本教材受江苏大学留学本科生英文授课课程教材出版基金资助

A Brief History of Translation

翻译简史

主　编　李崇月　张　璘
编　委　（按姓氏音序排列）
　　　　戴文静　冯瑞贞　姚　琴
　　　　曾景婷　张明权　张伟华

东南大学出版社
SOUTHEAST UNIVERSITY PRESS
·南京·

内容提要

本书从中国学者的视角,以翻译文本类型(如宗教、科技、文学、社科等)和翻译的方向(译入、译出)为经,以历史上有影响的翻译事件和翻译思想为纬,勾勒中外翻译实践和翻译思想的发展脉络,在中外参照对比中突出中国丰富的翻译实践及其对中国文化发展的贡献。本书从总体框架设计、具体史料选择到对翻译史实的解读等都做到了宏观与微观结合、史实与史识相融,囊括了翻译史的主要内容,为我国翻译史的研究和教学提供了新视角。

图书在版编目(CIP)数据

翻译简史 / 李崇月,张璘主编. — 南京:东南大学出版社,2024.8
ISBN 978-7-5766-1391-9

Ⅰ.①翻… Ⅱ.①李… ②张… Ⅲ.①翻译-语言学史 Ⅳ.①H059-09

中国国家版本馆 CIP 数据核字(2024)第 081671 号

责任编辑:刘　坚(liu-jian@seu.edu.cn)　　责任校对:周　菊
封面设计:王　玥　　责任印制:周荣虎

翻 译 简 史　Fanyi Jianshi

主　　编	李崇月　张　璘
出版发行	东南大学出版社
出 版 人	白云飞
社　　址	南京市四牌楼 2 号(邮编:210096　电话:025 - 83793330)
经　　销	全国各地新华书店
印　　刷	广东虎彩云印刷有限公司
开　　本	787mm×1092mm　1/16
印　　张	20
字　　数	580 千
版　　次	2024 年 8 月第 1 版
印　　次	2024 年 8 月第 1 次印刷
书　　号	ISBN 978-7-5766-1391-9
定　　价	68.00 元

本社图书若有印装质量问题,请直接与营销部调换。电话(传真):025 - 83791830

江苏大学国家级一流专业"英语"专业建设成果出版编委会

总 主 编：李崇月
编委会成员：张明平　王　蕾
　　　　　　李加军　李　霞

总 序
FOREWORD

江苏大学是2001年8月经教育部批准,由原江苏理工大学、镇江医学院、镇江师范专科学校合并组建的重点综合性大学,是江苏省人民政府和教育部、农业农村部共建高校,也是首批江苏省高水平大学建设高校。

江苏大学英语专业的起源可追溯到1958年原镇江师范专科学校开设的英语教育(专科)专业和原江苏工学院1984年开设的英语师资班。历经几十年的建设,以英语语种为主体的外国语言文学学科已获得了长足的发展:2003年获批"外国语言学及应用语言学"二级学科硕士学位点,2018年获批"外国语言文学"一级学科硕士学位点,2021年获批"MTI英语笔译"专业硕士学位点;在近三年(2020、2021、2022)"软科中国最好学科排名"中,江苏大学外国语言文学学科稳居江苏省内高校前六位;得益于外国语言文学学科的有力支撑,近年来,江苏大学英语专业"四级"和"八级"一次性通过率远超全国平均水平;近三年来,本科毕业生考研录取率达35%;毕业生专业教学满意度在全校30多个文管类专业中连续多年位居前列;英语专业特色鲜明,专业建设成绩显著,2021年获批"国家级一流专业建设点"。

目前,江苏大学英语专业师资力量雄厚。近30位教师中,有教授10人、副教授10人。师资队伍中除了有多位英语语言文学博士外,还有传播学博士、外交学博士和逻辑学博士各1人。师资结构有力支撑了英语专业"国际事务与沟通"特色方向的建设。在新文科建设背景下,英语专业教师结合自己的教学及研究专长,紧扣一流专业建设目标,在教师发展研究、课程教材资源开发、教育教学研究等方面取得了一系列成果,现以专著或教材的形式由东南大学出版社出版。

《社会文化理论视角下高校英语教师学习叙事案例研究》（李霞著）基于社会文化理论，对高校英语教师学习经历、学习过程及学习影响因素进行深入系统的探讨，为推动高校英语教师发展提供参考和建议。该研究成果有助于增进学界对高校英语教师学习的了解，激发教师反思自身学习，优化教学实践，实现科学、高效、持久的专业发展，从而进一步推进一流本科英语专业内涵建设及人才培养的高质量发展。

英语文学教材《文学与科学：新文科英语文学》（毛卫强主编）吸纳英语文学跨学科研究方面的成果，在介绍英语文学如何表征、传播甚至参与建构自然科学领域的研究及发现的同时，结合第一手文献资料和具体案例，培养英语专业学生利用自然科学领域相关知识来批判性解读英语文学作品的能力，发展学生的跨学科意识，拓展学生的科学人文素养。

英文教材《翻译简史》（李崇月、张璘主编）从中国学者的视角，以翻译文本类型（如宗教、科技、文学、社科等）和翻译的方向（译入、译出）为经，以历史上有影响的翻译事件和翻译思想为纬，勾勒中外翻译实践和翻译思想的发展脉络，在中外参照对比中突出中国丰富的翻译实践及其对中国文化发展的贡献。教材从总体框架设计、具体史料选择及对翻译事实的解读上都做到了宏观与微观结合、史实与史识相融，囊括了翻译史的主要内容，为我国翻译史的研究和教学提供了新视角。

《世界经典寓言童话故事选读》（叶富莲编著）的选材来自世界经典寓言童话作家的作品，教材从题材、人物、结构、修辞、主题、语言、同类比较等方面对寓言和童话进行了系统化的说明和阐释，各单元包括文本、注解、练习、讨论和写作等内容。本教材一方面可以提高英语专业学生的语言实践能力，另一方面可以引导学生利用相关语言材料进行英语语言教学的模拟实践。

《如何清晰、理性地思维：逻辑与批判性思维能力培养教程》（闫林琼编著）提供了适合中国高校尤其是理工科院校英语专业学生、融合思政要素并且难易度适中的逻辑与批判性思维能力培养教材。教材包括英语专业学生逻辑与批判性思维能力培养的紧迫性,如何提问,如何论证,如何在多种课程教学中培养逻辑与批判性思维能力等内容,有利于弥补英语专业学生逻辑思辨能力的不足。

《中国参与联合国大会人权议程设置的论辩话语研究》(候璐莎著)从中国参与联合国大会人权治理进程的不同阶段出发,考察中国参与联合国大会人权议程设置多边谈判之中影响论辩策略的因素,阐明了中国运用论辩策略来提高谈判说服力、议程设置能力以及国际人权话语权的研究路径。本书有助于培养英语专业学生的批判性思维、国际沟通与应变能力,增强学生用英语合理且有效地表达自己观点的论辩与谈判能力,有助于使其成为具有全球视野、跨文化交际能力的一专多能复合型英语人才。

《镇江文化外宣》(万雪梅编著)体现英语一流专业建设的地方特色,致力于讲好江苏大学所在地镇江的故事。本书提炼镇江文化的精神标识和精髓,从镇江历史、山水、文物、教育、文学、艺术、科技、饮食、对外人文交流等方面展开,呈现可信、可爱、可敬的镇江形象,助推中华文化更好地走向世界。

《唐宋诗撷英新译》(万雪梅、弗雷德里克·特纳编译)选译了李白、杜甫、王维、范仲淹、苏轼等53位唐宋诗人的148首诗作。所选作品皆为唐宋诗中的经典之作,既有哲学意蕴,又有诗学之美。且诗中体现的儒释道情感与精神能够激发起读者和译者的共鸣,对中华优秀传统文化的阐释和传播颇有裨益。

《学术英语能力及其标准建设研究》(钟兰凤编著)收录学术论文13篇,旨在通过对英文学术话语进行分析,兼采用实验法和调查法,探讨学术英语能力标准建设的主要构件:学术英语能力表现研究、学术英语能力培养的路径及影响因素、学术英语能力标准建设的基本路径和设计原则。本研究成果可以直接应用于英语专业必修课"英语学术论文写作"的课程内容改革及教学方法改革。

以上是即将出版的英语专业建设成果,这些成果为江苏大学国家级一流专业"英语"的专业建设作出了极大贡献。我代表江苏大学外国语学院衷心感谢付出辛勤劳动的、从事英语专业教学的同事们,也要感谢教育部外国语言文学类专业教学指导委员会和英语专业教学指导分委员会多位委员长期以来对江苏大学英语专业建设的关心和指导,感谢江苏大学校领导和教务处对英语专业建设的关心和支持,感谢东南大学出版社刘坚老师编辑团队的默默付出。

江苏大学国家级一流专业"英语"专业点建设负责人
李崇月
2023 年 7 月 1 日

序 1 PREFACE

宏观微观结合　史实史识相融

中外翻译活动已经存在了数千年,翻译推动了文字的发展、知识的传播、文化的交流,它是全球化的重要助推器。在此过程中,翻译教育对翻译的发展功不可没。目前,我国教育从翻译专业本科、翻译硕士到翻译博士层次齐全,发展到了一个全新的阶段。而在翻译教育中,翻译史是一门必备的课程,它有利于我们了解翻译的发生与发展,探求社会文化与译者群体和个体之间的关系。

与翻译史相关的内容大致可以分为两个方面:翻译史与翻译史研究。翻译史研究涉及的领域众多,在此不赘述。这里,我们重点谈谈与翻译史相关的问题。翻译史的编写,大致可分为通史、断代史和专题史。通史方面,目前较多以国别或地域翻译通史的方式呈现,如马祖毅等的《中国翻译通史》,谭载喜的《西方翻译简史》等;断代史则截取某一历史时期进行研究,如王秉钦、王颉的《20世纪中国翻译思想史》;专题史则主要关注某一主题,如李亚舒、黎难秋的《中国科学翻译史》,孟昭毅、李载道的《中国翻译文学史》等。翻译史的书写还可将断代与主题结合,如王建开的《五四以来我国英美文学作品译介史(1919—1949)》等。

无论是通史、断代史还是专题史,其撰写需要处理好两对关系:宏观与微观、史实与史识。

所谓宏观,主要指阐述对象的全面性。我们知道,无论哪种类型的"史",都有特定的所指,因此在撰写中应尽可能囊括其主要内容,这是翻译史撰写的基本要求,我们可以称之为翻译史撰写的"宏观结构"。所谓微观,则指在具体阐述中,对某一阶段的重大翻译事件、重要译者及译本的描写,我们可以称之为翻译史撰写的"微观结构"。

在安排好翻译史撰写的"宏观结构"和"微观结构"的同时,还需处理好"史实"与"史识"的关系。这里的"实"指"fact"。在翻译史的撰写中,我们会面对各类信息,因此这里的"实"有两方面的含义:一是翻译史上的各类事实,二是翻译史作者依据编写方针据"实"选择的内容,这种选择决定了各类翻译史著作的内容的多少以及篇幅的大小。对各类翻译事实的选择是一项基本工作,但一部翻译史的写作,不仅仅是罗列或陈述各类现象,还需对之进行学理阐释,也就是不仅要说明是什么,还需要解释为什么,这就是"史识"(explanation)。

上面的宏观与微观侧重翻译史内容的范围的择选,史实与史识则强调对史料的描述与分析的结合。这两对关系处理恰当与否,决定了一部翻译史著作的质量的高低。

最近收到江苏大学李崇月教授牵头编写的《翻译简史》,拜读下来,认为本书从总体框架设计、具体史料选择及对翻译事实的解读上都很好地做到了宏观与微观结合、史实与史识相融。

从"宏观结构"看,本教材分为十章,涉及中西翻译发展时期、佛经及圣经在中国的译介、圣经在西方的译介、古希腊经典在欧洲的译介、中国的科技翻译、西方的科技翻译、中国典籍在西方的译介与传播、西方文学经典在中国的译介、西方非文学经典在中国的译介、翻译对中国文化的影响。由之可以看出,本教材囊括了翻译史的主要内容,尤其适用教材的使用者。

从"微观结构"看,本教材的各章都精选了相关主题下的主要内容,如第1章包含以下部分:1.1 Major Historical Stages of Translation in China, 1.1.1 From the Earliest Times to the Reign of Emperor Huan of Eastern Han, 1.1.2 Buddhist Translation from Emperor Huan of Eastern Han Dynasty to Song Dynasty (from 147 to 1279), 1.1.3 Translation of Christianity and Western Science since the 16th Century, 1.1.4 From the Opium War to the Founding of P. R. China, 1.1.5 Translation after the Founding of P. R. China; 1.2 Major Historical Stages of Translation in the West, 1.2.1 The First Stage: Translation in Ancient Times, 1.2.2 The Second Stage: Translation in the Middle Ages, 1.2.3 The Third Stage:

Translation during Renaissance, 1.2.4 The Fourth Stage: Translation in Modern Times (17th—19th Centuries), 1.2.5 The Fifth Stage: Modern Translation (1900—1945)。

从此处列出的目录可以看出,本章内容丰富、层次分明,用较小的篇幅对中国和西方翻译的发展史进行了简明扼要的勾勒。

从史实与史识融合的角度看,本教材也有不少精彩之处,如第7章在对《诗经》的外译进行较为系统的介绍后,作者说 In conclusion, the 19th century translators of *The Book of Songs* abandoned the influence of theology in favor of realness, seeking to unveil the original features of this ancient poetry collection. Sinologists reached a consensus on its literary and cultural values, and began to explore its ontology, literature and art, language and culture, and social folklore. Such endeavors mark the maturity of the Western studies on *The Book of Songs*.

The 20th century witnessed a deepening of the study of *The Book of Songs* in the West, characterized by a profound artistic analysis, ideological and cultural connotation, and the application of new methodologies. Numerous monographs were written on the styles, rhythms, metaphors and images of *The Book of Songs*. Almost all Western translations during this period were accompanied by comprehensive and theoretical reviews, some of which were research studies.

这两段话,既是对19世纪《诗经》译介的总结,也是对20世纪《诗经》译介的概述,其中融入了学界研究的精华和作者自己的理解。

当然,本教材的编写还有不少值得肯定之处,限于篇幅,不再赘述。概而言之,《翻译简史》是一部内容全面、层次清楚、适用性强的教材,值得推荐。

北京航空航天大学外国语学院
二级教授、翻译学博士生导师
文 军
2022年12月10日

序 2
PREFACE

The Importance of Translation History

As a translation student, many years ago, I was terribly interested in how to translate. By that, I had in mind the procedures of translation, what sorts of strategies I could use in response to challenges in the text, what sorts of resources to use to help me solve problems and so on. All of this should sound familiar to translation students. These aspects of translation are of course important and feel like the tangible aspects of translation training. Theory and history feel less straightforwardly useful and, yet, as I spend more time thinking about translation, I find both, and particularly history, more interesting and useful than ever before. Both in terms of getting me to think about how to translate in practice and thinking about translation might and could be, beyond what Naoki Sakai calls the current regime of translation[1]. That is, the current understanding of translation as the recreation of a text from one distinct language in another distinct language with the goal of the second text to be a usable stand-in for the first text. Translation history shows that there are other ways of translating, including more literal methods as well as freer renditions, and that what we consider a language is also a somewhat shifting terrain—this is particularly complex in relation to minoritized languages like Scots that are more or less

---

[1] Naoki Sakai, *Translation and Subjectivity: On Japan and Cultural Nationalism* (Minneapolis: University of Minnesota Press, 1997).

intelligible to speakers of majority languages such as English. Yet there is a long and worthy tradition of translation into Scots, which differs from the history of translation into English[①].

Translation theory is now a well-established field and a well-established part of translation programmes. Students are used to working their way through introductory texts such as Jeremy Munday's *Introducing Translation Studies* or Susan Bassnett's *Translation Studies* which give an overview of the whole field[②]. These texts often introduce students to ideas in translation studies such as the connection between language and culture, as theorised by Edward Sapir and Benjamin Whorf, or ideas of equivalence, which have been hotly debated in work on translation since Eugene Nida and J. C. Catford's work in the 1960s, and which remain live issues today. More advanced students might have taken on Anthony Pym's more theoretical *Exploring Translation Theories*, which explores how various schools of thought in translation studies have approached translation and equivalence, from more linguistic approaches of Nida and Catford, to the skopos theory and functionalist approaches to translation by scholars such as Hans Vermeer and Christiane Nord, through descriptive translation studies as practised by Gideon Toury among others[③]. Pym also takes in notions such as uncertainty, localisation and cultural translation (in Homi Bhabha's formulation). Other key approaches are also often discussed, such as the cultural turn, as exemplified by Susan Bassnett and Andre Lefevere, as well as postcolonial translation studies (for example, Eric Cheyfitz, Vicente Rafael, Tejaswini Niranjana) and feminist translation studies (for example, Sherry Simon, Luise von Flotow, and more recently scholars such as Olga Castro and Emek Ergun)[④]. As a translation student,

---

① John Corbett, *Written in the Language of Scottish Nation: A History of Literary Translation into Scots* (Cleveland: Multilingual Matters, 1998).

② Jeremy Munday, *Introducing Translation Studies: Theories and Applications*, 3rd edition (London: Routledge, 2012); Susan Bassnett, *Translation Studies*, 4th edition (London: Routledge, 2013).

③ Anthony Pym, *Exploring Translation Theories*, 2nd edition (London: Routledge, 2014).

④ Jeremy Munday, *Introducing Translation Studies: Theories and Applications*, 3rd edition (London: Routledge, 2012), pp. 191–214.

I remember first working my way through some of the writings in Lawrence Venuti's *The Translation Studies Reader*[1]. These were among the first primary texts of translation scholarship that I had read; some made sense instantly, others remained somewhat unclear. After reading Walter Benjamin's 'The Task of the Translator' countless times in different translations, I'm still not sure I understand it, or ever will[2]. Benjamin's "lovely little essay" (as I once heard it described at a conference) was one of the handful texts in Venuti's book that came from a time before translation studies existed as a discipline, though of course people have been writing about translation for thousands of years[3]. These earlier writings suggested some interesting different ways of thinking about translation, as well as ideas that have influenced current understandings of translation in Europe and North and South America as much as in Asia. Munday also discusses the history of translation theory, putting together all writers before the twentieth century in a single chapter[4]. In some ways it is interesting to see Saint Jerome next to discussion of Buddhist translation practices (as will also happen in this book) and Étienne Dolet next to Alexander Tytler and Friedrich Schleiermacher. I was reminded of the vibrancy of these ideas and their continuing influence on current thought when reading a recent speculative fiction novel by R. F. Kuang, *Babel*[5]. The novel posits a steampunk alternative past where language magic is activated by the difference in meanings between cognates (for example, *wúxíng* in Chinese and invisible in English)[6]. In this alternative past, the department of

---

[1] Lawrence Venuti, *The Translation Studies Reader*, 3rd edition (London: Routledge, 2012).

[2] Walter Benjamin, 'The Translator's Task', translated by Steven Rendall, in *The Translation Studies Reader*, 3rd edition, ed. by Lawrence Venuti (London: Routledge, 2012), pp. 75-83. The title in the body text, 'The Task of the Translator', is the canonical title used by Harry Zohn in his translation in *Illuminations*. Walter Benjamin, 'The Task of the Translator', in *Illuminations*, translated by Harry Zohn (London: Pimlico, 1999), pp. 70-82.

[3] For primary texts in the European tradition, see Douglas Robinson (ed.), *Western Translation Theory from Herodotus to Nietzsche* (Manchester: St Jerome, 1997). For primary texts in the Chinese tradition, see Martha Pui Yiu Cheung (ed.), *An Anthology of Chinese Discourse on Translation: Vol. 1: From Earliest Times to the Buddhist Project* (Manchester: St Jerome, 2006).

[4] Jeremy Munday, *Introducing Translation Studies: Theories and Applications*, 3rd edition (London: Routledge, 2012), pp. 28-56.

[5] R. F. Kuang, *Babel: An Arcane History* (London: Harper Voyager, 2022).

[6] R. F. Kuang, *Babel: An Arcane History* (London: Harper Voyager, 2022), p. 66.

translation at the University of Oxford has significant power. We see the protagonists learn about translation, both in theory and practice, as they advance through their undergraduate years. While the novel offers an interesting reflection on colonialism and the relationship between centre and periphery, what excited me as a translation scholar was seeing their discussions of Schleiermacher and Tytler and realising that these scholars—who I probably had not read since I was last a student—still had interesting and useful things to say about translation today.

The history of translation is, to some extent, then, the history of translation theory, and it is always not possible to understand a translation from a different period without first understanding the theories of translation that influenced the production of that translation. One of my classes when I was a master's student was about case studies of translation and was, essentially, an approach to the history of translation through specific texts. I remember being amazed at the way in which Simone de Beauvoir's *Le deuxième sexe* had been altered in translation in English, with some parts totally removed [1]. Why would a translator do that? I found, delving more into the history of translation, that such alterations in translation were not all that uncommon. Terry Hale wrote about translations in the late Victorian period that blurred the boundaries between adaptation and translation and which would look nothing like the translations we encounter today as translations[2]. Going further back, medieval translations before printing would often include commentaries and various forms of reworking, offering a very different understanding of translation to the current, equivalence-focused regime of translation[3]. This *longue durée* history of translation offers a whole world of different experiences and different thinking about

---

[1] Margaret A. Simons, 'The silencing of Simone de Beauvoir: Guess what's missing from *The Second Sex*', *Women's Studies International Forum*, 1983,6(5):559-564.

[2] Terry Hale, 'The Imaginary Quay from Waterloo Bridge to London Bridge: Translation, Adaptation and Genre' in *Translating French Literature and Film* II, ed. by Myriam Salama-Carr (Amsterdam: Rodopi, 2000), pp. 219-238.

[3] Rita Copeland, *Rhetoric, Hermeneutics, and Translation in the Middle Ages* (Cambridge: Cambridge University Press, 1991).

translation; one of the benefits of the current book is to allow an overview of translation history in China and in Europe.

Translation history offered me, as a student, different ways of doing translation that were not just theoretical possibilities, but visible and tangible: someone had translated this way before. This might be an idiosyncratic way of understanding translation history—and nowadays I might approach it differently—but that was the immediate effect as a student. Translation history has developed a lot since I was an undergraduate, becoming a more distinct part of translation studies[①]. A slew of publications, including Pym's *Method in Translation History*,[②] have helped to shore up and develop the understanding of translation history. Special issues of *Translation Studies* and *The Translator* from the early 2010s provided some more metatheoretical reflections on history in translation studies and the history of translation[③]. More recently, the *Routledge Handbook of Translation History* collects many key scholars' works in the field to provide a single reference point in the field, demonstrating the importance of history to translation studies and helping to consolidate the discipline[④]. It seems, translation history is more popular and more accessible to students than ever before. This brings us back to the book you are holding in your hands.

This is a book of translation history which gives an overview of the various practices of translation in China and in the West over time. It touches on religious translation, scientific translation and the translation of literary classics before concluding with the importance of translation for Chinese culture. This sort of overview gives you the chance to see what happened, when, who the important agents were, what the key texts are;

---

① Chris Rundle, 'Historiography' in *The Routledge Encyclopedia of Translation Studies*, 3rd edition, ed. by Mona Baker and Gabriela Saldanha (London: Routledge, 2020), pp. 232-237.
② Anthony Pym, *Method in Translation History* (Manchester: St Jerome, 1998).
③ Carol O'Sullivan, *Rethinking Methods in Translation History*, Special issue of *Translation Studies*, 2012, 5 (2); Christopher Rundle, *Theory and Methodologies of Translation History*, Special issue of *The Translator*, 2014, 20(1).
④ Christopher Rundle, *The Routledge Handbook of Translation History* (London: Routledge, 2021).

in other words, to get a sense of the important places, people and texts of translation history. It does so in a comparative framework, joining together Western (primarily European) histories and the history of translation in China. These are not entirely separate, however, as all of the chapters address the intercultural contact between China and European cultures in some forms or other, leading to a sort of *histoire croisée* (crossed history) of translation that explores the mutual and ongoing influence of European and Chinese cultures[①].

The first chapter reviews the historical stages of translation in China and the West, moving from antiquity to the present day, through periodisations that apply to each culture. That is, for China, from ancient times to Eastern Han Dynasty and Song Dynasty, from the Opium War to the Founding of P. R. China, and post-1949 China. For the West, from antiquity to the middle ages, the Renaissance, the 17th—19th centuries and 1900—1945. Importantly, the Western section includes works from Russia, which are often left out of these overviews. This chapter serves as an introduction to the wider works and gives the reader chances to understand the evolution of translation practices over the long duration.

Chapters 2 and 3 explore the translation of religious scriptures. The first of these two chapters focuses on Buddhist scriptures and the Christian *Bible* in China. This juxtaposition of an Eastern and a Western religion allows the reader to understand the changing roles of religion in China as well as the evolution of translation practices. Buddhist translation is among the older translation practices in China, dating back to Eastern Han Dynasty (25—220). This chapter covers a thousand years of history, from that dynasty to Song Dynasty (960—1279). The *Bible* was introduced much later in China, though Nestorian Christianity was first introduced in China in Tang Dynasty (7th century). The Roman Catholic church sent

---

① On *histoire croisée*, see Michael Werner and Bénédicte Zimmerman, 'Beyond Comparison: Histoire Croisée and the challenge of reflexivity', *History and Theory*, 45:1 (2006), 30–50.

missionaries to the court of Kubla Khan in 1245, and there follows a history of multiple attempts to introduce the *Bible* to China. The history of *Bible* translation in Europe is somewhat different, as it closely relates to the history of the church and the wider history of the continent.

Chapters 4 and 5 deal with scientific translation. The translation of science in China is said to begin in the second century, with the introduction of scientific knowledge from India. More knowledge came from the Arabic speaking countries, starting from the early Song Dynasty. Translation of science in the late Ming and early Qing dynasties took more European sources, often related to Christian missionary work. In the late Qing and early twentieth century, more translation came from European sources in order to understand Western technologies. In contrast, early scientific translation in the West brought knowledge from Egypt, and from Greece to Rome. In the Middle Ages, much ancient knowledge was translated into Arabic, and then from Arabic into Latin. Later, European translators translated both the classics and their contemporaries. Due to the increasing prominence of vernacular languages, works were not only translated into Latin but also those vernaculars so that more people could access them.

Chapters 6, 7 and 8 focus on the translation of ancient greek classics in Europe, before moving on to the Chinese classics in Europe and finally the Western literary classics in China. In chapter 6, we read about the ways in which literary translation took place in ancient Rome, featuring such well known translators and writers such as Cicero, Horace, Jerome and Augustine. There we see the translation from classical languages to the vernaculars in the Renaissance, following a similar pattern to the translation of scientific works. The chapter then looks at translation in Britain, France and Germany in the early modern period. Again, the discussion is focused around significant translators and their works. Chapter 7 focuses on how Chinese classics were translated in Europe. Changing the focus from translators, this chapter analyses the translation histories of important Chinese works such as *The Analects of Confucius*, *The Tao Te*

Ching and novels such as *The Dream of Red Mansion* and *The Water Margin*. Here we see Christian missionaries like Matteo Ricci try to introduce Confucianism to the West, and the translation of Taoist classics and Chinese novels. Chapter 8 first discusses the translation of English-language literatures, including poetry, fiction and drama, before moving onto Russian, French and German literature. Chapter 9 follows on chapter 8 by focusing on what we would now call social sciences and how they were translated from European languages to Chinese. These show the continuing dialogues between China and the West, highlighted by the stories of scholar translators such as Yan Fu.

Chapter 10 draws back from the specific histories of translation in China and the West to focus on the influence of translation on Chinese culture. This takes in the considerable influence of Buddhism on the modern Chinese language and literature, the influence of Christian missionaries and the connection of New Culture Movement and translation. Like the other chapters in this book, it demonstrates the importance of encounters between China and the rest of the world, highlighting the interconnections between cultures that extend far beyond the current age of globalisation.

Overall, this book shows us why translation can be an important entry point to understanding history. It will not only be of interest for people to study translation, especially between Chinese and European languages, but also for people to have interest in the ongoing dialogues between China and the rest of the world.

Dr Jonathan Evans
Senior Lecturer in Translation Studies
University of Glasgow. Jonathan. E. Evans@glasgow. ac. uk
January 27th, 2023

目 录 CONTENTS

Chapter 1　Historical Stages of Translation in China and the West 001

  1.1　Major Historical Stages of Translation in China 001

    1.1.1　From the Earliest Times to the Reign of Emperor Huan of Eastern Han 003

    1.1.2　Buddhist Translation from Emperor Huan of Eastern Han Dynasty to Song Dynasty (from 147 to 1279) 005

    1.1.3　Translation of Christianity and Western Science since the 16th Century 005

    1.1.4　From the Opium War to the Founding of P. R. China 007

    1.1.5　Translation after the Founding of P. R. China 013

  1.2　Major Historical Stages of Translation in the West 018

    1.2.1　The First Stage: Translation in Ancient Times 019

    1.2.2　The Second Stage: Translation in the Middle Ages 023

    1.2.3　The Third Stage: Translation during Renaissance 027

    1.2.4　The Fourth Stage: Translation in Modern Times (17th—19th Centuries) 031

    1.2.5　The Fifth Stage: Modern Translation (1900—1945) 040

  Questions for discussion 044

  References 044

Chapter 2 *Bible* Translation in the West 046

    2.1   Early *Bible* Translation and Dissemination of Christianity 046

        2.1.1   *The Septuagint* 046

        2.1.2   *The Vulgate* 047

    2.2   Religious Reformation and *Bible* Translation 048

    2.3   English Versions of the *Bible* 051

    Questions for discussion 055

    References 055

Chapter 3 Buddhist Scriptures and *Bible* Translation in China 056

    3.1   Buddha and Buddhism 056

    3.2   First Introduction of Buddhism to China 057

    3.3   Three Phases of Buddhist Translation 057

        3.3.1   The First Phase: Eastern Han Dynasty and Three Kingdoms Period (c. 148—265) 058

        3.3.2   The Second Phase: Jin Dynasty and the Northern and Southern Dynasties (c. 265—589) 061

        3.3.3   The Third Phase: Sui, Tang, and Northern Song Dynasties (c. 589—1100) 066

    3.4   *Bible* Translation in China 071

    Questions for discussion 077

    References 078

Chapter 4 Translation of Ancient Greek Classics in Europe 079

    4.1   Latin Translation of Ancient Greek Classics in Ancient Rome 080

    4.2   Translation of Ancient Greek and Rome Classics in Renaissance 087

        4.2.1   Translation in Germany 088

        4.2.2   Translation in France 096

       4.2.3 Translation in Britain ········· 099

  4.3 Literary and Philosophical Translation in European Countries ······ 105

       4.3.1 French Translation and Batteux ········· 108

       4.3.2 German Translation and Schleiermacher, Humboldt ······ 111

       4.3.3 British Translation and Dryden, Tytler ········· 115

  Questions for discussion ········· 118

  References ········· 118

Chapter 5 Scientific Translation in China ········· 120

  5.1 Scientific Translation in Ancient China ········· 120

       5.1.1 Scientific Translation before Ming Dynasty ········· 120

       5.1.2 Scientific Translation in the Late Ming and Early Qing Dynasties ········· 121

  5.2 Scientific Translation in the Late Qing Dynasty and Early Republic of China ········· 123

       5.2.1 The Pioneers ········· 123

       5.2.2 Institutions ········· 124

       5.2.3 Prominent Translators ········· 125

  5.3 Scientific Translation since the May 4th Movement ········· 127

       5.3.1 Before 1949 ········· 127

       5.3.2 After 1949 ········· 128

  Questions for discussion ········· 129

  References ········· 129

Chapter 6 Scientific Translation in the West ········· 130

  6.1 Scientific Translation in Ancient Greece and Rome ········· 130

  6.2 Scientific Translation of Arabic Literature in the Middle Ages ······ 133

       6.2.1 The School of Translators of Baghdad ········· 133

  6.2.2 The School of Translators of Toledo ················ 136

 6.3 Scientific Translation during the Renaissance and the Age of Reason ······ 137

 Questions for discussion ················ 139

 References ················ 139

Chapter 7 Translation and Circulation of Chinese Classics in the West ······ 140

 7.1 Translation and Circulation of *The Analects of Confucius* in the West
  ················ 140

 7.2 Translation and Circulation of *Tao Te Ching* and *Chuangtse* in the West
  ················ 145

 7.3 Translation and Circulation of "Four Masterpieces" in the West ············ 148

 7.4 Translation and Circulation of Classical Poems in the West ················ 163

 Questions for discussion ················ 168

 References ················ 168

Chapter 8 Translation of Western Literary Classics in China ················ 169

 8.1 English and American Literary Classics ················ 169

  8.1.1 Translation of Poetry ················ 170

  8.1.2 Translation of Fiction ················ 171

  8.1.3 Translation of Drama ················ 180

 8.2 Russian Literary Classics ················ 182

  8.2.1 Translation of Poetry ················ 182

  8.2.2 Translation of Fiction ················ 184

  8.2.3 Translation of Drama ················ 191

 8.3 French Literary Classics ················ 192

  8.3.1 Translation of Poetry ················ 192

  8.3.2 Translation of Fiction ················ 193

  8.3.3 Translation of Drama ················ 200

8.4　German Literary Classics ·· 201

    8.4.1　Translation of Poetry ·· 201

    8.4.2　Translation of Fiction ·· 203

    8.4.3　Translation of Drama ·· 203

Questions for discussion ·· 204

References ··· 204

Chapter 9　Chinese Translation of Western Non-literary Classic Works ······ 205

9.1　Chinese Translation of Western Classic Works in Politics ················ 207

    9.1.1　Chinese Translators of Western Classic Works in Politics in the Ming and Qing Dynasties ·· 207

    9.1.2　Chinese Translators of Western Classic Works in Politics after the May 4th Movement ·· 214

    9.1.3　Characteristics of the Translation of Political Works ············· 218

9.2　Chinese Translation of Western Classic Works in Philosophy ············ 221

    9.2.1　Chinese Translation of Western Classic Works in Philosophy ······ 221

    9.2.2　Characteristics of the Translation of Philosophical Works ········· 233

9.3　Chinese Translation of Western Classic Works in Law ···················· 235

    9.3.1　The Historical Development of Legal Translation in China ········ 235

    9.3.2　Prerequisites of a Successful Translator of Legal Documents ······ 239

9.4　Chinese Translation of Other Western Non-literary Classic Works ········· 240

    9.4.1　Chinese Translators of Other Western Non-literary Classic Works ··· 240

    9.4.2　Characteristics of the Translation of Western Non-literary Classic Works ··· 240

Questions for discussion ·· 242

References ··· 243

Chapter 10　The Influence of Translation on Chinese Culture ················ 244

 10.1　Buddhist Translation's Influence on Modern Chinese Literature and Language ·· 244

  10.1.1　Buddhist Translation's Influence on Modern Chinese Literature ·· 247

  10.1.2　Buddhist Translation's Influence on Modern Chinese Language ·· 254

 10.2　The Influence of Missionaries' Translation in the Late Ming and Early Qing Dynasties in China ··· 260

  10.2.1　On Ideology ·· 261

  10.2.2　On Science and Technology ························· 265

  10.2.3　On Chinese Language ································· 268

  10.2.4　On Education ·· 270

 10.3　Relationship between Translation and China's New Culture Movement ·· 273

  10.3.1　Translation and the Rise of China's New Culture Movement ··· 274

  10.3.2　Yan Fu's Translation Practice ······················ 277

  10.3.3　Lu Xun's Translation Practice ······················ 281

 Questions for discussion ·· 289

 References ·· 290

Postscript ··· 292

Chapter 1

Historical Stages of Translation in China and the West

Translation has a long history in both China and the West. Translation history cannot be explored exhaustively within a brief history textbook, since "translation history is a set of discourses predicating the changes that have occurred or have actively been prevented in the field of translation. Its field includes actions and agents leading to translations (or non-translations), effects of translations (or non-translations), theories about translation, and a long string of causally-related phenomena" (Pym, 1998)[5]. The present chapter exclusively deals with the time divisions (stages or periods) of translation history in China and the West, which can aid the readers to have a clear picture of the evolution of translation in both regions.

1.1 Major Historical Stages of Translation in China

According to Arnold Joseph Toynbee (1889—1975), a well-known British historian, every civilization undergoes a universal rhythm of rise, development, and decline, that is, no civilization can exist forever. An obvious exception to Toynbee's assertion is the Chinese civilization, which has survived for thousands of years. The secret to the survival of Chinese civilization, from ancient to modern times, lies in translation. "A civilization can be compared to a river. The Chinese civilization is a long river that has never gone dry, although its water has been sometimes abundant and sometimes not. The reason is that the river has been constantly replenished with fresh water. Of the two greatest water replenishments in Chinese history, one came from India and the other came from the West. These two greatest water replenishments were accomplished by way of translation, which is the elixir for the Chinese civilization to remain as fresh as ever. Translation is of great service to us" (Ji Xianlin, 2015)[9-10]. China boasts not only a time-honored civilization but a long history of translation. The activities of interpretation and translation can be traced back to remote antiquity. "In terms of either the historical length of translation practice or the amount of translation and the influence of translation, China is the No. 1 country in the world" (Ji Xianlin, 2015)[8].

So far, there has no universally-agreed division of the historical stages of translation in China. Different time divisions have been put forward from various perspectives. Eva Hung (2005)[14] divided Chinese translation history into two stages: the first one is Buddhist translation before the end of Tang Dynasty (618—907) and the second one is the translation of Western literature, philosophy and science since the end of Qing Dynasty (1616—1911). The first stage focused on knowledge about human spirit while the second stage centered on material culture, which was intended for national reform and development.

From the viewpoint of the translation's influence on Chinese language and literature, Guo Moruo (1892—1978), one of the leading writers of the 20th-century China and a prominent government official, divided translation history before the founding of P. R. China in 1949 into three stages: translation of Buddhist scriptures, translation of the *Holy Bible*, and translation of modern Western literary works (Chen Fukang, 2000)[401]. Zou Zhenhuan (1996) divided the Chinese translation history into three chronological stages: translation between Chinese and minority languages (*minzu fanyi*), translation of Buddhist scriptures, and translation of Western learning (*xixue fanyi*). Xie Tianzhen et al. (2009) adopted different criteria to periodize translation history. These are about the mainstream type of texts translated, the development of human knowledge of translation, and translation's social status and influence. The division includes: stage of religious translation (the mainstream texts translated are religious), stage of literary translation (the mainstream texts translated are literary and social science classics), and stage of non-literary translation (the focus is on practical texts).

Wang Kefei (1994) divided the history of Chinese translation into four periods: Buddhist translation from Han to Tang Dynasties (206 B. C. —907), science translation in the Ming and Qing Dynasties (1368—1911), translation of Western learning, and comprehensive translation of foreign texts.

A more detailed periodization was suggested. Wang Bingqin (2004)[3-4] divided the Chinese translation history into five periods: 1) Buddhist translation in Han-Sui-Tang-Song Dynasties (206 B. C. —1279); 2) science translation in Ming-Qing Dynasties (1368—1911); 3) translation of Western learning in the late Qing Dynasty and the early

Republic of China (roughly from 1900 to 1920); 4) Post-May 4th Movement translation of social sciences and literature; and 5) translation after the founding of P. R. China.

Ma Zuyi, the author of *A Condensed History of Translation in China before the May 4th Movement*(《中国翻译简史：五四以前部分》, *Zhongguo Fanyi Jianshi: Wusi Yiqian Bufen*), which is the first monograph about Chinese translation history, divided the translation before the May 4th Movement in 1919 into 5 periods: 1) translation practice from Zhou Dynasty to Eastern Han Dynasty (before Emperor Huan's rule) (from 1046 B. C. to 146); 2) translation practice from the late reign of Emperor Huan to Song Dynasty (roughly from 167 to 960); 3) translation practice in Yuan Dynasty (1206—1368); 4) translation practice from Ming Dynasty to the beginning of the Opium War (1368—1840); and 5) translation practice from the Opium War to the May 4th Movement (1840—1919). About 20 years later, Ma Zuyi published a multi-volume history of translation in China in 2006, in which 4 waves of translation in China were enumerated: Buddhist translation from Eastern Han Dynasty to Tang and Song Dynasties, translation of Western learning in the late Ming and early Qing Dynasties, translation of Western learning from the Opium War to the May 4th Movement, and translation in the 1980s—1990s after the launch of Reform and Opening-up Policy in 1978. Therefore, Ma Zuyi actually divided the history of translation in China into 6 periods or stages.

Sun Yingchun (2011) divided translation history into five chronological stages: 1) Embarkation and Buddhist translation; 2) Yuan and Ming Dynasties to pre-Opium War; 3) Opium War to the Pre-May 4th Movement; 4) The May 4th Movement to the end of 1970s; and 5) Chinese translation in globalization.

From the above examples of periodization of translation history in China, we can see that the most commonly-adopted division is made chronologically. Therefore, in this section, a chronological division of translation history is presented and each stage or period is introduced.

1.1.1 From the Earliest Times to the Reign of Emperor Huan of Eastern Han

China, a vast country with more than 50 ethnic groups, has probably witnessed translational activities including translating and interpreting since the first tribal battle or barter. Interpreting must have been the oldest form of translation. In ancient times, most of such activities, especially oral interpreting, were unrecorded once the primary purpose of serving for communications between parties speaking different languages was fulfilled.

There were no audio and video recording devices, so there was no record of the actual interpreting activities. There were no documents to indicate the translational activities in the primitive society. Although some documents from Xia (c. 21st—17th century B.C.) and Shang (c. 17th—11th century B.C.) Dynasties are available, they do not refer to any translational activities. As early as Zhou Dynasty in the 9th century B.C., there were special government officials in charge of translational activities. The following excerpt from "Wangzhi"(王制, Royal Institutions) in *The Book of Rites*(《礼记》, *Liji*) is one of the earliest historical records of the ancient perception of the function of what is today known as *fanyi*(翻译, interpreting/translating):

The Chinese original: 五方之民，言语不通，嗜欲不同。达其志，通其欲，东方曰"寄"，南方曰"象"，西方曰"狄鞮"，北方曰"译"。

> The people living in the five regions spoke different languages and had different customs, likings and preferences. To make accessible *da*(达) what was in the minds of different peoples, and to make their likings and preferences understood, there were functionaries for the job. Those in charge of the regions in the east were called *ji* (寄, the entrusted transmitters); in the south, *xiang*(象, likeness-renderers); in the west, *Didi*[狄鞮, they know the *Di*(鞮) tribes]; and in the north, *yi*(译, translators/interpreters) (Cheung, 2010)[46].

According to the extant literature, translational activities, both translating and interpreting, in the periods before Qin Dynasty (221—206 B.C.) were functional in nature rather than activities inspired by a genuine intellectual curiosity about other languages and cultures (Cheung, 2010)[46]. Before Qin Dynasty, the government officials in charge of the communication between different tribes were called *sheren* (舌人, tongue-men) and *xiangxu*[象胥, interpreting-functionaries: *xiang*(象), likeness-renderers; *xu* (胥), minor government officials]. "Tongue-men", the common name for interpreters in ancient China, were minor government officials mainly responsible for communicating with foreign tribes. The *xiangxu*'s duties were receiving the envoys from the tribes of *Man* (蛮), *Yi*(夷), *Min*(闽), *He*(貉), *Rong*(戎), and *Di*(狄), conveying the utterance of the king and explaining the meaning of the king's message to them. The terms *xiangxu*, *sheren*, *ji*, *xiang*, *Didi*, *yi*, which were used as official titles of government posts or as collective names for the people engaged in interpreting or translating, threw some light on the ancient perception on the activity now called *fanyi* 翻译 (interpreting/translating) (Cheung, 2010)[46-47].

Folk Song of the Yue People(《越人歌》, *Yuerenge*), the earliest surviving written translation, dates back to at least the 6th century B.C. As a love song for Yue old couples, it was sung by a boatman of the tribe more than 2,000 years ago. The Chu version of the song was the first translated poem in China. The original text in ancient Yue language was preserved in *Garden of Anecdotes*: *On Kindness*(《说苑·善说》, *Shuoyuan Shanshuo*) written by Liu Xiang(刘向) (Chen Yulan, 2020).

1.1.2 Buddhist Translation from Emperor Huan of Eastern Han Dynasty to Song Dynasty (from 147 to 1279)

There is no doubt that the first wave of translation in the history of China was the translation of Buddhist scriptures or sutras, which began no later than the middle of the second century. No reliable documents were preserved to exactly indicate when translation of Buddhist sutras started. It is universally agreed that the extensive translation of Buddhist sutras into Chinese did not begin until the end of the late Han Dynasty in the middle of the 2nd century. This was the time when Parthamasiris (安士高) and Lokaksema(支娄迦谶) came to Luoyang during the reign of Emperor Huan(桓帝) of Han Dynasty. The mid-2nd century witnessed the beginning of a massive Buddhist translation movement, which lasted for nine centuries. The Chinese translation from Sanskrit can be roughly divided into three phases: Eastern Han Dynasty and Three Kingdoms Period (c. 148—265), Jin-Northern-Southern Dynasties (c. 265—589), and Sui-Tang-Northern Song Dynasties (c. 589—1100). From Yuan Dynasty (1206—1368) to Ming Dynasty (1368—1644), the translation of sutras took on less importance.

1.1.3 Translation of Christianity and Western Science since the 16th Century

Yuan Dynasty (1206—1368) succeeded Song Dynasty (960—1279). In 1271, Kublai Khan(忽必烈) founded the former and united China five years later. The official languages were New Mongolian(蒙古新字) and Wei Wu Mongolian(畏吾蒙字), which were used correspondingly. With the Han nationality being the majority in China but the ruling class not speaking Chinese, translation became an important daily affair of ruling the whole country. *Tongshi*(通事, interpreter) was responsible for oral communications between the Mongolian people and the non-Mongolian speaking populace while *yishi*(译史) was in charge of written translation. Imperial government agencies were provided with *tongshi* and/or *yishi*. The translation activities in Yuan Dynasty were of great significance in ruling the empire but introduced limited cultural elements beneficial to the development of Chinese civilization.

The second wave of translation in Chinese history was also related to religious activities. It began with the arrival of Jesuit missionaries to China in the late 16th century. The Jesuits, notably Matteo Ricci(利玛窦, 1552—1610), decided that the best way to spread the Gospel was to cultivate China's educated class. For this aim, a large number of Western scientific works were translated into Chinese and circulated among Chinese scholars and government officials. This reality in turn facilitated the Jesuits' missionary activities. Many works were translated jointly by Western missionaries and Chinese scholars and/or government officials. Scientific ones fell into the following major fields: Mathematics, Astronomy, Geography, Physics and Religion. Xu Guangqi(徐光启, 1562—1633), the most distinguished Chinese translator, working with Jesuit missionaries, produced *Jihe Yuanben*(《几何原本》, *Euclidis Elementorum*). It is the Chinese version of *Euclidis Elementorum* by Clavius (1537—1612, German mathematician) and is regarded as one of the most influential translations in the history of China. The Jesuits and later missionaries were not only engaged in foreign-Chinese translation, but were also responsible for the initial introduction of Chinese philosophy and literature to the West, bringing the Chinese classics to Europe. The "Four Books" [*The Great Learning*(《大学》, *Daxue*), *The Doctrine of the Mean*(《中庸》, *Zhongyong*), *The Analects of Confucius*(《论语》, *Lunyu*), and *The Works of Mencius*(《孟子》, *Mengzi*)] and "Five Classics" [*The Book of Songs*(《诗经》, *Shijing*), *The Book of Documents*(《尚书》, *Shangshu*), *The Book of Changes*(《周易》, *Zhouyi*), *The Book of Rites*(《礼记》, *Liji*), and *The Spring and Autumn Annals*(《春秋》, *Chunqiu*)] were translated into Latin respectively by Ricci and Nicolas Trigault(金尼阁, 1577—1628). Some of the "Four Books" and the "Five Classics" were later retranslated by missionaries actively during Qing Dynasty. Around 1750, *Laotzu*(《老子》, *Laozi*) was introduced to Europe for the first time by means of a Latin version possibly produced by Jesuit missionaries. *The Orphan of the Zhao Family*(《赵氏孤儿》, *Zhaoshi Guer*), a Chinese drama written by Ji Junxiang(纪君祥) of Yuan Dynasty, was brought to the West by Joseph-Maria de Premare(马若瑟, 1666—1736), a Frenchman who came to China in 1698. *Hau Kiou Choaan* (《好逑传》, *Haoqiuzhuan*), a romance written under a pseudonym

Chapter 1 Historical Stages of Translation in China and the West

"Mingjiaozhongren"(名教中人) around the late 17th century, was translated into English by Thomas Percy and published by R. Dodsley in 1761. It was the first traditional Chinese novel translated into English and introduced to the West. *The Two Fair Cousins* (《玉娇梨》, *Yujiaoli*), a romance, was one of the "Ten Masterpieces by Talented Authors"(十大才子书) in Yuan, Ming, and Qing Dynasties. French sinologist Jean Pierre Abel Rémusat(雷慕沙, 1788—1832) translated this work into French in 1826, and it was the first full foreign version of the novel.

Jesuit missionaries, who introduced Western science and culture together with Christianity to China and who disseminated traditional Chinese philosophy and literature to the West, played an important role in and contributed a lot to the establishment of Sino-Western cultural relations.

1.1.4 From the Opium War to the Founding of P. R. China

"From the time of China's defeat in the Opium War of 1840, Chinese progressives went through untold hardships in their quest for truth from Western countries. Hong Xiuquan, Kang Youwei, Yan Fu and Sun Yat-sen represented those who had looked to the West for truth before the Communist Party of China was born. Chinese who then sought progress would have read some books containing the new knowledge from the West" (Mao Tse-tung, 1960). In the early nineteenth century, the trading incursions of the European powers, backed by military might, grew too insistent to be ignored by the Peking government. Lin Zexu(林则徐, 1785—1850) was dispatched to Canton in 1838 to deal with the situation. It was his insight, "to control the foreigners, we have to master their arts", that prompted the first official team of translators to tackle the English language (Baker, 2006)[369]. The team translated excerpts from the foreign press in the locale and various English pamphlets on Chinese matters and international laws. *Geography of the Maritime Nations* (《海国图志》, *Haiguo Tuzhi*), which was based on Murray's *Encyclopedia of Geography* (1834) and published in 1844, was the translation team's major achievement. In 1862, the School of Combined Learning(同文馆, Tongwenguan) was founded in Peking to offer students 8-year programs of languages (initially English, then French, Russian, and German), natural and social sciences. This institution trained students for diplomatic affairs. Additionally, it translated and published books on laws, politics and natural sciences. In Shanghai, Jiangnan Arsenal(江南制造局, Jiangnan Zhizao Ju) set up its own translation agency in 1865 concentrating on translations of technical manuals and a broad scope of Western sciences. Many Chinese translators working at the agency were scientists in their own right such as Li Shanlan(李善兰, 1811—1882). Foreign experts were employed to work collaboratively with Chinese translators and later became known as "China hands" in their home countries (Baker, 2006)[369].

The main force of translation at that time was either official or foreign. A third force in the translation of Western works emerged in the 1890s and was composed of Chinese native intellectuals. They were headed by political reformists, and the prominent among them were Kang Youwei and Liang Qichao(梁启超, 1873—1929). "To impress on their compatriots who needed to struggle if they did not wish to perish, they introduced the ominous lessons of other empires in world history; they also undertook translations in the fields of politics and sociology as a way of ensuring national survival" (Baker, 2006)[370]. The reformists' newspapers and magazines carried translations of items from the foreign press. The most prestigious of the newspapers were *The Chinese Progress*(《时务报》, *Shiwu Bao*) in Shanghai, edited by Liang Qichao, and *National Register*(《国闻报》, *Guowen Bao*) in Tianjin, edited by Yan Fu (1854—1921). Yan's Chinese version of Thomas Huxley's long essay, *Evolution and Ethics*, was first published in *National Register* in 1897, before being issued in the book form with the title of *Tianyanlun* (《天演论》, *On Evolution*). Its publication was a milestone in the Chinese translation history because aside from the book's content and translation style, there was the three-character translation principle which Yan Fu laid down in the preface of the book: *xin* (faithfulness), *da* (expressiveness), and *ya* (elegance). *Tianyanlun* was the Chinese translation of the first two chapters of Huxley's *Evolution and Ethics* and other essays. Yan Fu began his translation career with *Tianyanlun*. In the next ten years, Yan translated works of Western philosophers in social sciences such as Adam Smith's *An Inquiry into the Nature and Causes of the Wealth of Nations*(《原富》, *Yuanfu*, 1901—1902), Herbert Spencer's *The Study of Society*(《群学肄言》, *Qunxue Siyan*, 1903), John Mill's *On Liberty*(《群己权界论》, *Qunji Quanjie Lun*, 1903) and *System of Logic*(《穆勒名学》, *Mule Mingxue*, 1905), E. Jenks' *A History of Politics*(《社会通诠》, *Shehui Tongquan*, 1904), Charles Louis de Secondat Montesquieu's *L'esprit des Lois*(《法意》, *Fayi*, 1904—1909), and W. S. Jevons' *Logic* (《名学浅说》, *Mingxue Qianshuo*, 1909). Yan's influence on the modern Chinese mind and contributions to the ideological development in the 20th century China by means of translation are beyond dispute. He remains an inspiration to Chinese translators of today who debate on the translation principles he set in the preface of *Tianyanlun*.

Chapter 1 Historical Stages of Translation in China and the West

As a translator, Lin Shu(林纾, 1852—1924), a contemporary of Yan Fu, was equally well-known. Lin was a novelist, poet and painter, but he was better known as a literary translator in the history of Chinese literature. Lin was a master of classical prose, though he did not know a word of English or any other foreign languages. He produced translations with the help of an oral interpreter. The latter read and explained the original while Lin took notes hurriedly of what he heard on the spot, which needed some revisions. In collaboration with interpreters, he translated more than 170 Western literary works in about 30 years. These could not be expected to be free of errors. *La Dame aux Camelias* (《巴黎茶花女遗事》, *The Legacy of the Paris Camellia Woman*) was the first Western work Lin translated and it was an immediate success. The Western writers whose works he translated included French writers like Balzac, Dumas Pere, Dumas Fils, and Hugo; British writers such as Shakespeare, Defoe, Fielding, Swift, Scott, Dickens, Charles Lamb, L. Stevenson, Sir Arthur Conan Doyle, Sir Henry Rider, and Haggard; American writers like Washington Irving and Harriet Beecher Stowe; and the likes of Aesop (Greek fabulist), Cervantes (Spanish writer), Leo Tolstoy (Russian writer), and Ibsen (Norwegian dramatist). Lin's best-known translations are, among others, *Sakexun Jiehou Yingxiong Lüe*(《撒克逊劫后英雄略》, *Ivanhoe*), *Kuairou Yusheng Shu*(《块肉余生述》, *David Copperfield*), and *Heinu Yutian Lu*(《黑奴吁天录》, *Uncle Tom's Cabin*).

Both Yan and Lin were famous personages in the history of Chinese translation. "Just as Yan Fu's introduction of the capitalist ideology played a part in ushering in reform and revolution and civil war and a bigger revolution, so the translations of the old Chinese classical scholar prepared the ground for the radical social novels of the more turbulent times to come" (Wang Zuoliang, 1981).

By 1911, Qing Dynasty had lost much of its influence on the provinces as local warlords declared sovereignty. The Revolution of 1911, also known as the Xinhai Revolution(辛亥革命), resulted in the abdication of the child Emperor Puyi on February 12, 1912 and the establishment of the Republic of China. The revolution, which was a part of extensive popular uprisings that had been occurring against Qing Dynasty (1616—1911) since the mid-1800s, was caused by a number of factors including Chinese intellectuals' growing exposures to Western schools of thought.

In 1919, the May 4th Movement, a great anti-imperialist, anti-feudal revolutionary movement, marked the beginning of the new democratic revolution in China. It was, at once, a patriotic political and new cultural movement. The cultural movement before the May 4th Movement had prepared ideological conditions for the breakout of the patriotic movement while this rising patriotism also intensified the cultural movement. This paved way for its transformation from a movement characterized by old democracy into one of new democratic movements with the dissemination of Marxism as its main current.

As an important part of the May 4th Movement, New Literature Movement was a milestone in the history of Chinese literature, particularly during the period between 1917 and 1927, which is conventionally known as May 4th New Literature. Along with its prosperous development, foreign literature translation became unprecedentedly active. *Youth Magazine*(《青年杂志》, *Qingnian Zazhi*, later renamed *New Youth*), a primary symbol of New Culture Movement, not only advocated new literature but also actively introduced foreign literature. From 1915 to 1921, the magazine carried translations of foreign literary works from a dozen of countries: Russia, Britain, France, America, India, Japan, Norway, Spain, Poland, Denmark, Portugal, etc. Writers like Turgenev (1818—1883), Chekhov, Maupassant, Henryk Siekiewic, Ibsen, Andersen, Gorky, Artsybashev, Mushanokouji Saneatsu, and Wilde were introduced. The translators were Chen Duxiu(陈独秀), Hu Shi(胡适), Liu Bannong(刘半农), Lu Xun(鲁迅), Zhou Zuoren(周作人), Shen Yanbing(沈雁冰), Zheng Zhenduo(郑振铎), among others. The translations published by the *Youth Magazine* were intended to serve New Culture/ Literature Movement.

Literature Research Association (文学研究会, Wenxue Yanjiu Hui) was an important association in the history of both modern Chinese literature and Chinese translation. The association was founded jointly by a dozen of active and influential literary writers in 1921. Its co-founders, Shen Yanbin, Zhou Zuoren, Zheng Zhenduo, Geng Jizhi (耿济之), were not only well-versed in foreign literature, but also active in literary research and translation. The group attached great importance and contributed much to the development of foreign literary translation in China. *Short Story Magazine*(《小说月报》, *Xiaoshuo Yuebao*), which started in 1910, became the official organ of the association in 1921. From January 1921 to December 1926, of the works published in *Xiaoshuo Yuebao*, 33 were from Russia, 27 from France, 13 from Japan, 6 from India and 8 from Britain. Besides, Literature Research Association edited and published about 100 literary books of various national origins, schools and genres. The association's foreign literature introduction and translation mainly focused on the works of realist writers and the literature of small, weak, and oppressed nations. In 1921, *Short Story Magazine* carried 60 items of translations of literary works of such countries, accounting for 55% of the translations published. In 1922, the percentage increased to 59%. Two special issues of the magazine were published to offer a systematic introduction of the literature of such nations as Poland, Hungary, Czech Republic, Sweden, Israel, and Russia (Wang Gang, 2014). The association also cultivated a large number of translators.

The Creation Society(创造社, Chuangzaoshe) was another important literary group in the history of modern Chinese literature and translation. If the Literature Research Association had paved the way for the introduction and translation of foreign realist literature, Creation Society would have been instrumental to the translation of foreign romantic literature. The society was founded in Japan in 1921 and was closed by the Kuomintang in 1929. The leading members of the group included Guo Moruo(郭沫若), Yu Dafu(郁达夫), Cheng Fangwu(成仿吾), Zhang Ziping(张资平), Zheng Boqi(郑伯奇). From 1922 to 1929, the society carried out four kinds of works concerning translation. First, they translated books of poetry, novels, dramas, and literary theories. Second, they introduced various literary trends of thought, such as Romanticism, Symbolism, Futurism, and Expressionism. Third, they advanced their own ideas about translation. Fourth, they commented on translated texts. Their translations and introductions of foreign literary works were published in the periodicals *Creation Quarterly* (《创造季刊》, *Chuangzao Jikan*), *Creation Weekly* (《创造周报》, *Chuangzao Zhoubao*), and *Creation Daily*(《创造日》, *Chuangzao Ri*).

Another literary group Weiming (literally meaning *unnamed or unknown*) Society(未名社, Weimingshe) was founded in Beijing in 1925. The group was organized by Lu Xun. Its leading members were Lu Xun, Wei Suyuan(韦素园), Cao Jinghua(曹靖华), Li Jiye(李霁野), Wei Congwu(韦丛芜), and Tai Jingnong(台静农). Compared with other literary organizations, Weiming Society was unique because it regarded translating and introducing foreign literature as its duty. The society lasted for 6 years. Its outstanding contribution was the introduction of Russian literature and Soviet literature after the October Revolution.

In the first half of the 20th century, not a few outstanding translators made great contributions to the introduction of foreign literature. Lu Xun's major translations were

Yuwai Xiaoshuo Ji(《域外小说集》, *Collection of Foreign Short Stories*, 1909 and 1921), *Huimie*(《毁灭》, Fadeyev's novel *The Rout*, 1930), and *Si Hunling*(《死魂灵》, Gogol's novel *Deal Souls*, 1935).

Mao Dun(茅盾, original name Shen Yanbin, 1896—1981) produced 30 translations in 1920, produced 50 translations in 1921, and published a collection of translated short stories of small European nations. Also, Mao Dun wrote series of articles about translation theories.

Guo Moruo, a part-time prolific translator, produced a five-million-character Chinese translation. Roughly, his translations can be divided into three types: 1) Literary works. Most of his translation works are literary. Guo's major book-length literary translations were Goethe's *Faust*(《浮士德》, *Fushide*, first part, 1921; second part, 1947), Goethe's *The Sorrows of Young Werther*(《少年维特之烦恼》, *Shaonian Weite zhi Fannao*, 1921), German writer Storm's *Immensee*(《茵梦湖》, *Yinmenghu*, 1921), *Selected Poems of Shelly*(《雪莱诗选》, *Xuelai Shixuan*, 1923), Fitzgerald's English version of Persian poet Omar Khayyam's *Rubaiyat of Omar Khayyam*(《鲁拜集》, *Lubaiji*, 1922), Nietzch's *Also Sprach Zarathustra*(《查拉图斯特拉如是说》, *Chalatusitela Rushi Shuo*, 1923), Turgenev's *Virgin Soil*(《新时代》, *Xin Shidai*, 1924), Irish dramatist J. M. Synge's dramatic works(《约翰沁孤戏曲集》, *Yuehan Qingu Xiqu Ji*, 1924), and German writer Hauptmann's *The Heretic of Soana*(《异端》, *Yi Duan*, 1924). In 1926, Guo translated *Strife*(《争斗》, *Zhengdou*) written by Galsworthy. He also translated American writer Sinclair's novels: *King Coal*(《石炭王》, *Shitan Wang*, 1928), *The Jungle*(《屠场》, *Tuchang*, 1929), and *Oil*(《煤油》, *Meiyou*, 1930), altogether, one million words. In 1929, Guo published *Xin'e Shixuan*(《新俄诗选》, *Poems of New Russia*, co-translated with Li Yimang). He also published three volumes of Tolstoy's *War and Peace*(《战争与和平》, *Zhanzheng yu Heping*). In 1935, Guo worked on *Selected Japanese Short Stories*(《日本短篇小说集》, *Riben Duanpian Xiaoshuo Ji*). In 1936, he translated Schiller's *Wallenstein*(《华伦斯太》, *Hualunsitai*) and Goethe's *Herman and Dorothea*(《赫曼与窦绿苔》, *Heman yu Douliütai*). 2) Works in social sciences. Guo published *Social Organization and Social Revolution*(《社会组织与社会革命》, *Shehui Zuzhi yu Shehui Geming*) written by the Japanese Marxist Kawakami Haijime in 1924, *Critique of Political Economics*(《政治经济学批判》, *Zhengzhi Jingjixue Pipan*) by Karl Marx in 1931, and *German Ideology*(《德意志意识形态》, *Deyizhi Yishi Xingtai*) in 1938. 3) Works in natural sciences. In 1931, Guo began to translate the 1.2-million-word-long and multi-volume book *Science of Life* (《生命之科学》, *Shengming zhi Kexue*), which was published in 1949.

Ba Jin (巴金, 1904—2005) translated about 50 works in literature and social sciences from the languages of English, French, Russian, German, and Esperanto. The writers of these works came from Russia, Britain, Germany, Poland, Italy, Japan, Hungary, Spain, Switzerland, America, and Bulgaria. Most of the works were written by Russian writers.

Zhu Shenghao (朱生豪, 1912—1944) spent almost a decade translating Shakespeare's plays into Chinese, having finished 31 by the time of his death in 1944. He began with comedies and then turned to tragedies and historical plays. Zhu chose to render Shakespear's blank verse into prose, and his translations have been praised for their linguistic elegance and richness.

Before the May 4th Movement, Western masterpieces were generally translated into classical Chinese except some being rendered into vernacular Chinese. The classical Chinese translations produced by Yan Fu and Lin Shu were popular among the Chinese literati. Not until the New Culture Movement (around the time of the New Literature Movement as promoted by the May 4th Movement) did the trend of translating Western works into classical Chinese get fundamentally reversed. Writing in vernacular Chinese became the main trend of literature. The classical Chinese translations were soon replaced by vernacular Chinese translations, which provided common readers with access to foreign works.

1.1.5 Translation after the Founding of P. R. China

The founding of P. R. China in October 1949 marked a new stage in Chinese translation history. Translation activities began to be planned, organized, and supervised by the government, which advocated socialist ideologies coming from Europe. Translating the works about socialist and communist ideologies had been one of the important tasks of Left-Wing Cultural Movement led by the Communist Party of China (CPC). Since the late Qing Dynasty, literature had been used as a weapon of struggle by various schools of thought and political parties, though its being instrumental was overemphasized. The Chinese translation of foreign literature was no exception. After 1949, the Chinese government strictly regulated and supervised translation activities for the development of P. R. China. Generally, the translation history since 1949 is divided into three periods:

the first 17 years (1949—1966), the 10-year Cultural Revolution (1966—1976), and the start of reform and opening up in 1978.

The first 17 years of P. R. China witnessed great achievements in the translation of works in social sciences, literature, science and technology. Partial statistics show that 530 works about the international communist movement were translated into Chinese before 1949. Among these, 86 were written by Marx and Engels, 188 were written by Lenin, and 210 were written by Stalin. From the founding of P. R. China to 1965, there was an influx of translations of works by the Marxist leaders. In 1953, Central Committee's Bureau of Compilation and Translation of Works by Marx, Engels, Lenin and Stalin of the CPC(中共中央马恩列斯著作编译局) was established for the task of producing Chinese versions of three complete collections of works: one by Marx and Engels, one by Lenin, and one by Stalin. Until 1958, 13 volumes of translated works originally written by Stalin, about 3.4 million words, were published. Until 1959, 38 volumes of translated works originally written by Lenin, about 15 million words, were published. Until 1974, the translation of all works originally written by Marx and Engels was completed, 39 volumes of which were published. Some classical Western works in philosophy, politics, economics, law, and history were translated. From 1956 to 1966, the Commercial Press published 129 translated books of philosophy, including Immanuel Kant's *Three Critiques* [*Critique of Pure Reason*(《纯粹理性批判》, *Chuncui Lixing Pipan*), *Critique of Practical Reason* (《实践理性批判》, *Shijian Lixing Pipan*), *Critique of Judgment*(《判断力批判》, *Panduanli Pipan*)] and Hegel's *Phenomenology of Spirit*(《精神现象学》, *Jingshen Xianxiangxue*), *The Logic of Hegel*(《小逻辑》, *Xiao Luoji*), *Elements of the Philosophy of Right*(《法哲学原理》, *Fazhexue Yuanli*), *The Philosophy of History*(《历史哲学》, *Lishi Zhexue*), and *Aesthetics*(《美学》, *Meixue*). Translated classics of economics included William Petty's *A Treatise of Taxes and Contribution*(《赋税论》, *Fushui Lun*), David Ricardo's *On the Principles of Political Economy and Taxation*(《政治经济学及赋税原理》, *Zhengzhi Jingjixue ji Fushui Yuanli*), John Maynard Keynes' *The General Theory of Employment, Interest and Money*(《就业、利息和货币通论》, *Jiuye, Lixi he Huobi Tonglun*). In 1957, 7 books written by Thomas Robert Malthus were translated for criticism, the most known being *An Essay on the Principle of Population*(《人口论》, *Renkou Lun*). In history, the important translated works were Herodotus' *The Histories* (《历史》, *Lishi*), Thucydides' *The History of Peloponnesian War*(《伯罗奔尼撒战争

史》, *Boluobennisa Zhanzheng Shi*), Publius Cornelius Tacitus' *Historiae* (《历史》, *Lishi*), Gottfried Spengler's *The Decline of the West* (《西方的没落》, *Xifang de Moluo*), Voltaire's *Philosophical Letters* (《哲学通信》, *Zhexue Tongxin*), A. J. Toynbee's *A Study of History* (《历史研究》, *Lishi Yanjiu*), and William Shirer's *The Rise and Fall of the Third Reich* (《第三帝国的兴亡》, *Disan Diguo de Xingwang*).

From the founding of P. R. China to the end of 1958, 5,356 literary works were translated into Chinese, much more than those translated from 1919 to 1949. In the first few years, P. R. China adopted the diplomatic policy of *yibiandao* (Leaning to one side, the side of socialism, here the Soviet Union). Hence, 3,526 out of 5,356 (65.8%) translations were from Russian and Soviet literature. In the 17-year period, the retranslated and newly translated works originally written by important Russian and Soviet writers included those of Pushkin, Gogol, Turgenev, Chekhov, Dostoevsky, Gorki, Mayakovsky, Sholokhov, Fadeyev, and Ostrovsky. Also, works of more than 100 Soviet writers were translated for the first time. The prosperous translation of Russian and Soviet literature came to an end in 1957 because of the bilateral hostile relationship between China and the Soviet Union. "Progressive" and "oppressed" realist literary works from more than 20 countries in Asia, Africa, and Latin America were translated and published. In contrast, no translation was made for the literature of European and American capitalist countries, except a few classics and critical realist works. Modernist literature, the greatest literary achievement of the 20th century in Europe and America, was completely ruled out. From 1949 to 1966, about 245 British literary works were translated into Chinese, 92 of which were novels. The foci of translation were classical and realist works such as, Swift's *Gulliver's Travels* (《格列夫游记》, *Geliefu Youji*), Henry Fielding's *The History of the Adventures of Joseph Andrews and of His Friend Mr. Abraham Adams* (《约瑟·安德鲁斯的经历》, *Yuese Andelusi de Jingli*), Jane Austin's *Pride and Prejudice* (《傲慢与偏见》, *Aoman yu Pianjian*), Thackeray's *Vanity Fair* (《名利场》, *Minglichang*), Dickens' *The Old Curiosity Shop* (《老古玩店》, *Lao Guwan Dian*), Dickens' *Hard Times* (《艰难时世》, *Jiannan Shishi*), Charlotte Bronte's *Jane Eyre* (《简·爱》, *Jian'ai*), John Galsworthy's *The Forsyte Saga* (《福尔赛世家》, *Fu'ersai Shijia*); Thomas Hardy's *Tess of the D'Urbervilles* (《德伯家的苔丝》, *Debojia de Taisi*), *The Return of the Native* (《还乡》, *Huanxiang*), *Jude the Obscure* (《无名的裘德》, *Wuming de Qiude*), *The Mayor of Casterbridge* (《卡斯特桥市长》, *Kasiteqiao Shizhang*), Joseph Conrad's *Lord*

Jim(《吉姆爷》, *Jimuye*), and Ethel Voynich's *The Gadfly*(《牛虻》, *Niumeng*). The poets whose pieces were translated were Shelley, Keats, and Robert Burns and the works of dramatist Bernard Shaw were prioritized. As for American literature, 215 works were translated, 136 of which were novels. The translated works originally written by important American writers included those of Mark Twain, Jack London, Theodore Dreiser, Howard Fast, and Albert Maltz. Literary pieces of poets like Longfellow and Langston Hughes and of the "progressive" dramatists such as left-leaning Clifford Odets were also translated.

About 300 French literary works were translated into Chinese. Much effort was devoted to the translation of works of the following writers: Moliere, Balzac, Hugo, Maupassant, George Sand, Zola, Romain Rolland, and Louis Aragon. The representative works of Francois Rabelais, Pierre Corneille, La Fontaine, Jean Racine, Denis Diderot, Stendhal, Montesquieu, Gustave Flaubert, and Alexandre Dumas Fils were also translated. The translation of German literature focused on classical writers such as Goethe, Schiller, and Heine. Only a few outputs of modern writers were translated. For contemporary German literature, translation focused on compositions of few writers of German Democratic Republic. Some literary works of Eastern, Southern and Northern Europe were translated but the number of translations was very small. Translations in the first 17 years after the founding of P. R. China covered many countries but the ideological criteria for selecting foreign literary works cast aside those of high artistic value.

Great importance was attached to scientific translation, for it was necessary for the development of P. R. China's economy and society. According to statistics, 16,000 scientific books were translated in the first 17 years. This figure is 6 times the total output of scientific translation in the 38 years before the founding of P. R. China. Among the translated books, 10,022 dealt with industry and technology, accounting for 62.6% of the scientific translations. 12,983 translations were produced from 1952 to 1960. In 1960, the Soviet experts who offered China the technical help withdrew from many Chinese projects and the projects came to a halt. Such withdrawal led to a steep decline in scientific translation outputs. 3,416 books from Soviet Union were translated while 304 books from America were translated (Ma Zuyi et al., 2006).

The Cultural Revolution (1966—1976) was a civil strife, which discouraged translation. In the first years of the revolution, there were almost no translation activities.

Chapter 1   Historical Stages of Translation in China and the West

There were no translations of philosophical and social scientific works before 1971. In 1971, two sets of books were translated under orders: a set on national histories and a set on national geographies. By the end of 1978, 171 translated books of the former and 50 translated books of the latter had been published. In 1972, when diplomatic relations between China and America were established, a few books about international politics were translated. In a decade (1966—1976), 1,100 books in the fields of natural sciences were translated, of which 66 books were about biology. 512 books concerning industry and technology were translated while 78 books on traffic and transportation were translated. In terms of origins, of 1,100, 253 books came from Soviet Union, 212 books came from America, 74 books came from Japan, and 72 books came from Britain. Works of social sciecnes and litrature, which were politically sensitive, were not translated and published as much as scientific ones. In the late years of Cultural Revolution, 6 Soviet literary works were openly published, namely, Maxim Gorky's *In the World*(《在人间》, *Zai Renjian*), *Mother*(《母亲》, *Muqin*), *January 9*(《一月九日》, *Yiyue Jiuri*), Alexander Alexandrovich Fadeyev's *The Young Guard*(《青年近卫军》, *Qingnian Jinweijun*), Nikolai Alexeevich Ostrovsky's *How the Steel Was Tempered*(《钢铁是怎样炼成的》, *Gangtie shi Zenyang Liancheng de*), and Aleksandr Serafimovich's *The Iron Blood*(《铁流》, *Tieliu*). These works were praised by Mao Tes-tung and Lu Xun and were regarded as genuinely proletarian revolutionary literary works. At the same time, 3 Japanese novels, 1 Japanese literary criticism, 1 Japanese literary history, and 10 literary books from socialist countries were openly published. Toward the end of the 1920s, Kobayashi Takiji(小林多喜二), a Japanese writer, became one of the leading representatives of proletarian literature. His novels *The Crab-Fishing Boat*(《蟹工船》, *Xiegongchuan*, 1929) and *The Absentee Landlord*(《在外地主》, *Zaiwai Dizhu*, 1929) were translated and openly published. In addition, *Wenjing Mifu Lun*(《文镜秘府论》), a collection of classical Chinese literary theories compiled by the Japanese Buddhist monk Ku Kai(遍照金刚, 774—835) and *History of Modern Japanese Literature*(《现代日本文学史》, *Xiandai Riben Wenxueshi*) written by Yoshida Seiichi(吉田精一, 1908—1984) were translated and openly published. 10 collections of short stories, poems, and movie scripts from socialist countries such as Albania, Democratic People's Republic of Korea, Vietnam, Cambodia, and Laos were also translated and widely circulated. The translation and open circulation of these works were not simply a literary activity but a diplomatic and political one. During Cultural Revolution, the number of internally distributed translations of foreign literary works was much bigger than that of the openly published and distributed ones. Among the internally distributed foreign literary works, 24 works were from Russian, 13 works were from Japanese, and 6 works were from American. In terms of the total translated literature, Russian and Soviet literature ranked the first. Japanese and American literature, which were scarcely translated in the first 17 years since 1949, became important and were introduced in Cultural Revolution.

After the Third Plenary Session of the 11th Central Committee of the Communist Party of China in 1978, the Chinese government shifted the focus of work onto economic development and introduced reform and opening up, thereby ushering in a new era of progress. The cause of translation, both foreign-Chinese translation and Chinese-foreign translation, became extremely active. Translation practice was unprecedentedly diversified and more efforts were devoted to translation studies, especially the introduction of Western translation theories. Currently, many people are engaged in translation practice and/or translation studies, and many Chinese universities offer bachelor's, master's and doctor's degree programs of Translation Studies.

1.2 Major Historical Stages of Translation in the West

Translation is a time-honored tradition in the West. To some degree, Western civilization has owed much to translators who have facilitated cultural, economic, and political contacts among countries throughout times, from Ancient Rome to the European Union and from the nation-state formation to the establishment of the United Nations. In a broad sense, the first translation in the West was produced in the 3rd century B.C., when 72 Jewish scholars in Alexandria translated the *Old Testament*. However, strictly speaking, the earliest translation is *The Odyssey*, which was translated into Latin in the mid-3rd century B.C. by Livius Andronicus (284—204 B.C.?) in Rome.

In Western history, there were six major stages of translation. The first was embarkation. The second was religious, which dated from the late Roman Empire to the early Middle Ages. The third was during the Middle Ages, between the 11th and 12th centuries, when Western translators gathered in Toledo, Spain to translate a slew of works from Arabic to Latin. The fourth occurred during the European Renaissance, between the 14th and 16th centuries, when translation practices pervaded the fields of ideology, politics, philosophy, literature, and religion. Translation in this stage involved great works from antiquity to the Renaissance and created a host of outstanding translators and excellent outputs. The fifth stage spanned the second half of the 17th century to the early 20th century during which translators not only continued to translate classical works, but also took interest in modern and contemporary ones. Numerous works authored by eminent writers such as Cervantes, William Shakespeare, Honoré de Balzac, Goethe, among others, were repeatedly translated into various languages. The sixth happened after World War II, during a period of significant changes in the translation community. In this stage, translation practice was prominent in science, technology and business in contrast to the conventional translation, which was concerned with literary and religious works. Translation had become an activity that was done not only by literary men, philosophers, and theologians, but also by specialized teams. Additionally, translation played a unique role, especially in the aftermath of the founding of the United Nations and the European Union. Translation serves as a conduit for contacts and exchanges in a variety of fields among Western countries. Finally, translation has developed in various ways since then: the inclusion of translation in higher education, the formation of translation organizations to pool resources, and the development of machine translation to complement traditional human translation.

1.2.1 The First Stage: Translation in Ancient Times

Around 3,000 B.C., formal text translation manifested in the Assyrian Empire, which was inextricably related to later European culture. The king asked the scribes, who were proficient in several languages, to inform the public about his great accomplishments in the empire's numerous languages. Additionally, the assistance of a large number of translators was required for many of the kingdom's political affairs. In the *Bible*, Esther made reference to ancient translators and Nehemiah recorded a unique type of translation that happened during his time.

The Greek version of the *Bible* was the first significant translation in the ancient West. The *Old Testament*, which was originally written in Hebrew, was Judaism's classic work. For a long period of time, the Jews were dispersed and drifted abroad. Over time, they lost touch with their ancestors' language and began speaking foreign languages such as Arabic and Greek, with speakers of the latter constituting the majority. In the 3rd century

B. C. , Egyptian King Ptolemy II requested the Bishop of Jerusalem to send translators to Alexandria, Egypt for the *Old Testament*. Between 285 B. C. and 249 B. C. , 72 "noble" Jewish scholars from 12 separate tribes of Israel met in the Library of Alexandria, Egypt and completed the *Septuagint*. This work is the product of collaborative efforts, establishing suh a precedent in the history of translation. Notably, the book is accorded a unique position in the history of translation as the translation is incredibly accurate and has been hailed as a masterpiece by believers, sometimes supplanting the Hebrew text as the "first original".

The Rosetta Stone, one of the most popular ancient translations associated with Western culture, is said to have been carved in the 2nd century B. C. , but it was not discovered until 1799 by Napoleon's army in Rosetta City, near Alexandria. The stone bears an inscription praising King Ptolemy V in three languages: ancient Egyptian hieroglyphics, popular hieroglyphics, and ancient Greek. This artifact is also used by archaeologists to compare and interpret the original text and translations, allowing for the translation and annotation of ancient Egyptian hieroglyphs and shedding light on the mystery-surrounding ancient Egyptian culture.

Translation in continental Europe dates back to the 3rd century B. C. , the time of Livius Andronicus, the first popular Roman translator. Since those times of the Roman Republic's heyday, its citizens had been transplanting Greek culture in the domestic sphere. Large-scale translation and absorption of Greek classics resulted to the first phase of significant growth in the history of Western translation. Livius Andronicus, the father of Roman epics and dramas, was the first translator in Rome. He translated Homer's epic poem *The Odyssey* into Latin. The output gave birth to the first Latin poem and made *The Odyssey* the first literary work translated into Latin. Additionally, Livius was the first to introduce Greek epics and dramas and to adapt Greek poetry and rhythm to the Latin language. He also translated or adapted 9 tragedies written by major Greek dramatists such as Aischylos, Sophocles, and Euripides, as well as 3 comedies by Menandros. After Andronicus, there were Naevius and Ennius. They were great dramatists, poets, and translators. Gnaeus Naevius (270—200 B. C. ?), mostly known as an ancient Roman historical dramatist, translated 6 tragedies and 30 comedies. Quintus Ennius (239—169 B. C.), the father of Roman literature, introduced the Greek hexapodic meter to Rome through translation and made significant changes to the composition of Latin poetry, thus, opening up new and expansive possibilities for Roman poetry.

Along with the above three major translators, there were numerous great writers engaged in translating Greek classics like Plautus (254? —184 B.C.), Terence (190? —159 B.C.?), Cicero (106—43 B.C.?), and Catullus (84? —54 B.C.?). For a long time, translation practice prevailed and no one but Cicero paid much attention to the study of translation theories and methods. He was not only engaged in translation practices but also advanced his own translation theoies, making him the first theorist in the history of translation in the West. Cicero was a celebrated orator, statesman, philosopher, and rhetorician. Also, he was a prolific translator whose works cover Homer's *The Odyssey*, Plato's *Timaeus and Protagoras*, Xenophon's *Oeconomicus or Economics*, Aratus' *Phenomena*, and other Greek masterpieces. Cicero's translation thoughts had a profound influence on subsequent translation theories and practices. His theories can be found in his works *De Optimo Genere Oratorum* (*The Best Kind of Oratore*, 46 B.C.) and *De Finibus Bonorum Et Malorum* (*On the Final Ends of Good and Evil*, 45—44 B.C.). Cicero said in *De Oratore* (*On the Orator*, 55 B.C.), "And I did not translate them as an interpreter but as an orator, keeping the same ideas and forms or, as one might say, the 'figures' of thought but in language which conforms to our usage. And, in doing so, I did not consider it necessary to render word for word but rather to preserve the general style and force of the language" (Robinson, 2014)[9]. This remark has become a famous, often-quoted aphorism in Western translation circles. His translation thoughts are as follows. First, translators should work as orators, expressing the content of foreign works in a language that adheres to Roman linguistic conventions to captivate and impress readers and listeners. Second, literal translation is a sign of incompetence. One should avoid translating word for word but retain the essence of the word, that is, its meaning. The translator's commitment is not to count words out to the readers like coins but to pay them by weight as they were. Third, translation is also a literary creation and anyone who attempts to translate Dimosini's works must be a figure like Dimosini. Fourth, it is a common phenomenon in language that sound and meaning are naturally connected or words and their meanings are inseparable in function. Since rhetorical devices are based on such a relation, they are identical across languages which demonstrate that style equivalence can be achieved by translation. Since the publication of his views, translation has come to be known as a literary creation. Issues such as the original and translated works, their form and content, as well as the translator's authority and responsibility, have always been issues of concern to the public. After Cicero, Quintus Horatius Flaccus (65—8 B. C.) proposed, "Do not worry about rendering word for word, faithful translator, but render sense for sense" (Lefevere, 2004)[15]. Marcus Fabius Quintilianus (35? —96?) held, "I would not have our paraphrase to be a mere interpretation but an effort to vie with and rival our original in the expression of the same thoughts" (Lefevere, 2004)[20].

The *Bible* translation is pivotal in the history of translation in the West. In ancient times, there were some significant religious translators and translation theorists. Philo Judaeus (20 B. C. ? —50?), the most influential religious translator, was a Greek-speaking Jewish philosopher who had formulated the first influential synthesis of Judaic theology and Greek philosophy. He was well-known in early religious circles for his statement that translating the *Bible* was sacred and that one cannot translate the *Bible* without the Holy Spirit's inspiration. These were his thoughts even though he was fluent in two languages. Only those who lead a pure religious life without "worldly impurity", such as theologians or devout religious believers have the authority to interpret the *Bible*.

In late ancient Rome, the ruling class of the Empire became more devoted to Christianity. Thus, religious translation reached its second apogee in the Western history of translation. The most prominent figures in this period were Jerome and Augustine. St. Jerome (347? —420) was revered throughout the Middle Ages and well into the modern era as the "official" translator of the *Bible* and the author of the Latin translation of the *Vulgate* that, in matters of doctrinal dispute, took precedence over all Hebrew and Greek texts until the 16th century and beyond. Jerome was one of the most influential translation theorists in the Western tradition. His statements on translation principles and methods influenced subsequent translation theories and practices significantly, which can be summarized in three points: first, translation is not word-for-word but sense-for-sense; second, literary translation and religious translation should be treated differently; and third, correct translation is contingent upon accurate comprehension.

St. Augustine (354—430) did not engage in a substantial amount of translation work. He only edited some parts of the Latin *Bible*. His main ideas about translation are summarized as follows. 1) Translators must meet the following requirements: they must be fluent in two languages, be familiar with and "empathize" with the subject matter being translated, and possess a certain level of collating capacity; 2) Three distinct styles must be considered when translating: plain, elegant, and solemn; 3) In translation practice, it is necessary for translators to understand the triangular relationship among "signified" "signifier", and their own "judgment"; 4) Word is the basic unit of translation; 5) *Bible* translation must be based on the divine inspiration.

The translation in the ancient West (except the translation in the ancient Assyrian Empire, the Babylonian Kingdom, and the *Old Testament* period) experienced two major periods of growth, from the heyday of the Roman Empire to its collapse that lasted more than 700 years. The first stage saw the introduction of ancient Greek literature to Rome, especially Homer's epics and dramas. This encouraged the emergence and growth of Roman literature, which served as a bridge for later European countries to inherit ancient Greek culture. In the second stage, the stage of large-scale religious translation, the translation of the *Bible* and other theological works was on a parity with the translation of secular literature and eventually surpassed it to become the mainstream translation activity in the West for a long period of time. With the fall of the Roman Empire, translation in the West gradually dwindled and entered the Middle Ages.

1.2.2 The Second Stage: Translation in the Middle Ages

The Middle Ages generally started from the collapse of the Western Roman Empire in 476 and ended with the Renaissance in the 15th century. In terms of the translation history, the Middle Ages has three major markers: Boethius (c. 480—524), who was a translator in the early period, the Toledo School of Translation in the middle period, and the translation in the national languages in the late period. In the late Roman Empire, religious translation, especially that of the *Bible*, dominated the translation field in Europe. After the fall of the Roman Empire, the situation changed. On the one hand, the church continued to organize the translation of religious documents to strengthen religious control. On the other hand, the new feudal landlord class intensified the translation and introduction of ancient Greek philosophical works to absorb political and philosophical ideas beneficial to the new feudal class. Important translators in the early Middle Ages were Cassiodorus, Gregory I, and Boethius. Cassiodorus (490—585), a historian, politician, and monk in the period of barbarian warfare, founded a monastery named Vivarium in 555. He collected a large number of manuscripts, organized monks to copy various theological and secular works, and carried out translation and research so as to protect and carry forward the cultural heritage of ancient Rome.

Gregorius I (540? — 604?) organized the earliest official translation agency to engage in the translation of religious and administrative documents of Eastern and Western Europe. Such an agency was the pioneer of various later ones. Manlius Boethius (480? —524?) was the most prominent theologian, politician, philosopher, and translator in the first few centuries after the fall of the Roman Empire and a central figure in the translation fields in the early Middle Ages. Boethius translated the *Categories* and *On Interpretation* in *Organon* of Aristotle, as well as the *Isagoge* written by Porphyrius for Aristotle's *Categories*. Through these translations, commentaries, and his important work *De Consolatione Philosophae* (*The Consolation of Philosophy*), he introduced the basic principles of Aristotle's *Logic* to Western Europe, causing a wave of research of Aristotle's philosophy. This had a great impact on the academic and theoretical circles in the Middle Ages. Boethius' main translation views are as follows: 1) Content and style are antagonistic to each other and the translator should keep either the style or the content; 2) Translation is centered on objective things and the translator should give up the right of subjective judgment. To express "uncorrupted truth", the translator should translate word for word.

The Toledo's translation activities in the middle of the Middle Ages represented the third peak in the Western translation history. In the 7th and 8th centuries, the Arabs expanded outward and conquered the Greek. A large number of Syrian scholars came to Athens, translated Greek works into Syriac language, and brought them back to Baghdad. Then, they translated these translations and some original Greek works into Arabic. Arab scholars came to Baghdad from all over the world to study Western culture and translate Greek works with great interest, making the city known as the Arab translation agency. Arab academic research began to decline in the 10th and 11th centuries and Arabic works poured into Spain in the 11th century. Toledo replaced Baghdad as the translation agency of Europe, in which a large number of Greek works were translated from Arabic into Latin. From the middle of the 11th century, scholars from various countries in the West went to Toledo and Cordoba, another city in Spain, to engage in the Latin translation, which reached a climax at the beginning of the 12th century. The Toledo translation agency has three characteristics: 1) Translation activities were generally patronized by the church; 2) The translated works were mainly Arabic translations of Greek works; and 3) Toledo was the educational and Muslim academic center of Spain at that time. The historical significance of Toledo's large-scale translation is as follows: 1) It marked a rare friendly contact between Christians and Muslims; 2) It brought Oriental ideas, spread ancient Greek culture, enlivened the academic atmosphere in the West, and promoted the development of Western culture; and 3) Since many translators were also scholars who taught all kinds of knowledge in Toledo, it became the educational center of Spain and even Western Europe at that time, and in a sense, became the predecessor of the first university in north central Spain.

By the end of the Middle Ages (13th—15th centuries), large-scale translations in national languages were evident. Primarily, the translation in national languages was related to the *Bible*, but it was not easy to carry out this translation. The early *Bible* translation was intended to guide the priests in preaching Christianity to the common people. The translation in national languages did not arouse people's opposition. By the 12th century, the cultural level of the laity had improved and they began to read and interpret the *Bible* according to their own understanding. The church opposed the translation of the *Bible* in national languages. This opposition and repression by the church could not restrain the strong desire of the people to read the translations in their own national languages. With the rise of humanism, translation of the secular literature and the *Bible* into national languages had been in climax in European countries since the 13th century. In France, interpreters were employed by the royal court to translate various Latin and Greek works. In Spain, influenced by the Toledo School of Translation, writers, historians, jurists, and natural scientists translated a large number of Arabic, Hebrew, Greek, and Latin works into Spanish. This promoted the development of Spanish culture and science. In Italy, translation in national languages was not large in scale but the great poet Dante's (1265—1321) elaborations on translation and national languages played an important role in solving the problems of translation in Italian national languages. The most influential translation theorist in Italy at the end of the Middle Ages was Leonardo Bruni (1370? —1444), an Italian humanist writer, translator, politician, and one of the pioneers of the European Renaissance. His academic career was mainly related to the translation of classics and historical research. He translated the works of Plato, Aristotle, Petrarch, and others into Latin. Bruni's contributions to translation theory made him an authority in Western translation theory at the end of the Middle Ages and the beginning of the Renaissance.

In Russia, the first major development stage of translation in national languages can be traced back to the Kiev period from the 11th century to the 12th century. During this period, large-scale translation began to take shape, with Greek and Latin works being the most widely translated. Although the translation in national languages had been widely carried out in Germany, Latin remained the significant. Critics praised the elegance of Latin language and complained about the vulgarity of the German language. They believed that German was neither mature nor inflectional. The grammatical categories of independent component usage, gerunds, antithesis, and infinitives in Latin were transplanted into German through translation and imitation in this period. At that time, word-for-word translation was dominant in Germany. To meet the needs of the era, most writers and translators translated a large number of Latin classical literary works. The most outstanding was Wyle, a translator and critic. Nicolas von Wyle (his date of birth and death unknown) was a university language teacher who translated dozens of ancient Roman works for his teaching. His preface to a collection of translated works showed his principles and methods of translation and has become one of the important documents about the early German translation theory. Wyle's main translation views are as follows: 1) Accurate translation of Latin can produce the most beautiful German style; 2) Word-for-word translation can promote Latin; and 3) To be faithful to the original text, the intelligibility of the translation can be sacrificed.

In Britain, with growing national consciousness, the desire for translation in national languages was stronger. In the 13th and 14th centuries, English was still a barbaric language in Western Europe. The British who wanted to read popular works at that time must be proficient in three foreign languages. The best English translator of this period was the great poet Geoffrey Chaucer (1340? —1400) who was fluent in Latin, Italian, and French. He translated many works of Boccaccio and all works of Boethius. Eustache Deschamps, a French poet at that time, praised Chaucer as a great translator. His translations opened a broad prospect for English translation and outstandingly contributed to the credibility of English as a literary language and the development of English literature. The literary atmosphere of medieval England was not very beneficial to translators. Firstly, English was underdeveloped. The readers of native languages were poor people without education and literary appreciation so the status of translators was quite low. Secondly, translators often could not choose works that met their own tastes because literary works only existed in the form of manuscripts at that time. Translators were often commissioned and funded for translation so most manuscripts were provided by funders. A large part of the English translations in the Middle Ages were legendary literary works and historical books. By the end of the Middle Ages, the second major translation was the translation of religious documents, most of which were short stories of legends of saints and certain abstract doctrines. The translation of religious works was different from that of legendary literary works. On the one hand, the original religious works usually came from Latin instead of French language. On the other hand, the translator emphasized the target audience. The purpose of religious translation was to provide understandable versions for people with no or low literacy. In the 15th century, religious translators, like literary translators, were particularly interested in the style of translation. The medieval English translators generally adhered to the principle that word-for-word translation was the primary method. Free translation could only be adopted according to the meaning of the sentence if word-for-word translation was not adopted. One of the most important translations of this period was the English translation of the *Bible*, which was initiated by John Wycliffe (1328—1384), a famous English theologian and philosopher in the 14th century. From 1380 to 1382, as the representative of the civil opposition and the founder of the English Reformation, Wycliffe presided over the translation of the *Bible*, which was a complete English translation. Such translation was supported by some people in the intellectual circle but his views and translation were strongly opposed by the church. Church authorities even banned translating in national languages but it took no effect. By the 15th century, Wycliffe's translation had been widely spread as the only English version. Throughout the Middle Ages, the study of translation theories was not systematic yet. Great advances in translation studies did not appear until the Renaissance.

1.2.3 The Third Stage: Translation during Renaissance

The Renaissance refers to the rediscovery and revitalization of the literature, art, and science of ancient Greece and Rome. The Renaissance began in Italy at the end of the 14th century and spread throughout Europe in the 15th and 16th centuries, especially in Western European countries. In the 16th century, the movement had spread from its birthplace, Italy, to other countries and gradually reached a climax. The Renaissance not only marked the great development of literature and art but also manifested an important milestone in translation history.

The translation activities in the 16th century in Germany were the same as those in the 15th century, mainly involving the translation between Latin and German. At the beginning of the 16th century, many Germans knew more about Greek and Hebrew languages and the status of these languages improved. Scholars began to realize that Hebrew, Greek, and Latin had different characteristics as German had its own unique ways of expression. German could not be translated into other languages word by word, nor could the reverse in the same manner. In the 15th century, the only reason that translators advocated free translation and opposed literal translation was that the word-for-word translation was not easy for readers to understand. In the 16th century, another significant reason for free translators to oppose literal translators was that German is an independent language with its own rules and must be respected. German has its own language style, which cannot be destroyed by imitating other languages. The translation in the 16th century Germany mainly focused on German proverbs, which were collected and translated into Latin while classical Latin literature and religious texts were translated into German. The translated Latin literary works include those by Cicero, Horace, Pliny, Cato, et al. The translation of religious texts focused on the *Bible*. Notable translators and theorists are Emser, Dietrich von Pleningen, Sebastian Brant, Leo Juda, Johannes Reuchlin, Desiderius Erasmus, Luther, among others. Martin Luther's translation of the *Bible* was the peak of German translation in the 16th century. Luther was the leader of the Reformation Movement and a translator in Germany. With the help of collaborators, the *New Testament* was first translated from Greek into German and published in 1522, and then the *Old Testament* was translated from Hebrew into German and published in 1534. The publication of the *Bible* enabled the German peasants and the poor to cite the chapters and sentences directly in defending their class interests so it was known as "the first Bible of the people". It not only had a profound impact on the life and religion of the Germans but also created a literary language form accepted by the people, which played an inestimable role in the unification and development of the German language. It is the first translation work that had a huge and direct impact on the development of national languages and was regarded as the superb in Western translation history. Luther's main translation views are as follows: 1) The language of common people must be used for translation; 2) Translators must pay attention to the connection between grammar and meaning. Translators should follow the essentials of grammar while focusing on the comprehension and expression of meaning; 3) Translation must be based on collective wisdom. As far as the essence of the translation theory was concerned, Luther discussed translation issues from the perspective of a theologian rather than a humanist.

Before the 16th century, French translation was mainly related to religious documents such as the *Bible*. At the end of the 15th century, a large number of literary works by such Italian humanists as Dante, Petrarch, and Boccaccio were introduced to France, which opened French people's eyes. French humanists translated numerous classical works and works of the Italian Renaissance into French. Although translation began to reach a climax, it was not high in quality or influential. In the climax of French translation, two people's contributions were very outstanding: "prince of translators" Amyot and translation theorist Dolet. Jacques Amyot (1513—1593), a university professor and bishop, translated some Greek and Roman literary classics. His translations reflected an overriding concern for absolute clarity. He was acclaimed for his contributions to the French language. Amyot's translation of Plutarch represented the supreme effort for the French language to equal the languages of antiquity. The Larousse Dictionary characterizes him as "one of the creators of classical prose" (Delisle et al., 2018)[41]. Amyot's translation principles are as follows: 1) The translator must have a thorough understanding of the original text and make great efforts in the translation of the content; 2) The translation must be simple and natural, without any ornament. Amyot made indelible contributions to the purity and standardization of French through his translation. Etienne Dolet (1509—1546) was a French humanist printer, translator, and scholar who is often referred to as the first martyr of the Renaissance, specifically as the first martyred translator. In addition to several translations and monographs on Greek and Latin, his contribution to translation was in his paper *La maniere de bien traduire d'une langue en autre* (*The Way to Translate Well from One Language into Another*, 1540). According to Dolet, translating well requires five main things: 1) The translator must perfectly understand the sense and matter of the author he is translating; 2) The translator has perfect knowledge of the language of the author he is translating and is likewise excellent in the language into which he is going to translate; 3) In translating, the translator must not be servile to the point of rendering word for word; 4) Don't be content with the vulgar and common tongue; 5) Observe rhetorical numbers, join and arrange terms with such a sweetness that not only the soul is pleased, but also the ear is delighted and never hurt by such harmony of language. His five principles of good translation are not original from him but they were influential (Robinson, 2014)$^{95-96}$.

In the Elizabethan Age, from the mid-16th century to the early 17th century, the British Renaissance reached its culmination and translation experienced its first great development in British history. Many translators, who were not scholars and were free from the restriction of translation theories, enjoyed freedom in what and how to translate. Both the scope and the quantity of translation were unprecedented. The translation of ancient historical classics, which were popular with both translators and readers, was flourishing. Because the theories of ancient philosophers and ethicists served the interests of the Tudor Dynasty (1485—1603), the works by Aristotle, Boethius, Cicero, Seneca, Demosthenes, Apuleius, and Aurelius were translated. Except a Greek drama by Euripides, almost all drama translations were confined to ancient Roman works. The translations of neoteric works were numerous, including Italian, French, and Spanish Renaissance works. The 16th century was destined to be a great century for it boasted some prominent translators and translation theorists like Gavin Douglas, John Cheke, Nicholas Udall, Nicholas Grimald, Thomas North, John Florio, Philemon Holland, George Chapman, and William Tyndale. The most famous translation in the Elizabethan period was Thomas North's English version of *The Biography of Celebrity*. It is an epoch-making masterpiece with an elegant prose style that is neither rigid nor grotesque and stands as an enduring example in English translation history. The most distinguished translator in the 16th century was Philemon Holland whose translation works were much more than those of his contemporaries. Meanwhile, his works were diverse in languages and subject matters. Holland was honored as Translator General of the Elizabethan era. His translation demonstrated two features: translation served the social reality and translation might attach great importance to literary style. George Chapman was a poet and playwright but it was through his translations that he earned a great literary fame. His translations of *The Iliad* and *The Odyssey* became the literary masterpiece of the time. His translations played a role in connecting the 17th century with the 16th century, which was his greatest contribution to the English literature. Chapman advocated that translation should be neither too rigid nor too free. In the 16th century, biblical translation was flourishing. Prominent *Bible* translators were William Tyndale and William Fulke (1538—1589). William Tyndale was the most influential *Bible* translator in English language. The three major English *Bible* translations of the 16th and 17th centuries, the Geneva *Bible*, the Douay-Rheims *Bible*, and the King James *Bible*, were all heavily attributed to his uncompleted work of the 1520s and 1530s. His English version of the *Bible* was banned by the Church and he was martyred in the end. William Fulke made an enormous contribution to the biblical translation theory. In 1589, he published *Defence of the Sincere and True Translation of the Holy Scripture into the English Tongue*, in which he proposed that translation had nothing to do with one's religious beliefs and biblical translation must comply with the preferences of target languages.

In conclusion, a remarkable feature of Western translation during the Renaissance was that the national translations in Western Europe developed independently and simultaneously. The Renaissance marked the appearance of national translations in history and a significant step forward in the translation practice and theory in the Middle Ages.

1.2.4 The Fourth Stage: Translation in Modern Times (17th—19th Centuries)

Translation in Western countries further developed from the 17th century to the 19th century. Numerous ideological trends in France such as classicism in the 17th century, sinology in the 18th century, and introductions to contemporary literary works of Western countries in the 19th century all contributed to the booming of the translation. In the 17th century, translators continued to translate classical works and some of them intensely debated about the principles and methods in translating classical works. Some translators adapted classical texts to canons and genres through omissions and "improvements" while others urged fellow translators to show humility to the classical source texts and strive for fidelity in their translation (Baker, 2006)[411-412]. Perrot d'Ablancourt (1606—1664) was the most prominent French translator in the 17th century. He translated a large number of classical works, the most famous being Tacitus's *Chronicle*. This version was well-known and reprinted many times. Ablancourt advocated for free rather than literal translation. The main purpose of his translation was to cater to the readers' tastes. Regardless of its accuracy, the content was cut at will to make sure that the translation was readable and popular with readers. Under his influence, many translators followed his way and blindly pursued the beauty of the translation's style. Gilles Menage (1613—1692), a famous translation critic, was said to have commented on a translation of Perrot D'Ablancourt, "I called it 'la belle infidele' (beautiful and unfaithful), which is what I used to refer to one of my mistresses when I was young" (Delisle et al., 2018)[66]. However, the "la belle infidele" translations were popular with many readers. Michel de Marolles was a French translator whose translations were the most in quantity and the worst in quality. He translated 70 works of ancient Roman writers such as Seneca, Stachus, and others, but all the translations were sharply criticized. During the Renaissance, translators generally adopted inaccurate translation without any explanation. Until the 17th century, mainstream translation was still inaccurate but translators tried to explain and defend their methods theoretically. Late in the 17th century, there was a dispute about adapting or being faithful to the classical source texts. At the end of the 17th century, free translation was advocated by the majority of translators. Daniel Huet (1630—1721?), one of the most influential translation critics in the 17th century, proposed that the only goal of translation was to be accurate and the translator had no right to choose words or change the word order at will. Francois Mauriac (1619—1708) and Jacques de Tourreil (1656—1714) were two representatives of the transition from inaccurate to accurate in France. Maucroix was regarded as one of the most outstanding translators and the first one to have translated Demosthenes' works in the 17th century. He did not posit any systematic translation theory. He came to realize that one could both show respect to the classical source texts and adopt d'Ablancourt's 'la belle infidele' translation principle. Tourreil translated *Demosthenes*. At the beginning, his translations were more elegant than accurate and were criticized severely. He published three French versions of *Demosthenes* and the third version, unlike the first two, was exceptionally linguistically accurate and beautiful. In the 18th century, Charles Batteux (1713—1780), a professor of philosophy at the Royal Academy of France, made the greatest contribution to the study of translation theories. He edited and published a variety of translated works, including many classical works of ancient Greece and Rome like those of Aristotle and Horace. Batteux's *Principes De La Litterature* was an influential book in the field of translation. It was an important milestone in the development of translation theories in the 18th century, which illustrated various thoughts and views on translation issues with fresh positions and good arguments. Another climax of French translation was in the 19th century when a large number of English, German, Italian, Spanish, and Latin literary works were translated.

Chapter 1　Historical Stages of Translation in China and the West

　　Translation in Germany also made great strides from the 17th century to the 19th century. A large number of works of ancient Greek and Roman authors and of modern or contemporary literary masterpieces from Britain, France, Spain, and other countries were translated into German. Such outputs turned Germany into another center of translation theory research and translation practice in Europe. Christoph Martin Wieland (1733—1813), an important writer during the Enlightenment, translated 22 plays of Shakespeare. Famous writer Friedrich von Schiller (1759—1805) was also a well-known translator whose translations included Shakespeare's *Macbeth*, Picard's *Parasite* and *Nephew as Uncle*, Racine's *Phaedra* and so on. The poet Johann Heinrich Voss (1751—1826) translated Homer's *The Odyssey* and *The Iliad*, as well as the works of Virgil, Ovid, and Horace. August Wilhelm Schlegel (1767—1845), the greatest German translator in the 18th and 19th centuries, followed the principle that the translation might be accurate and represent the original style. He translated 17 plays of Shakespeare, the Spanish plays of Pedro Calderon de la Barca (1600—1681), as well as works of many Italian writers. Johann Gottfried von Herder (1744—1803), the forerunner of German romanticism and a leading figure in the Sturm and Drang (storm and stress) movement, proposed that the task of a translator was to make foreign books understandable to the readers who did not know the relevant foreign languages.

　　Wolfgang von Goethe (1749—1832), one of the greatest German writers and the major figure in German romanticism, was well-versed in several languages and qualified in translating several languages. Some of his translations were the most influential and excellent in the European literature. Goethe was also a great translation theorist. His major points on translation are as follows (Robinson, 2014)[222-225].

　　1) A simple translation is the best for common readers who have to feel an effect. The translations produced by experts that compete with the original only serve as entertainment for scholars.

　　2) Meter and rhyme should be honored, for that is what makes a writing a poem, but the part that is really, deeply, and basically effective, and the part that is truly formative and beneficial, are parts of the poem that remaind when it is translated into prose.

　　3) There are two maxims for translation: one requires that the foreign author be brought over to us so that we can look upon him as our own; the other requires that we cross over to the foreign country and find ourselves inside its circumstances, its modes of

speech, its uniqueness. Both approaches have their strong points.

4) There are three kinds of translation. The first is informative translation, which familiarizes us with the foreign country in our own terms. The second is adaptation, in which one seeks to project oneself into the circumstances of the foreign country, but in fact, he only appropriates the foreign meaning and then replaces it with one's own. And the third is interlinear translation, in which one seeks to make the translation identical with the original so that the one would no longer be in the stead but in the place of the other.

5) Translators should be considered as busy matchmakers, praising a half-veiled beauty worthy of our love. They excite an irresistible yearning for the original.

More famous than Goethe in the field of linguistics and translation theories are Schleiermacher and Humboldt. Friedrich Daniel Ernst Schleiermacher (1768—1834) was a German theologian who is generally credited with the creation of modern Protestant theology. Schleiermacher's importance for the romantic theory of translation cannot be overestimated. In 1831, he expounded the principles and methods of translation in *Ueber Die Verschiedenen Methoden Des Uebersezens* (*On the Different Methods of Translating*). It is the major document of romantic translation theory and one of the major documents of Western translation theory in general. The main points of the treatise are (Robinson, 2014)[225-238] as follows.

1) There are two kinds of translation: the interpreted works in the field of commerce while the translated proper works in the fields of scholarship and art. Verbal art and scholarship require writing to render their works permanent.

2) Translation may be mechanical or true. Translating the business-related texts is a merely mechanical task that can be performed by anyone who is moderately proficient in the source and target languages. The true translation refers to the translation of poetic and philosophical texts.

3) The translator must have a good command of the dialectic relationship between language and thinking.

4) A translator must choose between taking the reader back to the original source or bringing the original source to the reader. "Either the translator leaves the author in peace, as much as possible, and moves the reader towards him. Or he leaves the reader in peace, as much as possible, and moves the author towards him".

Chapter 1 Historical Stages of Translation in China and the West

Schleiermacher's reflections on the theories of language and of translation have influenced the linguists and students of translation to the present day.

At the turn of the 18th century, Germany became the center of translation studies in Western Europe. Wilhelm von Humboldt (1767—1835), a linguist, philosopher, and educational reformer, had special contributions to translation studies. The German romantic trend marked not only the great development of literature but also a turning point in the history of translation. Under the influence of Romanticism, Humboldt published two works successively: *A Comparative Study of Language in Different Ages of Language Development* and *On the Differences of Human Language Structure and Its Influence on the Development of Human Spirit*. He also wrote a theoretically profound preface to his translation of *Agamemnon*. His contribution to the translation theory was reflected by his linguistic theories: 1) Language determines thought and culture; 2) The languages are too different to be translatable; 3) A dialectical relationship exists between translatability and untranslatability. Humboldt's greatest contribution was his dualistic view of language that was very influential in the 20th century. According to his dualistic view, language can be analyzed from two aspects of "language system" (Langue, Sprache, language, competence) and "speech act" (Parole, Rede, speech, performance). Such view is conducive to solve the problem of language translatability and untranslatability.

In the 19th-century Germany, the poet Friedrich Holderlin (1770—1843) also had a great influence on the translation field. He translated works or fragments of Homer, Pindar, Sophocles, Euripides, Virgil, Horace, Ovid, Lucan (39—65) and the like. Holderlin did not write about translation theories specifically but only made some comments on his translation of Sophocles' works, which touched the essential issues of language and translation and occupied a special position in the history of Western translation theory.

Translation in Britain developed on an unprecedented scale in the Elizabethan Age. From the 17th century to the 19th century, translation in Britain flourished, and many great translations of classic works were published. Studies on translation theory in the 17th and 18th centuries surpassed those in the Elizabethan Age. King James Version of the *Bible* (Authorized Version) published in 1611 was the most important translation in the 17th century and even in the entire history of British translation. For a long period of time, it was the only well-known translation in Britain and almost everyone had a copy of it. The translation was plain, solemn, and vivid in language. This work greatly expressed the beauty of phonology, giving play to the characteristics of the British national languages. And this had an immeasurable impact on the development of British prose, language and culture. The King James Version was the result of a collective translation completed by 47 people in groups. The main reasons for the success of this translation are as follows: 1) All 47 people participating in the translation were the best scholars and theologians at that time, who had the superb comprehension of the *Bible* and excellent language skills; 2) The 47 translators were closely collaborative to give full play to the collective wisdom; 3) Reference to the existent translations of the *Bible* was made; 4) The general principle was faithful to the original text; 5) The translators drew on Hebrew, Greek, and Latin language styles appropriately.

The 17th century, a period of remarkable achievements in literary translation, produced some influential translators including Thomas Sheldon (dates of birth and death unknown), Charles Cotton, John Stevens, Roger L'Estrange, Tom Brown, John Phillips, and Peter Anthony Motteux. John Dryden (1631—1700) was the predominant English literary figure of his day. His influence on English literature for the next one or two centuries was massive. As the greatest translator in the 17th century, Dryden made greater contributions to translation, with a large number of translated works and his systematic translation theory, than his predecessors and contemporaries. He did not write lengthy knit-browed treatises on translation but his short treatises and prefaces on translation were later collected in *Essays of John Dryden* in 1900. His main translation principles and views are as follows: 1) Translation is an art; 2) The translator must have a good grasp of the features of the original works; 3) The translator must be considerate of the readers; 4) The translator must be absolutely obedient to the original works; 5) All translations may be reduced to three types: metaphrase, paraphrase, and imitation. Dryden's translation theory is illuminating, not only dominating the second half of the 17th century, but also deeply influencing the translation studies in Britain in the 18th, 19th and 20th centuries.

When it comes to the 18th century translators, the first translator who comes to mind is Alexander Pope (1688—1744). Pope, an English poet, satirist, and translator, has been the best remembered for his eminently quotable couplets and for his brilliant translations of Homer. Pope's Homer has been attacked as it is not homeric, and it sounds more like Pope and generally like an 18th-century Englishman than it does like an ancient Greek (Robinson, 2014)[192]. He translated *The Iliad* and *The Odyssey*. For quite a long time, his translations were regarded as the standard English translations and were very popular with the readers. Compared with the previous centuries, the 18th century had some achievements in translation studies but made no substantial progress. By the end of the 18th century, there was a breakthrough in the history of translation studies. Theoretical research was no longer limited to sporadic impressionistic views about translation. George Campbell (1719—1796), dean of Marischal College in Aberdeen, Scotland, published *A Translation of the Four Gospels with Notes*, including two volumes. The second volume is the translation of the *Bible* and the first volume is his 500-page introduction. This is a monograph on translation. In the book, he made a careful and systematic analysis of the translation of the *Bible* and believed that the translation of the *Bible* should serve two different purposes, namely literature and religion. Campbell's theoretical elaboration was far more extensive and profound than his previous scholars and his breakthrough in theory was mainly manifested in: 1) Explaining the function and purpose of translation; 2) Describing and analyzing the actual process and skills of translation; and 3) Commenting on the relationship between purposes and skills. At the same time, he advanced three principles of translation for the first time: 1) Accurately reproducing the meaning of the original text; 2) Transplanting the spirit and style of the original author as far as possible on the premise of conforming to the linguistic features of the translated text, and 3) Making the translated text as natural and fluent as the original. These three principles were of epoch-making significance.

In 1790, Alexander Fraser Tytler (1747—1814) published his monograph *Essay on the Principles of Translation*. In addition to this, he published several volumes of local, legal and universal history in the 1780s and 1790s. He was a professor of universal history at the University of Edinburgh and a lawyer. Tytler presented three principles of translation: 1) The translation should give a complete transcript of the ideas of the original work; 2) The style and manner of writing should be of the same character with that of the original; 3) The translation should have all the ease of the original composition (Robinson, 2014)[209]. Tytler's translation theory is comprehensive and systematic. It is a milestone in the history of English translation and Western translation. Influential translators in the 19th century are Thomas Carlyle, George Eliot, Byron, Shelley, Fitzgerald, among others. In this century, there was no such a monograph on translation studies as that written by Tytler. However, in the second half of the 19th century, there was a famous debate on the translation of Homer's epics, which was triggered by the translation of *The Iliad* by Francis W. Newman (1805—1897). The poet and critic Matthew Arnold (1822—1888) published *On Translating Homer* in 1861 and commented on Newman's translation and its preface. Newman was not convinced and wrote *Homeric Translation in Theory and Practice: A Reply to Matthew Arnold* (1861) in response. Arnold wrote *Last Words on Translating Homer: A Reply to Francis W. Newman* (1862) to further criticize Newman. Arnold's views are listed below: 1) Understanding Homer before translating Homer; 2) Retaining Homer's basic characteristics; 3) Having the poet's insight; 4) Being equipped with the insight of a poet; 5) Having the same appeal as the original; and 6) It is the scholars, not the readers, who test the appealing quality of the translation. For Newman, his main points are as follows: 1) Homer is an ancient man and the translation should have the characteristics of the ancients; 2) The standard of translation is mainly the response of the ordinary readers rather than the scholars; 3) Translation is a compromise. The more outstanding the original is, the less comparable the translation is. The arguments of Arnold and Newman do not concern general translation skills or knowledge of the language. The key to their disagreement is their different translation principles and methods.

In the hundreds of years before the 18th century, Russian translation had expanded in scale. But compared with those of several Western European countries, both Russian translation practice and theory were inferior. The beginning of the 18th century heralded the era of Peter the Great, in which Russia actively developed economic and cultural exchanges with Western European countries. The number of translated works in the 18th century increased significantly, making the period an extremely important turning point in Russian translation history. The following are the characteristics of translation in this era: 1) The translation activities were supported by the royal courts; 2) The literary writers were keen on translation; 3) The activities were well organized to a certain extent; 4) Translation theories were given importance. Translation covered a wide range of works, including scientific and literary works. Many outstanding writers, such as Trejakovsky, Lomonosov, Sumarokov, Fonvizin, and Radishev, enthusiastically participated in the translation. With the support of the Russian Queen, the Association for Translating Foreign Books, the earliest professional organization in Russian translation history, was established in 1768. In the history of Russian translation, the brilliant study of translation theory began with Lomonosov and his contemporaries. Through his own translation and creation of scientific works, Lomonosov made great contributions to the purity and unification of Russian scientific terms.

Russian translators in the 18th century held that translation was creative in nature. But this optimism and the popular "adaptation to Russian taste" resulted in liberalism in translation practice, which meant that translators could change the original freely. When it comes to Russian translators in the 19th century, people may first think of the greatest poet Pushkin. His major translations include the satirical poems by French poets in the 17th and 18th centuries, odes of Horace in ancient Rome, fragments of lyrics in ancient Greece, fragments of Italian poet Alosto's works, narrative poems and the preface of the long poem *Konrad Wallenrod* written by Polish poet Mitskovitch, and fragments of *Koran* and the *Bible*. Pushkin's highly artistic translation and insightful views about translation were a powerful impetus to the translation in Russia and made him a milestone in the history of translation. Vasily Rukovsky (1783—1852), the pioneer of Russian lyric poems, made outstanding contributions to translation in Russia. His literary writing was not as much as his translation and adaptation of foreign works, including works of Schiller, Goethe, Hebel, Scott, and Byron. Rukovsky's translation was highly appreciated by Pushkin and Belinsky (1811—1848). Mikhail Yuryevich Lermontov (1814—1841), the great poet, showed his talent in translation in his short life. He translated works of Byron, Schiller, Heine, and Chenier, et al. The political and ideological strife in the Russian literary community became increasingly grave in the mid-19th century. This was between "art for the people" and "art for art's sake". The former was advocated by revolutionary democrats while the latter was supported by the reactionary nobles and bourgeois liberals who worshiped the capitalism of Western Europe. The struggle was reflected in the field of translation and manifested in the selection of texts to be translated. Revolutionary democratic translators like Plexeyev (1825—1893), Mikhailov (1829—1865), Kurochkin (1831—1875), and Minayev (1835—1889), among others, translated ideologically progressive works. While translators of reactionary nobles and bourgeois liberalism such as Fett (1820—1892), Mikov (1821—1897), Pavlova (1807—1893), and Tolstoy (1817—1875) translated works with negative contents. Some works translated by the two opposing parties were the same but these were translated and interpreted in quite different ways. In the 19th century, many outstanding Russian writers and literary critics showed strong interest in translation issues. They realized the significance of translation to the development of literature and explored problems concerning translation. Progressive writers, from Pushkin to Belinsky, Turgenev, Chernishevsky (1828—1889), and Pisalev (1840—1868), expressed their opinions on translation issues. These views are important and they are different from the traditional Western European translation theories. They expounded the following points with advanced ideology: 1) The ideological content and literary value are the first criterion for selecting literary texts to be translated; 2) A good translation must be a unity of content and form; and 3) Translation should be reader-oriented and serve the people. Revolutionary ideology was embodied in the translation theories for the first time in the history of Western translation. The main feature of Russian translation in the late 19th century was the unprecedented expansion of translation practice rather than a breakthrough in translation theory. Weinberg (1831—1908), the greatest contributor in the late 19th century, translated a large number of foreign works including Shakespearian plays and Heine's proses and lyrics from the standpoint of Russian progressive literature at that time.

The above is a review of the translation in some major European countries from the 17th century to the 19th century, which is an important stage for the development of translation theories.

1.2.5 The Fifth Stage: Modern Translation (1900—1945)

The period from the beginning of the 20th century to the end of World War II can be regarded as the modern period of translation history. The two world wars in the first half of the 20th century seriously disturbed the translation cause but translation in some fields and countries had special features. For example, translators of classic works no longer put emphasis on the elegant style of the original works and broke away from the tradition of translating poetry into poetry by translating poetry into prose. Many prominent translators from various countries translated modern and contemporary literary works, especially those of Russia and Northern Europe. Constance Garnett (1861—1946), the most famous female translator in Britain in the first half of the 20th century, translated almost all the classical Russian novels and has been regarded as the most important English translator of

Chapter 1 Historical Stages of Translation in China and the West

Russian literature. She was the first who translated the works of Turgenev, Dostoevsky, and Chekhov into English and translated all the main works of Turgenev, Gonzalov, Dostoevsky, Tolstoy, Gogol, and Chekhov. Garnett translated 70 Russian works in her lifetime. Aylmer Maude and his wife Louise translated twenty-one volumes of *The Collected Works of Tolstoy*. Their English translation of *War and Peace* gained them a reputation as authoritative English translators of Tolstoy's works. Though they could not be compared with Garnett in terms of the number of works translated from Russian to English, the couple were not inferior in influence. Among those English translators who translated works of Tolstoy, Dostoevsky, Turgenev, Chekhov, Goncharov, and others, R. S. Townsend, R. Edmonds, Samuel S. Koteliansky, Ethel C. Mayne, Boris Brasol, Richard Renfield, D. Magarshack, Doris Mudi, Edward Wasiolek, K. Fitzlyon, J. Coulson, and M. Josephson are more well-known.

During the first half of the 20th century, in addition to the enthusiasm about the translation of Russian literature, Western European translation circles also developed a great interest in Nordic literature and drama, such as Andersen's, Ibsen's and Strindberg's works. During Andersen's lifetime, one of his works was translated into fifteen languages at the same time including almost all major languages in Western Europe such as English, German, French, Italian, and Spanish. Later, all his works were successively translated into various languages and there were many versions in England, France, Germany, and other countries. The main English translators who translated Ibsen's plays were William Archer and James McFarlane. From 1906 to 1912, William Archer translated twelve volumes of *The Collected Works of H. I.*, including all of Ibsen's plays and some of his unpublished papers. McFarlane compiled eight volumes of *The Oxford Ibsen* from 1960 to 1977. F. E. Garrett translated *Lyrics and Poems from Ibsen* in 1912; Mary Morison translated *The Correspondence of H. I.* in 1905; and Evert Sprinchorn translated *H. I. Letters and Speeches* in 1964.

In Germany, the standard German version of Ibsen is the 10-volume *The Collected Plays of H. I.* edited and published by G. Brandes, J. Elias, and P. Schlenther from 1898 to 1902. The standard French version is the 16-volume *The Collected Works of H. I.* translated and published by P. G. La Chesnais from 1914 to 1945. Strindberg's works were translated into English in 1912, and since then, a lot of people have studied and translated his works. The main English translators were E. Schleussner, Walter Johnson,

M. Sandbach, Elizabeth Sprigge, and Michael Meyer. In Western European countries such as Germany and France, Strindberg's plays were translated into the native languages. Besides, his plays were brought on stage.

In Western European countries, the mutual translation of modern literary works was quite vibrant. From 1900 to 1906, the well-known French writer Marcel Proust (1871—1922) translated and introduced the works of John Ruskin (1819—1900), an English art critic and writer. From 1922 to 1931, C. K. Scott Moncrieff and Stephen Hudson translated Proust's great work, seven-volume *The Remembrance of Things Past*. Jackson Mathews compiled *The Collected Works of Paul Valery*. Besides, many works caused a strong reaction among British and American readers. Examples of such are *The Collected Works of Paul Valery* compiled by Jackson Mathews, Baudelaire's works translated by Arthur Symons, Jonathan Mayne et. al., and Sartre's works translated by K. Black, F. Williams, H. E. Barnes, and others. H. T. Lorow Porter (1876—1963) was the first translator who translated the works of modern German writer Thomas Mann (1875—1955) into English. From 1916 to 1961, Porter translated and published almost all of Thomas Mann's works.

With the craze for Sinology, Western countries started translating a lot of Chinese literary works. At the end of the 16th century, Chinese works were introduced into Europe. In the 20th century, the West became more and more interested in Chinese culture. After the 1950s, with the rise of international prestige of China, the craze for China and the translation of Chinese literature continually emerged in the West. Not only the classics—"Four Books" (四书, Sishu), "Five Classics" (五经, Wujing), *The Romance of the Three Kingdoms*(《三国演义》, *Sanguo Yanyi*), *The Water Margin*(《水浒传》, *Shuihuzhuan*), *The Journey to the West*(《西游记》, *Xiyouji*), *The Dream of Red Mansion*(《红楼梦》, *Hongloumeng*), and Li Bai's (李白), Du Fu's (杜甫) and Bai Juyi's (白居易) poems were translated into English, French, and German, but also the works of modern writers Lu Xun, Ba Jin, and Mao Dun were introduced to Western countries. Arthur Waley (1889—1966), the most outstanding British sinologist in the 20th century, translated *Hanshi Xuanyi*(《汉诗选译》, *Chinese Poems*) in 1916. It was his first translation. He also published *Hanshi Yibai Qishi Shou*(《汉诗一百七十首》, *One Hundred Seventy Chinese Poems*) in 1918. Besides, in 1942, Waley finished the abridged translation of *Xiyouji*(《西游记》, *The Journey to the West*) and published the other four Chinese-English translations. His works were prominently regarded in the history of translation in England, especially in the translation of Oriental culture. In the 20th century, another eminent sinologist and translator in the West was Franz Kuhn (1884—1961) from Germany. In 1919, he published his first translation, *Maiyoulang Duzhan Huakui*(《卖油郎独占花魁》, *The Oil Seller and the Song Girl*). Up to 1961 before he passed away, Kuhn translated and published more than 40 works of ancient and modern Chinese literature, including *Haoqiuzhuan*(《好逑传》, *Biographies of Good Spouses*), *Erdumei*(《二度梅》, *Second Blooming Plum Blossom*), *Jinpingmei*(《金瓶梅》, *The Plum in the Golden Vase*), *Shuihuzhuan*(《水浒传》, *The Water Margin*), *Yuqingting*(《玉蜻蜓》, *Jade Dragonfly*), *Ziye*(《子夜》, *Midnight*), and so on. Like Waley, Kuhn made no remarkable contribution to translation theory and did not put forward important views about translation.

Translation in Soviet Union was unique. After the October Revolution in 1917, the Russian nation entered the Soviet era and the fundamental changes in the political system led to great changes in translation activities. Translation in socialist Soviet Union and that of the capitalist Western Europe and North America experienced two completely different development routes. Translation in Soviet Union had the following features. First, Marxism-Leninism was the guide for translation practice and theory. Second, the translation and publication of foreign literature was organized, planned, and systematic. Third, the selection of texts to be translated was strictly based on the ideology, art, and intellectual value of the original work. Fourth, the translation between different national languages in Soviet Union developed greatly. Finally, translation activities generally followed the principles of fidelity, accuracy, and not translating literally.

Since the end of the Second World War, the world has entered into a relatively peaceful period. The history of translation has been ushered in the contemporary phase. With the revitalization of translation in Europe and the United States, new translation theories emerged one after another. Both translation practice and translation studies have advanced significantly.

Questions for discussion:

1. What do you think is the secret to the survival of Chinese civilization, from ancient to modern times?

2. What are the major historical stages of translation in China?

3. What are the major historical stages of translation in the West?

References:

陈福康,2000.中国译学理论史稿[M].修订本.上海:上海外语教育出版社.

Chen Fukang, 2000. A draft history of Chinese translation theory[M]. Shanghai: Shanghai Foreign Language Education Press.

陈玉兰,2020.《越人歌》楚译的象征主义审美表现及其对诗歌翻译的启示[J].浙江师范大学学报(社会科学版)(6):25-35.

Chen Yulan,2020. The symbolistic aesthetic expression of the Chu translation of folk songs of the Yue people and its inspiration on poetry translation[J]. Journal of Zhejiang Normal University(Social Science Edition)(6):25-35.

季羡林,2015.季羡林谈翻译:典藏本[M].北京:当代中国出版社.

Ji Xianlin,2015. Ji Xianlin talks about translation: Collected edition[M]. Beijing: Contemporary China Publishing House.

孔慧怡,2005.重写翻译史[M].香港:香港中文大学翻译研究中心.

Eva Hung, 2005. Rewriting Chinese translation history[M]. Hong Kong: Research Centre for Translation, Chinese University of Hong Kong.

毛泽东,1960.毛泽东选集(第四卷)[M].北京:人民出版社.

Mao Tse-tung, 1960. Selected Works of Mao Tse'Tung (Volume Ⅳ)[M]. Peking: People's Publishing House.

马祖毅,等,2006.中国翻译通史[M].武汉:湖北教育出版社.

Ma Zuyi et al. ,2006. A history of translation in China[M]. Wuhan: Hubei Education Press.

孙迎春,2011.翻译简史[M].天津:天津教育出版社.

Sun Yingchun,2011 . A brief history of translation[M]. Tianjin: Tianjin Education Press.

王秉钦,2004. 20世纪中国翻译思想史[M].天津:南开大学出版社.

Wang Bingqin,2004. A history of translation thought in the 20th Century China[M]. Tianjin: Nankai University Press.

王钢,2014. 场域斗争·民族心理认同·西学救国:欧美弱小和被压迫民族文学"中国化"的深度分析[J]. 东北师大学报(哲学社会科学版)(4):118-123.

Wang Gang, 2014. A deep analysis on "China localization" of small and weak and oppressed Euro-American national literature[J]. Journal of Northeast Normal University (Philosophy Social Science Edition)(4):118-123.

王克非,1994. 论翻译文化史研究[J]. 外语教学与研究(4):57-61.

Wang Kefei, 1994. On the study of cultural history of translation[J]. Foreign Language Teaching and Research(4):57-61.

王佐良,1981. Two early translators reconsidered[J]. 外语教学与研究(1):12.

Wang Zuoliang, 1981. Two early translators reconsidered[J]. Foreign Language Teaching and Research(1):12.

谢天振,等,2009. 中西翻译简史[M]. 北京:外语教学与研究出版社.

Xie Tianzhen, et al., 2009. A brief history of translation in China and the West[M]. Beijing: Foreign Language Teaching and Research Press.

邹振环,1996. 影响中国近代社会的一百种译作[M]. 北京:中国对外翻译出版公司.

Zou Zhenhuan, 1996. The 100 Chinese translations that influenced modern China[M]. Beijing: China Translation and Publishing Corporation.

Baker M, 2006. 翻译研究百科全书[M]. 上海:上海外语教育出版社.

Cheung M P Y, 2010. 中国翻译话语英译选集(上册):从最早期到佛典翻译[M]. 上海:上海外语教育出版社.

Delisle J, Woodsworth J, 2018. 历史上的翻译家[M]. 北京:外语教学与研究出版社.

Lefevere A, 2004. 翻译、历史与文化论集[M]. 上海:上海外语教育出版社.

Pym A, 1998. Method in translation history[M]. Manchester: St. Jerome Publishing.

Robinson D, 2014. Western translation theory: From Herodotus to Nietzsche[M]. New York: Routledge.

Chapter 2

Bible Translation in the West

The *Bible* is the most important and influential document in the world, especially in the West. A religious work as it is, it is also a work of history, literature, and other fields. It is the most translated work in history.

2.1 Early *Bible* Translation and Dissemination of Christianity

The *Bible* was originally the holy work of the Jews. Eventually, it became the *Holy Scripture* for the Christians. With the spread of Christianity, it was translated into many different languages. One of the earliest languages it was rendered into was Greek and its result was the *Septuagint*.

2.1.1 *The Septuagint*

As one of the sources of the Western civilization, the *Bible* was handed down via oral tradition among the Jewish tribes throughout time, which began around 600 B.C. No written Hebrew texts existed from that time. Although it is unknown when the Hebrew *Scripture* was written down, the Dead Sea Scrolls indicates that the *Scripture* was written in Hebrew, Aramaic, and Greek in the 3rd century B.C.

When Ptolemy II Philadelphus came to power in 283 B.C., Israel was under Greek rule and many people spoke Greek rather than Hebrew. The king tried to expand his library at Alexandria and asked for a Greek translation of the Hebrew Law. The Jewish tribes were more than willing to accept the task for they wanted those who did not understand Hebrew to have access to the *Scripture* in a language they could understand.

It is said that the 12 Jewish tribes each sent 6 scholars to fulfill the responsibilities of Ptolemy II's commission in writing and translating the Hebrew Law into Greek. These scholars worked on their translations independently. As the story goes, every single one of them had exactly the same output! This work was the *Septuagint*, "the translation of seventy". Other books were translated over the next 3 centuries and the entire process had been finished by 132 B.C.

Chapter 2　*Bible* Translation in the West

　　The *Septuagint* was the source of many later translations including the Latin *Vulgate*. It is the version of the *Scripture* quoted by most *New Testament* authors and has profound influences on the formation of early Christian vocabulary. Even today, the Orthodox Church still prefers the *Septuagint* as its basis for translating the *Old Testament* and uses the untranslated version of the *Septuagint* in places where the liturgical language is Greek.

2.1.2　*The Vulgate*

　　After the Roman Empire was established, people in the eastern part spoke Greek while those in the west used Latin. As Christianity spread through Greek-speaking cities and made its way across the empire, the growing Christian church needed Latin translations of the *Scripture*.

　　Such translations were all primarily based on the *Septuagint* and Greek manuscripts of the *New Testament* but were, more often than not, word-for-word translations. Some even retained the Greek word order, making them almost indecipherable in Latin.

　　In 382, Pope Damasus I commissioned Jerome (347—419/420) to render a better Latin translation of the *Bible*, in other words, a standard, authoritative translation.

　　St. Jerome was born to a wealthy family in Stridon, a village in today's Croatia, on March 27, 374. He traveled to Rome with his friend Bonosus to pursue rhetorical and philosophical studies, in which Jerome learned Latin and Greek. He led a daring life, which he often regretted, and as a result, he frequented the sepulchers of the martyrs and the catacombs of the Apostles. He was initially skeptical of Christianity but was eventually converted and baptized in the year 366 by Pope Liberius.

　　A few years later, Jerome went to Gaul with Bonosus and settled in Trier. In about 373, Jerome and his peers embarked on a journey through Thrace and Asia Minor to northern Syria. He stayed mostly at Antioch due to an illness that had killed two of his friends and a vision of devoting himself to God. With this, Jerome had to forego his secular studies.

　　He studied the *Bible* under Apollinaris of Laodicea and was inspired to live like an ascetic, for which Jerome spent some time in the desert of Chalcis and learned Hebrew from a converted Jew. Before Jerome's return to Antioch in 378 or 379, he had copied a Hebrew Gospel and translated parts of it into Greek. He, then, spent two years studying the *Scripture* under Gregory Nazianzen in Constantinople before serving as a secretary to Pope Damasus I in Rome for three years.

After the latter's death in December 384, Jerome was removed from his position. However, his work on the *Scripture* continued. After completing the project, Jerome took it upon himself to revise the Latin translations of the *Old Testament* with the *Septuagint* as basis. In 390, he began translating the *Bible* from the original Hebrew source.

There were mainly three principles guiding Jerome in his Latin translation from Hebrew, namely, to make the text intelligible, to avoid slavish renderings, and to take cognizance of the elegance of diction.

As a result, the Latin *Bible* had been the most authoritative version for Christians for more than 1,000 years. And on April 8, 1546, the Council of Trent declared the *Vulgate* as authentic. But this does not exclude minor mistakes from it. Instead, the declaration presupposes the *Vulgate* to be free from substantial errors, at least in matters pertaining to faith and morals.

2.2　Religious Reformation and *Bible* Translation

The Roman Catholic Church had ruled Europe for a long time that it became bureaucratic and corrupted. The church controlled the explanation of the *Bible* and the ordinary people had no access to the Holy *Scripture* except the *Vulgate*. Dissent within the church gained momentum so the people protested and called for reform, ushering the Protestant Reformation in the 16th century. The Reformation was more than a religious one. It was also a political, intellectual, and cultural upheaval that splintered Catholic Europe, setting up the structures and beliefs that would define the continent in the modern era. In northern and central Europe, reformers like Martin Luther, John Calvin and others challenged the papal authority and questioned the Catholic Church's ability to define Christian practice. They argued for the redistribution of religious and political powers among *Bible*/pamphlet-reading pastors and princes.

Although John Wycliffe (1328—1384) was known as the "morning star of the Reformation", this historical juncture is generally believed to begin with Martin Luther's "95 Theses" in 1517 and to end anytime from the Peace of Augsburg in 1555 to the Treaty of Westphalia in 1648. The former allowed for the coexistence of Catholicism and Lutheranism in Germany while the latter ended the Thirty Years' War.

Martin Luther was born on November 10, 1483 to a relatively prosperous mining family in Eisleben in the Holy Roman Empire. His father, Hans, gave him a good education with the intention for Martin to become a lawyer so that he could help with the family business. In 1501, Martin entered the University of Erfurt where he was exposed to Aristotle's teachings, nominalism, and humanism and earned his Master of Arts degree in 1505. However, he quit his legal training later in the same year and chose, instead, to enter the Augustinian monastery at Erfurt, much to the annoyance of his father.

As a monk in the monastery and a temporary lecturer at Wittenberg, Luther's education continued. In 1512, he replaced Staupitz at the university in Wittenberg as the professor of the *Bible*, a position he was to hold until his death. Earlier in the same year, he had his only excursion beyond German lands, travelling on behalf of Staupitz to Rome where he witnessed those religious rituals and practices (such as indulgences) incompatible with his principles.

Dissatisfied with the Pope's sale of reprieves from penances or indulgences, Luther nailed a copy of his "95 Theses" on the door of the Wittenberg Castle Church on October 31, 1517. His ideas were written in a remarkably humble and academic tone, questioning rather than accusing. However, the overall thrust was, nonetheless, quite provocative. The "95 Theses" would later become the foundation of the Protestant Reformation.

The publication of the document eventually led to Luther's excommunication in 1521. He was summoned to defend his beliefs before the emperor at the Diet of Worms but he refused to succumb and was thus declared an outlaw and heretic. Fortunately, Luther had the protection of powerful German princes. The key figure among them was Frederick Ⅲ of Ernestine Saxony (Frederick the Wise) whose sheltering enabled Luther to translate the *Bible* into German.

Such translation is one of the greatest contributions of Luther to the church. Luther was not the first one to render the *Holy Scripture* into German but was, no doubt, the greatest translator of the German *Bible*. He and the German *Bible* are inseparable inasmuch as Jerome is with the Latin *Vulgate*. Luther threw the older translation into the shade and has not been equaled or surpassed by another. There are more accurate versions for scholars but none can rival his popular authority and use as his work transformed and ennobled the German language.

Luther's first attempt to translation was to render seven penitential psalms into German. This work was published in March 1517, six months before his famous "95 Theses". He, then, tried to translate several sections of the *Old Testament* and the *New*

Testament, for which he was urged by his friends, especially by Melanchthon, to translate the whole *Bible*.

He began with the *New Testament* in November or December 1521 and had completed it in March next year, before he left the Wartburg. It took him just 3 months to finish the translation, which indicates that he made judicious use of the earlier German versions. He thoroughly revised this output on his return to Wittenberg, with the effectual help of Melanchthon, who was a much better Greek scholar, and two other friends. The translation was then hurried through three presses and appeared on September 21, 1522 but without Luther's name.

He, then, proceeded to the more difficult task of translating the *Old Testament* and published it in parts as they were ready. In the progress of the work, he founded the Collegium Biblieum and a *Bible* club. Each member contributed to the work with his special knowledge and preparation. Sometimes, they barely mastered three lines of the Book of Job in four days and searched for a single word in two to four weeks. Unfortunately, no record of the discussions of this group exists. Finally, in 1534, the translation of the whole *Bible* was completed and printed using numerous woodcuts.

Luther continuously amended his translation. Besides correcting errors, he improved the unrefined and confused orthography, fixed the inflections, removed obscure and ignoble words, and made the whole more symmetrical and melodious.

Luther's German *Bible* helped make modern High German as the common book language, bringing order out of the confusion caused by the German language. When Luther was doing the biblical translation, German language had many dialects and none served as unifying. People from different regions could hardly understand one another. Each author wrote in the dialect of his area. It was in such a milieu that Luther selected the Saxon dialect as the basis. It was bureaucratic, stiff, heavy, involved, dragging, and unwieldy. He adapted this dialect to theology and religion and popularized it. He enriched the dialect with the vocabulary of the German mystics, chroniclers, and poets. He made it intelligible to the common people in all parts of Germany. Luther modified the words to the capacity of the Germans, often at the expense of accuracy. This move brought out the whole wealth, force, and beauty of the German language. Luther's German *Bible* is the first German classic as the King James Version is the first English classic. These conjunctures anticipated the golden age of German literature as represented by Klopstock,

Lessing, Herder, Goethe, and Schiller.

Luther's publication of the German *New Testament* in 1522 started a new era of vernacular biblical translation. Soon, the Dutch vernacular *Bible* was produced, followed by William Tyndale's (1494—1536) English *New Testament* in 1526 and a complete French *Bible* in 1530.

2.3 English Versions of the *Bible*

Although partial translations of the *Bible* into Anglo-Saxon had existed long before Wycliffe's translation, John Wycliffe's version is credited as being the first translation of the entire *Bible* (both the *Old Testament* and the *New Testament*) into English in the 14th century. What prompted him to do the work was that the Czech wife of England's Richard II had the *Scripture* in her native language.

John Wycliffe was born on an inland sheep farm 200 miles from London sometime between 1325 and 1330. He left for Oxford University in 1346 but was not able to earn his doctorate until 1372 because of periodic eruptions of the Black Death. Nonetheless, by then, he had been already considered as Oxford's leading philosopher and theologian.

Wycliffe believed that every Christian should have access to the *Holy Scripture* (only Latin translation was available at the time) so he began to translate the *Bible* into English in 1380.

He did not work alone as others helped him. He translated the Four Gospels (Matthew, Mark, Luke, and John) and, possibly, the entire *New Testament* while his associates handled the *Old Testament*. The *New Testament* was finished in 1382 and the entire *Bible* was translated in 1384.

The Church was furious at rather than welcoming the translation. At the Council of Constance in 1415, Wycliffe was declared a heretic. It decreed that all his works should be burned and his remains was exhumed. And in 1428, 43 years after his death, Wycliffe's corpse was disentombed and burned at Pope Martin V's command. His ashes was cast into the River Swift, which flows through Lutterworth where he preached.

Despite such posthumous treatments for its translator, the Wycliffe's *Bible* would ultimately survive, with about 250 individual copies or revisions available in various libraries and museums today. Although each manuscript had to be hand-written because of the Church's wish to destroy the translation wherever it was, the survival of the work proved its popularity. It laid the groundwork for further translations of the *Bible* into English. In fact, the King James Version retains much of the same wording as in the Wycliffe's *Bible* and continues the latter's legacy.

No new English translations were produced between Wycliffe's and Tyndale's due to the 1408 British law against any *Bible* in English. It would be risky enough just to make a copy of Wycliffe's *Bible*!

William Tyndale was born in Gloucestershire around 1494. He was trained in Greek and Hebrew. He earned his bachelor's degree from Oxford in 1512 and his master's degree in 1515. He later studied at Cambridge. At that time, he became fluent in six or seven languages. His English style was unparalleled.

As he was contemplating a new translation of the *Bible* in the 1520s, he felt that it was impossible to do this work in England for the 1408 British law against *Bible* translation was still in effect. Besides, Tyndale could not find anyone who knew Hebrew in England. So he traveled to Germany where he was introduced to rabbis from whom he learned Hebrew. While on the Continent, he translated much of the *Bible* into English. By 1525, he had completed his first translation of the *New Testament* but was unable to had it printed until 1526.

Tyndale later revised the *New Testament* substantially, producing a masterpiece of translation. He even coined certain new words that found their way to the English lexicon in the next five centuries such as "passover" "peacemaker" "scapegoat", and even the adjective "beautiful". Altogether, he produced five editions of the *New Testament*, though the third edition in 1534 was the one most remembered.

Tyndale translated a large part of the *Old Testament* before he was kidnapped in Antwerp in 1535 and burned at the stake for heresy the next year. The irony was that he was charged with a corrupt translation of the *Bible* even though he produced a superb one.

It is impossible to overestimate the significance of Tyndale's translation because it was the first English *New Testament* after the age of printing and was translated directly from Greek. Also, the work was the first translation to use italics for words that were not in the text and greatly influenced the King James Version. In 1940, Prof. J. Isaacs wrote about Tyndale's accomplishment: "His simple directness, his magical simplicity of phrase, his modest music, have given an authority to his wording that has imposed itself on all later versions... Nine tenths of the authorized *New Testament* is still Tyndale's and the best is still his" (Wallace, Lecture 1).

Soon after Tyndale's *Bible* came three more translations, the Coverdale's *Bible* (1535), the Matthew's *Bible* (1537), and the Great *Bible* (1539). These were all inferior to Tyndale's but, nevertheless, important milestones in the history of the *Bible* in English. Other important later translations of the *Bible* were the Geneva *Bible* (1557 [NT], 1560 [whole *Bible*]), the Bishops' *Bible* (1568), and the Douay-Rheims Catholic *Bible* (1582 [NT], 1609—1610 [whole *Bible*]) before the arrival of the authorized King James Version in 1611.

In January, 1604, King James I of England summoned the religious leaders of the country to Hampton Court to make a translation of the whole *Bible* that should be almost like the original Hebrew and Greek.

King James was enthusiastic about the translation that he formulated the rules of whom the translators should be, how they should be organized, and what principles they were to follow. But he did not do any actual translation. Instead, he divided the 47 scholars into six panels to do the work: three for the *Old Testament*, two for the *New Testament*, and one for the Apocrypha. Two panels met at Oxford, two at Cambridge, and two at Westminster Abbey.

The translators did not follow the King's rules to the letter. For example, King James ordered that although the translators were to rigorously consult the Greek and Hebrew texts, they should retain the wording of the Bishops' *Bible* whenever possible. But this rule was ignored more often than not.

The Authorized Version was not well-received at first. It took about 50 years for the translation to surpass the Geneva *Bible* in popularity. The Authorized Version was criticized for being too simple, too easy to understand, and from the perspective of some, being inaccurate.

But it has endured the test of time. It is regarded as "the single greatest monument to the English language". A scholar claimed that "The supremacy of the King James is one of style, not of scholarship". "The men who made it did not set out to manufacture a literary classic—classics are seldom made to order. Yet they did produce one: perhaps the only classic ever turned in by a committee..." (Wallace, Lecture 2). The Authorized Version has rhythm, balance, dignity, and force of style that is unparalleled in any other translations.

This version had been unchallenged for 270 years until the publication of a revision of the Authorized Version in 1881. This aimed at accuracy in representing the meaning of the original but the language was often unnatural. It turned out to be a dismal failure although it launched a new era—the era of accuracy.

In 1901, the American Standard Version was produced. It was still a revision of the King James *Bible* and the language was stilted but passable, significantly better than that of the Revised Version. The American Standard Version was the most literal translation ever done in English that prompted readers to accept its English.

In 1952, the Revised Standard Version was published, selling 1 million copies on the day. It was very much in the spirit of the Authorized Version and should be regarded as another revision of the King James *Bible*. The Revised Standard Version was powerful in its simplicity and directness. It is still one of the most popular translations ever done but also the most hated English translation of all time.

Unlike the first half of the 20th century, the second half was teemed with new translations. The first major reaction to the Revised Standard Version was the New American Standard Version, produced by the Lockman Foundation in La Habra, California—a theologically conservative organization.

In 1970, the New English *Bible* was produced to achieve dynamic equivalence rather than formal equivalence. The version was conceived in 1946 but not completed until 1970. It was done by British scholars, perhaps as an overreaction to the failure, that was, the Revised Version. Nevertheless, the New English *Bible* is a very fresh and readable translation, the most beautiful translation of the 20th century.

If the New American Standard Version was the first major reaction to the Revised Standard Version, the New International *Bible* would be another evangelical reaction. It was highly readable but hardly elegant.

In 1979, the New King James *Bible* was published. It was much more accurate than the old version but lost the beauty, making it look almost like the New American Standard Version.

A decade later, the New Revised Standard Version came into circulation to adapt to the new discoveries in the past 40 years. Changes in English language, itself, and culture caused it to become one of the first gender-inclusive translations of the *Bible*.

The year 2001 saw the publication of two new translations of the *Bible*: the Holman

Christian Standard Version, representing a fractured evangelical community where bibles seemed to be political and religious pawns again, and the English Standard Version, which was a reaction to the New Revised Standard Version and a work consciously in line with the Authorized Version.

With the advances brought by the Internet, a new version, the NET *Bible*, appeared in 2001. This strove to be as accurate as the formal equivalent translations, as readable as the dynamic equivalent translations, and more elegant than either.

Questions for discussion:

    1. Why is the first Greek version of the *Bible* called the *Septuagint*?

    2. Why and how did Saint Jerome produce the *Vulgate*?

    3. What contributions did Luther's translation of the *Bible* make to the German Language?

    4. What is the relationship between the Authorized Version and the English language?

    5. How about the English translation of the *Bible* in recent years?

References:

Wallace, Daniel. "Lecture 1: From Wycliffe to King James". https://www.biblicaltraining.org/transcriptions/lecture-1-wycliffe-king-james

"Lecture 2: The Reign of King James (The Era of Elegance)". https://www.biblicaltraining.org/transcriptions/lecture-2-reign-king-james-era-elegance

Chapter 3

Buddhist Scriptures and *Bible* Translation in China

Generally, the translation of Buddhist scriptures, which began no later than the middle of the second century, is regarded as the first wave of translation in China. The Chinese translation of the *Bible* occurred much later than that of the Buddhist scriptures and influenced the Chinese language much less than the translation of Buddhist scriptures.

3.1 Buddha and Buddhism

Buddha means "awakened one" or "enlightened one". In Sanskrit, the term *buddha* has traditionally been used to refer to "one who has awakened from the deep sleep of ignorance and opened his consciousness to encompass all objects of knowledge" (Buswell et al., 2013)[315]. In Chinese, *fo*(佛) is the transcription of the first syllable of *buddha*, and *fotuo*(佛陀) is the full transcription of *buddha*. *Buddha* is often transcribed as *fo*(佛), not semantically translated into *juezhe*(觉者, the awakened one). In addition to Shakyamuni(释迦牟尼), there are many other buddhas named in the Buddhist literature. Although different Buddhist schools have not agreed on the precise nature of buddhahood, it is universally agreed that "a buddha is a person who, in the far distant past, made a previous vow to become a buddha in order to reestablish the teaching at a time when it was lost to the world" (Buswell et al., 2014)[315]. In the Mahayana(大乘, Great Vehicle) Buddhist traditions, the name *Shakyamuni* is used to distinguish the historical buddha from the myriad of other buddhas who appear in the sutras. The ākyas were a tribe in northern India in which the man who would become the historical buddha was born. The Sakya clan flourished in the foothills of the Himalayas, near the border between present-day Nepal and India. Shakyamuni lived in northern India between the mid-6th and mid-4th centuries B.C.. Buddhism is the religion and philosophy that developed from the teachings of the Buddha Shakyamuni. Spreading from India to Central and Southeast Asia, China, Korea, and Japan, Buddhism has played a central role in the spiritual, cultural, and social life of Asia.

3.2　First Introduction of Buddhism to China

No one knows for certain when or how Buddhism entered China. A commonly accepted account of the introduction of Buddhism to China placed that event in the Yongping(永平) era of the reign of Emperor Ming(汉明帝, reigned 58—75) of Western Han Dynasty (25—220). According to *The History of the Later Han*(《后汉书》, *Houhanshu*), the official history of the dynasty, Emperor Ming showed a considerable appreciation for the teachings of Buddhism, for a younger brother of Emperor Ming paid homage to Buddhist images and there lived some Buddhist monks and lay Buddhist believers in his territory. The Buddhist faith first took root in China in the first century, specifically during the time of Emperor Ming.

No reliable historical record indicates exactly when and how the religion was first introduced to China, but there are two possibilities: Buddhism was transmitted directly from India by persons journeying to China by sea, or was introduced from the countries of Central Asia by Chinese envoys or foreign missionaries traveling over the Silk Road that linked China with the West. The latter seems much more likely. The countries in Central Asia were the intermediaries in transmitting Buddhism from India to China because many important Buddhist terms such as *shamen*(沙门, shramana or recluse) and *chujia*(出家, become a monk) seemed to have not directly come from Sanskrit words but from terms used in the languages of the Central Asian countries (Ikeda, 1986)[13]. The opening of the Silk Road paved a way for the cultural contacts between China and Central Asia. New plants and foods were brought to China by the travelers on the Silk Road so it is very likely that Buddhism entered China by the same route. As can be speculated from available evidence, Buddhism spread from India, passed along the Silk Road running through Central Asia, and was introduced to China. Buddhism, founded by Shakyamuni Buddha, spread beyond the country of its origin and was received in China, a country with a wholly different cultural background five hundred years after its founder's passing away.

3.3　Three Phases of Buddhist Translation

The Buddhist scriptures were written in Sanskrit and Pali, two languages totally different in structure from the Chinese language. It was not realistic to expect ordinary Chinese people to learn to read the *Scripture* in Sanskrit or Pali. Hence, it became necessary to translate the *Scripture* into Chinese if the religion was to be extensively accepted. The monks from Central Asian countries served as mediators between the Chinese and Indian languages.

The Chinese translation of the Buddhist scriptures in history can be roughly divided into three phases: the first phase (initial stage): Eastern Han Dynasty and Three Kingdoms Period (c. 148—265); the second phase (development stage): Jin Dynasty and the Northern and Southern Dynasties (c. 265—589); and the third phase (prosperity stage): Sui, Tang and Northern Song Dynasties (c. 589—1100) (Baker, 2006)[366].

3.3.1 The First Phase: Eastern Han Dynasty and Three Kingdoms Period (c. 148—265)

According to historical documents, Chinese translation of the Buddhist scriptures in great numbers did not begin until the end of the Later Han Dynasty, around the middle of the second century, when Parthamasiris(安世高, c. 148 – 180) and Lokaksema(支娄迦谶, c. 178 – 198) came to Luoyang, the capital of China.

The task of translating the Buddhist scriptures in earnest did not start until a century and a half after the religion was introduced to China. In the reign of Emperor Huan(汉桓帝, reigned 147—167) of the Later Han, such a task was initiated by Parthamasiris, a Parthian monk who arrived in Luoyang in 148, and carried on by later arrivals such as the Yuezhi monk Lokaksema. The monk translators from Central Asia enjoyed the patronage of rulers like Emperor Huan.

Parthamasiris, a prince of the royal family of Parthia, relinquished his right to the throne to his younger brother after the death of his father and gave himself up to the study of Buddhism. He came to China in 147 and spent more than twenty years translating Buddhist texts into Chinese. He was an early Buddhist missionary in China and the first major translator of Indian Buddhist materials into Chinese. Because of his renown as an early translator, later Buddhist scriptural catalogues in China ascribed many works that did not carry translator's attributions to Parthamasiris. Many of the earliest translations of Buddhist texts into Chinese are credited to Parthamasiris, but few can be determined with certainty to be his works. His most famous translations are *Renbenyushengjing*(《人本欲生经》, *Mahanidanasuttant*), *Anbanshouyijing* (《安般守意经》, *Anapanasatisutta*),

Chapter 3 Buddhist Scriptures and *Bible* Translation in China

Yinchirujing(《阴持入经》), and *Daodijing*(《道地经》). His transcriptions, rather than translations, of some seminal Buddhist concepts are still in use, such as the Chinese transcription *fo*(佛) for *buddha*, *pusa*(菩萨) for *bodhisattva*.

Lokaksema, an Indo-Scythian monk from the Kushan kingdom in northwest India, was active in China sometime in the last quarter of the second century, soon after Parthamasiris. He is often known in the literature by the abbreviated form Zhi Chen(支谶). Fourteen Chinese translations in twenty seven rolls are ascribed to him, of which twelve are generally presumed to be authentic. These include the first Chinese renderings of sutras from some of the earliest strata of Indic Mahayana (摩诃衍那, 大乘), such as *Astasahasrika Prajnaparamita*(《小品般若经》, *Xiaopinbanruojing*), *Kasyapaparivarta* (《遗日摩尼宝经》, *Yirimonibaojing*), *Pratyutpanna Buddha Sammukhavasthita Smadhi Sutra*(《般舟三昧经》, *Banzhousanmeijing*), and *Aksobhya Tathaga Tasya Vyuha*(《阿閦佛国经》, *Achufoguojing*). It is possible that Zhi Chen produced the Chinese versions for a community of Kushan immigrants who had lost their ability to read Indic languages, because the texts were translated into pidgin Chinese.

Zhi Qian (支谦, c. 220—252), a descendant of an Indo-Scythian émigré from the Kushan kingdom in northwest India, was a great Buddhist translator after Parthamasiris and Lokaksema. Zhi Qian fled northern China in the political chaos that accompanied the collapse of Han Dynasty, eventually migrating to the Wu Kingdom in the south. He first settled in Wuchang and later in Jianye(建业, currently Nanjing, the capital city of Jiangsu Province), the capital of Wu Kingdom. He became the first to translate the Buddhist scriptures in the south of China instead of in Luoyang. In Jianye, he completed the majority of his translations. Many of his Chinese translations were noted for a fluent style that did not strive to adhere to the exact meaning of each word and phrase, but sought to convey the insights of the text for the Chinese audience in an accessible fashion. The translations that can be credited with certainty to Zhi Qian are the early renderings of *Vimalakirtinirdesa*(《维摩经》, *Weimojing*), *Pusa Benye Jing* (《菩萨本业经》), *Sukhavativyuha Sutra*(《无量寿经》, *Wuliangshoujing*), *Astasahasrika Prajnaparamita*(《小品般若经》, *Xiaopinbanruojing*), and a primitive recension of *Avatamsaka sutra*(《华严经》, *Huayan Jing*). He is also thought to be one of the first Buddhist commentators in the East Asian tradition.

Kang Senghui(康僧会, ?—280), a Sogdian monk and early translator of mainstream

Buddhist texts into Chinese, came to Jianye, the capital of Wu Dynasty (222—280), in 247. Kang's translations included *Avadanas*(《六度集经》, *Liudujijing*), and he wrote an important preface and commentary on *Anapanasatisutta*, a Chinese recension of the Smrtyupasthana sutra.

The initial period of Buddhist translation has the following features. A large number of early Chinese translations of the Buddhist scriptures were produced not directly from the Sanskrit texts but indirectly from sources written in the monk translators' mother languages. The bulk of the translators were monks from Central Asia or descendants of people from Central Asia. Most of the translators from Central Asia were respected for their religious knowledge, but they had to rely on their Chinese pupils or the native Chinese translators for assistance because of their poor command of the Chinese language. Translation Forums, or *Yichang*(译场), were set up to ensure an accurate understanding of the original texts and remedy the foreign monks' deficiency in Chinese language. A highly revered Buddhist monk served as the chief translator or *yizhu*(译主) of the forum. The foreign monks were responsible for a detailed explanation of the precise meaning of the original texts. Collaboratively working with the foreign monk were one or more interpreters [*chuanyan*(传言) or *duyu*(度语)] who orally interpreted the monk's explanation into Chinese. Usually, a big audience listened to and took notes of the foreign monk's explication. The Chinese version of a text was then compiled by the recorder (*bishou*, 笔受), who wrote down the interpreter's words in Chinese.

The early Chinese translations of Buddhist texts, which almost all were produced by monks from Central Asia, were faithful enough to the original texts, but they were often difficult for Chinese readers to comprehend. In rare cases where the translators succeeded in making the essence more easily comprehensible for Chinese, it was usual and inevitable that they departed from or distorted the basic meaning of the original texts. Literal translation, the regular method adopted by the early Buddhist translators, seemed to have been approved by the later critics. According to some critics, the translations were "simple but not vulgar" (质而不野), "the original substance is highly valued and ornamentation excluded" (贵尚实中,不存文饰), "the original gist has indeed been obtained without any ornamentation" (皆审得本旨,了不加饰), "elegance is abandoned to retain the substance" (弃文存质,深得经义), and even "simplicity will be close to the original" (朴则近本) (Yang Yan, 1992)[11].

3.3.2 The Second Phase: Jin Dynasty and the Northern and Southern Dynasties (c. 265—589)

In 265, Sima Yan(司马炎), a minister of Wei Kingdom, usurped the throne and established Jin Dynasty(Western Jin Dynasty, 西晋). The invasion of the northern "five barbarian states" and the internal serious strife among the royal families for power threw the whole empire into great disorder. In 317, the Jin court was forced to move to Jianye in the south and began Eastern Jin Dynasty (东晋). At the end of Jin Dynasty, there appeared 16 states. Political instability and ideological confusion pushed people to religion for comfort. The rulers advocated and promoted the religion, which created a favorable environment for the spread of Buddhism. Because of the incessant wars in the north of China, the traditional center of Buddhist introduction and translation moved from north to south. Then, Buddhist translation entered the phase of development. In this phase, outstanding Buddhist translators, including Dharmaraksa(竺法护, 231—308), Dao'an (道安), Kumarajiva(鸠摩罗什, 343—413), Dharmaksema(昙无谶, 385—433), Yan Cong(彦琮, 557—610), Faxian(法显, c. 337—422), Huiyuan(慧远, 334—416), and Paramārtha(真谛, 499—569), made great contributions to the development of Buddhist translation[①].

1) Dharmaraksa

Dharmaraksa, one of the most prolific translators in early Chinese Buddhism, played an important role in transmitting the Indian scriptural tradition to China. Born in Dunhuang in far western China, he was called the Dun-huang Bodhisattva or the Yuezhi Bodhisattva because of his descent. He grew up speaking multiple languages. Because of his multilingual ability, he was able to supervise a large team in rendering the Buddhist scriptures into Chinese. 150 translations of over 300 fascicles are attributed to him, including the first translation of *Saddharmapundarika Sutra*(《法华经》, *Fahuajing*), *Vimalakiritinirdesa*(《维摩诘经》, *Weimojiejing*), *Lalitavistara*(《佛说普曜经》, *Foshuopuyaojing*), *Bhadrakalpika Sutra*(《贤劫经》, *Xianjiejing*), and some of the Prajnaparamita literature. He is generally considered as the most important translator of the early Chinese Buddhist samgha.

2) Dao'an

In 383, a Buddhist translation center was founded with the patronage of Fu Jian(苻

---

① Notes: The introduction of Buddhist translators in this section is based on Buswell Jr. and Lopez Jr. (2014)

坚), ruler of the former Qin Kingdom(前秦). The center became an official enterprise instead of a private one. Eminent Chinese and foreign Buddhist monks were invited to the place to work collaboratively. The task of translation was spearheaded by Dao An who publicly declared that "the cause of Buddhism will go nowhere without the support of the monarch."

Dao'an, a native of Fuliu in present-day Hebei province, was a monk exegete and pioneer of Buddhism during Eastern Jin Dynasty. Fleeing from the invasions of the northern minorities, Dao'an migrated frequently with his teacher Fotudeng(佛图澄) who was a famous Kuchean monk and thaumaturge. Dao finally settled down in Xiangyang(襄阳), a prosperous city in Hubei province and taught there for fifteen years. Learning of Dao'an's great reputation, the former Qin ruler Fu Jian amassed an army and captured Xiangyang. After its fall, Fu Jian invited Dao'an to the capital Chang'an and honored him as his personal teacher. Dao'an, who was ignorant of Sanskrit and languages in Central Asia, made the following contributions: 1) He compiled *Zongli Zhongjing Mulu*(《综理众经目录》), a catalogue of scriptural translations. This is not only the first catalogue of translated scriptures but also the first catalogue of translations. 2) He presided over the Buddhist translation and expounded the Buddhist sutras for big audiences. In collaboration with eminent Chinese and foreign monks, he translated 14 texts in 180 rolls. Dao An advocated "translating according to the original features"(案本而传), which put him in the school of literal translation. 3) He composed various prefaces and commentaries and his exegetical technique of dividing a scripture into three sections (*Sanfenkejing*, 三分科经)—"preface" (*xufen*, 序分), "text proper" (*zhengzongfen*, 正宗分), and "dissemination section" (*liutongfen*, 流通分)—is still in wide use in East Asian scriptural exegesis even today.

3) Kumarajiva

Dao'an ever urged Fu Jian to invite the renowned central Asian monk Kumarajiva to China. Kumarajiva was born in Kucha, a central Asian kingdom. His father Kumarayana, who came from a distinguished family in an Indian kingdom, renounced his right to the post of prime minister because of political disappointment, became a monk, and came to Kucha in Central Asia. Kumarayana married the younger sister of Kucha's king. Their marriage bore a son named Kumarajiva. When he was nine years old, Kumarajiva returned to his father's hometown with his mother. There he studied under an esteemed Buddhist master. In spite of his great youth, Kumarajiva's reputation began to spread throughout India and the nations of Central Asia. At the age of 12, he, with his mother, embarked on a return journey to Kucha. He moved from place to place with his mother. In addition to his studies of Buddhist works, Kumarajiva studied texts on specialized subjects such as medicine, astronomy, exegetics, technology, and logic. Without this academic background, he might never have been able to understand such an encyclopedic text, *Treatise on the Larger Perfection of Wisdom* (Mahāprajñā Pāramitā Śāstra,《大智度论》), much less render it into Chinese. At the age of 51, he came to Chang'an in the third year of the Hongshi era of the Later Qin Dynasty(后秦弘始, in the year of 402). After that, he entered the most fruitful period of his life. Counting both retranslations and first translations, Kumarajiva is believed to have translated over fifty works in more than three hundred volumes. The whole process of Buddhist translation was a corporate undertaking sponsored by the government. Yao Xing(姚兴), who was the second ruler of the Later Qin Dynasty and an avid student of Buddhism, was Kumarajiva's patron and spared no effort to encourage and assist Kumarajiva's translation. Kumarajiva made greater contributions to Chinese Buddhist translation than his predecessors. His sufficient learning and understanding of the Buddhist texts enabled him to avoid errors that the earlier translators had made and rectify such mistakes when these came to his attention. He has been universally recognized for the excellence of his translations. He was well-known for ensuring that the Buddhist teachings were correctly transmitted into Chinese and the beauty of translation language and translation skills were superbly done. *The Lotus Sutra*(《妙法莲华经》, *Miaofalianhuajing*), *The Larger Perfection of Wisdom Sutra*(《大智度经》, *Dazhidujing*), and *The Vimalakirtinirdesa*(《维摩诘经》, *Weimojiejing*), which are basic Mahayana texts, came to be widely studied and revered throughout China not only because of the superior nature of the ideas in these texts but also because of Kumarajiva's powerful and compelling language in the Chinese versions.

4) Fa Xian

Fa Xian was a Chinese monk of Eastern Jin Dynasty. In 399, with the company of fellow monks, he left the Chinese capital Chang'an for India to produce a complete recension of an Indian Vinaya. In his *A Record of Buddhist Kingdoms*(《佛国记》, *Foguoji*), Fa Xian provided a detailed record of his journey across numerous kingdoms in Central Asia, arduous pathes through the Himalayas, and various pilgrimage sites in central India. In India, he studied Sanskrit and copied various sutras and vinayas. A few years later, he left India for Sri Lanka. On the voyage back to China, Fa Xian was trapped on the island of Java for 5 months. In 413, he returned to Jiankang(建康, present-day Nanjing in Jiangsu province). He devoted the rest of his life to translating the Buddhist texts that he brought back from overseas. In collaboration with the Indian monk Uddhabhadra, Fa Xian completed the Chinese translation of 6 texts in 63 rolls, including *Mahasangha-vinaya*(《摩诃僧祇律》, *Mohesengqilü*), *Mahā-parinirvāna*(《大般泥洹经》, *Dabannihuanjing*).

5) Dharmaksema

Dharmaksema, an Indian Buddhist monk, was well-versed in the mainstream Buddhist texts. At the end of Western Jin Dynasty, he carried with him the first part of *Mahaparinirvana Sutra*(《大般涅槃经》, *Dabanniepanjing*) as he left India and arrived in the Kucha kingdom in Central Asia. He, then, moved to China and had lived in the western outpost of Dunhuang for a few years. Juqu Mengxun(沮渠蒙逊), the ruler of Northern Liang Dynasty(北凉), brought Dharmaksema to his capital Guzang(姑臧, now Wuwei in Gansu province) where he engaged in a series of translation projects under the patronage of the ruler. With the assistance of Chinese monks, he produced many influential Chinese translations such as *Dabanniepanjing*(《大般涅槃经》, *Mahaparinirvana Sutra*) in forty rolls, the longest recension of the sutra extant in any language; *Jinguangmingjing*(《金光明经》, *Suvarnapprabhasottama Sutra*) in four rolls; and *Pusadichijing*(《菩萨地持经》, *Bodhisattvabhumisutra*) in ten rolls. His translation of Indian Buddhist texts into Chinese have impacted significantly on Chinese Buddhism, in particular, the doctrine that all beings have the buddha-nature (*foxing*, 佛性).

6) Paramārtha

Paramārtha, an Indian Buddhist monk, translator, and exegete, became prominent after arriving at Jiankang, capital of Liang Dynasty in 546. Under the patronage of the emperor and the local rulers in the south, he completed the translation of many Buddhist scriptures. His translations were *Suvarnaprabhasottama Sutra*(《金光明最胜王经》, *Jinguangming Zuishengwang Jing*), *Anuttarasraya Sutra*(《佛说无上依经》, *Foshuo wushangyi jing*), *Madhyantavibhaga*(《辩中边论》, *Bianzhongbianlun*), and *Vimsatika* (《唯识二十论》, *Weishi Ershi Lun*). Paramārtha died in 569 while translating *Abhidharmakosabhasya*(《阿毘达磨俱舍论》, *Apidamo Jushe Lun*). According to *A*

Chapter 3 Buddhist Scriptures and *Bible* Translation in China

History of Buddhism in China(《中国佛教史》, *Zhongguo Fojiao Shi*) by Ren Jiyu(任继愈), the variety of Buddhist scriptures that Paramārtha translated is greater than that of all the other Buddhist translators in history.

From the above, it can be seen that, in this second phase, Buddhist translation has the following characteristics:

1) It began to be highly organized and sponsored by the imperial government. Collaborative translation grew in scale and often became state-sponsored translation assemblies, with lay people as the majority of participants. Rulers like Fu Jian, Yao Xing, Yang Jian(杨坚) were some of the official patrons of translation while Dao An, Kumarajiva, Yan Cong were outstanding organizers and supervisors of the collective translation work.

2) A growing number of Chinese people participated in the translation and study of the Buddhist scriptures. Many translations were completed with the assistance of the native Chinese who were not necessarily familiar with Sanskrit. Dharmaraksa did his translation with the help of many native Chinese. Dao'an and his disciple Hui Yuan contributed greatly to Buddhist translation although they were ignorant of the relevant foreign languages.

3) Retranslations were done to satisfy the expectations of increasingly sophisticated audiences, especially those of the imperial patrons. The earlier Chinese translations were often based on isolated fragments, incomplete versions or heavily edited versions of the original. Retranslations were produced to rectify the earlier errors and misconceptions about the understanding of the original and to improve the readability of the translation.

4) The criteria for Buddhist translation were diversified and the studies of translation principles and criteria were more systematic and profound than before. The traditional preoccupation with quality and style of translation in the first phase was reflected in the divided views about refined (*wen*, 文) translation and unhewn (*zhi*, 质) translation. Topics dealt with fleetingly in the first phase were given more in-depth treatments. More concepts about the translation style and quality were advocated, such as "stay close to the source" (*shouben*, 守本), "yield to the source" (*yiben*, 依本), "elaborate" (*fan*, 繁), "simple" (*jian*, 简), "coarse" (*ye*, 野), "flowery" (*hua*, 华), "plain" (*pu*, 朴), "felicitous/skillful/contrivance" (*qiao*, 巧), "embellish (*shi*, 饰)", "tedious" (*fan*, 烦). Dao'an suggested "Five Stances of Losing the Source" (*wu shiben*, 五失本)

and "Three Difficulties" (*san buyi*, 三不易), which concern the qualities of "unhewn", "refined", and "wordy" (*fan*, 烦). Yan Cong studied his predecessors' translation practices and views systematically and attempted to establish a model for Buddhist translation in his well-known treatise *On the Right Way*(《辩正论》, *Bianzheng Lun*).

3.3.3 The Third Phase: Sui, Tang, and Northern Song Dynasties (c. 589—1100)

In 581, Sui Dynasty(隋朝, 581—618) was founded and in 589, Chen Dynasty(陈朝) came to an end. China got reunited under the reign of the founder of Sui Dynasty, Emperor Yang Jian. This ended almost 300 years of internal division and turmoil. Yang Jian, a Buddhist, established a translation forum at Great Xingshan Monastery(大兴善寺) in Chang'an and set up a translation bureau in the capital Luoyang. Although Sui Dynasty lasted for a short period of 40 years, some 59 Buddhist scriptures, including 262 fascicles, were translated. In 618, Sui Dynasty was overthrown and Tang Dynasty(唐朝, 618—907) was founded. It heralded the splendid flourishing of Buddhist translation in China. In this phase, the leadership of Buddhist translation enterprises was taken over by the eminent Chinese Buddhist monks who were experts not only in Buddhist doctrines but also in both Sanskrit and Chinese languages. The following are some of the outstanding translators in the third phase.

1) Yan Cong

Yan Cong, a native of the present-day Xiping County in Henan province, was proficient in Sanskrit. In 583, he was summoned by the emperor to translate the Buddhist texts from *Xiyu*(西域, Western Regions). In 592, he took charge of the Buddhist translation affairs at Great Xingshan Monastery. Yan Cong was greatly respected by Yang Jian, the founder of Sui Dynasty. At the order of the monarch, Yan compiled *A Catalogue of Buddhist Scriptures*(《众经目录》, *Zongjing Mulu*) and *Annals of the Western Regions* (《西域志》, *Xiyu Zhi*). He worked at the Translation Bureau(翻经馆) after its establishment to compile a catalogue of over 1350 Sanskrit scriptures discovered in *Xinpinglinyi*(《新平林邑》). In his life, he translated 23 Buddhist scriptures in more than a hundred fascicles. In his well-known treatise on translation, *Bianzheng Lun*, Yan Cong summarized his own and his predecessors' translation experiences. He suggested a translator's "Babei"(八备, eight prerequisites for Buddhist translators):

First, a translator must love the truth sincerely and devote himself to spreading the Buddhist faith and wisdom to others.

Second, he must hold fast to the rules of abstinence and not arouse scorn or laughter in others to prepare himself for enlightenment.

Third, he must be well-read in the Buddhist canon and understand both Mahayana and Hinayana Buddhism and he should not be deterred by the difficulties he encounters.

Fourth, he must also study Chinese classics and the Chinese history and make himself well-versed in letters so that his translations will not be clumsy and awkward.

Fifth, he must be compassionate, be open-minded and be keen to learn and must not be biased or stubborn.

Sixth, he must devote himself to practicing the truth, think lightly of fame and fortune, and harbor no desire to show off.

Seventh, he must study the *Fan* language (Sanskrit) until he knows it thoroughly and must learn the correct methods of translating so that he will not lose the meaning of the doctrines.

Eighth, he must also acquaint himself with the lexicons in ancient Chinese writings and the development of the Chinese scripts so that he will not misuse words in his translations(Cheung, 2010)[142].

2) Xuan Zang

Xuan Zang(玄奘, 602—664) is one of the two most influential and prolific translators of translating Indian Buddhist texts into Chinese, along with Kumarajiva. At the age of 10, he entered the monastery of Jingtusi(净土寺) in Luoyang and fled the capital in 618 when Sui Dynasty collapsed. At the age of 20, he was fully ordained as a monk. By this time, he had studied the earlier Chinese translations of *Mahayanasamgraha* (《摄大乘论》, *Shedachenglun*), *Jnanaprasthana* (《发智论》, *Fazhilun*), and *Tattvasiddhi*(《成实论》, *Chengshilun*) but doubted the accuracy of the translations. When Xuan Zang was 25 years old, he embarked on an epic journey to India to resolve such doubts. He visited various Buddhist pilgrimage sites in India and spent years at Nalanda monastery studying Buddhist doctrines and the Sanskrit language. At the age of 43, he returned to Chang'an, the capital city, with over 657 Sanskrit manuscripts that he had collected in India. The Emperor Taizong(唐太宗) honored Xuan Zang with the title of Tripitaka-master(*sanzang fashi*, 三藏法师) and established translation bureaus in the capital. In such institutions, Xuan Zang supervised a team of monks to transcribe the texts, clarify their meanings, compile the translations, polish the renderings, and certify both their meanings and syntax. In 19 years, 75 sutras and treatises in a total of 1,335 fascicles were translated into Chinese under his supervision. Xuan Zang initiated the "new translation" period in the history of Chinese Buddhist translation which is in distinction from the "old translation" period in which Kumarajiva was the most influential translator.

Xuan Zang and his group created an etymologically precise set of Chinese equivalents for Buddhist technical terms. Such translations were known for their rigorous philological accuracy. Xuan Zang set down "*wubufan*" (五不翻, five guidelines for non-translation of a term). A term will not be translated if ① it partakes the occult; ② it has multiple meanings; ③ the object represented by it is inexistent in the world; ④ a past rendering of it has be established and accepted; and ⑤ it elicits positive associations. Based on his years of translation experience and exposures to translations by other Buddhist monk translators, these guidelines represent Xuan Zang's views on the important topic of how to handle terminologies in translation.

Besides, under Xuan Zang's supervision, the organization of Translation Forum/Bureau and the division of the translation work were further made efficient. In Tang Dynasty, 11 duties were established for the translation: ① *Yizhu* (译主, chief translator), who was the head of the forum; ② *Zhengyi* (证义, in charge of rectifying the meaning), the assistant of the chief translator who reconciled differences in meanings between the Chinese translations and the Sanskrit originals; ③ *Zhengwen* (证文, in charge of rectifying the text) or *Zhengfanben* (证梵本, in charge of rectifying the Sanskrit text), who was responsible for spotting errors in the original Sanskrit texts; ④ *Duyu* (度语, interpreters), who transliterated the Sanskrit texts; ⑤ *Bishou* (笔受, recorder), who turned the transliteration into the first draft of translation; ⑥ *Zhuiwen* (缀文, in charge of modifying the draft), who improved the draft into grammatically acceptable Chinese; ⑦ *Canyi* (参译, those participating in the translation), who proofread the original Sanskrit texts for possible errors and determined whether these texts were ambiguous for Chinese translation; ⑧ *Kanding* (刊定), who deleted redundant expressions caused by the differences between Chinese and Sanskrit; ⑨ *Runwen* (润文, polisher), who refined the Chinese translation rhetorically; ⑩ *Fanbei* (梵呗), who recited the Chinese translation in a manner similar with the Sanskrit texts to see whether the work sounded natural and appropriate for the monks to recite or not; and ⑪ *Jianhu Dashi*(监护大使), the official or imperial envoy who supervised the translation process.

During Xuan Zang's time, the Chinese translation of Buddhist scriptures reached its peak.

3) Vajrabodhi

Vajrabodhi(金刚智, 669—741) was a south Indian brahman native. In 721, he and his famed disciple Amoghavajra(不空, 705—774) arrived in the capital Chang'an. Vajrabodhi played a major role in the introduction and translation of seminal Buddhist texts of esoteric traditions in China. Under the patronage of Emperor Xuanzong of Tang Dynasty (唐玄宗, reigned 712—755), Vajrabodhi translated *Vajrasekhara Sutra*(《金刚顶经》, *Jinggangdingjing*) and other related texts. During his stay in China for more than twenty years, he introduced about 20 texts belonging to the Vajrasekhara textual line.

4) Amoghavajra

Accompanying his mentor Vajrabodhi, Amoghavajra arrived in Chang'an in 721 and spent most of his career there. Following his mentor's death in 741, he went to India and Ceylon (present-day Sri Lanka) with the permission of the emperor of Tang Dynasty. In 746, he brought back 500 new Buddhist texts. His influence in Tang Dynasty reached its height when he was summoned by the emperor to construct a consecration altar on the monarch's behalf. As one of the four greatest Buddhist translators (the other three are Kumarajiva, Xuan Zang, and Paramārtha) in the history of Chinese Buddhism, Amoghavajra translated 110 texts and a total of 143 fascicles into Chinese, of which the most important are *Sarva Tathagata Tattva Samgraha*(《一切如来真实摄大乘现证三昧大教王经》, *Yiqie Rulai Zhenshishe Dacheng Xianzheng Sanmei Dajiaowang Jing*) and *Bhadracaripranidhana*(《普贤菩萨行愿赞》, *Puxian Pusa Xingyuanzan*).

In Chinese history, the development of Buddhism met several setbacks when the religion was banned by the rulers. Emperor Wuzong of Tang Dynasty(唐武宗, reigned 841—846) dealt a serious blow to Buddhism in 845. The progress of Buddhist translation entered a period of decline as few monks showed interest in the translation of Buddhist texts. Almost all available Buddhist sutras had been translated into Chinese by the end of the progressive period while the transformation of Indian Buddhism into Chinese Buddhism was already ongoing. More importantly, the change in imperial policy led to a rapid decrease of Buddhist translation activities. No translation forums were sponsored by the imperial government, so most of the Buddhist translations produced in Song Dynasty were the works of individuals instead of the collective efforts of a royally-sponsored translation group. In Song Dynasty(宋朝, 960—1279), the quantity of Buddhist translation declined along with the quality. 284 Buddhist sutras in 758 fascicles were translated into Chinese but the translation quality was much inferior to those produced in Tang Dynasty, especially to those rendered by Xuan Zang.

APPENDIX 1: Key events in ancient China's Buddhist translation history (Raine, 2016)

Period	Key translation events
c. 150—265 (Later Eastern Han and Wei Dynasties)	• Central Asian monks come to China to spread Buddhism • Sutra translations begin in 148 by Parthamasiris, a Parthian
265—420 (Jin Dynasty)	• Large-scale translation work by Central Asian monks begins • By 317, over 1,100 sutras has been translated • Period of *ge-yi* (concept matching) • Large translation forums are held
420—589 (Northern and Southern Dynasties)	• The first persecution of Buddhism (431—454) • Emperor supports Buddhism (502—549) • The second persecution in 574 • Official sutra translation begins in 582
581—618 (Sui Dynasty)	• Sutra translation academy is established • In 594, 2,257 translations are cataloged • In 602, the catalog lists only 688 extant works
618—907 (Tang Dynasty)	• The Muslims invade Central Asia, Buddhism then declines • The Government's control over Buddhism completes • *Kaiyuan* catalog in 730 lists, 1,076 translated works • There are 176 translators from 148 to 730 • Indian monks begin to translate • The third persecution of Buddhism (840—846)
907—960 (Five Kingdoms period)	• The translation activity declines, and the period of political turmoil starts • There are no translations of Buddhist texts from 810 to 970
960—1279 (Song Dynasty)	• Emperor orders compilation of Chinese canon in 971 • Translation forums are revived, and systematic imperial government-sponsored translation process is implemented • 284 tantric texts are translated by Indian monks from 982 to 1111 • The translation activity ends in the 13th century • A total of at least 2,200 texts are translated by 194 translators

3.4 *Bible* Translation in China

The Buddhist translation marked the first wave of translation in China. The translation of the *Holy Bible* and of Western science heralded the next. The *Bible* contains the sacred scriptures of Judaism and Christianity. The Christian *Bible* consists of the *Old Testament* and the *New Testament* while the Hebrew *Bible* only includes the books known to Christians in the *Old Testament*. The *Old Testament* is about God and the laws of God while the *New Testament* is about the doctrines of Jesus Christ. *Testament* means the agreement between God and his people.

The introduction of Christianity to China can be divided into four periods (Ma Zuyi, 2004)[261]. The first period is Tang Dynasty, in which Nestorian Christianity or Jingjiao(景教) was introduced to China in the 7th century. The second period is Yuan Dynasty, in which the Roman Catholic Pope sent missionaries to the Mongol court at the invitation of the Emperor Kublai Khan. The third period is the late Ming and early Qing Dynasties, when Roman Catholicism was brought into China. And the fourth period begins in 1807, when a Jesus-dominated brand of Christianity started to be spread in China.

According to Cen Zhongmian (1982)[320], Olopen(阿罗本), a Persian Nestorian missionary, arrived in Chang'an with some scriptures in 635 and was permitted by the emperor to do missionary work in 638. Olopen converted 21 people to Christianity, who were mostly high officials and noble lords of Tang Dynasty. They called the religion Jingjiao. The first *Bible* translator in China was Jing Jing(景净), a Persian missionary who was the author of the 1870-character writing inscribed on the Nestorian Tablet(大秦景教流行中国碑). This artifact was erected in Chang'an in 781. Jing Jing translated 35 Nestorian scriptures into Chinese language. These were selected from the 530 scriptures in Syrian language brought to China by Olopen. No one knows for sure how much of the *Bible* was translated into Chinese during Tang Dynasty, but there is evidence that the *New Testament* began to be translated into Chinese during the first half of the 7th century. Besides the Chinese translations by Jing Jing, other works are *Book of Jesus Messiah*(《移鼠迷师诃经》, *Yishu Mishi Hejing*), *On Lokajyestha's Donation*(《世尊布施论》, *Shizun Bushilun*), and Li Bai's poem *Shangyunle*(《上云乐》) in which the story of Genesis was told. The early Nestorian translators, who did not translate the Biblical texts literally, represented Christian ideas with Buddhist terms in the same way as the early Buddhist translators replaced Buddhist ideas with Taoist and even Confucian terms. For example, *fo* (佛, Buddha) was used for *Almighty God*, 世尊 (*shizun*, Lords of Worlds) for *Savior*, *zhufo* (诸佛, buddhas) was used for *saints* or *angels*, and *pudu* (普度, universal ferrying across) was used for *redemption*. This translation strategy was adopted for the reason that the initial acceptance of a new religion by a society, where another religion is popular, depends on its compatibility with the former (Yang Yan, 1992)[31-32]. In 842, Emperor Wuzong of Tang Dynasty began to confiscate the properties of Buddhist temples and ordered the Buddhist monks to resume their secular lives in 845. Nestorianism was unavoidably affected by the banning of Buddhism because Nestorian monks, two to three hundred in total, were forced to do the same. The spread of Christianity came to a halt and nearly 500 years had passed before it came to China again (Yang Yan, 1992)[32].

In 1245, entrusted by the Roman Catholic Pope, Friar John de Plano Carpini visited the Great Khan in China and appealed to stop the brutal killing by his troops in the European Christian states. Consequently, the contact between China and the Roman Catholic Church was established. In 1294, Friar John of Monte Corvina who was sent by the Pope to the Yuan capital Dadu (大都) resumed Christian missionary work. At that time, 4 chapels were constructed in the city, 6000 people were baptized, and as many as 1500 people learned Greek and Latin. Corvina translated the *New Testament* into Mongol, conducted the service according to the Latin rite, and recited the *Bible* and *Genesis* in Mongol in the chapel (Yang Yan, 1992)[33]. Michael Ruggieri (罗明坚, 1543—1607) and Matteo Ricci, both from Italy, were the first Jesuit missionaries who directly went to the hinterland of China. Michael Ruggieri set foot on China in 1580, arrived at Zhaoqing in Guangdong in 1583, and built a chapel there. In 1584, his compilation titled *Tianzhu Shengjiao Shilu* (《天主圣教实录》, *Veritable Records of the Holy Catholicism*) was published in Guangzhou. This book, a summary of the *Bible*, talks about God's creations of people and things, the immortal spirits, the Ten Commandments, the Seven Sacraments, and relevant tenets. Matteo Ricci came to China in 1583 and went to Beijing in 1601. He established a church in Beijing so that Catholicism gained a legal status in China. Although no evidence shows that Matteo Ricci directly translated the *Bible*, he solved the important problem of how to translate the Latin word *Deus* (corresponding the English word *God/Lord*) in his most important Chinese writing *Tianzhu Shiyi* (《天主实义》, *The True Meaning of the Lord of Heaven*),

Chapter 3 Buddhist Scriptures and *Bible* Translation in China

which was firstly published in 1595. The book narrates an imagined debate on the similarities and the differences between Christianity and Eastern beliefs in a dialogue context, that is, between a gentleman from the East and a gentleman from the West. From the book, we can learn the main ideas in the *Bible*. At the turn of the 16th and 17th centuries, not a few foreign Jesuit missionaries made Chinese adaptations of the *Bible*. The relatively important ones are: *Tianzhu Shengjiao Yueyan*(《天主圣教约言》) by the Portuguese Jean Soerio(苏若望, 1566—1607) in 1601, *Shengjiao Rike*(《圣教日课》) by the Italian Niccolo Longobardi (his Chinese name Long Huamin, 龙华民, 1559—1654) in 1602, *Tianzhushengjiao Qimeng*(《天主圣教启蒙》) by the Portuguese Jean de Rocha(罗如望, 1566—1623) in 1619, *Qike Daquan*(《七克大全》) by the Spanish Diego de Pantoja(庞迪我, 1571—1618) in 1614, and *Jiaoyao Jieliie*(《教要解略》) by the Italian Alfonso Vagnone (高一志, 1568—1640) in 1626. In a Chinese adapted translation *Tianzhu Jingjie*(《天主经解》, 1628), Jacobus Rho (罗雅谷, 1593—1638) rendered the *Bible* into "主经" (*zhujing*), which is the closest to "圣经" (*Shengjing*) in the wording of the book title. In 1636, Emmanuel Diaz (阳玛诺, 1574—1659), a Portuguese missionary who came to China in 1611, published *Shengjing Zhijie*(《圣经直解》) in Beijing. As far as we know, this is the first time "圣经" was used to render "the Bible" (Xu Zongze, 2006)[17-19]. A direct and full Chinese translation of the *Bible* was completed by the French missionary Louis Poirot (贺清泰), who came to China in 1770 and was well-versed in both Chinese and Manchu languages. Unfortunately, this work was unpublished.

There had been no complete Chinese translations of the *Bible* until Robert Morrison (1782—1834), the first Protestant missionary to China, came to the country in 1807. He and his colleague William Milne (1785—1822), the second missionary to China in 1813, were both sent by London Missionary Society. They collaboratively produced the first complete Chinese version of the *Bible*, which was published in 1823.

The Chinese version by Feng Yasheng(冯亚生, 1792—1829) in 1834 was the first one produced by a local. In 1816, Feng, a native of Guangdong, went to Europe and proceeded to Berlin, Germany in 1823. In 1826, he was summoned to the German court where he finished the Chinese translation of *The Gospel of Mark* and *The Gospel of Luke*. In

1834, he presented his translation manuscripts to the German Royal Library. Feng's translation was a reproduction of the foreign missionaries' earlier work but it was the first Chinese version of the *Bible* by a Chinese translator (Zhao Xiaoyang, 2021). He Jinshan's (何进善, 1817—1871) work was the first Chinese version that was both translated and published by a Chinese native. When he was a boy, He Jinshan of Guangdong lived with his father in Malacca, Malaysia and learned English, Greek, and Hebrew from James Legge there. Later, He became a missionary and preached Christianity in Foshan, Guangdong. He translated *The Gospel of Matthew* in 1854 and *The Gospel of Mark* in 1856 and got these published in Hongkong after James Legge's revision. To reiterate, He Jinshan's work was the first Chinese version conscientiously translated and published by a local, which indicated that Chinese Christians would shoulder the task of translating the *Bible* into Chinese since then (Zhao Xiaoyang, 2021).

The foreign missionaries paid much attention to the written style of the translation. In the second half of the 19th century, the demand for Chinese versions of the *Bible* surged because the Protestant missionaries were allowed to do missionary work in the Chinese coastal and hinterland cities. Chinese versions varied in their linguistic styles. These styles were *Wenli* (文理, the style of classical Chinese), Easy *Wenli* (浅文理), and Mandarin (官话). The foreign missionary societies produced their own Chinese versions but expected to have a universally acceptable one.

From the 1850s to the 1910s, the foreign Protestant missionaries in China published a number of Chinese translations of the *Bible* which were widely distributed among the Chinese people. The American Bible Society and the British and Foreign Bible Society circulated at least 155,600,833 copies of the Chinese *Bible*, including complete Bibles, Testaments and biblical portions from 1877 to 1936 (Mak, 2017)[1]. The following are the major Chinese translations of the Protestant *Bible* (Mak, 2017)[9–17].

1) The Shanghai Version (the *New Testament*, 1856). After the completion of the Delegates' Version of the *New Testament*, which is a translation in classical Chinese, Walter Henry Medhurst (麦都思) and John Stronach (施约翰) began its Southern Chinese language version with the help of Chinese assistants. The complete *New Testament* translation got published for the first time in Shanghai in 1856.

2) The Beijing Version (the *New Testament*, 1872). Joseph Edkins (艾约瑟,

Chapter 3 Buddhist Scriptures and *Bible* Translation in China

1823—1905) began to revise the Shanghai Version in 1860 so that the offshoot would be intelligible to Mandarin speakers in North China. Supported by other Beijing-based Protestant missionaries, Edkins formed an interdenominational translation committee comprising himself, Schereschewsky, William A. P. Martin(丁韪良, 1827—1916) of the North American Presbyterian Mission, John Shaw Burdon(包尔腾或包约翰, 1826—1907) of the Church Missionary Society, and Henry Blodget(白汉理或柏亨利, 1825—1903) of the American Board of Commissioners for Foreign Missions. With the help of a Chinese teacher or assistant, each of them translated a section of the *New Testament* and sent his first draft translation to others for corrections. The final revised edition was published in 1872 and was the most popular one before the Union Version.

3) Schereschewsky's(施约瑟) Mandarin *Old Testament* (1874). The source text for this Mandarin version was the Hebrew Masoretic Text, although he also consulted the King James Version, Wilhelm Martin Leberecht de Wette's German version, the *Septuagint*, the *Vulgate* and etc. Schereschewsky's complete work came out in 1874.

4) Schereschewsky's revised Mandarin *Bible* (1908). Schereschewsky did revisions in his Mandarin *Bible* to achieve greater clearness and smoothness. In 1899, Schereschewsky's revised Mandarin *Old Testament* was published with the Beijing Version in one volume. He made further revisions of this volume before his death in 1906. In 1908, his final version of the 1874 Mandarin *Old Testament* and his revision of the Beijing Version were published in a one-volume edition with references.

5) Griffith John's Mandarin *New Testament* (1889). In 1885, Griffith John(杨格非, 1831—1912) published his Easy Wenli translation of the *New Testament*. Considering the differences between Northern Mandarin and the Mandarin prevalent in Central China, John reproduced such work in Mandarin and published his Mandarin *New Testament* in 1889, which is stylistically closer to the Southern Mandarin.

6) Mandarin Union Version (1907/1919). Various Chinese versions of the *Bible* had been produced and distributed in China but none of them was generally accepted by all Protestant denominations in the country. The General Conference of the Protestant Missionaries of China held in Shanghai in 1890 resolved that the Union Version of the Chinese *Bible* should be produced in three different forms of the Chinese language: Easy Wenli, High Wenli or Shen Wenli(深文理), and Mandarin. An executive committee for

each of the three translations was established to select translators and supervise their work. 16 Protestant missionaries and their Chinese assistants participated in the translation work. The Mandarin Union Version was based on Greek and Hebrew texts underlying the English Revised Version as the translators consulted the previous Chinese versions constantly and carefully. Each translator sent his own draft translation to his colleagues for criticism and corrections. The complete Chinese translation of *New Testament* in one volume was first published in 1907 while the complete Mandarin Union Version appeared in 1919. The latter is still popular among Chinese Christians.

From 1842 to 1859, with the assistance of local Chinese Christians, some missionaries produced versions in Chinese dialects. The following are some examples: Chinese Version in Shanghai Dialect (1847), Chinese Version in Ningbo Dialect (1847), Chinese Version in Xiamen Dialect (1847), Chinese Version in Fuzhou Dialect (1852) and Vernacular Chinese Version (1857) (Wang Dan, 2019).

In 1908, Yan Fu, a renowned translator, was invited by the British and Foreign Bible Society to translate the *Bible* into Chinese. Without foreign missionary's assistance, Yan Fu translated English Revised Version's first four chapters of *The Gospel of Mark* into classical Chinese *Make Suochuan Fuyin*(《马可所传福音》). And in the same year, Yan's version was published by the Commercial Press in Shanghai. This version was not only the first Chinese translation independently produced by the Chinese but also the first one completed by a non-Christian Chinese translator. *The Absalom Sydenstricker-Zhu Baohui's Version*(《赛兆祥-朱宝惠新约译本》, *Sai Zhaoxiang-Zhu Baohui Xinyue Yiben*) was the first Chinese version co-produced by two bible scholars from the East and the West. Absalom Sydenstricker (赛兆祥, 1852—1931), an American Presbyterian missionary and the father of Nobel laureate Pearl Buck, came to China in 1880 and did missionary work in Hangzhou, Suzhou, and Zhenjiang. Zhu Baohui (朱宝惠, 1886—1970), born into a Christian family in Shandong, was an educator of theology and translator of theologian texts. In 1920, both men worked together to translate the Greek *New Testament* into Chinese. Their work *Xinyi Xinyue Shengjing Chuanzhu Zhujie*(《新译新约圣经串珠注解》, *A New Chinese Translation of New Testament with Annotation*) was published by Nanjing Theological Seminary in 1929. A few years later, Zhu Baohui translated the *Old Testament* into Chinese by himself and published his *Chongyi Xinjiuyue Quanshu*(《重译新旧约全书》, *A New Chinese Translation of Old and New Testaments*) through Nanjing Jingxin Publishing House in 1939. In 1933, Qingdao China Christian Society published Wang Yuande's(王元德) Chinese version of the *New Testament*, which was the first of such a kind by a Chinese Christian and the first work with modern punctuation marks. Zheng Shoulin(郑寿麟, 1900—1990), a famous scholar, got his doctorate in Germany and worked as a professor in certain universities in China. He and Heinrich Ruck(陆亨理, 1887—1972), a German missionary, collaborated to translate the *Bible* from Greek into Chinese. Their *Xinyue Quanshu*(《新约全书》) was published by Beiping Xinjiuku Press in 1939. The first full Chinese translation independently produced by Chinese Christians was Lü Zhenzhong's version. Lü Zhenzhong(吕振中, 1898—1988), a native of Nan'an, Fujian in southeast China, obtained his bachelor's degree at Hongkong University in 1921 before moving to Yenching University College of Religion(燕京大学宗教学院) to study theology, Greek, and Hebrew. In 1925, Lü got a bachelor's degree in theology. After that, he worked as a teacher in some universities. In 1946, Yenching University College of Religion published his *Lüyi Xinyue Chugao*(《吕译新约初稿》, *A First Draft of Lü's Chinese Translation of the New Testament*). The Hongkong Bible Society published Lü's *Xinyue Xinyi Xiudinggao*(《新约新译修订稿》, *A Revised New Chinese Translation of New Testament*) in 1952 and *Shengjing Quanshu*(《圣经全书》, *The Complete Version of the Bible*) in 1970.

From the 17th century to the 19th century, *Bible* translation in China was conducted mainly by foreign missionaries. Since the late Qing Dynasty, especially during the Republic of China, Chinese Christians became the major translators of this holy book. The Chinese *Bible* translators graduated from theological seminaries, got systematic trainings in theology or had experiences of assisting foreign missionaries in *Bible* translation. Gradually, the foreign missionary translators were replaced by Chinese translators.

Questions for discussion:

1. What are the main features of the first phase of Chinese translation of Buddhist scriptures?

2. What are Xuan Zang's major contributions to the introduction of Buddhism?

3. Briefly introduce the major Chinese versions of the Protestant Bible.

References:

岑仲勉,1982.隋唐史[M].北京:中华书局.
Cen Zhongmian,1982. A history of Sui and Tang Dynasties[M]. Beijing:Zhonghua Book Company.

马祖毅,2004.中国翻译简史:"五四"以前部分[M].北京:中国对外翻译出版公司.
Ma Zuyi,2004. A condensed history of translation in China:Before May Forth[M]. Beijing:China Translation and Publishing Corporation.

王丹,2019.众川归一:近代汉译《圣经》事工的变迁[D].上海:上海大学.
Wang Dan,2019. Streams merge into a river:The vicissitudes of modern Chinese Bible ministry[D]. Shanghai:Shanghai University.

徐宗泽,2006.明清间耶稣会士译著提要[M].上海:上海书店出版社.
Xu Zongze, 2006. Synopses of Chinese translations by Jesuits in Ming and Qing Dynasties[M]. Shanghai:Shanghai Bookstore Publishing House.

赵晓阳,2021.晚清民国华人翻译圣经译本研究[J].宁波大学学报(人文科学版),34(2):8-16.
Zhao Xiaoyang,2021. A study on Chinese translations of Bible in the Late Qing Dynasty and the Republic of China[J]. Journal of Ningbo University(Humanity and Science Edition),34(2):8-16.

Baker M,2006.翻译研究百科全书[M].上海:上海外语教育出版社.

Buswell R E, Lopez D S,2013. The princeton dictionary of Buddhism[M]. Princeton:Princeton University Press.

Cheung M P Y,2010.中国翻译话语英译选集(上册):从最早期到佛典翻译[M].上海:上海外语教育出版社.

Ikeda D,1986. The flower of Chinese Buddhism[M]. New York:Weatherhill.

Mak G K W,2017. Protestant Bible translation and mandarin as the national language of China[M]. Boston:Brill.

Raine R,2016. The Buddhist translation histories of ancient China (c. 150—1276) and Tibet (c. 617—1750):A comparative study[J]. Asia Pacific Translation and Intercultural Studies,3(1):2-21.

Yang Yan,1992. A brief history of Chinese translation theory[D]. Austin:University of Texas.

Chapter 4

Translation of Ancient Greek Classics in Europe

This chapter covers three parts. The first part introduces the Latin translation of ancient Greek classics in ancient Rome. The main translators in this period were Andronicus, Cicero, Horace, Quintilian, Jerome, and Augustine. They formed three schools, with Cicero and Horace belonging to sense-for-sense school, Philo and Augustine belonging to word-for-word school, and Jerome belonging to the compromise school between them. Admittedly, all of them showed a profound understanding of the theoretical issues of translation, which had a deep effect during the subsequent periods as well as modern times. However, it must be noted that throughout the ancient times, the study of the translation theory was far from being systematic, and there were no experts or monographs. Writers and theologians mentioned translation while discussing other topics, or translators gave their opinions on translation in the preface or postscript of their translated works.

The second part focuses on the translation of ancient Greek and Rome classics in Renaissance. On the whole, one of the most important features of the translations of Western Europe during this period is that translations of every country developed in a balanced way. Though the use of Latin was prominent, it was merely a branch of literary works or translations. Before the Medieval and the Renaissance, Western translations were mainly connected with Latin translation. However, with the formation of Western European nations in Post Medieval including the Renaissance, the native languages became chief means in translations. Accordingly, the Renaissance was a turning point for the Western translation. This epoch signified that the theory and practice of translation had departed from the "dark time" of the Medieval Age and made great progress.

The third part sheds light on the history of literary and philosophical translation among European countries. A brief narration is emphatically given in several sections on translation in Germany, France and England in 17th and 19th centuries. It should be pointed out that this is a very important developmental period especially in translation theory studies, with further advances being achieved in comparison with that in the Renaissance.

4.1 Latin Translation of Ancient Greek Classics in Ancient Rome

Ancient Western translation, except for the Greek translations of the *Old Testament*, mainly refers to the Latin translation in ancient Rome from the 3rd century B. C. to the 5th century, when the Roman Empire collapsed. The main translators in this period were Andronicus, Cicero, Horace, Quintilian, Jerome, and Augustine.

The first important ancient Western translation was the Greek translation of the *Old Testament*, which was originally the scripture of Judaism written in Hebrew. In the 2nd century B. C., an unknown Jew wrote an epistolary article entitled *Letter of Aristeas*(《阿里斯狄亚书简》). This was a significant document related to translation, reflecting the author's views on the translation methods and procedures employed in translating the *Old Testament*. The article had earliest descriptions of the criteria for translating the *Bible* and revealed traditional views on translation.

With the early translation becoming prevalent, literary works were translated continuously and the translator's main purpose was to introduce the Greek culture and entertain the Roman audience by offering them translated literary works and plays. As for the theory, even if there were fragments about it, they were just a counterattacks on criticisms against one's own translated work, and few touched upon any research on the translation theory before Cicero. He was undoubtedly the most well-known translator in Western history for his translation of the *Vulgata*(《拉丁文圣经》), which was also known as the *Editio Vulgata*(《通俗拉丁文本圣经》).

Marcus Tullius Cicero(马尔库斯·图利乌斯·西塞罗, 106—43 B. C.), born in Arpinum to a local wealthy family, was generally considered to be one of the most versatile minds in ancient Rome. He introduced the Romans with the chief schools of Greek philosophy and created Latin philosophical vocabularies, distinguishing himself as a linguist, translator, philosopher, and statesman. He was also widely regarded as one of the greatest orators and prose stylists in ancient Rome.

During this period in Roman history, if one was to be considered "cultured", it would be necessary to speak in both Latin and Greek. The Roman upper class often preferred Greek to Latin in private correspondence, recognizing its more refined and precise expressions and its greater subtleties and nuances. This was partly due to the greater range of Greek abstract nouns. Cicero, like most of his contemporaries, was educated with the teachings of the ancient Greek philosophers, poets, and historians. The most prominent teachers of oratory at that time were Greek. Cicero used his knowledge of Greek in translating many of the theoretical concepts of Greek philosophy into Latin, thus translating Greek philosophical works for a larger audience. It was his precisely broad education that tied him to the traditional Roman elite.

Cicero was the outstanding representative of scholars who claimed that translation might surpass the original and the translator might do better than the author. In a sense, it was Cicero who changed the habitual pattern that translation was only confined to the practice and had nothing to do with the theory. He clearly advanced his views on translation and was the first translation theorist in the history of Western translation.

Cicero's contributions to translation theory cannot be overestimated. Translation thus began to be seen as a literary and artistic creation after him. Issues covering such areas as the source text and the target text, form and content, rights and duties of translators, etc., have remained issues since his time. In his two writings, *De Optimo Genere Oratorum*(《论最优秀的演说家》, *The Best Kind of Orator*) and *De Finibus Bonorum Et Malorum*(《论善与恶之定义》, *On the Final Ends of Good and Evil*), Cicero expressed his opinions on translation. In particular, he proposed two translation methods that are to translate as an interpreter or an orator or to do it word-for-word or sense-for-sense, which determined the direction of translation development for future generations. Such opinions had an impact on Horace, Quintilianus, Jerome, Luther, Tytler, Schleiermacher, among others. A clear line, which consists of writers, translators, and linguists discussing translation criteria, methods, and techniques, has run through the history of Western translation theory (Grimal, 1998)[11-45].

Below are discussions about two of the major ancient translators and translation theorists after Cicero, Horace, and Quintilianus.

Quintus Horatius Flaccus(昆图斯·贺拉斯·弗拉库斯, 65—8 B.C.), known in the English-speaking world as Horace, was the leading Roman lyric poet during the time of Augustus. Born in the small town of Venusia in the border region between Apulia and Lucania, he was the son of a freed slave who spent considerable amount of money for his son's education.

Horace's *Ars Poetica* (also known as *The Art of Poetry* or *Letters to Piso*, 《诗艺》), published around 15 B. C., was a treatise on poetics. In this work, he attempted to analyze the nature and form of "poetics" with a view of making poetry recognized in ancient Rome as an art at the same level as painting. Influenced by Cicero's theory on literary criticism and translation, Horace delved a lot into the use of language in creation and translation issues. He held that translation must adhere to sense rather than word and maintained that native language could be enriched by loanwords.

Ars Poetica occupies an important place in the history of Western literary theory, which has profoundly affected later literary creations and promoted the study of translation theory. His remark—"Do not worry about rendering word for word, faithful translators, but rendering sense for sense"—has been frequently quoted ever since by people who prefer the same. When Horace speaks of "a faithful translator", he has the person in mind much more than the work that person produces. In his view, translators thrive on the trust of their patrons and the public. They do not have to translate "word for word" because both patrons and audiences literally "take their word" at face value (Robinson, 2006)[20].

Both Cicero and Horace told their readers not to rework foreign texts in Latin word for word like slavish translators but freely like an orator or someone claiming private property in public ground. Translators in those days were thought as blind literalists, and both Cicero and Horace wanted to remind those translating orations or literary works from Greek into Latin against acting slavishly. In other words, translators should not obey the implicit translation norm but develop a freer and more creative norm.

Marcus Fabius Quintilianus(马库斯·法比尤斯·昆体良, 35—100), usually referred to as Quintilian in English version and born in Calahorra, La Rioja in Hispania, was a Roman rhetorician who was widely esteemed in medieval schools of rhetoric and in Renaissance writing. His father, a well-educated man, sent him to Rome to study rhetoric early in the reign of Nero. In Rome, Marcus cultivated friendship with Domitius Afer who was a more austere, classical, and Ciceronian speaker than those common at the time of Seneca. Domitius might have inspired Quintilian's love for Cicero. In 88, Quintilian became the head of the first public school of Rome. According to Jerome, Quintilian evidently took Afer as his model and listened to him speak and plead cases in the law courts.

Around 90, Quintilian retired from teaching. He then wrote *Institutio Oratoria*(《雄辩术原理》), his twelve-volume textbook on rhetoric, which was published around 95. This work not only dealt with the theory and practice of rhetoric but also with the foundational education and development of the orator himself. The book was regarded as "a treatise on education, a manual of rhetoric, a reader's guide to the best author, and a handbook of the moral duties of the orator". Although much of what Quintilian wrote was similar to Cicero, Quintilian emphasized education and rhetoric, exerting a strong influence on the schools throughout the Empire.

He also expressed his views about translation, "I do not want a translation to be a paraphrase but rather a struggle with and an emulation of the original which renders the same sense". He maintained that translation itself was a creation, which must be comparable with or even exceed the original, preferably not causing any meaning-loss in substance(He Libo, 2009)[14-17].

In the late years of ancient Rome, literary translation was not as vigorous as before due to the decrease of creative literary activities. To save the collapsing empire, the ruling class intensified the use of Christianity to lull the people. In this way, religious translation has become increasingly important and has been further developed. It can be safely concluded that religious translation at this stage constitutes the second climax in the history of Western translation. During this period, the most influential figures in the translation community were Jerome and Augustine.

St. Jerome(哲罗姆, 331—420) or Eusebius Sophronius Hieronymus, the patron saint of translation and one of the early four greatest Western Christian theologians, is still considered as one of the greatest translators in history for rendering the *Bible* into Latin. He was born in Stridon on the borders of Dalmatia and Pannonia to a well-to-do Christian family. His parents sent him to Rome to further his intellectual interest. He acquired knowledge of classical literature and was baptized in 365. He then journeyed to Trier in Gaul and to Aquileia in Italy where he began to cultivate his theological interest with those who were ascetically inclined like himself. When Jerome returned to Rome, Pope Damasus I appointed him as the confidential secretary and librarian and commissioned him to begin rendering the *Bible* into Latin. However, after the death of Damasus in 384, Jerome fell out of favor and decided to go to the East for the second time. He briefly visited Antioch, Egypt, and Palestine. In 386, Jerome settled at Bethlehem in a monastery established for him by Paula. She was a wealthy Roman woman who was his spiritual adviser and lifelong friend. In such a place, Jerome began his most productive literary period and remained for 34 years until his death. It is in such a period that he did his major biblical commentaries and the bulk of his work on the Latin *Bible*, covering Church administrations, monastic rules, theologies, and letters. He is best known for his *Chronicles of Eusebius* (380), *Works of Origen* (381—390), and the *Vulgate* (383—406) (Tan Zaixi, 2004)[27].

Jerome's greatest accomplishment was his translation of the *Bible* into Latin, the edition known as the *Vulgate*. It is a Latin version of the *Bible* in the early 5th century and largely the result of Jerome's effort. He was commissioned by Pope Damasus I in 383 to revise the old Latin translations. Jerome renewed the Latin *Bible* for Christians after twenty-three years of diligence. Prior to Jerome's *Vulgate*, all Latin translations of the *Old Testament* were based on *the Septuagint*. Jerome's decision to use a Hebrew text instead of the *Septuagint* went against the advice of most other Christians, including Augustine who considered the Septuagint as the inspiration. Unavoidably, the *Vulgate* had stirred much controversy at first since it was so different from the *Septuagint*, which was perceived as sacred and inviolable. By the 13th century, the revision had been called the version *Vulgata*, that is, the "commonly used translation". Ultimately, it became the definitive and officially promulgated Latin version of the *Bible* in the Roman Catholic Church and remains the classical Latin *Bible* to this day.

In his *Apologeticum Ad Pammachium* (《致帕玛丘的护教信》, *The Letter to Pammachius*) in 1935, Jerome launched an attack on literalism and coined the term "sense-for-sense translation". The idea was a faithful middle ground between the faithful literalism Cicero and Horace censured and the free imitations they defended, even if they also defended literal translations of the *Scripture* problematically. In the letter, Jerome remarked that, "For me, myself, not only admit but freely proclaim that, in translating from Greek, I render sense-for-sense and not word-for-word, except in the case of the *Holy Scripture* where even the order of the words is a mystery". His letter was largely a series of examples in which the *Septuagint* translators and the evangelists' translated passages from the Hebrew *Old Testament* loosely, freely, and sense-for-sense into Greek. This is strange because there are contradictions in the letter. This is probably evidence that even Jerome, despite his thoroughgoing radicalism, had not totally demystified the sacredness of the word order of the source language.

For the next 15 years, until he died, Jerome had produced a number of commentaries on the *Scripture*, often explaining his translation choices. His commentaries aligned closely with the Jewish tradition and he indulged in allegorical and mystical subtleties after the manner of Philo and the Alexandrian school.

Jerome's translation principles and methods had a great impact on later translation theory and practice. Especially in the medieval West, when the *Bible* was translated into the vernacular languages, many of his ideas were inherited. By articulating a narrow range of the freer approach, Cicero opposed word-for-word translation and coined it for the term of "sense-for-sense" translation. Jerome set the stage for the three-term taxonomy that has reigned in the mainstream thinking about translation since the late medieval/early modern period: word-for-word, sense-for-sense, and free. He had a large number of followers, among whom many were engaged in secular literary translation. They agreed that style is an essential and integral part of content (Bassnett, 2004)[30-50].

Aurelius Augustinus(奥勒留·奥古斯丁) or St Augustine (354—430), a Church father, theologian, writer, and philosopher in late Roman Empire, was one of the most important figures in the development of Western Christianity. He was born in the city of Thagaste, the present-day Souk Ahras in Algeria, to a pagan father named Patricius and a Catholic mother named Monica. Aurelius was educated in North Africa and resisted his mother's pleas to become a Christian. In his early years, he was heavily influenced by Manichaeism and, afterwards, Neo-Platonism(新柏拉图主义) of Plotinus(普罗提诺). Living as a pagan intellectual, he took a concubine and became a Manichean(摩尼教徒). Later, he converted to Catholicism and became a bishop of Hippo in North Africa. When the Roman Empire in the West was starting to disintegrate, Augustine developed the concept of the Church as a spiritual City of God, distinct from the material City of Man. In the Catholic Church and the Anglican Communion, he was a saint, a pre-eminent Doctor of the Church, and the patron of the Augustinian religious order. Many Protestants, especially Calvinists, considered him to be one of the theological fathers of Reformation who taught on salvation and divine grace.

Augustine studied Greek and Roman literature and served as the professor of rhetoric. His masterpieces are *De Civitate*(《上帝之城》, *The City of God*), *Confessiones*(《忏悔录》), and *De Doctrina Christiana*(《论基督教育》, *On Christian Education*), *On*

Christian Doctrine（《论基督教教义》）. The last one discusses linguistics from the theological point of view. Although such was aimed at helping Christians learn and understand the *Bible*, the discussion was either directly or indirectly related to general issues of language and translation, which could be considered as an important document of ancient linguistics and translation theories.

Despite not having done much translation work himself, Augustine was involved in editing parts of the Latin *Bible* and had a lot of reflections on language. Besides *De Doctrina Christiana*, he expressed his opinions on translation in his papers on his interpretation of the Psalms *Bible* and two letters, one of which was for his son Adeodatus.

Undoubtedly, it was because of his political and religious services that Augustine strongly advocated that only those who were inspired by God could translate the *Bible*. Nevertheless, Augustine's theory of language and translation does have a considerable impact on language and translation studies of the future generations. His semiotic theory is regarded as a common property for both philosophers and linguists and still plays a role today (Chadwick, 2001)[48-125].

To sum up, ancient Western translation (excluding those of ancient Assyrian Empire and Babylonian kingdom) and the period of translating the *Old Testament* covered 700 years, from the heyday to the demise of the Roman Empire. During that time, there were two major stages of great development. In the first stage, the ancient Greek literature, especially Homer's epic and drama, was first introduced to Rome, thereby contributing to the emergence and development of Roman literature and playing an important role as a bridge for European countries to inherit the ancient Greek culture. In the second stage, a stage of large-scale religious translation, the *Bible* and other theological works of translation gradually were on a par with secular literary translations. The former had surpassed the latter for a long time, becoming the mainstream of Western translation.

Early translation methods, to a large extent, was subject to the power relationships between Rome and Greece. Later, Cicero explicitly advanced the dichotomy of word-for-word translation versus sense-for-sense translation, about which writers and translators had discussions. There were three schools, with Cicero and Horace belonging to sense-for-sense school, Philo and Augustine belonging to word-for-word school, and Jerome belonging to the compromise school between them. Admittedly, all of them showed profundity on the theoretical issues of translation, which had a deep effect on the subsequent periods as well as modern times.

However, it must be noted that throughout the ancient times, the study of the translation theory was far from being systematic, and there were no experts or monographs. Writers and theologians mentioned translation while discussing other topics, or translators gave their opinions on translation in the preface or postscript of their translated works.

With the decline of the Roman Empire, translation in the West gradually came to a low ebb, passing over to the Middle Ages.

4.2 Translation of Ancient Greek and Rome Classics in Renaissance

The movement of the Renaissance first took place in Italy at the end of the 14th century and spread to Europe, especially to Western Europe, in the 15th and 16th centuries. It is a movement rediscovering and reviving the literature, art, and science of ancient Greece and Rome, thus translation played a very important role in the period.

The climax of the Renaissance occurred in the 16th century. At that time, the spirit of conquering the world was prevalent in Europe. Thus, the field of translation was affected by this. The translators found new literature fields and cultural legacies and tried to transplant them to their own countries. The bulk of translated works were concerned with politics, philosophy, social systems, and the classics of literature and arts of ancient and contemporary great powers. These provided a critical thought for the target-language countries. The national self-awareness was further strengthened in Germany and the linguists came to realize the particular expression style in their language. Translation of meaning thus took the place of word-for-word translation in German. In the religious world, Martin Luther led the reformation of religion and translated the *Bible* employing the native dialect. This was popularly accepted by common Germans for the first time since the version satisfied the common people's desire to read a *Bible* that was easily understood. The translated *Bible* played a very important role in unifying Germany and laid the basis for the formation and development of modern German language.

In the same period, doctrines of the ancients began to prevail around France. The ancient language and writings became parts of the canon. Accordingly, translation remarkably shifted to classical literature from religious works, with the period becoming one of the climaxes of translation in French history.

Though the Renaissance in Britain occurred later than that in other European countries, it had a tendency to develop in a positive and swift way. The development benefited from the rapid growth of the capital economy and laid a solid basis for literature and translation in Britain. The translation activity was flourishing in that period, which started in the middle of the 16th century when Elizabeth was enthroned and greatly influenced the political stage. While religious translation was in the ascendant, the bulk of literary works of ancient Greece, Rome, and relevant nations were put into English. This circumstance was one of the peaks of translation in Europe. Literary translation was very broad in scope, varying from history and philosophy to poetry and drama. The translators of religious books, influenced by the thought of humanism and religious reformation, had a new understanding of the *Bible* and translated it with a new approach. Therefore, many new *Bible* translations, totaling nine, appeared from 1525 to 1911. Among these, the versions of Tyndale and Regius were outstanding.

In the following parts, brief reviews of the translation activities in Germany, France and Britain in the climactic time of the Renaissance will be given respectively.

4.2.1 Translation in Germany

As in the 15th century, German translation in the 16th century was mainly concerned with the rendition from Latin to German or vice versa. Therefore, an argument on literal or free translation arose in Germany. The mere reason held by those who stood up for translating meaning was that translating word for word was difficult for readers to understand.

At the beginning of the 16th century, more and more Germans came to know Greek and Hebrew and some scholars observed that there was a kinship among German, Greek and Hebrew rather than between German and Latin. By studying the three "sacred" languages—Hebrew, Greek, and Latin, scholars commonly agreed that Roman derived its basic thoughts from Greek and Greek was in turn from Hebrew. Meanwhile, scholars recognized that Hebrew, Greek, and Latin had different features respectively. Thus, owing to the understanding of the nature and differences of these languages, there was an intensified feeling towards national identity and an aspiration to develop the native language. A large number of historians and scholars began to pay more attention to customary German expressions than follow examples of Latin expressions. This trend of thought could be found in a variety of books published in Germany in the 16th century. At that time, a number of Latin grammar books were published to teach people how to learn elegant Latin and discuss how to translate the customary German expressions into Latin or vice versa. When the readers understood that there was no corresponding relationship between Latin and German and the translators dealt with Latin definite articles, adjectives, etc., they should follow the German ways rather than use Latin grammar mechanically. That is, a verbatim translation was not recommended.

At that time, collections and translations of proverbs became a common practice. In 1507, Heinrich Bebel wrote a book about German proverbs, which was translated into Latin. The translation, retaining the unique German style, was refined and elegant. In 1513, Antonicus Tunnicius compiled a collection in which 1362 German proverbs were included and a six-step rhyme Latin translation was also attached for improving the level of Latin of German students. Though Antonicus Tunnicius did not discuss the principles of translation, his work showed his adoption of free translation over literal translation. In addition, Ottomar Luscinius and Hauer et. al. compiled and published similar books of proverbs.

It should be stressed that all such books were for teaching Latin rather than German. This was the possible reason why the differences between German and Latin were made noticeable. Under such circumstances, the translation theories in early 16th century made their way ahead. Johannes Aentinus, in the preface to one of his translation, pointed out that the problems of translation at the end of the 15th century lay in the fact that some translators misinterpreted German, some inserted single Latin words into German sentences, and others used circuitous expressions. All of these made translated texts difficult to understand. Still, some translators imitated the Latin writing pattern, which was improper for each language has its own usages and features. Just as Latin should not follow the rules of German language, Latin words should not be inserted in German works without any reason, and German should not imitate another language in style. Therefore, translators should seek new theories and methods to solve this problem, and take into account the characteristics of the target language rather than the source language.

Supporters of free translation gradually gained an edge over the proponents for literal translation who used to have the upper hand in debates in the 15th century. The former raised a profound reason against literal translation: German was a unique and respectable language with its own rules and styles which should not be sacrificed for imitating other languages. This new trend of thought dominated the German translation field in the 16th century.

In addition to the above-mentioned translation of German proverbs, the mainstream of translation in Germany in the 16th century was that of classical literatures including the works of Cicero, Horace, Pliny, and Cato, among others, and religious works with the *Bible* as the prominent work. The well-known translators and theorists were Emser, Dietrich von Pleningen, Brent, Leo Juda, Erasmus, and Luther. Luther's work on Bible translation was the most important.

Sebastian Brant(赛巴斯蒂安·布兰特, 1457—1521), a famous poet and translator in Germany from the end of the 15th century to the beginning of the 16th century, first wrote many poems in Latin and then translated many into German verses. This kind of translations, viewed as special works written by bilingual poets, revealed the kinships between the two languages. The world of translation caused a sensation immediately after the publication of Brant's poems written in two languages. It impressed the readers deeply with regard to the faded art, using poetry to translate poetry. In 1508, Brant translated the poem of Cato, one of ancient Roman poets, into German. Sebastian Brant demonstrated his approach in translating poems in the preface of the translation in Latin and pointed out that as long as the rhythm was translated properly in poetry translation, a word-for-word approach should be adopted to highlight a poem's features. However, as seen from his translations, it is hard to believe that his viewpoints were practiced for not a slightest trace of verbatim translation can be found in his works. For example, the translations of Cato's didactic poems with a beautiful style and profound meaning seem to be the bilingual poems created by Brant.

Johannes Reichlin(约翰内斯·罗赫林, 1455—1522), whose writings were mainly in Latin, was a famous humanistic writer in Germany in the Renaissance. In 1506, he compiled the *De rudimentis Hebraicis*(《论希伯来语的基本规则》, *The Basic Rules of Hebrew*), which triggered the great interest in the language in the academic circles. In 1515, he compiled *Epistolae Obscurorum Virorum*(《鄙人书翰》, *Letters of the Obscure Men*), which simulated ignorant theologians' tone and their poor Latin to expose scholastic scholars and monks' narrow-minded ignorance and lead to a heated debate between reformers and conservatives in church. Reichlin did quite a lot of researches on translation theories. In his mind, translation was intended to guide the readers to the original because its integral thought was not possible to be expressed in any translation. As indicated in the first volume of the *Old Testament*, the bridge between God and humanity is the language, that is, only Hebrew rather than any other languages, for God hopes to tell mortals his secrets through Hebrew. As a result, anyone who would like to interpret the *Bible* should first be familiar with the Hebrew grammar so as to comprehend the true meaning of each word in the *Bible*. In 1508, Reichlin stated in a letter that anyone who spoke Latin should first understand the expressions in the *Old Testament* before the individual could accurately interpret the *Old Testament*. In translating, the "essence" of the original in Hebrew was bound to get lost. Thus, he relied on reading the *New Testament* in Greek and the *Old Testament* in Hebrew rather than on translations by others. He made commentaries by himself not by studying commentaries of others. Reichlin's profound knowledge of Hebrew and basis of his writings made him believe that he had a more proper understanding of the *Bible* than the traditional interpretations. In *The Basic Rules of Hebrew*, he criticized a lot of *Bible* translations in Latin and the interpretations of clerical theoreticians so much so that none of them had escaped his criticism. He knew that he was more of a linguist than a theologian. And as a linguist, Reichlin thought that his mission was to find the truth in "the language chosen by God".

Different from the literal translation in the 15th century, which merely stressed imitating the rhetoric forms of the original, Brant and Reichlin adopted free translation. This focused on the value of the rhythm and the differences between the original and the target languages. In particular, Reichlin held that the original form, closely integrated with the meaning, was not retainable in the target language. He pointed out that Homer's works could only be read in Greek; if translated into any other languages, the aesthetic value of such works would doubtlessly be lost. The goal of literary translation was not to imitate the original author's style but to enable the reader to pay attention to the original style and grasp its literary value.

Desiderius Erasmus(德西德里乌斯·伊拉斯谟, 1466—1536), a Dutch Renaissance humanist, Catholic theologian, and exemplar of employing new approaches in literary studies and translation theories, was born into a pastoral family in Rotterdam on October 28, 1466. In his early school years, he was influenced by the Augustinian canon. Later, he studied at the University of Paris and sojourned in England, Germany, Italy,

Switzerland, and certain places where he was exposed to Humanism which was opposed to Scholasticism. In the process, he became the most famous scholar in Nordic Renaissance. He had a great learning and was good at language research, especially on Greek and Latin literatures. His arguments on literature and style attracted great interest.

Erasmus translated the literary works of Libanius, Lucian, and Euripides, among others, from the ancient Greek. In 1516, Erasmus published the annotated the *New Testament*, which was virtually the first Greek text and contained his own translation into Latin. This bilingual version has caused the attention of the academic world in Western Europe, deeply influencing the research and translation of the *Bible* of later generations.

In 1506, Erasmus translated two dramas by Euripides: *Hecuba*(《赫库巴》) and *Iphigeneia Hē En Taurois*(《伊菲革涅亚在陶洛人里》). In the preface to *Hecuba*, Erasmus highlighted the difficulty in translating such excellent Greek works into elegant Latin. These works written by classical poets were full of vagarious personalities, uncommon dramatic plots, and concise and elegant expressions, which were hard to be sustained in the target texts. Euripides' works had unique rhetorical devices, sharp styles, profound chorus words, though his manuscripts were in disarray. Hence, Erasmus thought that works of ancient Greek poets such as Euripides had never been translated successfully. Basically, adopting the approach of literal translation, he paid attention to the style. This was different from the earlier verbatim translation which stressed the use of proper words while ignoring the problem of style.

In the preface to *Iphigeneia Hē En Taurois*, Erasmus first pointed out that the style of the play was fresh and rich in language, which was sharply contrasted with the plain and sharp style in *Hecuba*. These two different styles required two different translation approaches. Such a consideration was the reason why he translated *Iphigeneia hē en Taurois* in a bold and decisive manner, employing various rhetoric devices on the premise of being faithful to the original. This was different from the conscious and meticulous way that he adopted in translating *Hecuba*.

Erasmus' principles of translation are as follows: style was the important element of translation, and rhetoric devices of Greek were to be shown in translation, and poetry was to be translated by poetry, word by word, plain language by plain language, and elegant style by elegant style.

Chapter 4 Translation of Ancient Greek Classics in Europe

Martin Luther(马丁·路德, 1483—1546), a great translator and leader of the religious reform in Germany, was born into a peasant family in Thuringia. Specializing in theology in an abbey in his early years, he later obtained his doctor's degree of theology in Wittenberg University(维登堡大学) and began to work as a professor. In 1521, he was arrested several times because of his refusal to Charles V who tried to change his views on religious reform in vain. Luckily, Luther was helped and hidden at Wartburg. Since then, he went on translating the *Bible* with a collaborator. At first, he translated the *New Testament* from Greek and published it in 1522. Then, he translated the *Old Testament* from Hebrew and published it in 1534. Luther followed the translation principles of popularity, conciseness, and extensive acceptance by common Germans. He made his version the model of German by basing on the unified documentary language around Thuringia area, absorbing the essence of the eastern and south-central dialects and creating many new words and expressions. The birth of Luther's version enabled the German peasants and common people to defend their class interests by quoting directly from the *Bible*. Thus, such a version was praised and regarded as the first *Bible* for the common people. It not only brought a great influence on the life and religion of Germans but also created popular forms of literary language which played an inestimable role in unifying and developing the German language. Luther wrote modern German essays and composed words and melodies of the hymn full of enthusiastic confidence which could be regarded as the *Marseillaise*(《马赛曲》) in the 16th century.

The German version of the *Bible* by Luther was the first translated work which tremendously and directly affected the evolution of the national language in Western translation history. This work rose in popularity as the *Septuagint* of ancient Greece, *The Odyssey*(《奥德赛》) by Andronicus who was the first translator of ancient Rome, the *Vulgate* by Jerome, and the later Authorized Version.

Besides the *Bible*, Luther also translated *Aesop's Fables* (《伊索寓言》) and its literary value was not to be underestimated. Furthermore, his views on translation could be summarized in the following points.

In translation, to comprehend the viewpoint that the language of common people should be adopted, it was necessary to be familiar with the historical background of that time. In the later period of the Middle Ages, the Church opposed the translation of the *Bible* by secular men, arguing that they had limited knowledge of theology and would distort the *Bible* towards paganism. The Church fiercely forbade such pagan versions and even attacked those written in national language. However, if the versions were in accordance with orthodox ones, the Church would merely accepted rather than advocated for these. Before the Reform and after the invention of the printing press, the medieval German *Bible* was more frequently printed than any other, except the Latin *Vulgate*. No less than seventeen or eighteen editions appeared between 1462 and 1522 at Strassburg, Augsburg, Nürnberg, Cöln, Lübeck, and Halberstadt. Among them, fourteen were in the High German dialect, and three or four were in the Low German dialect. Most of them were in large folio in two volumes, and were illustrated by woodcuts. These editions presented one and the same version, or rather two versions that one was the High German and the other was the Low German. The revisers were as unknown as the translators. Another point was that translation theories were greatly influenced by Erasmus, the authority of academics. Impacted by political and social factors, people all over the world gradually paid attention to their own national languages to go against Latin, which was preferred by the court and the Church. Faced with these changes, even the most conservative Latin grammarians had to inspire their people in learning the expressions and features of their own languages. Though, some scholars such as Wyle and others were in favor of translating word for word to imitate the style of Latin, a lot of translators began to realize that translation must be done in people's oral language.

As Reuchlin and Erasmus, Luther held the linguistic viewpoints of humanism, believing that each language had its own features which could not be translated word for word. To reconstruct the literary forms and styles of the original text, Luther used authentic German as the original. He thought that it was possible to reconstruct the spiritual essence of the *Bible* to some extent.

In 1516, the publication of Erasmus' Greek *New Testament* allowed Luther to access the Greek original with the attached Latin version and commentaries on the *Vulgate* for the first time. Enlightened by Erasmus' linguistic methods, Luther began to focus on connotations of words and phrases, accepting Erasmus' understanding on grammar, style, literary expressions, and rhetoric forms. Luther agreed with humanists' basic principles that the prerequisite condition of making commentaries on the *Bible* was to give priority to the original. Hence, he concentrated on the Hebrew and the Greek original and studied the linguistic phenomenon of them carefully. In 1532, he wrote *Table Talk*(《桌上谈》).

When translating, he was a strong adherent to the principle of grammar. Those who was familiar with such a principle knew how to translate the words of the *Bible*, even if they failed to convey its spirit. Luther firmly believed that there was a close connection between the words of the *Bible* and theology and the Gospel could only be given by God to human beings which could only be delivered through human language. Therefore, Luther opposed the view that translation completely depended on the divine inspiration. He thought that if we neither had the specific research on words nor analyzed the wording of the *Bible* carefully, it would be impossible for us to discern the human fallacy or the inspiration of God. Luther underscored that the comments of Church priests were no substitute for careful studies of the original language, "for in comparison with the glosses of the Fathers, the languages are as sunshine to darkness". This means that translators should analyze the language of the original by themselves rather than believe in the traditional explanations easily. However, linguistic and grammar analyses were not the most important aspects in translation. In *Table Talk*, he wrote from March 25 to 27, 1532 that grammar was necessary for the noun cases, verb variations, and the structures of the sentences but the meaning and topics must be given the priority. This indicated that Luther not only realized the values of grammar but also its deficiencies. His view can be summarized as follows: a translator should stick to grammar and to the comprehension and expression of meaning.

There are seven principles to be followed. To make readers fully understand the translation, Luther adopted free translation, advocating for the translation principles especially the meaning of the *Bible* and for the seven rules of translation which formed a system: 1) The word order of the original can be changed; 2) Modal particles can be employed so long as they are logically justified; 3) Necessary conjunctions can be added; 4) The words of the original which have no equivalents in the target language can be omitted in translation; 5) Phrases can be used to translate single words; 6) Non-metaphors can be translated by metaphors or vice versa; 7) Variations in forms and accuracy in glosses are in need of attention.

Luther's principles and methods of translation made great influences in the history of translation, owing to his success in translation and prominence in European religious reform in the 16th century. Both William Tyndale in Britain and Reina in Spain referred to and partly adopted such principles and methods when they translated the *Bible* into English and Spanish respectively.

Principles reflected above are Luther's unique opinions. However, as far as the essence of his whole theory was concerned, Luther dwelled on translation problems from a theologian's perspective rather than a humanist's perspective. Even though he broke from the Roman Catholic Church and lashed out at scholasticism, he did not accept humanism entirely but merely drew on certain points to serve theology. He agreed that Erasmus' linguistic method should take the prior place when theologians attempted to interpret the *Bible*. Conversely, Luther specified that the same method could not be used to explain the spiritual essence of the *Bible* and enable people in deeply understanding its meaning. In his mind, there was an element, similar to that in the translation method once used by Augustine who took "divine inspiration" as indispensable, which cast the mystery on translation and was criticized by humanists like Erasmus.

Luther's version also received various criticisms, especially from Roman Catholics. After his *New Testament* was published, Hieronymus Emser published a version catering to Catholic readers' taste in 1527. In 1534, Diefenberger combined Hieronymus Emser's *New Testament*, Luther's *Septuagint*, and Juda's *Pseudepigrapha*(《伪经》) and published the comprehensive *Bible*. In the same period, many Greek and Roman works of secular literature were published successively. However, Luther's translation of the *Bible* enjoyed the greatest popularity and regard in Germany.

4.2.2　Translation in France

The translation activities on the *Bible* and other religious literature constituted the bulk of translation in France before the 16th century. However, there were few influential translators and translations in the country in that period of time. The climax of translation activities in France did not come until the 16th century. At the end of the 15th century, a lot of literary works by Italian humanists such as Dante, Petrarca, Boccàccio(薄伽丘) were introduced into France, thus promoting the development of French humanism. The idea of going back to the ancients prevailed around France so scholars adored the ancient Latin and Greek writers. The humanists attracted by the classical cultures tended to devote themselves to the study of classical literary works. Consequently, they translated a lot of classics and Italian works into French.

Since the classical literary works became the focus of translation, new issues emerged. It was generally believed that translating literary works was much more difficult than that of religious ones. A general feature stood out in the translation activities of this period—with the new climax of translation, most of the translated works were byproducts produced by the litterateurs in their spare time. Therefore, the translations were barely of basic quality and slightly of impact. However, two persons contributed a lot to translation in the 16th century: Jacques Amyot(雅克·阿米欧, 1513—1593) and Etienne Dolet (艾蒂安·多雷, 1509—1546).

Born into a business-oriented family, Jacques Amyot studied the languages and cultures of ancient Greece and Rome in a French college in his early years. He was famous for his several translations of masterpieces. These translations were so influential and his slogan that "translation can be a match for the original" was so resounding that Amyot was generally accepted as a writer in the history of literature.

The most famous translation of Amyot was *Vies Des Hommes Illustrus*(《希腊罗马名人比较列传》, *Plutarch Lives of the Noble Grecians and Romans*, referred to as《名人传》for simplicity), which was produced in 1559. In the process of translating it, he was greatly supported by the king. To ensure the accuracy of the translation and the clarity of the words blurred in the original, Amyot had been to Venice and Rome to search for and study ancient manuscripts. Though the book was not very long, Amyot spent about 17 years finishing the translation. This work was so successful that it provided materials for the masterpieces of contemporary and later Western writers such as Racine and Shakespeare.

Amyot followed the following translation rules: 1) Translators must understand the original thoroughly and transfer the meaning of the original conscientiously; 2) Translations are to be simple and natural, without too many embellishments. He stressed the unity of form and content and of literal and free translation. With this principle, he combined the language of common people with that of the scholars, making the translation natural and simple and forming a unique style of translation. Therefore, Amyot's translation was considered both flexible and creative. Thus, *Vies Des Hommes Illustrus* was regarded as Amyot's own. In the process of translating, he borrowed words and expressions from Latin and Greek, creating plenty of terms related to politics, philosophy, science, literature, music, etc. At that time, there was not a unified French language yet. Undoubtedly, Amyot contributed greatly to the purity and standardization of French through translation. His translation's unique literary style was imitated by writers at the end of the 16th century, widely contributing to the improvement of the form of French classical essays and the development of readers' literary interest. Though Amyot contributed tremendously to French culture, he was a translator rather than a theorist.

The fame of an important translation theorist belongs to Etienne Dolet who wrote a brief and creative essay about translation research. He was the first to put forward a systematic translation theory in the Western translation history. As a linguist, scholar and publisher in Lyons, Dolet was born in Orleans and schooled in Paris in his early years. He later sojourned in Italy and returned to France at the age of 21 to participate in the humanistic movement. He wrote, translated, and published many works on language, history, and philosophy. Since he published new thoughts of humanism, the Church and the University of Paris reacted angrily and arrested him many times. Dolet's thirteen works and translations were burned as he was considered an enemy. He was accused of misreading one of Plato's works in his translation, in which Dolet denied that the soul could be variable. As a consequence, he was indicted of believing in paganism and hanged. His contributions to translation were mostly manifested in the essay *La Manière De Bien Traduire D'une Langueen Autre*(《论如何出色的翻译》, *On How to Make an Excellent Translation*), which was published in 1540. The basic principles of translation applied in the essay are:

1) Translators must understand the meaning of the original thoroughly.

2) Translators must have a good command of the original and the target language.

3) Translators must avoid translating word for word since such a way cannot transfer the original thoroughly and damages the beauty of language.

4) Translators must adopt the idiomatic forms of language.

5) Translators must endow his translation with a suitable tinge by selecting words and adjusting the word order.

The first item is the basic principle of translation, which is concerned with faithfulness to the original meaning. The second gives demands for the language to be used. Dolet thought that excellent translators must master the original and the target languages with the same proficiency. The third principle shows that he advocated free translation rather than mechanically literal translation. The remaining principles indicate that Dolet proposed to use idiomatic phrases and keep the style of the original intactly. His purpose was to enable common people to understand translations. In general, Dolet paid attention to all aspects of translation, which are still followed by most modern translators and theorists to a large extent. However, all of these are merely principles, which are short of systematically theoretical illustrations (Tan Zaixi, 2004)[68-69].

4.2.3 Translation in Britain

The Renaissance began to flourish in Britain at the beginning of the 16th century, reaching its climax from the middle of the 16th century through the early years of the 17th century. It is the first period of great development in British translation history. At that time, manufacturing in Britain developed rapidly and politics, economy, and academics prospered accordingly. In such a situation, the field of translation also followed the trend. Many translators aimed to serve the country by translation, providing not only serious thoughts for the Queen and statesmen but also scenarios and interesting materials for dramatists and readers. Many translators were not restricted by strict translation theories and translated anything that they could find. Outcomes were indirect translations, which were translated from some other translations rather than from the original.

Historical works were favored by both translators and readers. In 1550, a goldsmith named Thomas Nicolls in London translated Thucydides'(修昔底德) famous works such as *Peloponnesian War*(《伯罗奔尼撒战争》). The propositions of ancient philosophers and moralists fitted the interest of Tudor Dynasty so these were favored by the translators. Most of the translated works were from Aristotle and the like.

Operas were mostly translated from ancient Rome. There was only one Greek work, an opera by Euripides, which was translated indirectly from Italy. Numerous translations of neoteric works by Boccaccio et. al. were also produced, mostly from Italy, France, and Spain. It was a trend to add forewords and postscripts in works in the literary world in the 16th century, which naturally spread to the translation field. Almost all the translators stated their purposes and methods in forewords and postscripts. This kind of theoretical discussions became quite popular when Elizabeth ascended the throne in the middle of the century. However, there was not such a thing like Dolet's essay which was focused on translation principles. That is to say, all the forewords and postscripts were unsystematic intuitions and thoughts.

Below is a brief review of the main personages of the British translation field in the 16th century. Gavin Douglas was a famous Scottish poet and literary translator who translated Virgil's historical poem *The Iliad*. It was published at the beginning of the 16th century. In the preface of the first volume of *The Iliad*, Douglas discussed a translator's responsibility, combining viewpoints in the 16th century with those in the Medieval Times. He first praised Virgil but then severely criticized free translation in the Medieval Times, stating that the translation of *Aeneid* by William Caxton from the French version was as unfaithful as "the difference between the devil and St. Austin". To illustrate such a point on free translation over the verbatim, Douglas took Caxton's wording as example—if difficult words, sentences, and rhymes were encountered, deviations from the original were unavoidable. Douglas' translations, therefore, were usually longer than the Latin originals for he believed that skillful treatments were permitted in translation. He thought that a Latin word could be translated into several English words sometimes since the original words had many meanings and connotations.

John Cheke(约翰·奇克, 1514—1557) was a classical scholar, statesman, and notably, the first Professor of Greek at Cambridge University. He translated many Greek works as well as the *Bible*. As a translator, he merely adopted pure English words or the ones which originated from the Saxon language. He never used any loanwords from other languages, believing that English was rich enough for translation. For this reason, he had to use vulgar, stale and rare words in his translation, which sometimes contributed to his blunt style.

Though Cheke's translation theories did not influence later generations much, such frameworks affected the contemporary translators deeply as many of them referred to Cheke's erudition and viewpoints in their works. The judgment criterion for translation then was whether the language was natural and easily understandable or not. At the same time, studies on grammars of foreign languages and comparative words became significant in language research. In one of his books published in 1520, it was demonstrated how a translator render Latin into English. He meant to turn the version into a textbook for the students who learnt language and translation to imitate.

A well-known proponent of the new vitality of the theory of translation in the middle of the 16th century, Nicholas Udall(尼古拉斯·尤德尔, 1504—1556), was an English playwright, cleric, schoolmaster, and the author of *Ralph Roister Doiste*(《拉尔夫·劳伊斯特·道伊斯特》). This work was generally regarded as the first comedy written in the English language. From 1542 to 1545, Udall was in London, being engaged in work as a translator. In 1542, he published a version of Erasmus' *Apopthegmes*(《箴言录》). Udall was employed by Catherine Parr, who shared her enthusiasm for the Reform to spearhead the translation of Erasmus' *The Paraphrases* of the *New Testament*. The first volume published in 1548 was about *The Gospel of Luke*. In various prefaces and dedications contained in the translation of *The Paraphrases*, Udall tackled essential concerns on stipends of translators, the augmentation of the English vocabulary, the sentence structure in translation, the style of Erasmus, and the unique quality of the style of every writer. These issues were treated lightly and undogmatically though. According to Udall, translation should not conform to iron rules. He was steady on the diversity of methods exhibited in *The Paraphrases*. "Though every translator," he wrote, "follows his own vein in turning the Latin into English, yet none of them willingly swerve or dissent from the mind and sense of the author, albeit some go more near to the words of the author and some use the liberty of translating at large, not so precisely binding themselves to the straight interpretation of every word and syllable". In his own share of the translation, Udall was inclined to the free method rather than to the literal method. He was not "fully to discharge the office of a good translator" partly because of his wishes to be understood by the unlearned and possess the ornate quality of Erasmus' style. Udall was less scrupulous as he could when translating the text of the *Scripture*, though he was guilty of the heretical opinion that "if the translators were not so precise as they are but had some more regards to expressing the sense, I think in my judgment they should do better". However, it can be noted that Udall's advocacy of freedom is an individual reaction, not a repetition of a formula. The preface to his translation of Erasmus' work helps to redress the balance in favor of accuracy. The rest of the preface shows that Udall, in his concern for the quality of English, did not make "following the sense" an excuse for undue liberties. Writing "with a regard for young scholars and students who get great value from comparing languages" made him most careful in noting such slight changes and omissions he did in the text.

The most famous translation in the time of Elizabeth is the English version of *The Lives of the Noble Grecians and Romans*, which was translated by Thomas North(托马斯·诺斯, 135—1604). He studied at Cambridge in his early years. While working in London, he made friends with a lot of translators and became interested in translation. The first edition of his translation was published in 1579. There are three features:

1) Since it was done through intermediate French rendering, the translation style was

different from that of the original. The former was plain while the latter was elegant.

2) The style of translation was also different from that of Amyot, which was the French original. That is to say, *The Lives of the Noble Grecians and Romans* is like his North's own work.

3) Though he had an average knowledge of classical languages, he was a master in using English. His translation was plain, fluent, elegant, and natural. Hence, he was praised by Shakespeare. The translation formed the source from which Shakespeare drew materials for his *Julius Caesar*, *Coriolanus* and *Antony and Cleopatra*. It is in the latter that Shakespeare followed *The Lives of the Noble Grecians and Romans* most closely, with whole speeches being taken directly from North.

John Florio(约翰·弗洛里欧, 1552—1625), born in London and of Anglo-Italian origin, was famous as the translator of Montaigne's *Essays* into English. In 1580, Florio translated the French voyager Jacques Cartier's *Navigations and Discoveries*. In 1598, Florio published the well-known dictionary *A World of Words*. In 1603, he translated *Essays* with wonderful imaginations. Though the work was translated in the essay style, it was quite different from that of the original. The original was ingenious yet plain while the translation was fine yet complicated. *Essays* was favored by Shakespeare who used certain parts of it in his play *Tempest*. The greatest contribution of *Essays* was that it made the British writers know that essay could exist independently as a kind of literary style.

Philemon Holland(菲尔蒙·荷兰德, 1552—1637) was the most prominent British translator in the 16th century, having translated books more than those of any other scholars. His father, John Holland, was a clergyman who fled the Kingdom of England during the persecutions of Mary Ⅰ. Philemon was born in Chelmsford, Essex and educated at King Edward Ⅵ Grammar School, Chelmsford where a house was named after him more than three hundred years later. He then studied at Trinity College, Cambridge. He finished with a degree in medicine and moved to Coventry around 1595 where he practiced his profession for the poor and devoted most of his energy to translating. In 1628, Philemon became the headmaster of a local free school but served for less than a year. He was indigent in his last years, though he was awarded a pension by the city council of Coventry in 1635. Holland was extremely productive. His best-known translations are Pliny the Elder's(老普利尼) *Natural Historie*(《博物学》), Plutarch's (普鲁塔克) *Moralia*(《道德论集》), Xenophon's(色诺芬) *Cyropaedia*(《居鲁士的教

育》), and William Camden's(威廉·康登) *Britannia*(《不列颠志》). In certain cases, Holland's work on Pliny's is superior to English translations commonly available in the 20th century despite the use of antiquated language. There are passages in Holland's translation of the work *Plutarch*(《普鲁塔克》), which have hardly been excelled by any later prose translator of the classics.

Holland paid much attention to the style of the translation, writing in a slow rhythm which made the translation longer than the source text. He tried to ensure that the translation was natural and without foreign accent. As written in the preface to his translation of Livy's work, he framed his pen not to any affected phrase but to a mean and popular style and if he was to use some old words, it was because of his love for his country's language. In conclusion, Holland left a lot of excellent translations with distinguished styles for later generations, thus giving joy to contemporary readers.

The quality of poetry translations in Elizabethan era was inferior to that of the prose versions, for most of the translators were more of scholars than poets who were more qualified to translate poems. Ancient poets like Virgil, Ovidius, and Homer were very popular at that time. In 1558, Thomas Phaer began to translate Virgil's *Aeneid* and finished it in 1583. In the same period, the famous translator Marlowe translated Ovidius's *Elegies* and George Chapman's translation of Homer's *The Iliad* and *The Odyssey*.

Chapman(查普曼, 1559—1634) was born at Hitchin in Hertfordshire. There is a conjecture that he had studied at Oxford but did not take a degree course. However, there is no reliable evidence to affirms this. From 1598 to 1611, he translated Homer's *The Iliad* and finished the translation of the same poet's *The Odyssey* in 1616. Chapman's translation of *The Odyssey* was in iambic pentameter while that of *The Iliad* was in iambic heptameter. Both were literary masterpieces at that time. His versions of Homeric works in the final years of the 16th century and the early years of the 17th century linked the two periods. He referred a lot to dictionaries of mythology and the early comments on Homer's works in his translations. However, Chapman's translation only fit in with the original partially in meaning and style. What's more, the personalities of the characters were modified and didactic elements were added. As a translator, Chapman had imperfections, but as a poet, he is beyond blame. His creativity and talents in language as a poet contributed to his great success in translation.

Some of the deficiencies of the 16th century theory were pointed out by Chapman, who himself applied with ardent zest so as to lay down the principles which should govern the poetical translation in his opinion. He attacked both excessively rigid and loose methods of translation. He was always conscious, "how pedantical and absurd an affectation it is in the interpretation of any author (much more of Homer) to turn him word for word, when (according to Horace and other best lawgivers to translators) it is the part of every knowing and judicial interpreter not to follow the number and order of words, but the material things themselves and sentences to weigh diligently and to clothe and adorn them with words, and such a style and form of oration, as are most apt for the language in which they are converted." Chapman thought this literalism was the prevailing fault of translators. However, he believed that it was possible to overcome the difficulties encountered in translation. He held that it required judgment to make Greek and English agree in sense and elocution.

In the 16th century, *Bible* translation prospered. The English version of the *Bible* took its shape under unusual conditions, which impacted the excellent quality of the final outcome. Appealing to all classes as it did, it had its growth in the vital atmosphere of strong intellectual and spiritual activities. From the scholar who is alert to controversial details to the simple layperson who cares only about his/her soul, such a work is relatable. Then, it was the translator's task to attain scholarly accuracy combined with practical intelligibility. The representatives of *Bible* translation were Tyndale and Fulke.

William Tyndale(威廉·廷代尔, 1494?—1536) was a Protestant reformer and scholar of the 16th century who translated certain parts of the *Bible* into the Early Modern English. He was influenced by works of Desiderius Erasmus and Martin Luther. While a number of partial and complete Old English translations had been made from the 7th century onward, Tyndale was the first English translator to draw directly from Hebrew and Greek texts and the first to take advantage of the new medium of print, which allowed for the wide distribution. In 1535, Tyndale was arrested and jailed in Vilvoorde castle outside Brussels for over a year. He was tried for heresy, being strangled and burned at the stake. Much of Tyndale's work eventually found its way into the King James Version (or "Authorized Version"), which was published in 1611. The work of 54 independent scholars, revising the existing English versions, drew significantly from Tyndale's translation.

The success of Tyndale's translation lay in its combination of scholarship, simplicity and literariness together, among which the simplicity was given more significance. He created the unique style of English *Bible* translation. Tyndale exerted so much effort to use "natural" expressions and common forms of vivid and concrete descriptions in his translation so that his language was simple and natural. Like other *Bible* translators, Tyndale was very serious and conscientious with his job, feeling the need for revision. When opportunities came, he would correct and polish the version.

If Tyndale made practical contributions to *Bible* translation in the 16th century, William Fulke(1538—1589) would complete theoretical ones. In 1589, he published his *Defence of the Sincere and True Translation of the Holy Scriptures into the English Tongue* (《为忠实英译〈圣经〉辩护》), in which he gave the most elaborate discussions on techniques in *Bible* translation. This work was his reply to the viewpoint of Gregory Martin (格列高里·马丁), a *Bible* scholar and translator, who wrote a book entitled *A Discovery of the Manifold Corruptions of the Holy Scriptures by the Heretics of Our Days*(《当代异教徒对〈圣经〉的误译面面观》) in 1582. He fiercely attacked all *Bible* translations by the Protestants. Fulke thought that Martin's perspectives were obscure so he expressed his analyses and criticisms paragraph by paragraph in his work.

On the whole, one of the most important features of the translations in Western Europe during the Renaissance is the balanced development of translations in every country. Though Latin was used extensively, it was merely a branch in literary works and translations. Before the Medieval and the Renaissance, Western translations were mainly connected with Latin translation. However, with the formation of West European nations after the Medieval period, especially in the Renaissance, native languages were chiefly employed in translations. Accordingly, the Renaissance became a turning point for the Western translation. In brief, the Renaissance signified that the theory and practice of translation had departed from the "dark time" of the Medieval (Tan Zaixi, 2004)[71-83].

4.3 Literary and Philosophical Translation in European Countries

The translation from the 17th century to the 19th century was not as great as that in the Renaissance in strength and impetus and the translated materials belonged to different fields. This marked a golden age for the entire study of translation theory.

England and France were much more powerful than other countries in Europe during the 17th century. More and more people wanted to read, write and translate, as the production developed rapidly, the economy prospered each day, and the educated population continually increased. It was certainly advantageous for translation to further develop and for researches on translation theory to dig deeper.

Classicism was so strong that not only literary creation was greatly influenced but also the field of translation. Then, translators rendered classical works on a large scale. There was a fierce debate on preferences for modern ways versus ancient ways. Also, the issue on paraphrase or metaphrase was closely connected with the question on stressing the past instead of the present and vice versa.

The 17th century saw the publication of the Authorized Version of the *Bible* in England, which was well known throughout the world. Collectively endeavored by 47 scholars, the book was a magnificent feat in the British history of translation. The work was like Martin Luther's German version of the *Bible*, which has contributed to the progress of modern English in history. The scale on which literary translation was done in the 17th century was smaller than that in the 16th century. Brilliant translators and translated works appeared such as *Don Quixote* rendered by Thomas Shelton. Translation theory research gradually gained momentum especially in the latter half of the 17th century. Roscommon published his *Essay on Translated Verse*, which discussed the principles to be applied in poetic translating. Armed with extensive translation knowledge and deep insight, John Dryden wrote many theses and prefaces concerning translation theory. He expounded translation principles and methods in-depth and raised new ideas, which made him the most conspicuous in the field of translation theory at that time.

The background and conditions of the 18th century were different from those of the 17th century. Classicism continued to dominate in England, Alexander Pope and William Cowper were the prominent figures in two different schools of translation. Pope's English translation of Homer's epics was regarded as standard for a certain period. In France, although the Enlightenment provided a vigorous and continuous development of translated classics, the period was first characterized by introduction of British works. Nearly all Enlightenment writers had been to England and introduced the progressive British ideology, literature and art to France, with translations of Shakespeare's dramas standing out.

Beginning from the latter half of the 18th century, to a great extent, scientific and technical translation was the result of Industrial Revolution of United Kingdom and the development of modern science and technology to a great extent. As Latin translation of science actually ended as early as 1750, works in vernaculars prospered, thus contributing a lot to the spread and development of physics and social sciences in various countries. The most frequently introduced authors and scientists included the British philosopher J. Locke, the French Chemist A. L. Lavoisier, and the British physicist M. Faraday.

As far as translation theory is concerned, the 18th century witnessed an important period in the Western history of translation. Theorists began to go beyond the narrow traditional range of research by advancing comprehensive, systematic, and universal theoretical patterns. Charles Batteux(夏尔·巴特, 1713—1780) of France raised a set of principles of realizing accurate translation from pectives of literature and linguistics. The translation principles put forward by George Campbell(乔治·坎贝尔) and Alexander Fraser Taylor(1747—1814), a famous English translation theorist, are still of reference value today. In particular, Tytler's *Essay on the Principles of Translation*(《论翻译的原则》) could be taken as the first monograph of translation theory in the real sense in the Western translation history. Mikhail V. Lomonosov(1711—1765) of Russia proposed that foreign words were to be Russianized so that translation could become beneficial to the purification and unification of the Russian language.

As the romantic school of literary thought became influential, the emphasis of translation in the 19th century shifted from classical works to modern or contemporary ones. Works by Milton, Goethe, Schiller, Hugo were rendered into various Western languages, playing an active part in the development of Romanticism throughout Europe.

The translation of Homer's epics is also controversial. The heated debate between Arnold and Newman enlivened the academic discussion and enriched the theoretical research at that time.

However, the center of translation theory research in the 19th century was in Germany. Ever since the latter half of the 18th century, German translators and theorists had been extremely active in presenting ideas, with frequent translation research activities and great achievements being gained many times. Such well-known theorists as Goethe, Schleiermacher, Humboldt, Hölderlin, et al., probed into different layers of translation from perspectives of literature and linguistics, thus opening up new scientific approaches for translation(Tan Zaixi, 2004)[84-86].

4.3.1 French Translation and Batteux

In the 18th century, France began to turn its attention to the literature of other countries, such as United Kingdom, although its power was somewhat weaker than that in the previous two centuries and its culture was more mobile. The novels by Samuel Richardson(1689—1761), a sentimentalism British writer, were translated into French, thus producing a great influence upon the development of the sentimentalism literature in France. It was interesting that Chinese culture which was spread to Europe many years before became more active on French soil in the 18th century. Yearning for Chinese culture, quite a few writers introduced novel Chinese works and regarded ancient Chinese culture highly, resulting in an unprecedented peak of Sinology. The great man of letters Francois-Marie A. Voltaire(伏尔泰, 1694—1778) created the tragedy *A Chinese Orphan* (《中国孤儿》) based on the Chinese drama *Zhaoshi Guer*(《赵氏孤儿》, *Orphan of the Zhao Family*) of Yuan Dynasty. Many priests and philologists focused on translating Chinese works and compiled collections of Chinese books. Unfortunately, their importance in the history of translation has declined because their translations focus on content rather than language.

It was Charles Batteux who made the greatest contribution to translation theory studies in the 18th century. Having edited collections of translated works including Aristotle's, the scholar Batteux wrote a book entitled *On Principles of Literature*(《论文学原则》, 1747—1748), which was divided into six parts.

Batteux approached translation principles in terms of general language skills instead of literary creations. He believed that, in language, the universal governing factor was not grammar but word order and that grammatical structure was governed by it. Therefore, when contradiction occurred, grammatical structure should give way to word order.

In addition, he elaborated on the task of a translator, pointing out that one was to represent the things, ideas, diction, and style in the original without any amplifications or omissions and any alterations of the original meaning. In thought, the version ought to preserve the original color, degree, and minute differences. In style, the original ought to preserve the enthusiasm, interest, and vitality. In diction, the version ought to be natural, imaginative and persuasive, choosing expressions that are rich, varied, elegant, and refined. The author, as an absolute master of thought and diction, might write at his free will depending upon his natural talents and collected materials. If an idea or expression was inappropriate, he could try to look for another. However, the translator, was not a master but the author's "servant", having to follow the author in any case and truthfully reflect his ideas and style. Otherwise, the translator could no longer be called as such, but an author instead.

Batteux proposed a theory and applied it, which was fully embodied in his translation of Aristotle's *Poetics*(《诗学》). This version kept the word order of the original from start to end. The sentences used were very close to those of the original in length, thus realizing the formal equivalence. Although it was not without prejudice and defect for Batteux to prioritize form than content, his principles of translation have had an impact not only in France but in the countries of Western Europe to some extent.

Translation of Shakespearean works was a feature of French translation in the 18th century. The great man of letters Voltaire, stayed in London and translated Shakespeare's dramas into French from 1726 to 1729. He did these while studying British society and politics, Newton's scientific achievements, Locke's materialist philosophy, the language and drama. However, Laplace(拉普拉斯), was the first to introduce Shakespeare's dramas into France, publishing a book entitled *English Theatre*(《英国戏剧》) in 1745, which contained part of the author's dramas. Seven essays appeared in a newspaper introducing and commenting on the vision upon its publication. His achievements were widely recognized but the way he translated was controversial. Laplace gave a summary of the sections which were less interesting although he translated the fascinating paragraphs word for word and sentence for sentence faithfully. The style of prose was generally used with insertions of poetic lines. In the mind of most present-day readers, such a translation is faulty since it is usually regarded as "trans-editing" instead of translation in the full sense. However, it met the need of readers at that time.

Another Shakespearean translator that followed was Jean-François Ducis(让-弗朗索瓦·迪西, 1733—1816) who was a surprise due to his translations of celebrated works without knowing English. Taking the versions by Laplace as models, Ducis translated such well-known Shakespearean dramas as Hamlet by collaborating with other scholars. He intended to make Shakespearean style completely compatible with "the most splendid system of drama in the world", that is, the French dramatic system. Obviously, Ducis' versions could not possibly be faithful and accurate. However, the much-altered versions, satisfied the French spectators.

Letourneur(勒图尔纳), the first translator who noticed Shakespeare's original style of writing, translated *The Complete Works of Shakespeare* from 1776 to 1782, which set an example for the later translations of Shakespeare's works. Stressing faithfulness to the original even more than Voltaire's approach did not mean literal translation. On the contrary, Letourneur thought metaphrase could only lead to unfaithful versions. The faithfulness in his theory referred to the retention of the original spiritual essence. Instead of favoring omitting and rewriting to satisfy the French preference for elegance, his standpoint was to preserve vivid images and the popular language style in the original. Letourneur's propositions have led to a new attitude toward Shakespeare in the translation community.

The peak of French translation came in the 19th century, when a large number of British, German, Italian, Spanish, and Latin literary works were translated such as works by the British writers Shakespeare, Milton, Byron, and Shelley; the German writers Goethe and Schiller; the Italian writer Dante; and the Spanish folk songs. The most outstanding was still the translation of Shakespearean works. If the 18th century was said to be the silver age of the translation of Shakespeare in France, then the 19th would be the golden age. People in this age not only adored his works but also Shakespeare himself. In France from 1800 to 1910, there were at least eight translated sets of *Complete Works of Drama of Shakespeare*, of which the version by François-Victor Hugo(1802—1885) was the best. With the assistance of his father Victor Hugo, the great man of letters, François-Victor translated *Complete Works of Drama of Shakespeare*. Since the version faithfully kept the beautiful rhythm schemed peculiar to drama, it was honored by critics as the second milestone in the history of Shakespearean drama translation in France, with the part it played even greater than the famous version produced at the end of the 18th century by Letourneur.

Chateaubriand(夏多布里昂, 1768—1848) and Nerval(奈瓦尔, 1808—1855) were among the rest of famous translators. Chateaubriand's translation was both faithful and beautiful. His French version of Milton's *Paradise Lost* was literally turned out, beautifully rhymed, and full of poetic flavor. It was one of the most prominent translated works in France. Well-known for his version of Goethe's *Fausto*, Nerval translated the book in the style of prose. After reading his version in 1830, Goethe highly praised it, saying that this version was better than his original (Tan Zaixi, 2004)[97-102].

4.3.2 German Translation and Schleiermacher, Humboldt

German translation also developed quickly from the 17th century to the 19th century. Germany became another center of European translation theory research and translation activity. Particularly from the end of the 18th century to the beginning of the 19th century, there were greatly celebrated philological masters and theoreticians such as Herder, Goethe, Schleiermacher, Humboldt, and Hölderlin. Prominent translators like Voss, Tieck, Wieland, Schiller, and Schlegel introduced a lot of ancient Greek and Roman works and brilliant modern and contemporary literary works of Britain, France, Spain, etc.

The greatest achievement of German translation practice from the 18th century to the 19th century was considered to be the pratice of August Wilhelm Schlegel(1767—1845) who was an outstanding literary critic, linguist, and translator. He learned theology and philology at Georg-August-University of Göttingen(哥廷根大学) in his early years before he became a professor of literature of University Bonn(波恩大学) and the head of Bonn Museum. He was a versatile translator learned and profound, completing the translation of 17 Shakespearean dramas (with the help of Tieck from 1797 to 1810), Spanish dramas (by Pedro Calderón de la Barca from 1803 to 1809), and many other Italian works. With very clear translation principles, Schlegel gave versions that were fluent and beautiful. Schlegel's translations of Shakespeare's dramas were precious sources in the translation literature of Germany. His versions and studies of Sanskrit and other oriental languages greatly influenced his contemporaries and the later generations.

Regarded as the prominent figure in the Storm and Stress movement, Johann Gottfried von Herder(1744—1803) was very accomplished in language and translation, writing such monographs as *On the Source of Language* and *On the New German Literature*. In the former, he refuted the fallacy that had God as the source of language, believing it was an important task for the German national literature to improve the German language. Stressing the importance of language, von Herder deemed knowledge could only be acquired through the medium of language. In his book *On the New German Literature*, he profoundly expounded the responsibility and task of a translator, claiming translation was an activity that touched the essence of the work. He pointed out the task of a translator was to help those who did not know the foreign language to understand foreign books, that is, "interpretation", which was a kind of teaching by which the reader acquired knowledge as Augustine dealt with more than a thousand years before. Herder's exposition of problems pertaining to language and translation produced a far-reaching influence on philology and translation, with his views being conveyed to Goethe and other contemporaries.

Johann Wolfgang von Goethe(1749—1832) was the most brilliant man of letters in modern Germany. With the introduction of Herder, Goethe read Homeric and Shakespearean and the British realistic novels of the 18th century in his early years, strongly fascinated by translation all his life. Proficient in languages of many countries, he had the ability to translate Latin, Greek, English, French, Spanish, Italian, Middle High German, Persian, and some South Slavic languages. His versions of the Italian sculptor Benvenuto Cellini's *Autobiography*, the Spanish dramatist Calderon's dramas, and the French philosopher Diderot's *Rameau's Nephew*, etc., were recognized as model translations, which were the most influential in the whole European literature.

Goethe was not only a great man of letters and translator but also a great master of translation theory. His interest in translation problems was embodied in all of his translations, the most important ones being *Poetry and Truths*(《诗与真》), *West-East Anthology*(《西东合集》), and *Letter to Carlyle*(《致卡莱尔书简》).

He asserted that translation could be divided into three kinds:

1) informative translation, for instance, Luther's *Bible* translation;

2) adaptation or parody, which was near to creation;

3) interlinear translation, which consisted in writing the version linguistically below the original but closely resembling the original text to represent the essence. Interlinear translation was a sentence-to-sentence translation, not a word-for-word mechanical imitation.

Of these, Goethe convinced that interlinear translation could result in a perfect version. It is just like genetics for the target and source languages to merge into one in a perfect translation, producing a new form without abandoning their respectively original elements. If Goethe is internationally well-known chiefly for literary creation, it will be Schleiermacher and Humboldt who enjoy a greater reputation in the fields of philology and translation theory.

Friedrich Schleiermacher(弗里德里希·施莱尔马赫, 1768—1834) was an influential German Protestant philosopher, theologian, and classical philologist. He entered Halley University in pursuit of philosophy of various schools in 1787, especially fascinated by Aristotle and Kant. Schleiermacher became a professor of the same university from 1804 to 1806 and a professor of theology in Berlin from 1810.

Familiar with Greek and Latin, he translated Plato's works in 1796. It was on June 24, 1813 when Schleiermacher read a thesis of more than 30 pages entitled *On Translation Methods* at the academic symposium held at Berlin Royal Academy of Science. It is a theoretical work on translation principles and methods, which has exerted a great influence on Germany translation theory.

Schleiermacher's theory was extremely influential in the 19th century and is still significant today. He was the first who distinguished between written and oral translation, but his view toward the latter was inappropriate. Contemporarily, oral translation is by no means a mechanical activity but a skill similar to written translation as both require a high-level language expression and artistry. Since oral translation is done impromptu, without much time for careful thinking, such type is no less difficult than written translation in many respects.

Wilhelm von Humboldt(维廉·洪堡, 1767—1835) was a philologist, philosopher, and education reformist. He made special contributions when Germany became the center for translation theory research in Western Europe from the end of the 18th century to the beginning of the 19th century. Influenced by Romanticism, he published two philological monographs and wrote an important foreword for his own translation of *Agamemnon*(《阿伽门农》). In these academic works, Humboldt gave a profound discussion on language problems, in which his contributions in translation theory were stressed.

There is an obvious dialectical element in his views. Like Schleiermacher, Humboldt combined the concept of language as a "system" and a "process". Getting insights from his own translation practice, he thought that there were both individual and general characters in languages and all of them could be mutually translated. In his analysis, he regarded language as a symbolic instrument employed in communication, taking the untranslatability of language lightly.

Summarizing the above, it could be seen that Humboldt's greatest contribution is to raise a dualist view on language, which escaped the attention of the 19th century theorists but had a great influence in the 20th century. This dualist view was held in language research by modern linguists like de Saussure, Walter Porzig, Alan Gardiner, and Noam

Chomsky, believing language could be analyzed in such dichotomies as langue vs. parole, Sprache vs. Rede, language vs. speech, and competence vs. performance. Thus, in the field of translation, the question whether translation was possible became the focal point again interested the translation theorists.

Friedrich Hölderlin（弗里德里希·荷尔德林, 1770—1843）was another important figure who was very influential in German translation of the 19th century. Second only to Goethe and Schiller as a poet in the period, Hölderlin was one of the prominent romanticist letters of men. Doing earnest researches in literary and philosophical works of ancient Greece, Rome, and modern Britain and France, he translated the works by the classical writers Homer, Pindaros, Sophocles, Euripides, Virgil, Horace, Ovid and Lucan. Hölderlin's translation of Sophocles' tragedies *Oedipus* and *Antigone* in 1804 were highly appraised in the literary sphere.

Without any special book or essay on translation theory, Hölderlin only gave some comments on his own translation of Sophocles' works. Touching upon the essence of language and translation, such comments were so insightful that these were specially remarked in the developmental history of Western translation.

Hölderlin thought every language was the embodiment of the "pure language". Therefore, translation is to look for the core element of this basic language, that is, the meaning. Since different languages are indeterminate collections that come from the unity, Logos(逻各斯), to which a translator has necessarily to refer if he is to complete a translation by fusing elements from different languages. When translating classical works, the translator should get the semantic kernel of the ancient language and see the creative revelation which is universal, overcoming the language and psychological barriers formed because of the temporal distance. Regarding the comprehension and expression processes as those of making an archaeological exploration into intuition, Hölderlin had greater efforts than any other philologists, grammarians, and translators in seeking for the universal source of poetry and language.

He adopted the method of word-for-word translation, intending to create a cultural and verbal intermediate zone between ancient Greek and modern German. Such a zone belonged to neither Greek nor German but was shared by almost all human languages. To realize this point, Hölderlin deemed one had to translate the original word for word. This idea seems right but actually groundless. In his reasoning, there is some truth. But in his conclusion that word-for-word translation was the final solution to the problem, there is none. Word and sense are two different things, though closely connected. What we are to obtain at any cost is sense instead of word (Tan Zaixi, 2004)[102–112].

4.3.3 British Translation and Dryden, Tytler

The scale on which translation was carried was unprecedented in the Elizabethan Great Britain. With British translation flourishing and celebrated translations continually being reproduced from the 17th century to the 19th century, huge achievements were attained from the 17th century to the 18th century, especially in translation theory research.

John Dryden(约翰·德莱顿, 1631—1700), the greatest translator in the 17th century, was the founder of the school of British classicism and a poet-laureate in the restored dynasty. Born into a rural gentleman's family, John went to school at Westminster, London when he was 13 and later to Cambridge for higher pursuit. The classical education he received in his early years was doubtlessly the source of his regard to and translation of works by ancient Greek and Roman writers. Dryden, with both a large number of translations and a systematic theory, surpassed scholars before him and his contemporaries in translation. He was skillful in turning classical texts into idiomatic English and in varying his style with authors. Having translated a lot of works by such classical authors as Homer, Virgil, Lucretius, Horace, Juvenal, Ovid, and recent ones like Chaucer, Boccaccio, and Du Fresnoy, Dryden was highly esteemed in literature and translation in the 17th century.

For him, metaphrase and imitation were "the two extremes" which ought to be avoided, and paraphrased the "mean between them"—the mode of translation which avoided the dangers of both extremes and combined their virtues of fidelity to the original and the fluency to the target language. In this, Dryden followed the orthodox tradition of translation theory since Jerome who first theorized sense-for-sense translation in the middle ground between Cicero's extremes: slavish fidelity and too free imitation (Baker et al., 2008).

Dryden was a brilliant translation critic. He articulated his views in a comprehensive and profound way. He clearly and systematically advanced his principles of translation in a large number of theses and prefaces which were collected in *Essays of John Dryden*, edited and published in 1900 by W. P. Ker(克尔).

In 1790, *Essay on the Principles of Translation* by Alexander Fraser Tytler was published in Britain. He raised three principles, which were practically the same as those put forward by Campbell. They floated these ideas anonymously at the time of publication, causing a misunderstanding between them. When accused by Campbell of plagiarism of his findings, Tytler wrote to him immediately claiming to be the author of the book and declaring that no plagiarism was involved since Campbell's work had not been known to him before he finished writing the book. Tytler thought that it was not surprising for two scholars, who were both well-versed in theories of criticism and embarked on the study on principles of translation, to arrive at the same findings. It was coincidental for them to have raised similar theoretical principles and ways. In general, scholars think that it is possible for two people to reach similar results when they pursue the same theoretical study at the same time. Judging from historical materials, Tytler's work far exceeds that of Campbell in influence.

Alexander Fraser Tytler was born in Edinburgh, Scotland, graduated from Edinburgh University, and became a history professor in the same university. In 1770, he turned to be a lawyer but he had always been deeply interested in literature and translation. In addition to *The Essay on the Principles of Translation*, he wrote many historical books and translated the works by the Italian poet Francesco Petrarca. Tytler read essays on translation and poem composition frequently at the Royal Society of Edinburgh. Such works were later collected to publish *Essay on the Principles of Translation* in 1790. Among young generations of Edinburgh, the manuscript of the book was very influential even before it came to press. Doubtlessly, Sir Walter Scott learned from Tytler, especially in collecting German romantic works.

In his *Essay on the Principles of Translation*, Tytler first gave a definition of "a good translation"—"that in which the merit of the original work is so completely transfused into another language, as to be distinctly apprehended and strongly felt by a native of the country to which that language belongs, as it is by those who speak the language of the original work" (Shen Yuping, 2002)[167]. Then, he put forward the "three principles of translation":

1) Translation should give a complete transcript of the ideas of the original work;

2) The style and manner of writing should be of the same character with that of the original;

3) The translation should have all the ease of original composition. Under each of these general laws of translation are a variety of subordinate precepts, which I shall notice in their order, and as well as the general laws, which I shall endeavor to prove and to illustrate by examples (Shen Yuping, 2002).

Detailed rules are given under these three. Citing examples from translation of well-known works in English and certain languages like Greek, Latin, French, Spanish, and Italian, Tytler tried to prove his principles and views. To give a complete transcript of the ideas of the original work, he deemed that the translator was to be familiar with the language in which the original is written and the subject matter to be translated, and both were indispensable requirements. When there is a ambiguity in the original, the translator has to give the meaning consistent with the context and the permanent ideological and writing style of the author. The translator enjoys the freedom of making certain additions and subtractions, which is closely connected with the original thought and makes translation more effective. When translating poetry, he may be even bolder in doing so, competing with the author in cleverness to keep the high level and surpass and improve the work to a certain extent, when possible.

According to Tytler's second principle, one has to recognize features of the original style. The translator has to distinguish among different styles and represent the features of the style by focusing on the target language. A version only with ideas faithful to the original but devoid of the original artistic features can only bring about distorted images. To imitate the original style and manner, one has to think the kind of style and manner he would have expressed himself if the author had written in the target language.

The most difficult part in translation is related to the third principle, in which Tytler compared the translator with the painter. Though both pursuing imitation, the two arts differ in many aspects. The painter may adopt the same colors as the original when copying a picture. The essence is how to faithfully imitate the style and form of the original. An appropriate imitation can bring about all features of the original. It is quite another story for translation since the translator has to employ his "picture" to produce similar force and effect without using the same colors. Not in a position to copy the language forms, he is to turn out a perfect copy in his own linguistic means. The more one tries to imitate carefully, the less it is possible to let the original fluency and spirit show.

Besides poetic translation, Tytler also raised the problem of idiom translation. Idiom represents a special language phenomenon, thus constituting an extremely knotty problem. When dealing with idioms, the translator should avoid adopting those which do not agree with the language and era of the original. For instance, he says, there is an ancient Greek proverb which carries the same meaning of "making an unnecessary move" as the English "to carry coals to Newcastle". The translator should not translate one into the other since these are of different backgrounds. Criticizing Denham's views, Tytler thought the translator ought not to let the author talk as if he (the translator) had lived in the same time and nation as the author. Linguistically, idioms are difficult to match with the target ones. The sole possible way is to express idioms into simple and understandable expressions while literal translation should be avoided. Idioms are untranslatable to a certain extent.

Tytler discussed the criteria for good translators at last. He believed a translator must be endowed with talents similar to the author. Of course, one cannot require the translator to become a great orator or philosopher like Cicero before he sets out on translating the works of the ancient Roman orators. The translator must see the complete value of Cicero's works, understand his thoughts and inferences, and savor all the beauty in his works.

Comprehensive and systematic, Tytler's translation theory was one of the important milestones not only in the history of British translation theory but in that of the Western world.

Questions for discussion:

1. What are the differences between the ancient Western translation and the earliest stage of translation in China?

2. What do you think of the theories of such scholars as Cicero and Augustine?

3. Could you give a brief account of Britain's achievements in *Bible* translation after the Renaissance?

References:

何立波,2009. 昆体良:古罗马最有影响的教育家[J]. 世界文化(5):14-15.

He Libo,2009. Quintilianus:The most influential educator in ancient Rome[J]. World Culture(5):14-17.

格里马尔,1998. 西塞罗[M]. 董茂永,译. 北京:商务印书馆.

申雨平,2002. 西方翻译理论精选[M]. 北京:外语教学与研究出版社.

Shen Yuping, 2002. Selections of Western translation theories [M]. Beijing: Foreign Language Teaching and Research Press.

谭载喜,2004.西方翻译简史[M].2版.北京:商务印书馆.

Tan Zaixi, 2004. A brief history of Western translation [M]. 2nd ed. Beijing: Commercial Press.

Baker M, Saldanha G, 2008. Routledge encyclopedia of translation studies [M]. London: Routledge.

Bassnett S, 2004. 翻译研究(第三版)[M].上海:上海外语教育出版社.

Chadwick H, 2001. Augustine: A very short introduction [M]. Oxford: Oxford University Press.

Douglas Robinson, 2006. 西方翻译理论:从希罗多德到尼采[M].北京:外语教学与研究出版社.

Chapter 5

Scientific Translation in China

Although sporadic translation can be found along with the translation of Buddhist sutra, large-scale translation of Western scientific and technological works did not begin until the late Ming Dynasty.

5.1 Scientific Translation in Ancient China

Technology has always been despised in the Confucian tradition so little importance has been attached to the development of science and technology in ancient China, let alone the translation of scientific and technological works. However, the latter did exist but as by-products lost in the extensive translation activities on the Buddhist sutra. In the Yuan and Ming Dynasties, purposeful translation of scientific and technological works began.

5.1.1 Scientific Translation before Ming Dynasty

The earliest translator of scientific and technological works was Parthamasiris(安士高) who was said to had introduced Indian astrology, mathematics, and medicine to China in the 2nd century. Since then, occasional scientific translation could be found on similar subjects like *Dabaojijing*(《大宝积经》, *Maharatnakuta Sutra*, the *Sūtra of the Great Heap of Jewels*, translated by Upasunya—a prince of Ujjayini—in 541) in which the Indian decimals were mentioned. The Indian astrological theories were of special interest in Chinese and Gautama Siddha of Indian descent translated the *Navagraha Calendar* (《九执历》) into Chinese in 718 as well as introduced the Indian numerals with zero to China as a replacement for counting rods. Besides astrology, Indian medical works were also appealing to the Chinese, with more than 10 works translated in the Sui and Tang Dynasties. Most of these works were lost, but their influence, especially that of ophthalmology, could be found in the writings of native Chinese doctors in the two dynasties.

With the development of commerce between China and the Arabian world, the Arabian astrological and medical theories were introduced into China. In the early Song Dynasty in 963, Ma Yize and Wang Chuna made a new calendar *Yingtian Li*(《应天历》)

based on Arabian astrology. This calendar introduced the Arabian knowledge of calculating solar and lunar eclipses and planetary movements for the first time, initiating the division of a night into five periods.

After the Mongols conquered the Arabian world, they brought Arabian documents and captives back to China, including Arabian scholars as trophies. It was through them that more Arabian knowledge entered China. A new calendar aligned with the Arabian system and new astrological instruments were made. A hospital was even established to house the Arabian doctors who were held captive. Arabian medical books were translated. 36 volumes of translation were done at the end of Yuan Dynasty and published in the early Ming Dynasty. Judging from what remained today, they were all inclusive and encyclopedic.

5.1.2 Scientific Translation in the Late Ming and Early Qing Dynasties

The scientific translation in the late Ming Dynasty began with the Christian missionary work. When the missionaries first arrived in China, they found it challenging to convert the Chinese to Christianity as the locals were strongly influenced by the traditional Chinese thoughts. So the missionaries chose to appeal to the Chinese with new scientific and technological findings as well as borrowings from and integrated elements in the tradition. The foremost of these missionaries was Matteo Ricci (1552—1610), an Italian who aroused the interest of Chinese officials and scholars by demonstrating his knowledge of astronomy, mathematics, and geography. He introduced them to European clocks, prisms, astronomical instruments, oil paintings, musical instruments, picture books and architectural drawings. In time, Ricci gained their respect and built rapports in cooperating with them.

Science and technology developed rapidly in the West in the 16th and 17th centuries. In such an environment, the missionaries were acquainted with the more advanced development of science and technology, which they used to attract and broaden the ken of Chinese officials and scholars—the Chinese society's "cream of the crop" at that time. The missionaries translated the scientific and technological works only to facilitate their missionary work. Their translation was often done in collaboration with the Chinese. So did Matteo Ricci.

Ricci's chief collaborator was Xu Guangqi (1562—1633), whom he came to know around 1593 and taught Euclid's *Elements*, especially after Xu passed the Imperial Examination in 1604. In the winter of 1606, they began to translate *Elements* and finished the first 6 books in the next spring. In the process, Ricci dictated the Chinese rendition while Xu wrote it down. Then, Xu would weigh the Chinese version word by word after a paragraph was done and if he found anything improper in the translation, Ricci would refer back to the original work in Latin and explained it again. As there were no equivalents in Chinese, Xu had to coin many of the terms like "dian(点)" for "point", "dun jiao(钝角)" for "obtuse angle", "rui jiao(锐角)" for "acute angle", "san jiao xing(三角形)" for "triangle", and "ping xing xian(平行线)" for "parallel lines". Some of the terms coined by Xu are not only used in China today but also in Japan and Korea.

After Ricci's death in 1610, he collaborated with other missionaries in scientific translation. In 1612, he and Sabbatino de Ursis (1575—1620) translated the book *Taixi Shuifa*(《泰西水法》, *Hydromethods of the Great West*) on hydraulic engineering, introducing Western reservoirs and hydraulic machineries to the Chinese for the first time. The book was later included in Xu's *Nongzheng Quanshu*(《农政全书》, *An Agricultural Encyclopedia*).

In 1629, Xu was finally assigned the task of making a new calendar after repeated requests to Emperor Chongzhen. Unfortunately, Xu's death in 1633 prevented him from further contributing to scientific and technological development in China. However, his scientific translation and experiments and his encouragement and support for other scholars earned him the distinction as the "Father of Chinese Scientific Translation" (Xie Tianzhen et al., 2009).

Besides the translators mentioned above, there were those who did translation on various subjects. In 1613, Li Zhizao compiled a mathematical book *Tongwen Suanzhi*(《同文算指》, *Selected Arithmetic Methods*) according to what he had learned from Matteo Ricci.

In 1620, Nicolas Trigault brought more than 7,000 Western books with him, the coursebooks used in European universities. Some Chinese scholars like Yang Tingyun hoped to translate all of them but failed. In 1623, Giulio Aleni wrote a summary of these books but aroused little attention unfortunately.

In 1626, Johann Adam Schall von Bell wrote a book *On Telescope*, introducing the optical principle, application, and the technology of making telescopes. In 1627, Johann Schreck (also Terrenz) and Wang Zheng wrote *Yuanxi Qiqi Tushuo*(《远西奇器图说》, *An Illustrated Guide to Western Equipment*), discussing mechanical principles and applications.

The translation of scientific and technological works survived the transition of dynasties and did not end until the reign of Emperor Yongzheng who adopted a close-door policy.

5.2 Scientific Translation in the Late Qing Dynasty and Early Republic of China

After about a century of isolationism, Qing Dynasty was knocked open by the Western ships and weapons in the Opium Wars, jolting it from the fancy dream of being the center of the world. In the face of Western threats, the Chinese tried to strengthen themselves by learning from their enemies, seeing the translation of Western scientific and technological works as an effective way to catch up with the Westerners.

5.2.1 The Pioneers

The first Opium War woke up some Chinese but not all. Among them was Lin Zexu (1785—1850) who had Hugh Murray's *The Encyclopedia of Geography*, a book given to Lin by a missionary from American Congregational Church, translated into Chinese. He renamed the work as *Sizhou Zhi*(《四洲志》, *Record of the World*) and even painstakingly polished it.

Like him, his friend Wei Yuan (1794—1857) did not do translation himself but was able to publish the 50-volume *Haiguo Tuzhi*(《海国图志》, *Illustrated Introduction to Countries over the Seas*) in 1863, based on available resources including Lin's *Sizhou Zhi*. Apart from Wei's own treatises on how to strengthen the country, he devoted many of his books to the geography, economy, science and culture of other nations. In 1847, he added knowledge about ship building, water mines, guns etc. to the same book and expanded it to 60 volumes. In 1852, he finally expanded it to 100 volumes with information about the USA and Switzerland. Such a work was used by the reformists as a coursebook to know the world despite its numerous errors.

Xu Jishe (1795—1873) published *Yinghuan Zhilue* (《瀛寰志略》, *World Geography*) in 1844. This was not a book of translation but a compilation, a result of his interviews with foreign missionaries, business professionals, and diplomats when he assumed his official position in Fujian. It is said that many of the reformists and revolutionaries in the late Qing Dynasty got to know the world through this book!

5.2.2 Institutions

The fiascoes on the Qing side during the Opium Wars, especially the 2nd one, forced the Chinese to face weaknesses in technology. "To learn from the barbarians in order to subdue them", the Chinese established various institutions to infuse Western knowledge, especially Western technology, into the minds of the young.

In 1862, right after the conclusion of the Opium War II, the School of Combined Learning was founded in Beijing as part of the Self-strengthening Movement. An English academy was established first. Later, academies of French, Russian, German, Japanese, astronomy, mathematics, and natural science were added. Attached to the School were press and translation bureaus as well as a chemistry laboratory, an observatory, and a museum. It is said that 26 books, including those on natural science, were translated and published by the School.

In the next year 1863, a similar school was established in Shanghai to train the desired translators and interpreters. It was originally called Shanghai Academy of Foreign Languages and Literature, which was later renamed as Shanghai Guang Fangyan Guan in 1867. At first, only an English academy was founded but academies of French and Arithmetic were established later.

In 1864, a school for English learning was founded in Guangzhou after that in Shanghai. This school was later called Guangdong or Guangzhou Tong Wen Guan. It was the first school to teach foreign languages in Guangdong.

Jiangnan Arsenal was opened in 1865. During the 1860s and the 1870s, it was the most successful arsenal in East Asia and one of the greatest in the world. Its translation bureau, directed by the Englishman John Fryer, translated more than 160 foreign works into Chinese. Some of the most important translators of scientific and technological books and treatises had worked for the Arsenal.

Missionary institutions also played an important role in the scientific translation. The most significant of all was Mohai Shuguan, founded in 1843, which translated and published scores of books on mathematics, astrology, physics, botany, and other subjects. Among the published were the final nine books of Euclid's *Elements*, De Morgan's *Elements of Algebra*, John Herschel's *Outlines of Astronomy*, and W. Whewell's *An Elementary Treatise on Mechanics*. The institution was the first to use Western typography in printing translated scriptures. It was regarded as a bridge for the Chinese to know the Western world.

Other prominent organizations were the American Presbyterian Mission Press, founded in 1860, which translated and published dozens of books of natural science such as coursebooks from algebra to mechanics and the Chinese Scientific Book Depot, founded by John Fryer in 1885, which translated and published many scientific and technological books, especially the Outline Series.

As for translating medical books, the translation agency of Canton Pok Tsai Hospital stood out, publishing works like *Vaccination*, *Encyclopedia of Surgery*, *Introduction to Western Medicine*, *Fevers*, and *Elementary Chemistry*. The agency's role in promoting Western medicine and training doctors in the Western-style could never be overexaggerated.

Finally, the role of the School and Textbook Series Committee should not be overlooked. This cultural organization established by missionaries published 104 textbooks in 10 years between 1877 and 1886.

5.2.3 Prominent Translators

Li Shanlan (1811—1882) was the greatest Chinese mathematician of 19th century who translated Western works and gave many summation formulas. In 1859, he, with Alexander Wylie, published the translation of *Elements of Analytical Geometry and of the Differential and Integral Calculus* by Elias Loomis. This was the first book which introduced Newton's calculus to China. Other mathematics books translated by Li included the final 9 books of Euclid's *Elements* and De Morgan's *Elements of Algebra*. However, Li Shanlan did not just translate mathematics books. He once worked with the protestant missionary Joseph Edkins on a translation of W. Whewell's *An Elementary Treatise on Mechanics*, the first introduction of Newtonian mechanics into China. And with Alexander Williamson and Joseph Edkins, he translated John Lindley's *Elements of Botany* in 1858. Li also translated John Herschel's *Outlines of Astronomy*.

Xu Shou (1818—1884), as the pioneer of modern chemistry, translated 13 books on chemistry and chemical technology. Among these, probably, the most important was *Principles and Applications of Chemistry* by David Ames Wells, which Xu titled as *Huaxue Jianyuan*(《化学鉴原》). He also drafted rules for translating the names of chemical elements and other scientific terms into Chinese that are still in use today.

Wang Tao (1828—1897) was one of the pioneers of modern journalism in China and an early leader of the movement to reform traditional Chinese institutions along Western lines. He was more of a thinker than a translator. He did do some scientific translation but was mostly of social works. Perhaps his greatest achievement in translation was his aid to James Legge in translating the "Five Classics" of Confucianism.

Hua Hengfang (1833—1902) was a mathematician but his translation was not confined to mathematical works. His personal struggles to understand mathematical materials helped him produce exceptionally lucid translations, particularly his fluent and accessible presentations of works on algebra and calculus. His translations included J. D. Dana's *Manual of Mineralogy*, C. Lyell's *Elements of Geology*, W. Wallace's *Algebra* and *Fluxions*, and J. Hymer's *A Treatise on Plane and Spherical Trigonometry*.

Zhao Yuanyi (1840—1902) was steeped in translating medical works. As his mother died of misdiagnosis when he was young, he decided to study medicine and became an expert in traditional Chinese medicine. In 1869, he was invited to work in the translation bureau of Jiangnan Arsenal. His translation focused on Western medicine and healthcare.

Xu Jianyin (1841—1901), the second son of Xu Shou, was a chemist and engineer. Together with John Fryer and others, he translated more than a dozen works covering various fields like engineering, drawing, electricity, ship and weapon building. In 1901, he died in an accident when he was experimenting with smokeless powder.

Ma Junwu (1881—1940) was one of the earliest individuals who introduced socialism to his fellow Chinese although he went to Japan to study chemistry in 1901. After returning to China, he was busy with writing and publishing anti-Manchu articles and calling for the revolution. In 1907, his activities were noticed by the authorities so he was forced to leave China. Ma studied in Germany where he earned a doctoral degree in metallurgy, the first for a Chinese. He was fluent in English, Japanese, French, and German and his translation ranged from social works to those of natural science which lasted for a long time. As early as in 1901, he translated and published a book on algebra. During his sojourn in Germany, he translated and wrote on plane geometry, differential equations, mineralogy, and botany, of which the most famous were his translations of Ernst Heinrich Philipp August Haeckel's *The Natural History of Creation* and *The Mystery of the Universe*. Ma was the first to translate Charles Darwin's *Origin of Species* in 1921 and his translation was reprinted 12 times within 16 years.

5.3 Scientific Translation since the May 4th Movement

The difference in the translation of terms by different translators is a standing problem in the translation of scientific and technological works. To solve this problem, the government and related academic societies initiated the term standardization project.

5.3.1 Before 1949

The national government in Beijing established the National Institute for Compilation and Translation, a governmental book compilation and translation institue, after the Qing tradition in 1920. Later, the Nanjing National Government reestablished and expanded the Institute as an organization under the Grand Academy and the Ministry of Education successively. The Institute was to translate and publish scientific and technological works, write or translate textbooks for secondary and tertiary education, provide standard translations for scientific and technological terms, and make dictionaries for different branches of science.

Besides the governmental organizations, academic societies also played their parts in standardizing the translation of scientific and technological terms.

The Chinese Medical Association (CMA) was established in Shanghai in February, 1915. The next year, the assembly decided that the Association's Department of Names assumed the function of participating in and examining the translation of medical terms. Between 1916 and 1926, the CMA sent its representatives to the annual assembly of the Examination and Approval Committee of Medical Terms (the Examination and Approval Committee of Scientific and Technological Terms after 1919) and participated in examining and approving terms in chemistry, medicine, anatomy, bacteriology, pathology, parasitology, biochemistry, organic chemistry, pharmacology, surgery, physiology, internal medicine, and pharmacology.

The Science Society of China (SSC), the first comprehensive Chinese scientific association, was actually organized in 1914 by a group of Chinese students at Cornell University in the United States to "promote science and industry, finalize scientific and technological terms, and spread scientific knowledge". The Society's Department of Writing and Translation was to "deal with the writing and translation of scientific and technological works". Before its end in 1958, the SSC organized many scientific translation projects.

5.3.2 After 1949

At the beginning, the People's Republic of China relied heavily on the Soviet Union in introducing advanced science and technology. As a result, many Chinese who could speak Western languages rather than Russian began to learn from and translate it. Many researchers and university teachers did Russian translation in their spare time. At the same time, national and local printing presses were all engaged in scientific translation from Russia. The huge volume of translated materials from Russian played an important role in scientific research, education, and economic construction. The journals founded during this time like *Translators Notes*, *Journal of Russian Teaching and Translation*, and *Journal of Russian Teaching and Research* became the platform for discussing the translation of Russian language.

Since 1978, when China was reopened to the outside world, scientific translation in the country has entered a stage in which exchanges between China and other countries were becoming increasingly frequent. Scientific translators had done much work and contributed in fields like scientific research, education, commerce, diplomacy, and economy.

The Committee for Chinese Science and Technology Translators under Translators Association of China and the Association of Chinese Science and Technology Translators under the Chinese Academy of Sciences were established.

Shanghai Journal of Translators for Science and Technology and *Chinese Science and Technology Translators Journal* were published.

Academic works like Li Nanqiu's *The History of Science Document Translation* and *The Historical Documents of Chinese Science Translation* and Lin Huangtian's *A Biographical Dictionary of Chinese Translators of Science and Technology* were published.

In addition to the publication of scientific translations by various presses, translation firms sprang up like mushrooms after rain. They churned out a lot of scientific translations per year. And with the advance of science and technology in China, hi-tech companies' demand for scientific and technological translation was always on the rise, creating a huge industry for science and technology translators. Unlike their predecessors who did everything manually, translators of today can take advantage of modern technology such as Translation Memory and Neural Machine Translation to translate swiftly and more correctly. The advent of the Internet has changed the working mode of traditional scientific translation, making it easier for translators to work with one another even at a distance. But the human translators are also challenged and facing the risk of being replaced by AI translators, like ChatGPT.

Questions for discussion:

1. Why was there not a large-scale scientific translation until the late Ming Dynasty?

2. Why were ancient scientific translators interested in astrology?

3. What role did the missionaries play in the science and technology translation in China?

4. Can machines replace human translators in science and technology translation? Why?

References:

谢天振,等,2009. 中西翻译简史[M]. 北京:外语教学与研究出版社.

Xie Tianzhen, et al., 2009. A brief history of translation in China and the West[M]. Beijing: Foreign Language Teaching and Research Press.

Xu Jianzhong. "Brief History of Science Translation in China". Meta. 2005(3).

Chapter 6

Scientific Translation in the West

Throughout recorded history, the translation of scientific knowledge from one culture into another has played an important role in shaping human civilization. However, the history of scientific translation has always been in obscurity as compared with the history of literary translation. Moreover, considering the early conceptualization of science in the West, the translation of philosophical works must be considered when exploring the ancient history of scientific translation in the West.

6.1 Scientific Translation in Ancient Greece and Rome

In ancient Greece, translation was involved in the process of absorbing scientific knowledge from other civilizations. The Greek knowledge of mathematics and astronomy was mainly influenced by the Mesopotamian and Egyptian civilizations. From ancient Egyptian and Babylonian civilizations, the Greeks learned scientific knowledge like the units and rules of measurement, simple arithmetic, almanac, and solar and lunar eclipses.

The conceptualization of Western science in ancient Greece can be said to have benefited from the translation of foreign literature on science and technology. From 600 to 500 B. C., the natural sciences developed in Hellenic Greece, when the ancient Greek idea of the universe was conceived.

Thales of Miletus (c. 625—545 B. C.) and Pythagoras of Samos (580—500 B. C. ?) pioneered geometry and astronomy based on the knowledge they had acquired from Egypt and Babylonia. In Egypt, Thales learned geometry and measured the height of pyramids by the length of the shadow they cast. He introduced this area of knowledge to Greece. Thales also visited Babylonia where he learned about astronomy. Historians such as Herodotus and Isocrates associated Pythagoras with Egypt so he might have also borrowed his mathematical knowledge from ancient Egypt. Other historical sources indicated that Pythagoras continued his education in mathematics and music in Babylonia as a "captive".

He became extremely proficient in mathematics and science as taught by the Babylonians.

Plato (427—347 B. C.) and Aristotle (384—322 B. C.) are generally regarded as the two greatest figures of Western philosophy. The scientific knowledge embodied in their philosophical works is of much interest to historians of science. Plato advocated the universalism of philosophy, putting forward a geocentric model of the universe. Though it was hard to associate Plato with any translation activity during his lifetime, his work *Timaeus* was later translated into the Latin language and became one of the few ancient Greek classics for the Church schools in the Middle Ages. Aristotle is more a logician and scientist than a philosopher. His scientific contributions are mainly on logic, physics, and biology. As a scholar of encyclopedic knowledge, he pursued the order inherent in the natural world and all aspects of human life. His presumptions about geocentrism and the circular motion of heavenly bodies set the precepts for pre-Copernican astronomy.

Unfortunately, until now, there has been little knowledge about whether Plato and Aristotle had absorbed knowledge from other civilizations in composition of their great works. Considering the linguistic environment of ancient Greece, translation must have been involved. It seems that both historians of science and translation are merely concerned with the translation of Plato's and Aristotle's works into the Latin and vernacular languages in later times. The reason may be ascribed to the lack of related literature on this matter.

Hippocrates (460—370 B. C.), the father of medicine in the West, was the greatest ancient physician to whom a great volume of writings was attributed. Many documents in his name were about detailed discussions on the brain, lungs, heart, liver, and blood and on recommended treatments. These became known as The Hippocratic Corpus (about 400 B. C.). Hippocrates was especially renowned for the theory of four humors: black bile, yellow bile, phlegm, and blood. This is another ancient Greek luminary whose works are waiting to be translated into other languages.

The importance of translation in the field of science became conspicuous in ancient Rome. Continuing the legacy of the Greek civilization, the Roman civilization would not have been so prosperous without translating ancient Greek works.

Early in the 6th century B. C., the Romans had been influenced by the Greek colonies in southern Italy. When the Romans conquered the central areas of Greek culture, their soldiers and officials began to communicate directly with educated Greek rulers and administrative officials. The vision of the Romans was reinforced by the Greek civilization they had direct contact with at that time.

In fact, what the Romans had taken up was a Hellenistic civilization that had broadened its influence with the conquest of Alexander the Great. The Museum established in 322 B. C. in Alexandria was an institution based on the Greek academia, comprising a library that boasted a collection of 500,000 to 700,000 books. The Museum embraced talents from the whole Mediterranean including philosophers, mathematicians, doctors, botanists, zoologists, astronomers, linguists, geographers, artists, and poets. It became a research and communication center for scholars from Europe, the Middle East, and India. Translation played its role in the environment of multiple languages. These translations included not only the Latin translation of ancient Greek classics but also those of other languages. Daily communication must have been conducted through interpreting and translating.

The scientists housed by the Museum in Alexandria were the famous mathematician Euclid (330—275 B. C. ?), the late Greco-Roman astronomer Claudius Ptolemy (c. 90—168), and the ancient Roman physician Galen (130? —200?).

Euclid's *Elements* is one of the most influential works of science in the history of humankind for its logical development of geometry and other branches of mathematics. Many scattered theorems and proofs were gathered from various aspects and compiled into an organized textbook form. This work has been translated into Arabic, Latin, Chinese, and many modern languages.

Ptolemy was the greatest astronomer before Copernicus. In addition to *Geography*, *Tetrabiblos*, and *Optics*, he wrote his most influential work called *Images*. It was regarded as the most important work in astronomy before Copernicus. This 13-volume encyclopedia of astronomy had been lost before the Arab scholar Hunayn Ibn Ishek rediscovered and named it *Almagest*.

What is of great significance to translation studies is that the ancient Roman works are mainly a translational synthesis of many earlier works. The most prominent example is *Naturalis Historia* by Pliny the Elder (23—79). This book has 37 volumes and quotes a lot of facts and observations from around 2000 previous works by previous authors, of which 146 are Romans and 326 are Greeks. Pliny the Elder did not identify the source of his data at all so he adopted the strategy of translation plus editing in his book.

In the medical field, this kind of translation also exists. Galen, an ancient Roman physician and one of the pioneers of anatomy, was influenced by Hippocrates' four humor theory and Aristotle's views on human nature in his writing. Galen had dominated the medical field until the modern times because his works have been better preserved than those of any other author in ancient times. 83 of his 131 medical works have been handed down due to translation conducted in Baghdad. In other words, his works have been preserved and expanded their influence with the help of translation.

As a consequence of the strategies popular with the Roman translators, the Roman readers were generally able to consider translation as a metatext in relation to the original. The translation effect was highlighted and translation was done for the purpose of competing with the original. Notable translation theorists during the Roman times were Marcus T. Cicero, Horatius Flaccus, M. F. Quitilianus, and Saint Jerome. Though they mainly explored literary and religious translation, these Roman theorists had certainly influenced scientific translation with their perspectives on the process.

6.2 Scientific Translation of Arabic Literature in the Middle Ages

6.2.1 The School of Translators of Baghdad

The translation of scientific and technical materials in the Middle Ages mainly comprises the translation of scientific and philosophical works in the Arab world in antiquity and the reverse translation of Greek and Roman scientific achievements preserved in Arab literature. In the early Middle Ages, the Arabs extensively translated Latin into Arab language. According to Mona Baker (2006), "The Arabs were credited with initiating the first organized, large-scale translation activity in history". They translated essentially scientific and philosophical materials from Greek but showed little or no interest in Greek drama and poetry. The translation activity reached its acme in the establishment of the School of Translation of Baghdad and the School of Translation of Toledo.

The translation activity in the Arab world grew with the rise of Islam. The exchanges between the Prophet and non-Arab rulers must have been conducted through translation. Borrowed words in the Qur'ān themselves showed the influences of Greek, Persian, Syriac, and Hebrew. Before the Arab conquest, many ancient philosophical and scientific texts had been translated into Syriac and Persian. The rulers of Caliphate had a great zeal for academic studies and translation so the Arab world soon became the center of science and translation in the Middle Ages.

In 661 A. D. , the Umayyad Caliphate was founded and accepted Greek culture from then on. Greek administrative documents were first translated into Arab and scientists were recruited to do the same to the ancient Greek scientific and philosophical works. These had a profound impact on the development of science and philosophy in the Arab world.

Later, a vast range of materials were translated under the Abbasids, including Ptolemy's *Geography*. Astronomy was also directly inspired by translation from either Greek or Syriac. The capital of Baghdad became the hub of all cultures at that time. The rulers of the Abbasid Caliphate favored paid translation. Legend has it that a translator was paid gold of the same weight as that of the book. The translation of medicine and philosophy aroused the most attention of contemporary translators. The choice of texts was determined by the political and cultural needs of the society.

The second Abbasid caliph Al-Mansur (reigned 754—775) was obsessed with astrology. The study of astronomy in Islam was said to have originated from the astronomical works of India. In 773, he requested the presence of the Indian astronomer Manka who presented him the Indian astronomical work *Siddhanta*. It contained profound knowledge in philosophy, astronomy, and medicine. Other Indian scientific works were also translated into Arab at that time.

In the early 9th century, Baghdad became the center of an ambitious translation enterprise sponsored by the House of Wisdom (Bayt Al-Hikmah). In 830, a library and a translation institute were established to translate Greek, Persian, Syriac, and Sanskrit works into Arabic. The translated authors included Pythagoras, Hippocrates, Socrates (470—399 B. C.), Plato, Aristotle, Euclid, Archimedes (287—212 B. C.), Plotinus (205—270), Galen, Sushruta (5th century B. C.), Charaka (born in 300 B. C.), Aryabhata (476—550), and Brahmagupta (c. 598—660).

Translation at the House of Wisdom was presided over by Hunayn Ibn Ishaq, who headed a group of more than 90 translators. Besides philosophical works, they also translated astronomical works by Ptolemy, and medical works by Galen. Hunayn's own knowledge of medicine laid a good foundation for the translation of Galen's works. According to Hunayn, he added interpretations to difficult passages in the process of translating Hippocrates' *Optics* for a pedagogical purpose. A medical work of Al-Razi (865—925), a student of Hunayn, was actually an encyclopedic collection of all medical knowledge of ancient Greece, Middle East, and India. This book may have been influenced by Chinese medicine.

The astrologist Abu Mashur at the House of Wisdom wrote the work *Great Introduction to Astrology* that had a great impact on later generations. The masterpiece was a philosophical demonstration of the validity of astrology, which was mainly based on the Aristotelian logic, but it has been lost now. Mashur was one of the most cited authoritative scholars in the Middle Ages. In the 12th century A.D., four of his works were translated into Latin.

It was also during this period that Al-Khwarizmi (780? —850?) introduced Indian numbers and algorithms into Arab countries, which later spread all over the world through Europe so that they are now known as "the Arabic numerals".

The golden era of translation under the Abbasids spurred on original writing in many fields including astronomy, alchemy, and geography, among others. Many of the original writings contained a substantial number of commentaries on Greek sources by writers who had little knowledge of Greek so they had to rely on existing translations to develop their own ideas. Among these scholars was Omar Khayyam (1048—1131), who was an encyclopedic author.

Omar is chiefly known to English-speaking readers through the translation of a collection of his quatrains in *The Rubáiyát of Omar Khayyám* in 1859. The translator was the English writer Edward FitzGerald. Omar was also a mathematician and astronomer. He wrote several pamphlets on arithmetic and music. Around 1070, he wrote an algebraic work and was invited by the Seljuk Sultan to head the Observatory of Isfahan (now part of Iran), where he was responsible for the reform of the calendar.

The House of Wisdom, established in 830, became the pivotal factor for Arabs to absorb the cultural wealth of China, India, Persia, and ancient Greece. A large number of translation activities persisted until the decline of the Arab empire in the 13th century. Translation had a strong impact on the development of science and philosophy throughout the Arab world. Later, the flowering of knowledge taking place in the Arab world provided impetus for the development of natural sciences in the West. Arab translations (often with editing) and commentaries on the scientific works of ancient Greece and Rome preserved a great deal of the ancient civilization that was revived later during the Renaissance period in Europe. As far as the historical significance is concerned, such dynamics signal the first friendly large-scale contact between Islamic and Christian cultures, introducing Eastern culture to the West and promoting the exchanges in science and technology between the two realms.

6.2.2　The School of Translators of Toledo

With the decline of Baghdad as an Arab cultural center, most Arab scholars migrated to Cairo in Egypt, especially during the Fatimid Caliphate. They flocked to the academy of science established by Al-Hakim (reigned 990—1020). Then, in the 12th and 13th centuries, the School of Translators of Toledo, as is popularly known, was established in Spain.

The most important translator in the 12th century was Gerard of Cremona (1114—1187). He went to Toledo from Italy to learn Arabic so he could read Ptolemy's astronomical work *Almagest* and translate it into Latin. Gerard remained in Toledo for the rest of his life and translated as many as 80 books from Arabic into Latin. Among works of other Greek authors, Gerard translated those of Aristotle, Euclid, and Galen from Arabic. He also translated Avicenna's *Canon of Medicine*, the key work of Islamic Golden Age of medicine, and introduced a few anatomical terms in Latin.

With the translation of scientific works from Arabic into Latin and later into vernacular European languages, a lot of scientific terms were borrowed by the European languages. The names of most stars and constellations were derived from Arabic, together with quite a few astronomical terms such as *azimuth*, *nadir*, and *zenith*. These terms are parts of the legacy bestowed to Europe by the Islamic culture.

The translation activity in the Middle Ages and earlier was fraught with creations and often not so restricted by the original texts. The political context and the handwriting are two factors that may have contributed to the creative feature of translation in early times.

Translators in the 12th century served the interests of the Church, who were actively involved in the discovery of the Greek and the Arab heritages. It seemed that the translators were not committed to be so informative and pedagogical in their translation. They were more concerned with creating the image of an erudite scholar through their translation so they were more willing to adopt literal translation by borrowing strange and complex lexicons from Latin, to rely on semantic borrowing to delineate the sense of an existing word in the target language, and to include a large quantity of abbreviations in the translated texts. More often than not, these efforts by the translators then made their translations even more difficult to understand. Original writing may be included in a translated book, such as in the translation by Adelard of Bath (c. 1116—1142).

The Spanish language started to be used in translating the Arabic and the Greek literatures so translation was endowed with the function of popularizing knowledge. Then, translation activity became more secular. The Spanish ruler Alfonso X (1221—1284) was one of the first to support large-scale translation in the West. During his reign, Alfonso exercised controls over translation and designated a series of texts to be translated into the national language. The series was later known as the *Book of Kings*. Alfonso X appreciated the easier translation, which was to be understood by the populace.

The translators in Toledo were patronized by the Church in the 12th century and then by the monarchs in the 13th century. These patrons highlighted the importance of acquiring knowledge through translation so they required the translators to subject foreign knowledge to the Latin framework in the 12th century. But the purpose was raised to establish the Spanish culture on such a basis.

The School of Translators of Toledo played an important role in the importation of science and philosophy into medieval Europe. Undoubtedly, the translators of that time completely changed the structure of knowledge in the West. The rediscovery of Aristotle inspired the academic thinking of emerging universities and the translated academic works broadened the vision of European scholars. The Western world rediscovered the ancient civilization through translation, absorbing the new knowledge of mathematics and astronomy produced by the Arabs. The translation activity of the School of Translators of Toledo promoted the creative activity of the scientists in the West.

6.3 Scientific Translation during the Renaissance and the Age of Reason

Scientific translation in the West entered a new era since the Renaissance. From the 15th century to the 16th century, the humanists did not want to perceive the classics of the antiquity through the "distorted lens" of the Muslims and scholastic philosophers. The humanists just intended to personally discover and read the original text. They started to study the original works of Plato, Aristotle, Euclid, Archimedes, Hippocrates, Galen, and the like.

Science had began to compete with religion since the 16th century. By the 18th century, scientific works had been available to more people due to the invention of printing and the wider use of vernacular languages in scientific exploration. In Renaissance perion in Europe, craftsmen were not as despised as they had been in the ancient and medieval eras. People respected the practical techniques of spinning, weaving, pottery, glass making, and especially the ever more important mining and metallurgy. The improvement of the status of craftsmen during the Renaissance strengthened the connection between them and the scholars. In the fields of pharmacology, chemistry, and physics, scholars began to introduce and translate works for readers who were not well-educated. In instructing non-professionals who did not know Latin, scientists and technicians had to use the national language certainly. Two translators, Jean Marcel de Boulenc and Nicholas Culpepper of the 17th century, were typical examples. Boulenc once translated a chemistry textbook by Oswald Croll into French by simplifying the content and describing the chemical reaction process step by step. Culpepper also simplified his translation of Galen's works so that the non-professionals could better understand the medical knowledge that used to be monopolized by the elite.

Technical translation was prevalent during the Age of Reason (1600—1750). Euclid's *Geometry* was translated several times: in England in 1650 by Isaac Newton and in 1703 by David Gregory. John Wallis translated works of Archimedes in 1676. There were many versions of the work of Hippocrates and most were written anonymously. The best known was that by John Friend in 1717.

Amsterdam and Geneva were translation centers then. The jobbing translators translated the latest works in all disciplines without considering copyright laws. This gave rise to the problem of intellectual piracy. Famous scientists participated in the movement against intellectual piracy. After 1700, scientific translation into Latin became sporadic and almost completely ceased in about 1750.

The rediscovery through translation of the scientific knowledge of the ancient Greek scientists and the updated technology of the craftsmen slowly changed the scientific paradigm of the time shortly after the Renaissance. Despite all setbacks and frustrations, the scientific revolution finally broke out, changing the direction of scientific translation in the West. The introduction of scientific knowledge to China in the 19th century served as an example of such a change.

The translation of scientific works declined in Europe in the 19th century but it does not mean that no scientific translation was done at all. Andrew Motte's English translation of the *Mathematical Principles of Natural Philosophy* by Isaac Newton deserves to be mentioned. It was given to Motte's brother, the publisher, soon after Newton's death. The work was published in 1729. Newton's scientific tome was also translated into French by Emilie du Chatelet (1706—1749), a female scientist of the Enlightenment period, who explained the Newtonian concepts to her French readers.

Another scientific monograph that may be of interest to a historian of scientific translation is Charles Darwin's *Origin of Species*. Heinrich Bronn, adding his own view on Darwin's ideas in an additional 15th chapter, provided a rather liberal interpretation in his first German translation of the book. The translator's interpretation of the original was later widely popularized by Ernst Haeckel. This phenomenon was long seen as the intellectual root of Social Darwinism in Germany.

In recent times, translation works continue to increase in the fields of science and medicine. However, the scientific translation in the West declined due to the hegemony of the English language. Even in the domain of technical terms, the adoption of scientific terms from other languages is rare, especially with the establishment of the Language Industry Certification System.

Questions for discussion:

1. What is the relationship between history of translation and history of science?
2. Why is the Arabic translation of scientific works important to the Renaissance?
3. Why could Toledo become a center of translators in the 12th century?
4. What causes the scientific translation to decline in the West in modern times?

References:

Baker M, 2006. 翻译研究百科全书[M]. 上海:上海外语教育出版社.

Chapter 7

Translation and Circulation of Chinese Classics in the West

Chinese culture is an extensive and profound treasure trove, replete with numerous classical literary masterpieces such as *The Analects of Confucius*(《论语》, *Lunyu*), *Tao Te Ching*(《道德经》, *Daodejing*), *Chuangtse*(《庄子》, *Zhuangzi*), *The Romance of the Three Kingdoms* (《三国演义》, *Sanguo Yanyi*), *The Water Margin* (《水浒传》, *Shuihuzhuan*), *The Journey to the West*(《西游记》, *Xiyouji*), and *The Dream of Red Mansion*(《红楼梦》, *Hongloumeng*). These works, along with Chinese classical poetry, have captivated the Western academic community and readership alike through their various overseas translations.

7.1 Translation and Circulation of *The Analects of Confucius* in the West

The Analects of Confucius, known as *Lunyu*(《论语》) in Chinese and "*A Collection of Dialogues*" in English, is a paragon of classical literature. It is an indispensable component of any introductory course on Chinese philosophy, as its subtle sayings are primarily attributed to the historical figure Confucius(孔子, 551—479 B.C.). *The Analects of Confucius* is believed to have been compiled by his first-generation and second-generation disciples centuries after his death. Confucius' ideology gained authority particularly during feudal eras, and has shaped the cultural, political, and legal norms of China and many other Asian countries. *The Analects of Confucius* continues to enlighten global audiences and communities to this day.

Over the past two thousand years, Chinese young men aspired to secure official employment in the imperial administration and excelled in rigorous imperial examinations, demonstrating their thorough knowledge of *The Analects of Confucius* and a comprehensive understanding of Confucius' teachings. Even today, the prestige traditionally attached to

Chapter 7 Translation and Circulation of Chinese Classics in the West

The Analects of Confucius resonates well with contemporary educated individuals of all ages, genders, and socioeconomic statuses.

Despite often being depicted as a dusty pedant whose meaning is left relatively obscure due to competing interpretations, Confucius is a multi-dimensional figure whose complete richness defies any singular attempt to render it. This has led to an ever-increasing number of new translations of *The Analects of Confucius*, with approximately 30 versions to date.

The translation and introduction of *The Analects of Confucius* to the West began with Westerners entering China. As a representative work of traditional Chinese culture, the spread of *The Analects of Confucius* to the West is closely related to Westerners' interest in China and China's international influence, forming several representative stages.

Matteo Ricci was the first to introduce Chinese Confucian classics to the West. His original intention of studying the classics was to understand the dominant ideas in the spiritual world of the Chinese people, so as to effectively spread the "Gospel" of God. He attempted to translate the Four Books of Confucianism into Latin, including *The Analects of Confucius* which is a collection of ethical maxims, but his efforts were not recognized by his peers. Some people in the Church believed that Confucianism and Christianity were irreconcilable. Moreover, this translation work would lead some Jesuit missionary translators to abandon their basic beliefs and integrate with the traditional Chinese ideology because of the influence of Confucianism. Such worries made Matteo Ricci's pioneering work controversial from the beginning, and this controversy grew day by day. Perhaps because of this argument, the existing Latin versions of *The Analects of Confucius* were not immediately translated into other European languages, affecting its spread.

About a century later, the first English translation came into being, titled *The Morals of Confucius, a Chinese Philosopher who Flourished Above Five Hundred Years before the Coming of Our Lord and Saviour Jesus Christ: Being One of the Most Choicest Pieces of Learning Remaining of that Nation*, 1691. No one seems to have mentioned who the translator was, only that it is not actually a translation of *The Analects of Confucius*, but rather a summary of the Latin version. The book, expressed in 80 short and uninteresting "proverbs", was treated as a series of moral preachings that did not clearly show Confucius' personality, and no one would be intrigued to learn more after reading it.

It was not until 1809, over one hundred years later, that another missionary, Joshua Marshman (1768—1837), translated parts of the works of Confucius, including a fragment of *The Analects of Confucius*. This was a prelude to the continuous translations in the English world that followed. Afterwards, there were many English versions.

The translation and acceptance of *The Analects of Confucius* in the English-speaking world have its special historical and cultural context. The English translations in the 18th and the 19th centuries were mainly for missionary purposes. The dawn and the middle of the 20th century saw a need for *The Analects of Confucius* to relieve the Western cultural crisis. In the late 20th century and the early 21st century, there was a desire for cultural diversity.

The translation and communication of *The Analects of Confucius* can be divided into the following four stages: 1) the stage of missionary translators' theological interpretation of Confucianism, 2) the stage of Western cultural centralism's interpretation of Confucianism, 3) the stage of the original Confucian cultural code interpretation, and 4) the stage of Chinese and Western cultural integral interpretation of Confucianism.

1) The theological interpretation of Confucianism by missionary translators during the period from 1809 to 1898, marked by the completion of English translations of *The Analects of Confucius* by Western missionaries, is a significant chapter in the history of Chinese Christianity. The earliest English translation, authored by Joshua Marshman, was a 742-page doctoral thesis on Chinese language and characters titled *The Works of Confucius*, published by the Mission Press in 1809. Despite never having visited China and spending most of his life as a missionary in India, Marshman played a pivotal role in this period.

James Legge's (理雅各, 1815—1897) translation, on the other hand, is criticized for its rigid wording and academic style, which has somewhat diminished its popularity and accessibility to readers.

Influenced by Christian theology, the missionary translators' interpretation of Confucianism reflects Western theological centralism. To disseminate Chinese Confucian culture among more missionaries and spread the word of God, they made efforts to demonstrate that the Chinese Confucian moral concept was equivalent to Western religious doctrine. Consequently, their main strategy for translating *The Analects of Confucius* was the so-called "Theological Regression."

2) The interpretation of Confucianism based on Western cultural centralism marks the period 1898—1979 when the first Western sinologist translated *The Analects of Confucius* after the era of the missionaries. Thomas Francis Wade (威妥玛, 1818—1895), a British diplomat and sinologist who served as a minister to China, authored the first English translation during this period. His version is concise and easily understandable, without a strong tendency towards Christianization. Arthur Waley (韦利, 1889—1966), an English sinologist, was the most outstanding figure in the field during the first half of the 20th century, despite never having visited China himself. He based his knowledge on older materials.

Ezra Pound (1885—1972), a renowned American poet, used his imagination freely while translating, which led to an unfaithful version of *The Analects of Confucius*.

H. M. Ku (辜鸿铭, 1857—1928) was a well-known Chinese translator who aimed to introduce Chinese culture and Confucianism to a wider audience. He made significant efforts to avoid Western cultural prejudice in his interpretation of *The Analects of Confucius*. However, he also excessively catered to the cultural and intellectual interests of Western readers, which resulted in a translation that deviated from the profound meaning of Confucianism.

Lin Yutang (林语堂, 1895—1976), a Chinese translator, injected vitality into the translation of Chinese classics, breaking the monopoly of Western missionaries and sinologists that had persisted for a long time. To overcome the communication gap between China and the West, he made valuable attempts to exhibit Chinese discourse power in the field of Chinese classics translation. *The Wisdom of Confucius*, compiled by him, was published by Michael Joseph Publishing Company in London in 1958, with a total of 238 pages. Lin's translation is more aligned with the cultural values of the English language by bringing the original work into the target culture. He sometimes filtered the oriental culture through Western cultural standards and wrote beautifully, but his translation was also selective and inappropriate in its recombination of segments at times.

3) The original interpretation stage of the Confucian cultural code (1979—1998) can be regarded as a transitional stage. For instance, D. C. Lau (刘殿爵, 1921—2010), a renowned translator in Hong Kong, employed semantic translation strategies to convey Confucian works and disseminate Confucian culture to English readers. He gave considerable attention to Chinese exegesis and English diction and inherited James Legge's

tradition of prioritizing textual research and interpretation. However, his approach was to integrate notes into the translation as much as possible, resulting in brief notes and sometimes lengthy translations, which affected the readability. Moreover, his writing was more precise but less accessible. For instance, Zeng Zi(曾子, 505—435 B. C.) stated, "慎终追远,民德归厚矣。"(... be careful in the end and pursue the future. The people's morality will be good), but Lau rendered it as," Tseng Tzu said, Conduct the funeral of your parents with meticulous care and let not sacrifices to your remote ancestors be forgotten, and the virtue of the common people will incline towards fullness. " (Lau, 1979) This equivalent seems somewhat cumbersome.

4) The Chinese and Western cultural integral interpretation of Confucianism stage (1998—present) is characterized by translators such as Roger T. Ames, Rosemont, and E. G. Slingerland. They primarily interpretted Confucianism from philosophical, psychological, and sociological perspectives and focused on the differences in cultures and readers between the East and the West. From a comparative philosophy perspective, Ames and Rosemont aimed to challenge the view prevalent in Western academic circles that China had lacked philosophy for a long time. They used the philosophical notion of "people to people" to liberate the misunderstood Chinese traditional philosophical culture from Legge's framework of "God and man" in Western philosophy.

Xu Yuanchong(许渊冲, 1921—2021) was an exemplary Chinese translator. His translation, presented in the form of English-Chinese comparison, highlighted that *The Analects of Confucius* attached great importance to morality and combined politics, ethics, and religion into a unified concept. The idea is that politics is public morality, ethics is private morality, and music or aesthetic feeling is used to replace religion, allowing individuals to experience a moral religious realm in daily life.

In conclusion, the translation and circulation path of *The Analects of Confucius* in the West can be succinctly summarized as the continuous reinterpretation of Confucian philosophical significance. This is primarily reflected in two aspects: 1) the evolution from interpretations of surface meanings to the dissemination of the underlying Confucian philosophy of the original texts, and 2) the shift from Western Confucianism emphasizing Christianization to the philosophical interpretation of Confucianism that highlights the common inheritance of humanity, with scholarly interest expanding in diverse directions.

7.2 Translation and Circulation of *Tao Te Ching* and *Chuangtse* in the West

Tao Te Ching, the philosophical work of Lao Tzu (also known as Li Er in the Spring and Autumn Period), is considered an essential source of Taoist philosophy. Comprised of two sections, Dejing and Daojing, the classic masterpiece contains 81 chapters and covers various aspects of self-cultivation, governance, military tactics, and health. The text mainly discusses the morality in the philosophical sense and emphasizes the "Sages Inside and Kings Outside" theory, which pertains to politics.

Tao Te Ching's broad and profound connotation has earned it the title of the "king of ten thousand Chinese classics." The text has significantly influenced traditional Chinese philosophy, science, politics, and religion. United Nations Educational Scientific and Cultural Organization (UNESCO) recognizes *Tao Te Ching* as one of the most widely translated and published cultural masterpieces, second only to the *Bible*. Up to 2010, there had been approximately 643 Western versions of *Tao Te Ching*, with nearly 200 in English.

English translations of *Tao Te Ching* can be categorized into three stages, each relating to specific historical environments. The first stage, which occurred from the 1870s to the beginning of the 20th century, saw a peak period of Chinese historical classic translations due to increased cultural exchanges between China and the West. Most of the English versions of *Tao Te Ching* from this period were translated from the perspective of Christianity, with James Legge's translation being a typical example.

The second stage began in the 1930s and lasted until the early 1960s, during which the Western world faced a social crisis. Western scholars sought wisdom from the East, and *Tao Te Ching* translations during this period were mainly approached from the standpoint of cultural comparison. In this period, Western scholars criticized Eurocentrism and Western cultural superiority, and *Tao Te Ching*'s philosophy of opposing war and advocating nature and harmony was seen significant in easing human conflicts. Therefore, the Christian elements in English versions were greatly reduced, and many translators adopted an objective cultural attitude to strive for a true understanding, despite inherent values, ways of thinking, and misunderstandings in the translated versions.

The representative work of this period is the translation of the *Tao Te Ching* by Arthur

Waley, who examined the *Tao Te Ching* within the context of the entire Chinese ideological system. He employed explanatory notes to provide a more comprehensive understanding of the text. Notably translators with cross-cultural backgrounds emerged in this period, allowing for more accurate translations of the *Tao Te Ching*.

The third period, which began in the early 1970s and continues to the present day, was marked by the discovery of a silk book of the *Tao Te Ching* in the Han Tomb at Mawangdui(马王堆汉墓) in Changsha. This prompted a "Laozi fever" around the world. Translators in this period avoided using Western terminologies in presenting Chinese philosophy, aiming to reproduce the original Taoist tradition and culture objectively. In terms of diction, more focus was given to literary grace and rhythm. Collaborative translations by scholars from both China and abroad, and from different disciplines, further enhanced the accuracy and diversity of the translations of the *Tao Te Ching*.

Overall, the evolution of English translations of the *Tao Te Ching* can be observed to have progressed from adaptations to Western culture to greater faithfulness to the original.

Thinkers such as Nietzsche and Tolstoy, as well as scientists like Joseph Needham and Einstein, have praised *Tao Te Ching*. It has become popular among common people in the West, as evidenced by the fact that German couples often exchange copies of the *Tao Te Ching* or wear clothing with the word "Tao"(道) on it. These examples demonstrate the widespread popularity of the *Tao Te Ching* in the Western world.

Chuangtse, written by Zhuang Zi(庄子, 369—286 B.C.), who was another sage of Taoism(道家, Daojia), consists of thirty-three chapters and is divided into three parts: "the Inner Chapters"(内篇), which address the fundamental principles of Taoist philosophy; "the Outer Chapters"(外篇), which provide supporting evidences; and "the Miscellaneous Chapters"(杂篇), which contain less than 70,000 words in total. Legend attributes a total of more than 100,000 words to additional chapters.

The seven-chapter Inner Part contains the writings of Zhuang Zi himself and is considered by most scholars to best reflect his thoughts. The 15-chapter Outer Part consists of Zhuang Zi's presumably unfinished works, which were completed later by his disciples. The 11-chapter Miscellaneous Part comprises works by Zhuang Zi's disciples on his ideas. Of the three parts, the Inner Chapters are widely considered the most authentic and therefore the most frequently translated.

Chapter 7 Translation and Circulation of Chinese Classics in the West

According to historical records from Japan, the teachings of *Chuangtse* were spread to Japan as early as the 5th century, and was introduced to Europe later. Since then, numerous versions of *Chuangtse* have emerged and circulated all over the world, including 26 English versions, 12 Japanese versions, 2 French versions, 1 German version, 1 Russian version, and 1 Hungarian version. Of these, the English version emerged at the end of the 19th century, matured in the 20th century, and new versions continue to appear in the 21st century.

Chuangtse has attracted scholarships from China, Britain, and America, resulting in dozens of English translations, complete works, and selective ones included since 1881. For example, from 1996 to 2010, approximately ten translated versions of *Chuangtse* were published, and the translating enterprise continues to this day. Translators come from a variety of professions, from missionaries such as Legge to sinologists like Giles(翟理思), scholars such as Lin Yutang, Palmer, and Watson, poets such as Merton(默顿) and Hinton(希顿), and philosophers such as Hochsmann. They each have their own translating purposes, individual understanding, translation methods, and strategies, resulting in distinctive translations.

Since the first translation by Frederic Henry Balfour (1846—1909), there have been important stages in the complete translation of *Chuangtse*. The first stage started at the end of the 19th century and was accomplished by the British, such as Giles and James Legge. The second stage began in the 1960s and was dominated by American translators like Weier and Watson(沃森). The third stage started in the 1990s and was characterized by a mix of multinational translators such as Palmer and Wang Rongpei(汪榕培). Each previous complete translation of *Chuangtse* provided valuable insights for later translators. Since the 1960s, an increasing number of selected English translations of *Chuangtse* have been printed.

The translators' remarks on *Chuangtse*, as indicated in the prefaces and introductions, vary from the historical backgrounds to the authenticity of *Chuangtse*, from the division of chapters to the themes.

For centuries, numerous English versions of *Tao Te Ching* and *Chuangtse* have appeared and gained popularity among Western readers. With the interactive development of research and translation activities at home and abroad, the interaction between China and foreign countries has promoted the continuous development of English translation and research on *Tao Te Ching* and *Chuangtse*, resulting in continuous improvements in translation quality.

The study of *Tao Te Ching* and *Chuangtse* in the English-speaking world has matured and progressed since the 1980s. Four landmark events can be identified: firstly, translations have continued to be improved, with diversified styles; secondly, scholars' research has evolved towards popularization and deepening; thirdly, numerous research papers have been published, leading to self-conscious and diversified research; and fourthly, an increasing number of Chinese scholars have participated in the introduction and research of these works in the West, with some even teaching the philosophy in American universities. The study of Taoism in China and the West has been characterized by an interactive exchange.

From the perspective of English translation studies and the dissemination of Chinese traditional culture, Chinese translators mainly focus on how *Tao Te Ching* and *Chuangtse* can enlighten people's thoughts, while their foreign counterparts mainly center on the perspectives of philosophy, religion, and literary thought.

As a result of the circulation of English versions, *Tao Te Ching* and *Chuangtse* have had a significant impact in Western countries. On the one hand, these Chinese classics have influenced Western religious philosophy, leading more Westerners to deeply reflect on problems in their lives. On the other hand, these works have also impacted the literary output of some Western writers, such as Wilde and Thoreau.

7.3 Translation and Circulation of "Four Masterpieces" in the West

The Romance of the Three Kingdoms, the first chapter-styled novel in the history of Chinese literature, exudes its ever-brilliant charm among the Four Masterpieces of the Chinese literary canon. During the Ming and Qing Dynasties(1368—1912), it was even known as "the First Talent's Book"(第一才子书).

The Romance of the Three Kingdoms spans nearly a hundred years from the end of Eastern Han Dynasty(东汉, 25—220) to the beginning of Western Jin Dynasty(西晋, 265—316). The novel primarily depicts the wars and narrates the story of the conflicts and alliances among Eastern Han Dynasty and the Three Kingdoms—Wei, Shu, and Wu. Eventually, Sima Yan(司马炎, 236—290) unified the Three Kingdoms and established

Jin Dynasty(265—420). The novel reflects the transformations of various social struggles and contradictions in the Three Kingdoms era, summarizes the significant historical changes in this period, and characterizes a group of powerful heroes of the Three Kingdoms.

The Romance of the Three Kingdoms has a profound influence on all aspects of China, particularly on the spiritual level of generations of Chinese people. It is a popular book among both the aristocratic literati and the common people and has been a bestseller since its publication. As a classic of Chinese literature, its influence not only exists in China but also throughout the world.

The original Chinese version of *The Romance of the Three Kingdoms* arrived in England in the early 17th century. However, in the 17th and 18th centuries, no sinologist in Britain could understand the sentence structure of this book, let alone read it, so *The Romance of the Three Kingdoms* had remained unheard of in the country for centuries.

There are approximately 20 foreign versions of *The Romance of the Three Kingdoms*, including those in Latin, English, Japanese, French, German, Russian, and others.

From *The Death of the Celebrated Minister Tung-cho* (《著名丞相董卓之死》) translated by Peter Perring Thoms (1790—1855) in 1820 to the latest English translation of *Three Kingdoms* translated by Moss Roberts in 1994, the English translation of *The Romance of the Three Kingdoms* had remained uninterrupted for 170 years. Batch after batch of scholars at home and abroad engaged in the translation and research of *The Romance of the Three Kingdoms*, which culminated in a peak in learning Chinese and Sinology research. To date, there have been as many as 20 English translational segments and complete versions.

The Romance of the Three Kingdoms, is the earliest and most comprehensive translation of the work. Translated by C. H. Brewitt Taylor (1857—1938), it was first published by Shanghai Kelly and Walsh Ltd. in December 1925. Taylor aimed to cater to the language preferences of Western readers by using authentic English and employing beautiful, vivid language. His translation did not include any arbitrary comments or summaries, which could potentially interrupt the reading experience. He painstakingly attempted to reproduce the original author's language while retaining the style and charm of the original work. Taylor's focus on presenting captivating plots ensured that Western readers could also enthusiastically appreciate this excellent work. The first printed edition of Taylor's version was more expensive than the typical books in the market, yet it sold out immediately due to the overwhelming demand. The influence of Taylor's translation persists today, as it had a significant impact in both the East and the West.

Moss Roberts' translation of *Three Kingdoms* is the latest and most exceptional version available. It offers a detailed account of the historical situation during the Three Kingdoms' period, and supplements the list of main characters, major events, titles, and duties. The book's illustrations, which include a map of the administrative divisions of that time and the road map of major campaigns, among others, make it easy for Western readers to understand. The academic nature of Roberts' translation has earned praise from sinologists worldwide.

The Water Margin (《水浒传》, *Shuihuzhuan*), another jewel among the Four Masterpieces of Chinese literary works, is distinguished by its unique vernacular style and its tremendous influence on later generations of Chinese literature. It is also one of the Chinese language and literature's epic works, with a far-reaching impact on narrative literature in China and even East Asia.

By portraying the great stories of the Liangshan heroes' struggle against oppression and rebellion on Liangshan Mountain, near a large area of mooring water of Song Dynasty (960—1279), the novel depicts the entire uprising of Song Jiang(宋江), from its inception, development, to its ultimate failure. The book profoundly exposes the social roots of the uprising while passionately extolling the resistance and social ideals of its heroes. The novel also details the internal reasons behind the uprising's failure.

There are many versions of *The Water Margin*, but three are the most popular：

1) The 100-chapter Edition, selected from the Rong Yu Tang version(杭州容与堂版本), is the earliest existing hundred-chapter Chinese version.

2) The 120-chapter Edition, also known as *The Complete Story of Shui Hu*(《水浒全传》), was published by Yuan Wuya(袁无涯) during Ming Dynasty (1368—1644).

3) The 70-chapter Edition, also known as the *Fifth Talent Book of Guanhuatang* (《贯华堂第五才子书水浒传》), is a critical edition by Jin Shengtan(金圣叹, 1608—1661) from late Ming Dynasty.

Shi Nai'an(施耐庵, 1296—1370) is generally considered the author or editor of the literary work. Most surviving copies are signed by either Shi Nai'an, Luo Guanzhong(罗贯

Chapter 7 Translation and Circulation of Chinese Classics in the West

中,1330—1400), or both.

As one of the earliest and most influential classics in China, *The Water Margin* has had a profound impact both domestically and abroad. This work belongs to the literary genre of heroic legend, and its rich language, vivid cultural information, typical characters, and unique narrative structure have all played significant roles in the development of Chinese literature.

In the mid-19th century, *The Water Margin* began to spread in the West. It was first translated into French, despite being only a fragment, which opened the door for people to understand Chinese culture. Since then, English and German versions have appeared and attracted the attention of local literary circles.

It is generally believed that the French version is the earliest in the West. A. P. L. Bazin's(巴赞,1799—1863) *Extraiats du Choui-Hou-Tschouen*(《水浒传摘译》) was published in the 57th and 58th issues of the *Journal of Asia*(《亚洲杂志》) in 1850 and 1851, respectively. The content of the translation includes the story of Lu Zhishen(鲁智深) in the first six chapters of the novel and the story of Wu Song(武松) from the 23rd to 31st chapters. This is the earliest translation of *The Water Margin* published in Western academic journals. In the second edition of *Chine Moderne*(《现代中国》) published in Paris in 1853 by Bazin, there are three excerpts of Bazin's translation, one of which is Jin Shengtan's preface in the name of Shi Nai'an and the other two are Jin's commentaries on the first chapter, "The Story of Wang Jin and Shi Jin"(王进和史进的故事) and the third chapter, "The Story of Lu Zhishen's Havoc in Wutai Mountain"(鲁智深大闹五台山的故事). *Les Chevaliers Chinois, Romans de Moeurs et d'Aventures*(《中国的勇士们》), published by Politique de Pekin(北京政闻报社) in 1922, is the first 12 chapters of *The Water Margin*. The 120-chapter *Au Bord de L'eau*(《水浒传》) was translated by Jacques Dars(谭霞客), a young sinologist trained after the establishment of diplomatic relations between China and France, and published in 1978. This caused a sensation in the literary world and was regarded as the most important literary.

H. Rudelsberger(鲁德斯贝格), a German sinologist, is credited with being the first to translate *The Water Margin* into German. In 1924, he compiled two Chinese novels: *The Story of Yang Xiong and Pan Qiaoyun*(《杨雄和潘巧云的故事》) and *The Story of the Unfaithful Wife of the Cookcake-seller Wuda*(《卖炊饼武大的不忠妇人的故事》). In 1927, Rudelsberger completed his translation of *The Water Margin* into seventy chapters, titled *Rauber und Solate*(《强盗与兵：中国小说》), which was a significant achievement. The protagonist of this book is Wu Song. As Rudelsberger did not know Chinese, he relied on a Chinese student to "interpret" more than 100 stories for him. While he found no unified structure in the original book, he used Wu Song as a unifying character. Rudelsberger thus created a structure that appeared to be unified, but he described Wu Song as a person with a contradictory character. Nevertheless, Rudelsberger made an immense contribution to the introduction of *The Water Margin* into German literature, and before his translation, no complete version was available in Western languages.

Franz Kuhn's (弗兰茨·库恩) translation of 120 chapters of *The Water Margin*, titled *Die Rauber vom Liang Shan Moor*(《梁山泊的强盗》), was published in 1934. Its popular paper book was found suitable for young people in 1955. In 1964, Maxi Mlian Kern published *Wie Lu Da unter die Rebellen kam*, and in 1968, Johanna Herzfeldt published *Die Rauber vom Liangshan*. These translations further contributed to the dissemination of *Shui Hu* in German literature.

The first English version of *The Water Margin* was published in the first volume of *China Review* (1872—1873) in Hong Kong. This contained excerpts from Lin Chong's story. In 1923, H. A. Giles published *The History of Chinese Literature*(《中国文学史》), which included another translation of Lu Zhishen's story. In 1929, Geoffrey Dunlop's translation, which he based on a German translation, was circulated in the United States.

Pearl S. Buck (赛珍珠) was the first person to translate *The Water Margin* into English. Using Jin Shengtan's 70 chapters as a basis, she completed the translation in four years and published it in two volumes in 1933, entitled *All Men Are Brothers*(《水浒传》, *Shuihuzhuan*), a title borrowed from a famous saying in *The Analects of Confucius*. In her opinion, this title fully and profoundly expressed the spirit of the chivalrous people portrayed in the novel.

Buck's work was very popular in the United States and quickly climbed the list of the monthly authoritative book club in the United States. She chose to translate this book in the hope of showcasing Chinese thought and the narrative mode of Chinese novels, with the goal of dispelling prejudices and negative impressions of Chinese novels in Western literary circles that had persisted for ages. She praised the superb technique of the original work, which vividly portrayed the 108 heroes and heroines. Buck believed that *The Water Margin* was incomparable to Western novels and enlightening to Western literature. She aimed to make the translation as similar to the original as possible, so that readers who cannot understand Chinese can experience the feeling of reading the original.

However, Buck exhibited a strong subjectivity in material selection. For example, she deleted the content of "*Liangshanpo Heroes' Nightmare*" which indicated the evil omen of the volunteers. Instead, she depicted a successful ending in which all 108 Liangshanpo (梁山泊) heroes gathered together, presenting it to Western readers.

In 1937, a 70-chapter abridged translation of *Shuihuzhuan*, known as *Water Margin* (《水浒传》, *Shuihuzhuan*), was published by J. H. Jacksonin and released by the Shanghai Commercial Press.

The only complete translation of the 100-chapter edition was published in 1980 by Foreign Language Publishing House in Beijing under the title *Outlaws of the Marsh*(《水浒传》), translated by Sidney Shapiro. It is considered by many to be the most authoritative translation.

From 1994 to 2002, the Chinese University of Hong Kong Press published a five-volume English translation of *The Water Margin*, entitled *The Marshes of Mount Liang* (《水浒传》, *Shuihuzhuan*), translated by John Dent Young. Young was a distinguished English translator who graduated from Cambridge University and taught in Myanmar, Spain, and Thailand before dedicating his life to translation in London. His son, Alex Dent-Young, who graduated from the University of London and the University of Chicago, studied Chinese in Taiwan and currently resides in London.

The *The Water Margin* novel is comprised of 120 chapters, with the following titles: "The Broken Seals" (揭封走魔), "The Tiger Killers" (打虎英雄), "The Gathering Company" (梁山聚义), "Iron Ox" (铁牛), and "The Scattered Flock" (鸟兽散). The first volume covers chapters 1—22, the second volume covers chapters 23—43, the third volume covers chapters 44—62, the fourth volume covers chapters 63—90, and the fifth volume covers chapters 91—120. In 2011, the Chinese-English aligned version was jointly published by the Shanghai Foreign Language Education Press and the Chinese University of Hong Kong Press.

In the foreword, the translators state that their aim is to make the English version readable for ordinary readers who do not know Chinese. They assure readers that they have not deleted or altered any content, preserved the taste of ancient China, reduced notes to a minimum, and expressed Chinese dialects and idioms in fluent English. The translators have largely achieved their goal, and it is worth noting that they translated 75% of the poems in the original novel.

This English version builds on the strengths of previous translations, including French versions, and surpasses them in many aspects. It not only spreads Chinese culture abroad but also provides excellent materials for Chinese readers to learn English.

Journey to the West(《西游记》, *Xiyouji*), one of the Four Masterpieces of Chinese literary works, is a pinnacle of Chinese magic and romantic novels. The book follows the pilgrimage of the Monkey King(孙悟空), Tang Seng(唐僧), Zhu Bajie(猪八戒), Sha Seng(沙僧), and Bai Longma(白龙马) as they journey to retrieve Buddhist scriptures. Along the way, they experience hardships and dangers, subdue demons, and eventually arrive to see the Buddha(如来佛祖). They become the Five Buddhist Saints(五圣成真).

The English translations of *Journey to the West* can be classified into two categories: segment translation and whole translation. Samuel I. Woodbridge(伍德布里奇) was the first to translate fragments of *Xiyouji* into English. His translation, called *Golden-Horned Dragon King or The Emperor's Visit to the Spirit World*(《金角龙王,皇帝游地府》), was based on a pamphlet compiled by Williams, a famous American sinologist. The contents of the pamphlet were selected from the 10th and 11th chapters of the popular version.

In 1900, Herbert A. Giles, a famous British sinologist, translated a passage from Chapter 98 of *The Journey to the West* which he included in Chinese Literature, a compilation he put together.

In 1905, James Ware(詹姆斯·韦尔) translated two sections of *Xiyouji* in the fourth volume of *East of Asia Magazine*, published by the Shanghai North-China Herald Agency(上海华北捷报社). The first section was derived from the first seven chapters of *Xiyouji*(《西游记》, pp. 80 – 83), and the second section covered the ninth through fourteenth chapters. The title of the two translations is *the Fairyland of China*(《中国的仙境》).

In 1921, Richard Wilhelm(卫礼贤), a German sinologist and translator of Chinese classical literature, compiled a collection of Chinese myths and stories titled *The Chinese Fairy Book*(《中国神话故事集》), which included the 17th chapter entitled *Yang Oerlang*(《杨二郎》, pp. 42 – 44), the 18th chapter *Notscha*(《哪吒》, pp. 45 – 53), the 69th chapter *The Monk of the Yangtze-Kiang* (pp. 243 – 251), and the 74th chapter *The Ape Sun Wu Kung* (pp. 292 – 329). Each chapter provided a comprehensive translation of a plot, with the original translations being in German and later translated into English by Wilhelm himself.

In 1922, E. T. C. Werner, a British scholar and researcher of Chinese history, authored Chapter 16 of the book *Myths and Legends of China*(《中国神话传说》), which included a special chapter entitled "How the Monkey Became a God" (pp. 325 – 369). The chapter excerpted fragments of the main plots of *Xiyouji*. The book was illustrated with two images of the Black River Demon (p. 352) and the Five Saints (p. 368).

In 1946, George Kao(高克毅, 1912—2008) compiled *Chinese Wit and Humor*, which included the English translations of the first seven chapters of *Xiyouji* as translated by Chi-Chen Wang(王际真).

The January 1961 issue of *Chinese Literature*, published by Foreign Languages Publishing House in Beijing, contained chapters 59, 60, and 61 of *The Journey to the West* as translated by Yang Hsien-yi(杨宪益, 1915—2009) and his wife Gladys Yang(戴乃迭, 1919—1999).

The May 1966 issue of *Chinese Literature*(《中国文学》) also included their translation of chapter 27 of *The Journey to the West* and an illustration of Monkey King.

The earliest complete English translation of *The Journey to the West* was done by Timothy Richard, titled *A Mission to Heaven*, which included full translations of the first seven chapters and selected translations of the succeeding chapters. The book was published by Shanghai Christian Literature Association(上海基督教文学会) in 1913 and republished in 1940. Timothy Richard also translated *Romance of the Three Kingdoms and A Mission to Heaven*, which was published by Shanghai Beixin Book Company(上海北新书局) in 1931. *A Mission to Heaven* comprised the second half of the book (pp. 115 – 265).

In 1930, *The Buddhist Pilgrim's Progress: The Record of the Journey to the Western Paradise*(《西游记》), translated by Helen M. Hayes, and a collection of selected translations of 100 chapters were published by John J. Murray Press in London and New York E. P. Darden Press (105 pages).

In 1942, Arthur Waley (1889—1966), a renowned British sinologist, translated approximately 30 out of 100 chapters of *Xiyouji*. He adapted the book and titled it *Monkey*, which featured smooth and vivid writing and quickly gained popularity in the

West. Waley also created an English version for children called *The Adventures of Monkey*, which was published in 1944 (143 pages) and illustrated by Kurt Wiese.

In 1944, Plato and Christina Chan(陈智诚与陈智龙) translated a selection of *Xiyouji* entitled *The Magic Monkey*, which included illustrations.

In 1958, Foreign Language Publishing House in Beijing translated and published an English version of *Xiyouji* titled *Flaming Mountain*(《火焰山》).

In 1964, George Theiner's English translation of *The Journey to the West*, based on a Czech selected translation and titled *Monkey King*(《猴王》, Houwang), was published in London.

From 1977 to 1983, Anthony C. Yu, a Chinese-American scholar and professor at the University of Chicago, accomplished the first complete English translation of *Xiyouji*. This work, *The Journey to the West* in four volumes, allows English readers worldwide to appreciate the entire picture of the novel.

The Journey to the West(《西游记》, *Xiyouji*) follows the quest of Tang Monk(唐僧) and his disciples for *The True Sutra*(真经) amidst numerous challenges, and it explores the evolution and character of Monkey King(孙悟空) in particular. As a stubborn stone monkey, his tenacious and persistent spirit of personal struggle led him to become a successful Buddha saint. This narrative aligns well with the common theme of "adventure and growth" in world literature and the value orientation of Western readers. Additionally, the strong depiction of oriental gods and demons can evoke a powerful aesthetic resonance in the West. The novel also reveals the unique survival experience and cultural ecology of the Chinese nation, including the integration of Confucianism(儒教), Taoism(道教), and Buddhism(释教), rich and colorful oriental folk customs, complex human emotions and worldly wisdom in Chinese life, and even ancient poems that create an atmospheric setting for the plot, all of which provide insights into ancient Chinese civilization.

The Dream of Red Mansion(《红楼梦》, *Hongloumeng*), the foremost pearl among the Four Masterpieces of Chinese literary reservoir, is a love novel with global influence. It is recognized as the pinnacle of Chinese classical novels, an encyclopedia of Chinese feudal society, and the grand integrator of Chinese traditional cultures.

The novel portrays the rise and fall of the Jia(贾), Shi(史), Wang(王), and Xue(薛) families as the backdrop, with Jia Baoyu's(贾宝玉) perspective as the primary

Chapter 7 Translation and Circulation of Chinese Classics in the West

focus. The central storyline revolves around the love and marriage tragedies of Jia Baoyu, Lin Daiyu(林黛玉), and Xue Baochai(薛宝钗). The novel depicts the lives of a group of boudoir beauties whose knowledge surpasses that of men, revealing the true beauty and tragedy of human nature. It can be hailed, without exaggeration, as an epic work that showcases the beauty of women and the state of ancient Chinese society from various perspectives.

The Dream of Red Mansion has been circulated in Europe and America for over 300 years, which can be divided into three stages: from 1830 to the end of the 19th century, from the beginning of the 20th century to the end of the 1950s, and from the 1960s to the present day.

In the first stage (1830—1900), four English versions of *The Dream of Red Mansion* emerged. John Francis Davis(戴维斯), a member of the Royal Society of England and later the British minister to China and the second governor of Hong Kong, translated two poems from the third chapter of *The Dream of Red Mansion* into English in 1830. These poems subtly and ironically described Baoyu's personality and occupied a significant portion of *The Dream of Red Mansion*. The translations of the poems were included in *On Chinese Poetry*(《中国诗歌》), a lengthy article written by Davis that was published in the Royal Asiatic Transactions and in a single edition by the East India Company in 1834. Although there is only a one-sentence introduction and two-poem translation in the full text of *Hongloumeng*, this marked the beginning of its English translation.

In 1846, Robert Thom, the British Consul in Ningbo, translated selected fragments of the sixth chapter of *Hongloumeng* into English. The translation was published in *The Chinese Speaker*(《正音撮要》or《官话汇编》), a textbook for foreigners learning Chinese in China. It was published by the Presbyterian Mission Press(基督教长老会出版社) in Ningbo(宁波). The translation contained 27 pages and was entitled *Extracts from the Hung-Low-Mung*.

In 1868, Edward Charles Bowra, an Englishman who served in the Customs and Revenue Department of Qing Dynasty(1616—1912) imperial government, translated the first eight chapters of *Hongloumeng* into English. The translation was serialized in *China Magazine*(《中国杂志》) from 1868 to 1869 and was much longer than the previous two translations, but it was not published as a single book.

From 1892 to 1893, Kelly and Walsh Ltd. in Hong Kong(香港别发洋行) and Typographia Commercial in Macao(澳门商务排印局) published the first systematic English translation of *Hongloumeng*. The translation was split into two volumes, titled *Hongloumeng* or *The Dream of The Red Chamber*(《红楼梦》, *Hongloumeng*), and was carried out by H. Bencraft Joly, the British Vice Consul in Macao. The first volume comprised 378 pages, while the second volume spanned 583 pages, covering the first 56 chapters of the original text. Despite his intention to complete the translation, Joly passed away before he could do so.

Several noteworthy features characterised the English translation of *The Dream of Red Mansion* during this phase. Firstly, all four translators were British diplomats in China. The first translator, who translated two poems, had an academic background in the Royal Society. The other three were regular diplomatic officials. Secondly, the translation aimed to provide language learning or pleasure reading materials for foreigners in China. Thirdly, distribution and publication of translations were inconsistent, with a limited circulation scope that primarily catered to foreigners in China.

In the second phase (1901—1960), four additional English versions of *The Dream of Red Mansion* were published. These were Wang Liang-chih's(王良志) work in 1927, Chi-chen Wang's(王际真) versions in 1929 and 1958, and Florence and Isabel McHugh's in 1958.

Wang Liang-chih's English translation, titled *The Dream of the Red Chamber*, was published in New York in 1927. Dr. Arthur Smith wrote the preface for this version. Wang was a graduate of Peking University, studied in the United States, and taught Chinese classical literature at New York University. His translation comprised 95 chapters with approximately 600,000 words, and primarily focused on Jia Baoyu(贾宝玉) and Lin Daiyu(林黛玉)'s love story.

Wang Chi-chen's English version was published by Doubleday Doran Co., Ltd. in New York and Routledge Co., Ltd. in London in 1929, titled *The Dream of the Red Chamber*. Wang worked at the Metropolitan Museum of New York and later became a professor of Chinese at Columbia University. His version spans 39 chapters, 371 pages, and is divided into three volumes. The first two volumes cover the first 57 chapters of the original book, while the third volume contains excerpts and translations of chapters 58 to 120. Arthur Waley, a renowned sinologist, wrote the preface followed by Wang's

Chapter 7 Translation and Circulation of Chinese Classics in the West

introduction to the novel. This translation had been the most widely read version of *Hongloumeng* in the English-speaking world until the 1960s, with numerous copies still present in British and American libraries.

In 1958, Wang expanded the content of the novel in his 1929 translation and published his second translation, titled *Dream of the Red Chamber*, through Twayne Publishers in New York. After nearly 30 years of supplementation and revision, numerous essential details were added to the translation, resulting in a work comprising 60 chapters and 574 pages. In the same year, an abridged version of the translation, spanning 329 pages, was published by Anchor Books in New York. This version was later reprinted by Anchor Books in 1989 and continued to be widely popular.

In 1957, Florence and Isabel McHugh's translation, *The Dream of the Red Chamber*, was published by Pantheon Books Inc. in New York, followed by Routledge & Kegan Paul in London in 1958, and reprinted by Greenwood Co., Ltd. in 1975. The work inspired by a German version by Kuhn, a renowned German sinologist, comprised a total of 582 pages. McHugh's translation was as well-known as Chi-chen Wang's second translation in the English-speaking world.

During this period, all four versions aimed to cater to common readers in the West, with the original text being significantly compressed and adapted. The translators focused on the "exotic flavor" of the original text, employed a specific method to render the names of the characters, and emphasized the Chinese customs and context. These approaches were intended to appeal to Western readers' tastes at that time and capture their imagination of China, thus achieving long-term market effects.

In the third stage (1961 to the present), three more English versions of *Hongloumeng* were published. From 1973 to 1980, Penguin Group published the first 80 chapters of the work in three volumes, translated by David Hawkes (1923—2009), a British sinologist and professor of Chinese at Oxford University. The three volumes have a general title of *The Story of the Stone*(《红楼梦》, *Hongloumeng*), with subtitles for each volume: "The Golden Days" (1973), "The Crab-Flower Club" (1977), and "The Warning Voice" (1980). From 1982 to 1986, John Minford(闵福德) translated the last 40 chapters and published them in two volumes under the same general title, with subtitles "The Debt of Tears" (1982) and "The Dreamer Wakes" (1986).

This translation embodies high academic contents, which are first reflected in the prefaces. The informative introduction in the first volume is an outstanding research paper on *The Story of the Stone*, demonstrating high academic standards. The preface of each volume also discusses relevant academic issues. The translators of the above 5-volume version did not provide footnotes but explained the cultural phenomena that may cause difficulties for readers in the form of appendices. Preceding the main text of each volume are spelling instructions using the International Phonetic Alphabet to explain the phonetic notation of the Chinese Pinyin system, aiding readers in understanding the pronunciation of the characters' names in the book. Additionally, after the main text of the five volumes, there are genealogical charts of the Jia and Wang families, including character names and descriptions.

The first volume's appendix contains a detailed description of the "Twelve Beauties of Jinling" (金陵十二钗). The second volume's appendix includes descriptions of the rhythm of Chinese metrical poetry, knowledge about Chinese Dominoes (骨牌), mechanics of Jia Mu's (贾母) card game, and answers and explanations for unsolved mysteries in the volume. The third volume's appendix provides information about the servant system, textual research on the whereabouts of You Laoniang (尤老娘) and other important figures and explanations of certain details. The fourth volume's appendix features the preface written by Chinese writer Gao E (高鹗), an introduction to Chinese eight-part essays and musical instrument Qin (琴), or Chinese Lute, and the legendary story of "Knowing the Sound", and an explanation of specific translation methods. These appendices and contents demonstrate the translators' serious attitude towards the details of the original work and related cultural phenomena.

Translator David Hawkes paid great attention to the artistic value of the translation.

Firstly, he made significant efforts to select the appropriate version of the original text. In the first preface, he states:

"In translating this novel, I have felt unable to faithfully stick to any single text. I have mainly followed Gao E's version of the first chapter as it is more consistent, albeit less interesting than the others. However, I have frequently followed a manuscript reading in subsequent chapters, and in a few rare instances, I have made minor emendations of my own." (Hawkes, 1973)

Secondly, he aimed to achieve a full translation. In the same preface, he continues:

"One of my abiding principle has been to translate everything, even the puns.

Although this is an 'unfinished' novel in the sense I have already indicated, it was written by a great artist with his very lifeblood. Therefore, I have assumed that whatever I found in there is for a purpose and must be dealt with somehow or other. I cannot always pretend to have done so successfully, but if I can convey even a fraction of the pleasure this Chinese novel has given me to the reader, I shall not have lived in vain." (Hawkes, 1973)

Based on these principles, Hawkes has truly achieved his goal of "translating everything". He has reproduced all kinds of rhetorical devices, proverbs, and poems from the original text in different ways in the translation. Some details of the original text may have presented difficulties and obstacles to understanding, but Hawkes' approach can convey the author's meaning more perfectly without affecting the aesthetic taste and readability of the translation. However, when dealing with certain cultural images such as "red" which symbolizes "youth" "spring" or "prosperity", Hawkes distorted their meanings. In the first preface, he explains:

"One bit of imagery which Stone-enthusiasts will miss in my translation is the pervading redness of the Chinese novel. One of its Chinese titles is red, to begin with, and red as a symbol, sometimes of spring, sometimes of youth, and sometimes of good fortune of prosperity, recurs again and again throughout it. Unfortunately, apart from the rosy cheeks and vermeil lip of youth, redness has no such connotations in English and I have found that the Chinese reds have tended to turn into English golden or green ('the green spring' and 'golden girls and boys' and so forth). I am aware that there is some sort of loss there, but have lacked the ingenuity to avert it." (Hawkes, 1973)

Thirdly, Hawkes resigned as a professor of Chinese at Oxford University to devote himself to the publishing contract signed with Penguin Publishing House to translate *The Story of the Stone* wholeheartedly. The form, appearance, and binding of the published work reflect the publisher's position that *The Story of the Stone* is a classic literary work for readers of different levels, reflecting their pursuit and attempt to canonization.

Upon its completion in 1986, *The Story of the Stone* gained an authoritative position in the relevant academic circles in the English-speaking world. Almost all academic interpretations of *Hongloumeng* in the English world used this translation as the source of citation, and all monographs and relevant contents on *Hongloumeng* include it in their bibliographies.

Another complete English translation of *Hongloumeng*, entitled *A Dream of Red*

Chamber, was completed by Yang Hsien-Yi and his wife Gladys Yang and published by Foreign Language Publishing House in Beijing. The first and second volumes were published in 1978, and the third volume was published in 1980. The translators also carefully selected the appropriate version of the original text. Yang's publication notes indicate that:

Our first eighty chapters have been translated from the Photostat edition published by People's Literature Publishing House in 1959 from movable type edition of 1792. The *Chi Liao-sheng*(《戚寥生序本》) manuscript of the first eighty chapters is one of the earliest copies extant. In our translation, certain minor errors and omissions made by the man who copied the original manuscript have been corrected according to other versions. (Yang Hsien-Yi et al., 1978)

In 1991, Foreign Language Publishing House published a shorter English version of *Hongloumeng*, entitled *A Dream in Red Mansions: Saga of a Noble Chinese Family*(《红楼梦:一个中国贵族家庭的传奇》) and translated by Huang Xinqu(黄新渠), to make it easier for Western readers to understand this masterpiece's content.

Certain interesting facts are worth mentioning. The first complete English translation of *Hongloumeng* was done by Reverend Bramwell Seaton Bonsall(布拉姆韦尔·西顿·邦斯尔, 1886—1968), an English missionary. Although he finished the translation, entitled *The Red Chamber Dream* around 1966, it had never been published and all that remained was a complete typewritten copy. Bonsall's family tried to negotiate with two publishing companies, but their efforts were unsuccessful. At the same time when Bonsall finished his translation, David Hawkes signed a contract with Penguin Publishing House to translate *The Dream of Red Mansion*.

Bonsall's translation closely follows the original text and includes appropriate notes. He translated for three hours a day with the Chinese Cheng Jiaben version(程甲本) starting at the age of 70. It took him 10 years to complete translating 120 chapters and he added 69 pages of "publication notes", "translator's preface", "catalogue", "translation notes", "terminology notes", "genealogy", and "list of names". Statistically, Bonsall's version is the longest English translation of *The Dream of Red Mansion*, with a length of 840,000 words, which is longer than Hawkes' version by 10,000 words and Yang's version by 210,000 words.

In summary, over the past few centuries, Western readers have gradually come to appreciate, though not fully, the lifelike characterization, subtle narrative techniques, superb descriptive powers, intricate structural plots, smartly-knit symbols, and unparalleled psychological penetration of the Four Masterpieces through various translations.

7.4 Translation and Circulation of Classical Poems in the West

Chinese poetry boasts a history of at least 3,000 years and has gone through many stages in its long development. Each stage has its own characteristics in terms of subject matter, zeitgeist, and poetic form, giving rise to a variety of poetic genres. Due to space limitations, this discussion will focus on certain classical poems that have been translated and circulated in the West.

Classical poetry is a profound aspect of Chinese culture and plays a crucial role in cultural exchanges between China and foreign countries. *The Book of Songs*(《诗经》, *Shi Jing*) is a collection of daily ballads, festival songs, and temple songs that had been completed before 8 B.C.. It is recognized as the oldest collection of classical Chinese poems, written in four-character forms with rigorous rhythms and rhymes. The book is a treasure of Chinese culture, representing the ancient Chinese civilization and an important cultural heritage of humanity. As many Western sinologists have noted, *The Book of Songs* stands in opposition to Homer's epics and Shakespeare's plays and holds immeasurable value in the treasure of world culture.

Since the 16th century, *The Book of Songs* has spread to the West and caught the attention of researchers overseas. The work was translated for European readerships by missionaries, whose translations from the 17th century to the 18th century were often influenced by strong allusions to church teachings. In this regard, it is somewhat similar to the traditional Chinese interpretation of its purpose, which is to promote the "King of the Holy way"(圣道王化).

During the 17th century, Western missionaries studied *The Book of Songs* to advance the Christian doctrine, utilizing the five Confucian classics, which often had touches of church teachings. For instance, Matteo Ricci's exposition of God quoted the terms "heaven" and "emperor" from "*Ode to the Zhou*"(《周颂》), "*Ode to the Shang*"(《商颂》), "King Wen"(《文王》), and "Daming"(《大明》) and compared these terms with the Christian concept of "God". The missionaries attempted to find the "evidence" of the Gospels in *The Book of Songs* to support the Christian doctrine and even to explain the signs of Jesus' coming to China.

In the 17th century, translations and introductions of *The Book of Songs* to the West were scattered and simplified, presenting a rudimentary form.

In the 18th century, the attention of capitalist Europe shifted to the East, resulting in an increased demand for understanding ancient Chinese civilization. This led to an intensified focus on learning about China and promoted the transition from religious to secular learning. L. P. Duhade(杜哈德), a prominent sinologist, classified the literary works in *The Book of Songs* into five categories: Praise of Human, Poetry of Dynasty Customs, Poems of Comparison, Odes of Noble Things, and poems that do not conform to Confucius' doctrine.

The French sinologist Pierre Martial Cibot(韩国英, 1727—1780) expounded the cultural and historical values of *The Book of Songs*. He believed that the collection of poems was intended for the king to understand the people, much like the princes, marquises, counts, and viscounts of the French provinces dedicated folk songs to the emperor. The style and melody of the poems were different, just as the songs of Lyons in France were different from those of Provence. Fibot described the contents of *The Book of Songs* as beautiful and harmonious, with customs and depictions that were simple and unique. He believed that they were sufficient to rival the authenticity of the information provided by historians.

The 19th century witnessed the rise of "Sinology Fever", which saw the translation and introduction of *The Book of Songs* flourish. Translation and research complemented each other. For example, regarding rhyme translation and free translation, the rhyme school focuses on the literary quality of *The Book of Songs* and translates it into a poem with appreciation value. However, the free translation school believes that it is necessary to stay close to the original sentence meaning, without additional or free translation. Both approaches have their pros and cons, but what they have in common is that they both require a thorough understanding of the content, language, and artistic style of the original text, as well as extensive knowledge. Only through the study of these aspects can high-quality translated versions appear one after another.

The French version by Seraphin Cogverur(顾赛芬, 1835—1919) presented a trilingual text in Chinese, French, and Latin. In his lengthy introduction, he not only introduced *The Book of Songs* in general but also regarded it as an encyclopedia to

Chapter 7　Translation and Circulation of Chinese Classics in the West

understand the ancient China and absorb the ancient Oriental knowledge. Moreover, he analyzed and summarized 20 items out of 300 articles, such as physique, clothing, architecture, and so on.

In conclusion, translators of the 19th century of *The Book of Songs* abandoned the influence of theology in favor of realism, seeking to unveil the original features of this ancient poetry collection. Sinologists reached a consensus on its literary and cultural values, and began to explore its ontology, literature and art, language and culture, and social folklore. Such endeavors marked the maturity of Western studies on *The Book of Songs*.

The 20th century witnessed a deepening of the study of *The Book of Songs* in the West, characterized by a profound artistic analysis, ideological and cultural connotations, and the application of new methodologies. Numerous monographs were written on the styles, rhythms, metaphors, and images of *The Book of Songs*. Almost all Western translations during this period were accompanied by comprehensive and theoretical reviews, some of which were about research studies. For example, James Legge's (1815—1897) translation of *The Book of Songs*, which includes a 200-page preface, is divided into five chapters that introduce relevant information on collections, compilations, circulation versions, basic contents, rhymes, and more. The annotations elaborate on myths and legends, historical geography, name and object systems, customs and habits, and other related topics.

In conclusion, *The Book of Songs* has been translated and circulated in the West for hundreds of years, going through three stages of development: initiation, maturity, and deepening.

Classical Chinese poetry saw its "golden age" during Tang Dynasty (唐朝, 618—907), in which many poets excelled and their works were considered to be the finest examples of Chinese poetry.

The spread of Tang poetry to the English-speaking world is a remarkable instance in the history of cultural exchanges between China and the West. In the 19th century and the early 20th century, a group of British missionaries and diplomats came to China, among them, Sir John Francis Davis, Edward Harper Parke, Herbert Allen Giles, and William John Bain Brigge Fletcher who were the forerunners of Tang poetry translation. Although their English translations may not have reached the highest level of quality, they all showed their love for the tradition of Chinese classical poetry, which laid the foundation for the entrance of classical poetry into the vision of Western culture.

By the 1920s, Western intellectual interests in China had grown, and a number of poetry collections translated from Chinese to English had emerged during this period, which had a wide impact on Europe and the United States. For example, Arthur Waley (1889—1966), a famous British sinologist, translated and introduced many oriental classical literary works in his lifetime. His poetry translations were very popular and produced countless prints, which had a great influence on the West. He creatively used the form of "jumping rhythm" to flexibly grasp the rhythm of the original poem without forcing rhyme. His translations revealed the beauty and profundity of Chinese classical poetry, which fascinated Western readership.

American sinologist Stephen Owen(宇文所安, 1946—present) is proficient in conveying the subtle beauty of classical poetry with poetic sensitivity, injecting new vitality into this ancient literary tradition. Other scholars, such as American sinologist Ronald Egan(艾朗诺), French sinologist Yves Hervouet(吴德明), and Chinese scholar Cheng Baoyi(程抱一), are not only interested in the aesthetic beauty of Chinese poetry but also adept at Western interpretation, playing a positive role in the dissemination of Chinese classical poetry overseas.

When literary historians discuss the influence of Chinese classical poetry on foreign literature, they often mention British and American Imagist poetry. In fact, Ezra Pound (1885—1972), the leader of the Imagist movement, and other Imagist poets were fond of Chinese classical poetry and were deeply influenced by it. Pound's translation of *Cathay* (《华夏集》, *Huaxaiji*) in 1915 caused a sensation upon its publication. This pamphlet, which only contains 19 classical poems, is regarded as Pound's "most enduring contribution" to English poetry. Thomas Stearns Eliot(1888—1965) even considered Pound the man who introduced Chinese poetry to the modern age.

Pound's contribution lies in bringing the tradition of Chinese poetry into Western modernist culture and promoting the development of a new American poetry movement. The Imagist Movement also set a precedent for modern British and American poetry, whose aesthetic core is based on imagery. The followers of this movement recognized that the implicit and concise treatment of imagery in Chinese classical poetry was consistent with the idea of Imagism, so they sought to learn from it eagerly.

Pound's "In a Station of the Metro", considered a representative work of

Imagism, reads: "The apparition of these faces in the crowd; Petals on a wet, black bough." (Pound, 1913) This poem clearly employs the technique of image juxtaposition, as the poet steps out of the subway station and suddenly sees many faces in the crowd, implying the fleeting feeling of the urban life and expressing the rationality and sensibility of the moment. The inner connection between the subway station and the wet black petal is difficult to imagine unless the poet possesses profound knowledge of Oriental literature.

"In addition, the 'Cold Mountain Fever' that swept Europe and America in the 1960s and 1970s could also have been influenced by Chinese classical poetry. Cold Mountain(寒山) was originally the name of a poet of unknown origin in the middle of Tang Dynasty (618—907). His poems were replete with reclusive and worldly thoughts, written in a simple style infused with philosophy. His collection of songs, translated by Gary Snyder and others, has received high praise. Some readers even perceive religious sentiment and advanced environmental awareness in his works. As a result, Cold Mountain was regarded as an idol by the "Beat Generation", which coincided with the "hippie" cultural trend of that time, and thus gave rise to a "Cold Mountain Fever" that had lasted for nearly 20 years, impacting many readers and writers.

However, in the process of translating Chinese classical poetry, foreign sinologists not only face the challenge of understanding the complex and profound linguistic and cultural barriers of ancient Chinese, but also the constraints of cultural differences. Therefore, misreading is inevitable in poetry translation.

Apart from misreading due to language and culture, there is also a form of intentional and creative misreading. For example, when Gary Snyder translated Cold Mountain's poems, he incorporated his own experiences and imagination of the mountains of California. This misreading was the result of the dual influence of American and Chinese cultures. In Snyder's translation, Cold Mountain's strange and erratic actions were preserved, creating a state of confrontation between the individual and the external world. Thus, Cold Mountain is not a paragon of virtue, but a "mass hero" of the "Beat Generation" in the context of American expectations.

From the early 20th century to the present, the translation of classical Chinese poetry into English has been in full swing in the West, especially in the United States, where reformers have been shaking off anti-European traditional poetic shackles and establishing new artistic and ideological appeals.

In summary, classical Chinese poetry has not only gained the popularity among English-speaking readers, but also challenged the conventional wisdom of English-speaking poetry and stimulated new literary formulations.

Questions for discussion:

1. Could you give a brief account of the four stages of translation of *The Analects of Confucius* in the West?

2. What do you think of the influence of *Tao Te Ching* and *Chuangtse* on the Western countries? Why?

3. Which of the translations of various versions of the Four Masterpieces impress you most? Why?

4. What do you think of the influence of Chinese classical poems on American Imagist poetry?

References:

Cao Xueqin, 1973. The story of the stone: Volume 1 (The golden days) [M]. Translated by Hawkes D. London: Penguin Books Ltd.

Confucius, 1979. Confucius: The Analects. Translated by Lau D C. New York: Penguin Group.

Cao Xueqin, Gao E, 1978. A dream of red mansions [M]. Translated by Yang Hsien-Yi and Gladys Yang. Beijing: Foreign Language Press.

Chapter 8

Translation of Western Literary Classics in China

The translation of Western literary classics began in the late Qing Dynasty and continued till now. At the initial stage, the classics were mingled with those with little or even no literary values as the early translators did not have the needed understanding of literature in the modern sense and were rarely able to distinguish the truly good works from the bad ones. As Chinese writers and translators became more acquainted with the notion of literature, the concept of classics and works with lasting literary values was understood, and increasing attention was then called to literary classics. At the same time, vernacular Chinese replaced traditional Chinese as the literary language, and the number of people who could speak foreign languages were on the rise and some chose translation as a career. With the advent of vernacular Chinese, the focus of translators changed. If they had cast their eyes on the writers from the more advanced nations in the past, they would have began to be drawn to the writers from the minor or oppressed nations, especially Russia and Eastern European countries. After the foundation of the People's Republic of China, literary translation was not just a personal choice; instead, it was more often than not the embodiment of mainstream ideology. So some classical works were purposefully selected for translation. Only after China adopted the Open Door policy did more inclusive translation of foreign literary works become possible. Many writers and works were translated into Chinese for the first time in this period.

8.1 English and American Literary Classics

Literary works written in English had always been the focus in the modern history of literary translation until they were replaced by Russian works after 1949. From the start, classics were accompanied by popular ones on their way to China. Since the 1920s, ideological consideration sometimes outweighed literary value in choosing the source texts.

During the Cultural Revolution (1966—1976), the translation of English and American literature was almost brought to a stop. After China was re-opened, the translation of literature in English experienced a retaliatory resurgence.

8.1.1　Translation of Poetry

The earliest translation of literary works from English was that of Henry Wadsworth Longfellow's "A Psalm of Life". This was perhaps done in 1864 by Thomas Francis Wade, a British diplomat and later the Ambassador to China, who turned to Dong Xun to polish his Chinese version.

Other poems had to wait for about 30 years to be translated into Chinese. Poetic translation could be found in Yan Fu's *Tian Yan Lun*(《天演论》) in 1897, the translation of Thomas Henry Huxley's *Evolution and Ethics*, in which the author quoted from Alexander Pope's "Essay on Man" and Alfred, Lord Tennyson's "Ulysses". The whole poem of Pope's "Essay on Man" was translated by Timothy Richard and Ren Yanxu in 1898, strange enough that this version was the only Chinese rendition of this poem.

In 1902, Liang Qichao translated parts of "The Giaour" by George Gordon, Lord Byron (1788—1824), a favorite to the late Qing readers. In 1908, Su Manshu published *Selected Poems of Byron*, perhaps the earliest collection of translated poetry, in Tokyo. This anthology contained five of Byron's poems, of which Huang Kan said two were his translations. Byron remained the favorite poet in the New Cultural Movement. Some of his poems, together with other English poetry, were translated and published in the 6th Volume of the 2nd Issue of the *New Youth* by Liu Bannong in 1917. On April 10, 1924, the 100th anniversary of Byron's death, *Fictional Monthly* even brought out a special commemorative issue, publishing eight translations: seven poems, one poetic drama and three papers on Byron. But large-scale and more comprehensive translation of Byron did not start until 1950s when "Corsair", "The Siege of Corinth", "Cain", "Manfred", *Selected Lyrics of Byron*, *Childe Harold* and *Don Juan* were published.

Besides Byron, Thomas Hood (1799—1845), a minor English poet, enjoyed great popularity as well in the late Qing Dynasty with his "Song of the Shirt". In 1907, Ma Junwu translated it into the traditional poetic form and published in a journal run by Chinese students in France. When the translation spread back to China, it was reprinted time and again in newspapers and magazines. When young Hu Shi read the translation and traced back to its origin, he was dissatisfied with Ma's translation. So he churned out his own rendition and published in a newspaper in 1908.

Whether Guo Moruo had read "Song of the Shirt" or not was unknown, but it was known that he admired Byron for his fighting spirit. But as a poet, he seemed to have a more affinity with Shelley. In the early 1920s, Guo came to know Percy Bysshe Shelley (1792—1822) when he was studying in Japan. He was fascinated by Shelley and translated and published his translation of Shelley's poems in magazines. In 1926, he published eight poems including "Ode to the West Wind" in *Selected Poems of Percy Bysshe Shelley*. In 1928, Guo Moruo published his *Translated Poems*, containing Thomas Gray's (1716—1771) and Percy Bysshe Shelley's works.

At about the same time, William Shakespeare's (1564—1616) poems began to be translated into Chinese. In 1936, Shakespeare's poems that had been translated and published by Qiu Tang, Liang Yuchun, Qiu Ruiqu, Zhang Jinchen, Zhu Xiang etc. in magazines were collected into *Fan Shi Liu Ji*(《番石榴集》) by The Commercial Press. But Shakespeare's long poems had to wait till Fang Ping's translation of *Venus and Adonis* in 1957.

The earliest translation of John Milton (1608—1674) was done by Zhu Weizhi, who published the Chinese version of *Paradise Lost* in 1934. In the mid-1930s, Fu Donghua also produced a version of *Paradise Lost*. But Milton's other works were not translated until the 1950s.

As for American poets, Walt Whitman (1819—1892) was one of the earliest poets that were introduced to Chinese readers. On July 5, 1919, the 100th anniversary of Whitman's birth, Tian Han wrote an article to commemorate the poet. In the article, Tian translated some poems from *Leaves of Grass*. In December of the same year, Guo Moruo, whose compositions were greatly affected by the American poet, translated "Out of the Rolling Ocean the Crowd". In 1944, Chu Tunan produced the translation of *Leaves of Grass* with 15 poems. In the following 40 years, he kept revising and adding more poems to his translation. After this version, there were at least six more versions with different number of poems. Among these versions, Zhao Luorui's translation in 1987 was the most noteworthy one by a Whitman specialist.

8.1.2 Translation of Fiction

Around 1870, a missionary translated the first part of Jonathan Swift's (1667—1745) *Gulliver's Travel* into Chinese as *Tan Yin Xiao Lu*(《谈瀛小录》), but this first translation of novel drew little attention from readers. A fuller translation of any English or American classic had to wait till Timothy Richard translated Edward Bellamy's (1850—1898) *Looking Back 2000—1887*, though a minor. Richard translated parts of the novel in 1891, and the stand-alone Chinese version was published in 1894. But at that time, the Chinese had no proper notion of the literary genre, fiction, and could not tell fiction from drama due to the traditional concept of "Xiao Shuo (fiction)" handed down from Han Dynasty. In fact, even in the 1920s, fictions were still mixed with dramas by some scholars.

In 1899, Lin Shu and Wang Shouchang rendered *La Dame aux Camélias* by Alexandre Dumas fils (1824—1895) into Chinese, marking the real beginning of literary translation. The huge success of the translation prompted Lin to embarked on a road he had never dreamed of in the past. Just a few years back, popular fictions were still something Confucian scholars despised and avoided. So when his first translation of the novel was published, Lin chose to disguise his true name with a pseudonym. In 1902, when Shen Zhufen published Daniel Defoe's (1660—1731) *Robinson Crusoe*, she did under the pen name of "a lame boy from Hangzhou".

The success of the translation of *La Dame aux Camélias* was a great encouragement to many as well as to Lin himself. Also in 1902, Liang Qichao blew the bugle of Chinese fictional revolution, reassessing the value of popular fictions. In such a background, Lin started his most productive journey of translation, creating a miracle of translating 181 (163 published and 18 unpublished) works as he knew no foreign languages. He had to rely on his partners in translation, from choosing the source texts to rendering into the target Chinese. As a result, his translated works mixed classics with the second-rate or even the third-rate writings, even though he was the greatest and most read translator in the late Qing period. Among the classics he brought to Chinese readers were Harriet Beecher Stowe's *Uncle Tom's Cabin* (1901), Charles and Mary Lamb's *Tales from Shakespeare* (1903), Daniel Defoe's *Robinson Crusoe* (1904), Walter Scott's *Ivanhoe* (1905), *Talisman* (1907) and *Betrothed* (1907), Daniel Defoe's *Robinson Crusoe* (1906), Jonathan Swift's *Gulliver's Travel* (the first half) (1906), Washington Irving's *Sketch Book* (1907), Henry Fielding's *A Journey from This World to the Next*, and Charles Dickens' *Nicholas Nickleby* (1907), *The Old Curiosity Shop* (1908), *Oliver Twist* (1908), *David Copperfield* (1908), and *Dombey and Son* (1909).

Lin Shu's success attracted many to the translation of foreign literature, though most were to that of popular works. Among them were Lin's partners, like Zeng Zonggong, Wei Yi, and Chen Jialin, who had some classical works translated into Chinese occasionally. Of the classical writers, like H. G. Wells (1866—1946) and Robert Louis Stevenson (1850—1894), they were often chosen for their strange and adventurous stories, such as *The Time Machine* and *Treasure Island*.

In 1909, Lu Xun and Zhou Zuoren, both enthusiastic readers of Lin's translations, published *A Collection of Overseas Short Stories*, aiming to bring something new to the Chinese literary circle. Contrary to their contemporaries, the two brothers were quite faithful to the original texts, leaving a milestone on the way of Chinese literary history, even though its meagre sale discouraged the brothers. In the same year, one more of Scott's novels were translated into traditional Chinese. Another was not published until 1917. After that Scott almost declined into oblivion till the 1950s when the interest in him was once again aroused and *Woodstock*, *The Surgeon's Daughter* and *Rob Roy* were published. But only in the 1980s and after did Scott enjoy a full comeback with almost all his works being translated and published.

As for Dickens, Chen Jialin with Xue Yi'e translated his *Little Dorrit*, and Wei Yi did *A Tale of Two Cities* between 1913 and 1914. *The Pickwick Papers* was translated in 1918. *The Christmas Carols* even had four different versions, published in 1910, 1912, 1913 and 1914 respectively.

In March, 1917, Zhou Shoujuan translated and published *A Collection of Famous European and American Short Stories*, containing 50 pieces, and many of which were translated for the first time in China. The quality of the translations of the book varies, but some are really good, even judging from today's criteria. In a sense, the publication of these short stories can be seen as the maturity of Chinese fictional translation (Zhang Lin, 2013).

The May 4th Movement brought the use of traditional Chinese to a halt. As a result, many novels that had been rendered in traditional Chinese were re-done in vernacular Chinese. For example, there were more than ten different versions of *Robinson Crusoe* between 1920 and 1940, even though most of them were partial translations. *Robinson Crusoe* remained the favorite among Chinese readers, so new translations kept coming. It is said that there were more than 30 new versions published after 1990. *Moll Flanders* by

Liang Yuchun in 1931 was turned into *Dang Fu Zi Zhuan*(《荡妇自传》, *An Autobiography of a Dissolute Woman*), and in 1958, with Wang Zhongying's proofreading, the title was transliterated.

But the New Cultural Movement ushered in more than retranslations. What is more important was that it helped the translators shift their focus from classical English writers to those of the oppressed nations. Of British and American novelists, especially contemporary writers, they were more drawn to realistic ones.

In such an environment, Guo Moruo translated Upton Sinclair's (1878—1968) *King Coal* under the pseudonym of Kan Ren in 1928 because he was moved by this muckraking work during his exile in Japan when he was wanted by the Kuomingtang Government and forced to leave his homeland. In the following year, he continued to work on Sinclair and published his translation of *The Slaughterhouse*. In 1930, he published another work by Sinclair, *Oil*. Guo was interested in the exposure of social evils in these works, so it was no wonder that he preferred Sinclair to other higher-achievers in literature.

Other realists or naturalists, like Jack London (1876—1916), were favored by Chinese translators as well. The translation of Jack London was concentrated between 1929 and 1936. The year 1929 saw the publication of two books of his: *The Iron Heel* translated by Wang Kangda, and an anthology of short stories *The Apostate* by Peng Ruisheng. In 1931, a bi-lingual version of *To Build a Fire* annotated by Fu Donghua was published. Next year, Qiu Yunduo published *The People of the Abyss*. In 1935, two versions of *The Call of the Wild* were brought out: one by Gu Feng and Ouyang Shan, and the other (in an anthology) by Liu Dajie and Zhang Menglin. In 1936, Zhang translated and published an anthology *A Piece of Steak*. The autobiographical *Martin Eden* was first translated by Zhou Hang in 1943. In 1947, *White Fang* was first translated by Su Qiao. In the following year, Jiang Tianzuo reworked it and *The Call of the Wild*. In the 1950s, London remained the favorite American writer. New translations of his works arrived: Qiu Zhuchang's *The Sea Wolf*, and his *Burning Daylight*, three versions of *Love of Life*: Li Liangmin's, Yin Fu's, and Wanzi and Yuning's; re-translations were published: Qi Ming's *The People of the Abyss*, Wu Su's *Martin Eden*, and Wu Lao and Lu Jin's *The Iron Heel*. A few anthologies of short stories were also made: Xu Tian's *The Strength of the Strong*, *Short Stories of Jack London* and *Selected Short Stories of Jack London*, and Chen Fu'an's *An Odyssey of the North*. Four anthologies of children stories were also published. What was interesting was that some of the stories were translated from Russian. But in the 1960s, enthusiasm for London began to decline, forever.

The father of English novels, Henry Fielding, was not translated until 1921 when his novella *A Journey from This World to the Next* was done by Lin Shu and Chen Jialin in traditional Chinese. Five years later, one of his truly great works *The Life and Death of Jonathan Wild, the Great* was translated by Wu Guangjian into vernacular Chinese. Another work *The History of the Adventures of Joseph Andrews and His Friend, Mr. Abraham Abrams* was published by the same translator in 1928. In 1937, *A Journey from This World to the Next* was retranslated by Ying Xiong. These novels were retranslated in the 1950s. In the 1980s and after, his masterpiece *The History of Tom Jones, A Foundling* were finally rendered into Chinese besides the reprinting of old versions of other works.

In 1936, two Chinese versions of Jane Austen's (1775—1817) *Pride and Prejudice*, by Dong Zhongchi and Yang Bing, were published respectively. But it took 13 years for her 2nd novel *Emma* to be translated and published by Liu Chongde in China in 1949. The 1950s saw the publication of Wang Keyi's *Pride and Prejudice* and Ma Qiaozhi's *Northanger Abbey*.

Dickens' rival William Makepeace Thackeray (1811—1863) did not have such a good fortune. When Dickens was enjoying great popularity in China, Thackeray had to wait patiently for Chinese translators to pick him up. And finally in 1931, Wu Guangjian started to translate his masterpiece *Vanity Fair*, but reduced the 67 chapters into 33. Fortunately, Yang Bi took the task to retranslate the work and published her Chinese version in 1957. The fluent language and faithful rendition of Yang's work had been appreciated ever since, making it a rare gem in the history of literary translation. Some other works by Thackeray were also translated in the 1950s, making him live up to his name of realist. In the 1980s and after, a dozen new versions of *Vanity Fair* were produced, and more of his works were translated for the first time.

The Brontë sisters were introduced to China earlier than their predecessor, Jane Austen. In 1924, Zhou Heizhang devoted a chapter to Charlotte Brontë (1816—1855) in *A History of English Fiction*. In 1927, Wu Guangjian had already finished the translation, though partially, of *Jane Eyre*, but was unable to publish it until 1935, making *Villette* the first work of Charlotte to be published in 1932. Li Jiye's version of *Jane Eyre* was also published in 1935, just a little bit earlier than Wu's, although he translated it two years ago. His *Jane Eyre* was the most read one till the advent of Zhu Qingying's in 1980. In the following years, many new versions were produced, but Li's and Zhu's versions had never lost their popularity. Emily's (1818—1848) *Wuthering Heights* were published by Wu Guangjian two years before *Jane Eyre* in 1933. In 1942 and 1945, Liang Shiqiu and Luo Sai produced their re-translations of the novel. In 1955, Li Jiye's and Yang Yi's translations were published at the same time. Of the two, Yang's version was reprinted by many Chinese presses. In the 1980s, more versions were produced and even Anne's works were finally translated.

Another realist Mrs. Gaskell (Elizabeth Gaskell, 1810—1865) fared better than Thackeray in entering China. As early as in 1921, Lin Jiashu translated her *Cranford* into traditional Chinese. The novel was retranslated by Wu Guangjian in 1927 and by Zhu Manhua in 1937. Another work of hers *Cousin Phillis* was translated by Xu Zhuoli in 1929. However, her great work *Mary Barton* was not translated until 1955 when Xun Mei and Yu Guitang finally rendered it into Chinese. After China was re-opened to the outside, new versions of Mrs. Gaskell's works were produced and some works were translated for the first time. However, her popularity could not be compared to Tkackeray's, let alone that of the Brontë sisters.

George Eliot (1819—1880) was first translated by an American missionary, Laura M. White, who published the Chinese version of *Romola* in 1932. *Silas Marner* was first translated by Liang Shiqiu in 1932 and retranslated by Shi Yingze in 1939. *The Mill on the Floss* was done by Zhu Jijun in 1939 and redone by Zhu Rong and Zheng Le in 1949. *Mr. Gilfil's Love Story* was translated by Liang Shiqiu in 1945, but her first novel *Adam Bede* was not translated until 1950 when Zhang Bilai finally turned it into Chinese. However, after 1980, *Adam Bede* was retranslated more than her other works, although all of them had new versions.

The earliest translation of Thomas Hardy (1840—1928) was done by Zhou Shoujuan in 1917 in *A Collection of Famous European and American Short Stories*. New translation of Hardy had to wait till 1921 when Li Bai published "To Please His Wife" in *Fictional Monthly*. In the following years, Hardy was translated by various translators and published in various journals. In 1928, his *Life's Little Ironies* was published by Zeng Xubai and Gu Zhongyi. This collection contained 8 stories, including "The Son's Veto", "For Conscience's Sake" and "The Tragedy of Two Ambitions". In 1930, Gu Zhongyi published a new anthology of four stories, including "The Three Strangers" and "Fellow Townsmen". In 1934, Luo Niansheng and Lu Muye brought out another anthology of four stories, including "A Tradition of Eighteen Hundred and Four" and "The Melancholy Hussar of the German Legion" as well as retranslated "The Son's Veto" and "For Conscience's Sake". The first translation of Hardy's novels was done in 1929. It was a partial translation of *Jude the Obscure*. Two years later, Gu Zhongyi published his translation of *Tess of the d'Urbervilles* in *Artistic Monthly*. In 1934, Lu Tianshi published *Tess of the d'Urbervilles* in a book form. In 1936, two new versions of the book were produced by Zhang Guruo and Yan Enchun respectively. This year also saw Zhang's translation of another novel, *The Return of the Native*. This book was also retranslated by Wang Shiwei in 1937 and Hai Guan in 1948. *Jude the Obscure* was first translated by Lu Tianshi in 1945. In the 1950s, *The Mayor of the Casterbridge* was translated for the first time besides the reprinting and retranslation of *Tess* and *Jude*. No new translations of Hardy could be found before he was reprinted and retranslated in the 1980s.

1928 was also the year when D. H. Lawrence's (1885—1930) *Lady Chatterley's Lover* was published, and it witnessed many advertisements of the novel in China. Two years later (1930), a magazine published a partial translation. In March of the same year, Wang Kongjia began to translate and publish the book, but only finished nine chapters due to the failure of the magazine that published it. In August, Rao Shuyi produced a full version of the book in Shanghai, but with little circulation. However, the real beginning of Lawrence's translation was in 1929 when Du Heng turned his "The Ladybird" into Chinese. In 1954, *The White Peacock* was translated by Xu Chongliang, signaling the last translation of Lawrence before his comeback 30 years later. In the 1980s, Lawrence regained his popularity among Chinese readers. His works, including *Lady Chatterley's Lover*, were translated and retranslated, and some of his works had more than 10 different Chinese versions.

Virginia Woolf (1882—1941) was translated as early as in 1935 when Shi Pu rendered her *Flush* into Chinese, only two years after its publication. *To the Lighthouse* was done by Xie Qingyao in 1945 and "A Room of One's Own" was done by Wang Huan in 1947. Then she elapsed into 40 years' oblivion till 1980s when her value was rerecognized and her works were translated and retranslated.

James Joyce (1882—1941) was mentioned by Mao Dun in *Fictional Monthly* in the

1920s, but as an American! The translation of Joyce was not started until 1942, in which year Fu Donghua's translation of "Counterparts" was included in a collection of foreign short stories. Then similar to the fate of Virginia Woolf, he was ignored till the early 1980s. In 1983, his *A Portrait of an Artist as a Young Man* was translated by Huang Yushi. In the 1990s, Jin Ti and the Xiaos produced their versions of *Ulysses*, and the Chinese rendition of *Finnegan's Wake* was finally produced by Dai Congrong in 1996!

Somerset Maugham (1874—1965) was first translated in 1938. In this year, Fang An published a collection of Maugham's short stories under the title *The Man with Red Hair*, containing five stories including "The Man with Red Hair" and "Rain". In 1944, *Up at the Villa* was translated by Lin Tongrui and in 1946, *The Moon and Sixpence* was translated by Wang Heyi. In the next 30 years, the writer had been almost forgotten. In the 1980s, he recaptured Chinese readers' attention, and translations of his works flooded. But in the 1990s, enthusiasm for Maugham abated.

As a novelist, John Galsworthy (1867—1933) was translated much later than he was as a playwright. Only after he received the Nobel Prize in literature in 1932, was *The Man of Property*, one of the Forsyte Saga, his prize-winning series, translated by Wang Shiwei in 1936 and re-translated by Luo Jinan in 1948. His novella *The Apple Tree* was translated by Lin Qi in 1941 and Duanmu Hongliang in 1945 respectively. In 1951, Luo Jinan's version of *The Man of Property* was published, but the series were finally translated by Zhou Xuliang: *The Man of Property* in 1958, *In Chancery* in 1961 and *To Let* in 1963. Yet only two of *A Modern Comedy* were translated into Chinese: *The White Monkey* (1958) and *The Silver Spoon* (1961), and one of *End of the Chapter*: *Flowering Wilderness*. In the late 1970s, Galsworthy was reprinted, ushering a new stage of translation. So far, almost all his fictions have been translated into Chinese.

The father of American literature, Mark Twain (1835—1910), was introduced to Chinese readers in the 1930s. In 1932, *The Adventure of Tom Sawyer* was first translated by Yueqi. Then, it was retranslated in 1933, 1939 and 1949. But his greatest work *The Adventure of Huckleberry Finn* was not translated until Zhang Zhensheng churned out his rendition in 1947. *The Prince and the Pauper* was translated by Li Baozhen in 1937.

In the 1950s, Mark Twain's popularity among publishers even surpassed that of Jack London. Besides republications and retranslations, many of his works were translated for the first time in this period. In 1950 and 1955, Bi Shutang translated *Life on Mississippi*.

In 1953, Liu Yizhu published *The Man Who Corrupted Hadleyburg*. In 1955, Hou Junji translated *Pudd'nhead Wilson*. Next year, Jiang Yiping rendered the novella *The Mysterious Stranger* into Chinese. Zhu Weizhi brought out *A Connecticut Yankee in King Arthur's Court*, and Zhu Fu brought out *Joan of Arc* in 1958. Some of these works were retranslated after their first translation. Chang Jian retranslated and published *Life on Mississippi*, *The Man Who Corrupted Hadleyburg*, and *Pudd'nhead Wilson* alone. Anthologies of short stories were also published, like *A Mysterious Visit* (1955), *Short Stories of Mark Twain* (1954), and *Selected Short Stories of Mark Twain* (1960).

After the Cultural Revolution, Mark Twain did not lose his favor with the publishers. Republication began with Zhang Yousong's translation of *The Adventure of Tom Sawyer* in April, 1978. In a few months, Zhang's *The Adventure of Huckleberry Finn* was republished. The translator compiled a new anthology of short stories, *Running for Governor*, as well in the following year. Afterwards, retranslations of Mark Twain sprang up like mushrooms!

As a realist, John Steinbeck (1902—1968) fared better than his contemporaries, whose value was only appreciated in the 1980s and after. He was introduced to China in the 1940s. In June, 1941, Qiu Chan translated one chapter of *The Grapes of Wrath* and published in *Literary Monthly*. A few months later, a complete version of the book was published by Hu Zhongchi. In the following years, Lou Feng translated *Of Mice and Man*. Steinbeck's other works, like *The Moon is Down* and "The Chrysanthemums", were translated and even retranslated within a few years, which was a rare treatment few writers received. After 1949, Steinbeck was reprinted with few works added, especially in and after the 1980s.

Finally, Ethel Lilian Voynich's (1864—1960) *The Gadfly* must be mentioned. The original work was not in the English literary canon, but its Chinese version was a classic of the Chinese translated literature. Its translator Li Liangmin was said to have the impulse of translating it in the 1930s, but the actual translation was not done until the early 1950s. In 1953, its Chinese version was brought to readers and became a hit. It was reprinted many times, with millions of copies being sold. Together with *How the Steel Was Tempered*, it affected several generations of Chinese readers. This single work firmly established the writer's position in the history of Chinese translated literature!

8.1.3　Translation of Drama

William Shakespeare's plays were staged in English long before they were in Chinese in China. As early as November, 1864, the LEWIS Company from Australia put *King John* on a Shanghai stage. In 1913, a girls' school in Shanghai staged a play *Nu Lu Shi* (《女律师》, *A Woman Lawyer*), a Chinese work Bao Tianxiao adapted from *The Merchant of Venice*. And this version of Bao's may be the first translation of Shakespeare.

In 1916, Lin Shu and Chen Jialin translated *Richard* Ⅱ, *Henry* Ⅳ, *Julius Caesar* and *Henry* Ⅵ and published on *Fiction Monthly* as novels.

A vernacular introduction of Shakespeare came after the May 4th Movement. In 1921, Tian Han translated and published *Hamlet* in *The Journal of Young China Association* (among the members were Mao Zedong, Li Dazhao, Deng Zhongxia, Yun Daiying and Zhang Wentian). In 1922, he had it republished as the 1st volume of *Masterpieces of William Shakespeare*. In 1924, he published *Romeo and Juliet*, as the 6th volume of *Masterpieces of William Shakespeare*. Unfortunately, the other 8 intended translations did not come out.

More of Shakespearean plays were translated after Tian Han, some of them were translated into traditional Chinese, like Shao Ting's *Hamlet*, but most of them were translated in vernacular Chinese, like Zeng Guangyun's *The Merchant of Venice*. In 1929, Zhu Weiji even translated *Othello* in the poetic form.

In the 1930s, new translations of Shakespeare kept arriving. In 1930 alone, four of Shakespeare's works were translated: Dai Wangshu's *Macbeth*, Zhang Wenliang's *Macbeth*, Gu Zhongyi's *The Merchant of Venice*, and Peng Zhaoliang's *The Twelfth Night*. In 1932, the poet Xu Zhimo also tried to render *Romeo and Juliet* in the poetic style. And it was in this period that the three most accomplished translators of Shakespeare embarked on their journey of translation: Zhu Shenghao, Liang Shiqiu and Cao Weifeng. Even the outbreak of the Anti-Japanese War was unable to halt their translation! Of the three, Zhu died young at 32 in 1942 but finished the translation of thirty and a half of Shakespeare's plays! But ever since their publication in 1947, Zhu's Shakespeare was the most read Shakespeare.

In the 1950s, the poetic translations of Shakespeare were published, like Cao Yu's *Romeo and Juliet*, Fang Ping's *Much Ado about Nothing*, *The Merchant of Venice*, and *Henry* Ⅴ, Lu Ying's *A Midsummer Night's Dream*, Bian Zhilin's *Hamlet*, Zhang Caizhen's

As You Like It, Wu Xinghua's *Henry* Ⅳ and Fang Chong's *Richard* Ⅲ. Of these, Bian's and Fang Ping's translations were worth special attention for their poetic test.

In 1957, *The Complete Works of William Shakespeare* (《莎士比亚全集》) were published by Taiwan World Bookstore, containing 27 of Zhu Shenghao's translations and Yu Erchang's translations of 10 Shakespearean historical plays. In 1967, the Bookstore published Liang Shiqiu's translations of Shakespeare's works, containing all the 37 plays.

After the New Cultural Movement, John Galsworthy's realistic theme made him a favorite in the Chinese translation circle. So even before he received the Nobel Prize in literature, he had been introduced to Chinese readers. In 1922, Deng Yancun initiated the translation of Galsworthy by rendering *The Eldest Son* into Chinese. In 1925 and 1926, Gu Delong (aka Gu Zhongyi) and Guo Moruo translated *The Skin Game* and *Strife* respectively. In 1927, Guo translated his *Justice: A Tragedy in Four Acts* and *The Silver Box*, and Xi Dichen and Zhao Song did *The Little Dream*. In 1930, Zhu Fu turned *The Mob* into Chinese and in 1937, Xiang Peiliang translated *The Fugitive*.

In 1923, Jin Benji and Yuan Bi published George Bernard Shaw's (1856—1950) *Plays Unpleasant* (*Widower's Houses*, *The Philanderer*, and *Mrs. Warren's Profession*). At about the same time, Pan Jiaxun published his translation of *Mrs. Warren's Profession* with two prefaces by the translator and Shen Yanbing (Mao Dun) respectively. In 1930 and 1935, two new versions of the play were brought out. Soon after, 3 versions of *Man and Superman* were produced. Besides, *Saint Joan*, *Village Wooing*, *The Devil's Disciple*, *Back to Methuselah*, *Geneva* and *Candida* had been translated by 1949. The 1950s and the early 1960s saw more of Shaw's works produced—in fact, 22 of Shaw's 55 dramas had been translated into Chinese so far, showing his popularity among the Chinese. After 1978, Shaw was reprinted and retranslated.

Eugene O'Neill (1888—1953) was introduced to Chinese readers when he was still at the peak of his creations. In 1928, *The Moon of the Caribbees and Six Other Plays of the Sea* was translated by Gu Youcheng. In 1932, Gu turned another play *Beyond the Horizon* into Chinese. In the next year, another Gu, Gu Zhongyi, finished his translation of this play. In 1939, it was republished with the translation of a new play *Emperor Jones*. Between Gu's two translations, Wang Shiwei translated *Strange Interlude* and Fan Fang *Before Breakfast*. In the 1940s, more of O'Neill's plays were rendered into Chinese: *Anna Christie* by Nie Miao and *Mourning Becoming Electra* by Zhu Meijun in 1948 and

Huangwu's retranslation of *Mourning Becoming Electra* in 1949. The other works that had been put into Chinese included *Bound East for Cardif*. Then the playwright disappeared from the public sight till the early 1980s. In 1980, Long Wenpei retranslated *Bound East for Cardif*, Bai Ye retranslated *Beyond the Horizon*, and Liu Xianzhi retranslated *Emperor Jones*. The next year witnessed the publication of *Desire Under the Elms* by Li Changwei and by Wang Yiqun separately. In 1982, an anthology of three plays was made: *Beyond the Horizon*, *Mourning Becoming Electra* and *The Hairy Ape*, all translated by Huangwu. Afterwards, more of O'Neill's plays were translated or retranslated, like *Long Day's Journey into Midnight* in 1985 and *The Iceman Cometh* in 1988. And it should be pointed out that O'Neill was one who had direct influence on modern Chinese playwrights like Hong Shen and Cao Yu, who modeled on his plays.

8.2 Russian Literary Classics

The translation of Russian literature reflects the ideological changes in China. At the beginning, there was little interest in Russian literature among Chinese translators. According to Xu Nianci who conducted a survey of the fictions had been published up to 1907, there were only two Russian works, compared to 32 English works, 22 American works, 9 French works and 8 Japanese works. The 1917 Russian Revolutionary not only worked as a beacon for those who wanted to strengthen the poor backward homeland, but also aroused the Chinese readers' interest in Russian literature. As a result, more Russian and Soviet works were introduced and translated. After the Communist Party of China established the People's Republic of China in 1949, the translation of Russian and Soviet literary works overwhelmed that of other foreign literature. Statistics show that from 1949 to 1958, 3,526 Soviet and Russian works were translated, accounting for 65.8% of all the translated literary works.

8.2.1 Translation of Poetry

The poet Alexander Pushkin (1799—1837) was recognized much later than the novelist whose work was introduced to Chinese readers as early as in 1903. The translation of his poetry began 30 years later. In 1933, Qu Qiubai translated most part of "The Gypsies" and the little unfinished part was done by Li He. The poem was later retranslated a couple of times: by Yu Zhen in 1949, by Ge Baoquan in 1980, by Feng Chun in 1981, by Zha Liangzheng in 1982, and by Liu Zhanqiu in 1984. Some of these translations were later collected in books of *Pushkin's Poetry*.

Pushkin's long narrative "Eugene Onegin" was first translated by Meng Shihuan etc. and collected in *Works of Alexander Pushkin*(《普希金文集》) in 1937. In 1942, Geng Fu retranslated it from Japanese. Two years later, Lu Ying churned out a new version. In 1954 and 1955, Zha Liangzheng's rendition and Chen Mian et al.'s were published successively. In the 1980s, three more new translations were produced: Wang Shixie's in 1981, Feng Chunlai's in 1982, and Zhi Liang's in 1985. But retranslation did not stop here. New translations arrived one after another. In 2012, there was even a shared edition to cater to online readers.

The first translation of "The Tale of the Priest and of His Workman Bald" was done by Ge Baoquan in 1947. In the 1950s, there were 3 retranslations.

In 1944, Lin Yun brought the first translation of "The Bronze Horseman". Then came Yu Zhen's translation in 1949. Five years later, Zha Liangzheng produced another new translation.

In 1957, Lin Lan published the first song of "Ruslan and Lyudmila". After the opening-up policy, new and full versions were produced.

And it should be remembered that most of these poems were collected in various *Works of Alexander Pushkin*.

In July, 1915, Ivan Turgenev's (1818—1883) four poems "The Beggar", "Masha", "The Fool" and "Cabbage Soup" were published in *Chinese Novel* by Liu Bannong. Afterwards, there were sporadic translations of his other poems. For example, "The Threshold" was found in Ba Jin's 1936 book, *Song of a Rebel*. In 1950, the same publishing house printed Ba Jin's *Threshold*, probably a duplication of his 1936 book under a different title. And finally in 1982, we found more poems by Turgenev in Huang Jingwei's *Love River—Prose Poems of Ivan Turgenev*.

Mikhail Lermontov (1814—1841), compared with a novelist, fared better as a poet. In 1942, Mu Mutian translated his "Demon" and published it in *Demon and Others*. In 1948, Yu Zheng published his first collection of Lermontov's poems, *Selected Poems of Mikhail Lermontov*. In 1951 and 1980, new *Selected Poems of Mikhail Lermontov* of his were published. In 1985 and 1991, Yu published two editions of *Selected Lyrics of Mikhail Lermontov*, containing as many as 455 poems. Another translator of Lermontov worth mentioning was Gu Yupu, who first published *Selected Poems of Mikhail Lermontov* in

1982, a new edition of *Selected Poems of Mikhail Lermontov* that contained 115 poems in 1985. During the period from 1994 to 1997, he worked out his *Complete Works of Mikhail Lermontov*.

Vladimir Mayakovsky (1893—1930) was hailed by Stalin as "the greatest and most gifted Soviet poet", a major founder of Soviet poetry. He was very friendly to China and wrote "No Interfering with Chinese Affairs" in 1924 when China was threatened by imperialism. But he was not translated until 1929 when Li Yimang rendered three poems of his from English and published in *Poetry of New Russia* translated by Li Yimang and edited by Guo Moruo. In 1937, a book of 20 poems, including "Left March" and "My Soviet Passport", was translated into Esperanto and published in Shanghai. After the founding of the People's Republic of China, a large scale of Mayakovsky translation began. And many of his poems, like the long poem "Lenin", were translated again and again. Between 1955 and 1956, a five-volume *The Collected Works of Vladimir Mayakovsky* was published. In 1984, this anthology was revised and republished in four volumes. Two years later, Fei Bai published a two-volume *The Collected Poems of Vladimir Mayakovsky*.

Sergei A. Yesenin (1895—1925) was a Russian lyric poet. Fragments of Yesenin's poetry were first found in Jiang Guangci's 1927 article "The October Revolution and the Russian Literature". Two years later, a poem of his, "Metamorphosis: the Third Part", was found in *Poems of New Russia*. In the 1930s and 1940s, besides a few poems translated by Dai Wangshu etc., nine poems of his were published by Ge Baoquan in 1947. Between 1949 and 1976, there were only four poems of Yesenin's published by Sun Wei in the Soviet Literature issue of *Translated Literature* in 1954. After the Cultural Revolution, interest in the Russian poet was aroused and at least four collections of his poetry were published: Liu Zhanqiu and Ru Xiangxue's *Selected Lyrics of Sergei A. Yesenin* in 1982, Lan Man, Fu Ke and Chen Ercheng's *Selected Poems of Sergei A. Yesenin* in 1983, Zheng Zheng's *Birch: Selected Poems of Sergei A. Yesenin* in 1991, and Ding Lu's *Selected Lyrics of Sergei A. Yesenin* in 1992.

8.2.2 Translation of Fiction

Alexander Pushkin was the first Russian writer whose work was translated into Chinese. As early as 1903, his novel *The Captain's Daughter* was turned into traditional Chinese by Ji Yihui from Japanese. When he was translated again, it was 17 years later.

Chapter 8 Translation of Western Literary Classics in China

In 1920, Shen Yin's translations of two short stories, "The Stationmaster" and "The Snow Storm", were found in *Short Stories of Famous Russian Writers*. In 1921, *Fictional Monthly* published a special issue "Study of Russian Literature", in which Zheng Zhengduo translated a short story of Pushkin's. In 1924, Zhao Chengzhi published *Short Stories of Alexander Pushkin*, containing "The Queen of Spades". The contributors to this collections included Chen Luyuan, Xiao Shan, Feng Chun, and Meng Shihuan, many of whom turned to be good translators. *Dubrosky* was translated by Qing Diqing in 1937, the 100th anniversary of Pushkin's death. This novella of adventure and revenge had been repeatedly translated ever since. *Works of Alexander Pushkin* was compiled as early as in 1947 by Luo Guofu and Ge Baoquan. Since then, many more collections had been published. After 1980s, there were even a number of complete works, and one of them was done by Feng Chun alone!

Leo Tolstoy (1828—1910), one of the greatest authors of all time, was not only among the earliest Russian writers that were introduced to Chinese readers, but also one whose works were largely translated. In fact, the first translation of his was done in 1905, only after Pushkin's *The Captain's Daughter*. In this year, *The Cutting of the Forest* was published in *Educational World* by an anonymous translator. The preface of the translation asserted that it was translated from Japanese. Another work of Tolstoy's, *Religious Fictions of Leo Tolstoy*, was the product of a German missionary and Mai Meisheng from the English book *Selected Fictions of Leo Tolstoy*. It is worth mentioning that the Chinese translation of Tolstoy's name is what we are using today!

1908 and 1911 witnessed the publication of two stories of his. And in 1913, there were two versions of *Resurrection*, one by Ma Junwu and the other unfinished. In the next year, Tian Xiaosheng brought out his translation of "How Much Land Does a Man Need" and Liu Bannong brought out another story of Tolstoy's. In 1915, Lin Shu and Chen Jialin worked out a collection of eight short stories, Xue Sheng translated "Master and Servant", and Zhu Dongrun "Two Hussars". In the next year, Ma finished another story, "Lucerne".

1917 not only saw the publication of Lin Shu and Chen Jialin's new anthology of "A Landowner's Morning" and "Two Hussars", and of "The Death of Ivan Ilyich" in a magazine, but also Chen Jialin and Chen Dadeng's *Anna Karenina*, and Zhu Shizheng's *Tales of Sevastopol*.

In 1918, Lin Shu and Chen Jialin translated *Childhood, Boyhood and Youth*, and

Zhou Zuoren translated "The Empty Drum".

Lin and Chen's cooperation continued into the next year when they brought out "The Kreutzer Sonata" and "Family Happiness".

So, together with those published in various journals by other translators, more than 30 works of Tolstoy's had been turned into Chinese before the May 4th Movement, nearly accounting for half of all translated Russian works.

After the Cultural Movement, the translation of Tolstoy continued. In 1921 and 1922, Taidong Bookstore produced a 2-volume *Fictions of Leo Tolstoy*, Qu Qiubai and Geng Jizhi published *Selected Short Stories of Leo Tolstoy*, Geng rendered *Resurrection* into Chinese and Yang Mingkai churned out a translation of the novella *The Forged Coupon*. In 1928, the 100th anniversary of Tolstoy's birth, a peak of translating Tolstoy arrived. In the following years, many works were translated or re-translated. *The Death of Ivan Ilyich* was retranslated by Gu Shouchang in 1930. *War and Peace* was translated by Guo Moruo between 1931 and 1933. *Anna Karenina* was retranslated by Zhou Mi and Luo Jinan. *Resurrection* was retranslated by Zhang Youji and Qiu Chang in 1938 and by Gao Zhi in 1943.

In the 1950s, Tolstoy remained a favorite Russian writer, whose works often had more than one translation in circulation. For example, there were three versions of *Anna Karenina*: Gao Zhi's, Zhou Mi and Luo Jinan's, and Zhou Yang and Xie Sutai's translated from English; two versions of *Resurrection*: Gao Zhi's, and Ru Long's; two versions of *War and Peace*: Dong Qiusi's translated from English and Gao Zhi's.

After the Cultural Revolution, Dong's *War and Peace* was republished in 1978. This initiated a new stage of translation: many of Tolstoy's works were translated or re-translated. By the early 1990s, *The Complete Works of Leo Tolstoy* was published by the People's Literature Press. Among the new translators, Cao Yin was worthy of our special attention. From 1978 to 1998, he committed himself to translating Tolstoy, and turned all of the Russian writer's works into Chinese. From 1992 to 1996, a 10-volume *An Anthology of Leo Tolstoy* of his was published by Shanghai Translation Publishing House. In 1997, an 8-volume *Fictions of Leo Tolstoy* was published by Foreign Languages Press. In 2004, his *Complete Fictions of Leo Tolstoy* was published by Shanghai Art and Literature Publishing House.

Mikhail Lermontov was one of the early but rarely translated Russian writers. In

1907, Wu Chou translated the first chapter of *A Hero of Our Time* from Japanese. In 1930, Yang Hui translated the full novella from English. In 1943, Xiao Wei retranslated the work and published it in two volumes. In 1978, Cao Yin brought out his version of *A Hero of Our Time*.

Nikolai Gogol (1809—1852) was mentioned for the first time in China in Lu Xun's article "On the Power of Mara Poetry" in 1907. He was even taken as a model when Lu Xun created his "Diary of a Madman", the first published Western-style story wholly written in vernacular Chinese in 1918. But he was still not translated. He had to wait till 1921, in which year Ye Jingfeng translated his story "The Overcoat" and published it in *Selected Short Stories of Russia*. In the 1930s, more of Gogol's fictions were put into Chinese. In 1933, *The Mysterious Portrait* was translated by Lu Yan from Esperanto, and the novella *Taras Bulba* was translated by Gu Minyuan and Yang Zhi from English. In 1934, Han Shiheng translated "Taras Bulba" and "How the Two Ivans Quarreled", both from English. Also in this year, Xiao Huaqing published *Selected Stories of Nikolai Gogol*, containing *Dead Souls*, *Diary of a Madman* and three others. In November, 1935, Lu Xun finally published his translation of *Dead Souls*, which was so popular that it had been reprinted 12 times by September, 1946. In 1936, an often republished collection *Mirgorod*, containing "The Old World Landowners", "Taras Bulba", "Viy" and "How the Two Ivans Quarrelled", was published by Meng Shihuan. After 1949, Man Tao was the most prolific translator of Gogol's works. And from 1951 onwards, he began to translate Gogol and others. His works included: *Evenings on a Farm near Dikanka* in 1955 and *Petersburg Tales* in 1957. The books included: *Mirgorod* in 1963, *Selected Fictions of Nikolai Gogol* in 1979, and *Selected Works of Nikolai Gogol* in 1983. Besides him, there were other translators committing to the translation of Gogol. New publications of Gogol kept coming. For example, an 8-volume *Completed Works of Nikolai Gogol* was published by Anhui Literature and Art Publishing House.

In 1915, Ivan Turgenev's (1818—1883) highly autobiographical novella *The Torrents of Spring* was translated by Chen Gu. In the next year, another novella *First Love* was translated. In 1917, Zhou Shoujuan translated "How the Russian Meets Death". All these were translated into traditional Chinese from English.

In 1920, Shen Yin (1873—1935) translated Turgenev's "The Dream" from Russian, the first part of *A Sportsman's Sketches*. Next year, Shen translated *On the Eve*.

This was the first translation of the work, and Qu Qiubai even wrote a preface for it.

In the 1930s, more works like *A House of Gentlefolk* translated by Gao Tao (1933), *Turgenev's Novellas* translated by Zhao Guhuai (1933), *Asya* translated by Kuai Sixun and Xi Dichen (1933), *Asya* translated by Wen Peiyun (1934), and *Asya* translated by Hu Kan (1935) were published. In 1939, Li Ni retranslated *On the Eve* from English. In 1949, the Culture and Life Press with Ba Jin as the editor-in-chief published 6 of Turgenev's novels in *Selected Works of Ivan Turgenev*.

Between 1949 and 1966, Turgenev was profusely published with both new and old translations. Just take the Culture and Life Press as an example, it published Ba Jin's *Virgin Soil*, Li Ni's *House of the Gentry*, and Geng Jizhi's *A Sportsman's Sketches* in 1950; Lu Li's *Rudin* in 1951; Li Ni's *On the Eve*, Ba Jin's *Fathers and Sons*, Lu Li's *Smoke*, and Feng Zikai's *A Sportsman's Sketches* in 1953. A few collections were also published in this period, like Liu Dajie's *A Desperate Man* in 1954, and Ba Jin and Xiao Shan's *Selected Novellas and Short Stories of Ivan Turgenev*.

In the 1980s, a new peak of translation of Turgenev's works arrived, which began with the publication of Chang Song's *The Torrents of Spring*. In 1981, Zhu Rong's translation of *The Torrents of Spring* and Ba Jin and Xiao Shan's *Selected Novellas and Short Stories of Ivan Turgenev* were published. 1982 saw the publication of the simplified version of *On the Eve* and *Asya*, and Huang Jingwei's *First Love—Selected Novellas and Short Stories of Ivan Turgenev*, and Zhang Yousong's *Selected Novellas and Short Stories of Ivan Turgenev*. Then flooded Turgenev's works. In 1983 alone, we could find the publication of Lu Li's *Smoke*, Huang Shang's *A Sportsman's Sketches*, Wang Jinling's *Smoke*, Lin Shutong's *The Duellist*, and Huang Jingwei's *A Sportsman's Sketches*.

In the 1990s and after, the publishers seemed dissatisfied with publishing separate works, so more collections and series of works were brought accordingly. For instance, soon after the People's Press brought out a 13-volume *Selected Works of Ivan Turgenev* in 1992, Hebei Educational Press published a 12-volume *Complete Works of Ivan Turgenev*.

Maxim Gorky (1868—1936), the pseudonym of Aleksey Maksimovich Peshkov, was first introduced to China in 1907 when Wu Chou rendered his story "Cain and Artem" from Japanese. In the next year, "Song of a Falcon" was translated into Chinese but published in Japan. But the translation of his next story, "Twenty-six Men and a Girl", had not been done until eight years later. In 1916, Liu Bannong translated and published this story in *Fictional Sea*. Next year, Zhou Shoujuan had "The Traitor's Mother" translated in *A Collection of Famous European and American Short Stories*. In the 1921 Russian Literature issue of *Fictional Monthly*, Shen Zemin published Gorky's first story "Makar Chudra".

The large scale translation of Gorky began in 1928, which witnessed the publication of three collections of Song Guihuang's *An Anthology of Marxim Gorky* with five short stories, Song Xi's *On Prairie* with four stories, and Xiao Xun's *A Green Cat* with three stories, all translated from English.

A peak of translation of Gorky's works was reached in the 1930s that saw his stories in at least 10 different collections, and his longer works such as *My Childhood*, *In the World*, *My Universities*, *The Man Who Was Afraid*, *The Artamonov Business* and part of *Life of Klim Samgin* series were translated. Among these works, *The Artamonov Business* was worthy of special attention because it had been retranslated several times.

The fever of translating Gorky's works did not abate in the 1940s. Apart from republishing those that had been translated, 15 new stories, 4 new novellas and 2 new novels were translated in the 10 years. Some were translated from languages other than Russian in this period, as it were in the previous decade. But it was also in this period that some important translators of Russian literature, like Geng Jizhi and Ru Long, came on the translation stage.

After 1949, Gorky was accessible to more readers as his works were hugely produced. Before 1960, *Selected Short Stories*, *My Childhood*, *In the World*, *My Universities*, *The Man Who Was Afraid*, *The Artamonov Business*, *Tales of Itality*, *Through Russia*, the *Life of Klim Samgin* series and his *Reminiscences*, had all been published. After the opening up, Gorky remained a favorite writer to Chinese readers. In 1981, the People's Press launched a project of publishing a 20-volume *Complete Works of Maxim Gorky* and finished it in 1986.

Alexander Fadeyev (1901—1956) was best known as the author of *The Young Guard*, but it was *The Rout* that was first translated into Chinese. In 1930, Lu Xun planned to publish his translation of the novel from Japanese in one of journals run by the League of Left-Wing Writers. As the journal was banned by the Kuomintang Government, the publication was interrupted. In the next year, he proofread his work in line with the Japanese and German versions and published it at his own expense. In a few months, it was reprinted under the pseudonym of Sui Luowen. It was banned time and again, but it enjoyed great popularity, leading to its numerous republications. It enlightened and encouraged many Chinese readers.

In 1947, *The Young Guard* was finally translated and published by Ye Shuifu. In 1954, Ye revised his translation according to the newly revised Russian text and had the revision published. The new translated novel was repeatedly printed to cater to the increasing readership.

So far, most of Fadeyev's works have been translated into Chinese. However, the difference between the reception of *The Young Guard* and *The Rout* in China and that in other countries illustrates the peculiar charm of translated literature: in the target culture, it does not equal to foreign literature!

Mikhail Aleksandrovich Sholokhov (1905—1984) was a Russian novelist, the winner of the 1965 Nobel Prize in literature. It was Lu Xun who introduced the Soviet writer and his *And Quiet Flows the Don* to Chinese readers. He asked Xu Shiquan to buy the German translation of the novel in Germany and send it back to him. After he got the book, he gave it to He Fei (pseudonym of Zhao Guangxiang) immediately, who promised him to do the translation. He also took pains to carefully proofread He's translation and wrote an afterword for it when this first book was published in 1931. The second book was translated by Zhao Xun and Huang Yiran from English as well as Russian in 1936. Three years later, the two translators published their translation of this second book. In 1941, Jin Ren translated all the four books from Russian. And before 1949, it had been reprinted 8 times.

Virgin Soil Upturned was published by Li Hongni just a few days before Zhou Libo churned out his version from Russian and Japanese, but the former was far less popular than the latter, which were reprinted many times. A new translation by Zhong Pu came in 1945. In 1948, Meng Hua rewrote the work for Chinese readers.

The unfinished epic tale *They Fought for Their Country* was translated and published in 1946.

Some of Sholokhov's short stories were also translated into Chinese. In 1933, Lu Xun translated his "Father", and Hu Sheng did "The Blue Field" in 1936. Cao Jinghua's collection of Russian stories in his 1939 included 4 stories of Sholokhov's.

After 1949, Sholokhov's works were translated and published at an unprecedented scale. In 1951, Jin's *And Quiet Flows the Don* was published for the 9th time. It was revised and published in 1956. The translator Cao Yin alone published his versions of *Fate of a Man*, *The Don Stories*, and *Virgin Soil Upturned* in the 1950s and the early 1960s. There was a version of *They Fought for Their Country* by Shi Ren, published in 1973!

In the 1980s and after, Cao's and Jin's translations were still published and read, but there were also new translations of Sholokhov.

Sholokhov affected several generations of Chinese readers through translation. Some Chinese writers like Zhou Libo openly acknowledged his influence.

Nikolay Ostrovsky (1904—1936) wrote only two novels, but these works exercised a tremendous influence on Chinese readers. In 1936, his first novel *How the Steel Was Tempered* was translated from Japanese by Duan Luofu and Chen Feihuang and republished in 1939, 1940 and 1946. But the more influential version translated by Mei Yi in 1942 was from English. This translation was reprinted numerous times and even simplified. In 1943, another rendition by Misha was brought out. In 1976, there was even a "collective" version of *How the Steel Was Tempered*. In the 1980s and after, besides the republication of Mei Yi's translation, other translators also produced new renditions. As one of the most influential foreign works, more than 5 million copies of this novel were sold if all versions were counted.

Another novel of Ostrovsky's, *Born of the Storm*, was put into Chinese by Wang Yujin in 1943, by Hejin in 1949, and by Fang Yu and Ji Xin in 1951. Later, all the translations were reprinted. Fang and Ji's was even reprinted in 1981.

Ostrovsky's short stories, letters, etc. were also translated into Chinese after 1949.

8.2.3 Translation of Drama

In 1920, Qu Qiubai initiated the translation of Gogol's plays. In the following year, He Qiming rendered *The Government Inspector*, the best known and most retranslated work, into Chinese. Thereafter, this work was retranslated many times. It was retranslated by Shen Peiqiu in 1937. Four years later, Geng Jizhi published *The Government Inspector and Others*, containing "The Government Inspector", "Marriage", "The Gambler" and 4 short plays. In 1941, Huang Ju brought out his version of *Marriage*. In 1948, Shi Zhi produced his translation of *The Gambler*. Other translations of Gogol included Fang Xin's in 1941 and Man Tao's rendering of "The Government Inspector" in 1963. In 1999, the fifth volume of *Complete Works of Nikolai Gogol* was devoted to plays.

From 1951 to 1954, Li Jianwu translated 9 plays of Turgenev's in 4 books: *Selected Plays of Ivan Turgenev*. All these were rendered from English. In 1956, Fang Xin published another play, *A Month in the Country*.

8.3 French Literary Classics

The translation of French literature would be smoother if it was compared with that of English and American literature that had ups and downs.

8.3.1 Translation of Poetry

Victor Hugo (1802—1885) as a poet was first translated in 1903 when Ma Junwu put his "Tomorrow at Dawn" into a traditional metrical poem. It was a rewriting rather than a translation, but its strict metrical form as well as strong emotions made it well received. Then Hugo had to wait for 9 more years for other poems to be translated. In 1912, Gao Jun translated "To My Daughter" in the traditional metrical form as well during the summer vacation. Next year, Ma Junwu brought out his own version of "To My Daughter". Other poems of Hugo's that were rendered into Chinese included "How Good are the Poor", translated by Liu Bannong in 1926. But it was in the 1980s that Hugo's poems were largely translated. Shen Baoji had *Selected Poems of Victor Hugo* and *Selected Lyrics of Victor Hugo* published in 1985 and 1986 respectively. The year 1986 also saw the publication of a two-volume *Selected Poems of Victor Hugo* by Zhang Qiuhong and *The Collected Poems of Victor Hugo* by Wen Jiasi. Cheng Zenghou published *Selected Poems of Victor Hugo* in 1986 as well and *The Flowering May: Selected Poems of Victor Hugo* in 1988. In 1992, Zhang Qiuhong published *100 Lyrics of Victor Hugo*.

Charles Baudelaire (1821—1867) was mentioned by Zhou Zuoren in the preface to his "Riverlet" in 1919, acknowledging his indebtedness to the French poet. Three years later, he published his translations of Baudelaire's "Invitation to the Voyage" and "Windows" in *New Youth*. This marked the beginning of the translation of Baudelaire's works, but the translation of the French poet in the 1920s was sporadic on the whole. "Be Drunken", together with "Invitation to the Voyage", was published by Zhou Zuoren in *Women* in 1922. Then "The Joyful Corpse" was independently translated by Jin Mancheng, Zhang Renquan and Xu Zhimo, and Jin's version and Zhang's version even came in the same journal though in different issues! More of Baudelaire's works were translated in the 1930s. In 1933, *The Crescent* even had a special issue for *The Flowers of*

Evil, publishing 10 poems of his, including "Correspondences", "Man and the Sea", "Music", "Autumn Sonnet", "The Broken Bell", "Spleen", "The Blind", "Travelling Gypsies" and "Meditation". In the same year, Xin Pengju published *Prose Poems of Charles Baudelaire*, which was reprinted in 1950. In 1935, Shi Min translated *Parisian Dream* from English. In 1947, Dai Wangshu retranslated *Parisian Dream* and published it under the title of *Gems from The Flowers of Evil*. After 1949, none of Baudelaire's poems were published until Chen Jingrong published 9 to commemorate the 100th anniversary of the first publication of *The Flowers of Evil*. After the Cultural Revolution, the translation of Baudelaire's works was restarted. Wang Liaoyi's (Wang Li), Qian Chunqi's and Guo Hong'an's versions of *The Flowers of Evil* were brought out in the 1980s. The translation of Baudelaire's works continued into the 1990s. In 1996, *The Complete Poetry of Charles Baudelaire* edited by Hu Xiaoyue was published. All the works in the anthology were new translations!

Paul Valéry (1871—1945) was first introduced to Chinese readers by Liang Zongdai in 1927. It was said that Liang was so impressed in a walk when Valéry tried to show him what "Narcisse" was about that he couldn't wait to render the long poem into Chinese and sent it back to be published in *Fictional Monthly*. In 1933, Cao Baohua was said to have published three poems of Valéry's and three years later, Bian Zhilin, a student of Liang's, translated "Le Vin Perdu" and "Le Bois Amical" into Chinese. The poet Dai Wangshu was also reputed to have his translation of "Le Vin Perdu". In 1979 and 1983, Bian produced more translations of Valéry, including "Le Cimetière Marin". In 1996, Ge Lei and Liang Dong brought out *Complete Works of Paul Valéry*, making the poet the first among the 20th century French poets to have a Chinese complete works.

8.3.2 Translation of Fiction

The translation of French fiction began with Lin Shu and Wang Shouchang's collaboration on Alexandre Dumas fils' *La Dame aux Camélias* in 1899. It was a huge success, "going ten thousand miles though legless", as was acclaimed by one scholar. It was republished time and again, even into the 1980s. The novel itself was retranslated by many translators, including Liu Bannong in 1926. In fact, retranslation of this French work had never been stopped ever since it was known to Chinese readers. There were a few other works by the French writer that had been translated into Chinese but their influence could be ignored if compared with that of *La Dame aux Camélias*.

After Dumas fils, Jules Verne (1828—1905) could be seen as the second popular French writer in the late Qing period. As early as 1900, Xue Shaohui published her *Around the World in 80 Days*. It was translated from English and brought out after the popular traditional Chinese novels. The first edition was only signed by Xue, but her husband's courtesy name was added to later editions, suggesting that the translation was the result of their combined work. Another novel of Verne's, *Two Years' Vacation*, was translated by Liang Qichao and Luo Pu in 1903. Liang had no intention to be faithful in translation, and was free to add and cut from the original work, earning him a bad name as a translator. But Liang was not alone. In fact, his method of translation was a general practice. A typical example was Su Manshu and Chen Duxiu's translation of Victor Hugo's *Les Misérables* in 1904—the two translators even added a new character to it. In the same year, Lu Xun translated *From the Earth to the Moon* and *Journey to the Center of the Earth* from Japanese. And he did no better than Liang although he was later known for his insistence on being faithful to the original work. But at that time, he just followed the general practice of translation. Thirty years later, he admitted to a friend that it was a rewriting rather than a translation. In 1915, *Around the World in 80 Days* was retranslated by Shu Zi. After that, interest in Verne abated, with only occasional retranslation of *Two Years' Vacation*. Since the mid-1950s, Verne came into sight of translators again because his works were interesting but did not deal with the social reality. Therefore, from 1956 to 1962, China Youth Press conducted a project of translating Jules Verne's works. *The Begum's Fortune* were done by Lian Xing, *The Children of Captain Grant* was done by Zhiren and Fan Xiheng, and *Doctor Ox* was done by Wang Wen from Russian in 1956; *The Adventures of Three Englishmen & Three Russians in Southern Africa* was done by Wang Wen from Russian, *The Lighthouse at the End of the World* was done by Zhou Xuliang from English and *The Mysterious Island* was done by Lian Xing in 1957; *Propeller Island* was done by Lian Xing and *Around the World in 80 Days* and *Twenty Thousand Leagues Under the Sea* was done by Sha Di in 1958; *Journey to the Center of the Earth* was done by Yang Xianyi in 1959; *Twenty Thousand Leagues Under the Sea* was done by Zeng Juezhi in 1961 (National Publishing Administration Residential Edition Library, 1980). In 1979, China Youth Press reprinted the series. It added more works to it till 1992. But the translation of Verne was not confined to China Youth Press. Other presses and translators had also been engaged in translating the writer's work since the 1980s.

Chapter 8 Translation of Western Literary Classics in China

Alexandre Dumas pere (1802—1870) was introduced to Chinese readers by Zeng Pu as a historical novelist in the July issue of *Xiao Shou Lin*(小说林, *Fictional Woods*) in 1902. Zeng discussed Dumas' plots and characterizations, but the translation of the "historical" novelist was done by another translator, Wu Guangjian, with his rendition of *Three Musketeers* in vernacular Chinese. Dumas' well-woven plots were very interesting to the late Qing readers, including the revolutionaries of *Fiction Circle*. He enjoyed significant popularity and attracted one translator after another. So since 1907, not only did Wu Guangjian continue with his translation, but also various translators, including Lin Shu, committed themselves to translating Dumas's works as well. In 1939, Huo Yiwen brought out the Chinese translation of *The Count of Monte Cristo*, and in 1947, Jiang Xuemo produced his version from English. Yet, no work of Dumas was published between 1949 and 1977 despite his previous popularity. And what was stranger was that *The Count of Monte Cristo* was a beloved work when readers had access to a few foreign literary works. It was said that the People's Press planned to reprint Jiang's version in 1972 but failed even though the plate had already been made. In 1978, this version finally come into Chinese sight again and was reprinted 15 times with a large sale of more than one million copies! *Three Musketeers* was then republished. In 1979, *The Black Tulip* was translated for the first time by Hao Yun. In the 1980s and after, more translators engaged themselves in translating Dumas's works, with new translations mingled with republications.

Victor Hugo first came to Chinese sight with Leng's translation of "Deaf Judge" in 1901. Two years later, Lu Xun, under the pseudonym of Geng Chen, produced his first translation in traditional Chinese from Japanese: a fragment from *Les Misérables*. In the same year, Su Manshu and Chen Duxiu worked out a partial translation of the same French novel. To publicize their revolutionary ideas, they created a new character in their translation, as was mentioned above. Since then, fragmentary or partial translations have not been rare. In 1905, Bao Tianxiao published *Bug-Jargal* as a standalone book and in 1906, *The Last Day of a Condemned Man* was published in a journal. Soon after the Bourgeois Revolution in 1911, Zeng Pu translated *Ninety-Three*, a novel about the French Revolution, to express his ideas about revolution. Nine years later, Lin Shu and Mao Wenzhong retranslated the work. A full translation of *Les Misérables* was finally done by Yu Hu in 1923. But retranslation of the novel never stopped. Retranslation of other works was the chief event in translating Hugo's works in the 1930s and 1940s except for a

Vietnamese's dictation of *The Hunchback of Notre-Dame* in 1946 and Chen Jingrong's translation of the same work in 1949. In the 1950s, many of Hugo's novels were reprinted or retranslated, like Chen Jingrong's *The Hunchback of Notre-Dame* in 1950 and Li Dan's *Les Misérables*. Then Hugo disappeared till April, 1978, when Li Dan's *Les Misérables* and Zheng Yonghui's *Ninety-Three* were republished. Afterwards, old translations were reprinted and new translations were churned out. In 1998, *Gems of Victor Hugo* and a twenty-volume *Complete Works of Victor Hugo* were edited by Liu Mingjiu, who wrote a long preface of 90,000 words for the latter. In 2002, the 200th anniversary of Hugo's birth, not only were old works reprinted, but a twelve-volume *Selected Works* was brought out.

Guy de Maupassant (1850—1893) was introduced, much earlier than his teacher Flaubert, to Chinese readers as early as 1904, when Chen Lengxue (Chen Jinghan) translated one of Maupassant's war stories and published in *New New Fiction*. In 1909, Zhou Zuoren had "Moonlight" translated in *A Collection of Overseas Short Stories*. The Duck and Butterfly School ushered in a new wave of Maupassant translation, with seven stories like "The Necklace" and "Souvenir" being rewritten rather than translated for their surprising stories but literary value between 1913 and 1914. Then the French writer was forgotten till 1919 when a new flood of Maupassant's stories arrived. The 1920s saw the publication of many Maupassant's collections, among which were Li Qingya's three volumes of *Short Stories of Guy de Maupassant*, published in 1923, 1924 and 1926 respectively. In 1929, Li began to work on a huge project: the translation of all Maupassant's works. Within three years, he had nine anthologies of Maupassant's stories published. Meanwhile, there were other translators working on the writer. In the 1950s, interest in him was not lost with not only old translations being republished but also some that had no Chinese versions being translated. Maupassant was almost immediately republished after China adopted its open-door policy in the late 1970s. Since then, republication and retranslation as well as translation of Maupassant's works had never been stopped. So far, all of Maupassant's works have been rendered into Chinese whether they were long or short.

In 1915, Honoré de Balzac (1799—1850) was translated for the first time by Lin Shu and his partner Chen Jialin. They produced a collection of 4 short stories in traditional Chinese, including "Farewell" and "The Red Inn". Two years later, his "El Verdugo" was found in Zhou Shoujuan's *A Collection of Famous European and American Short Stories*, in traditional Chinese as well. This story was retranslated by Zhongchi and published in *Fictional Monthly* in 1924. The 1930s witnessed the flourishing of Balzac translation. In 1935 alone, 6 stories of Balzac's were translated: "The Atheist's Mass" and "An Episode of the Reign of Terror" by Xu Xiacun and "The Unknown Masterpiece", "Farewell" and another two by Mu Mutian. One more collection and two more short stories arrived in 1936 and 1945 respectively. Meanwhile, Balzac's novels were translated. In 1936, Mu Mutian published his translation of *Eugénie Grandet*, ushering in a new stage of Balzac translation. With the Balzac translators Mu Mutian, Gao Mingkai, Fu Lei and Li Liewen, the important works in the *Human Comedy*, like *Father Goriot*, *Cousin Bette*, *Cousin Pons* were presented to Chinese readers. Gao Mingkai alone produced 21 translations and Fu Lei produced eight translations in the 1940s and 1950s. Of all the Balzac translators, Fu was best known for his idiomatic language. Since the Reform and Opening beginning in 1978, a new generation of translators had taken the stage and produced new versions of Balzac's works although some old translations were also republished.

Although the prop of the New Cultural Movement, like Chen Duxiu and Hu Shi, held Émile Zola (1840—1902) in high regard, it was the Duck and Butterfly writers who first translated his works into Chinese. Zola's "The Flood" was found in Zhou Shoujuan's 1917 book, *A Collection of Famous European and American Short Stories*. Three years later, he published two more stories of Zola's in *Fictional Monthly*. More translators were then drawn to the French naturalist and churned out more translations, including Liu Fu's (Liu Bannong) "The Cats' Paradise" in 1927, Mao Dun's *Department Store* in 1931, Wang Liaoyi's (Wang Li) *Nana* in 1934, *L'Assommoir* in 1937, Ni Ming's *Germinal* in 1944 and Li Qingya's *The Stomach of Paris* in 1949. In the 1950s, new translations of Zola continued despite the reprinting of some old translations. Then new translations of Zola disappeared from the public sight until his resurgence in the 1980s when new translations kept coming that almost all of Zola's works had been translated into Chinese.

Although articles about Gustave Flaubert (1821—1880) were published in 1921, he was not translated until 1925, in which year Shen Zemin and Li Jieren brought out their own versions of *Madame Bovary* independently. Two years later, Li Qingya's translation of the same novel was published. In 1931, Li Jieren published the Chinese rendition of

Salammbô. In 1936, Qian Gongxia finished his translation of *The Temptation of Saint Anthony*. Also in this year, the most important Flaubert translator, Li Jianwu, published *Short Stories of Gustave Flaubert*. Li, whose Chinese rendition of the name Flaubert is still used today, produced his translation of *The Temptation of Saint Anthony* in 1937 and *Madame Bovary* in 1949. By this time, almost all of Flaubert's works had been translated. In the 1950s, *The Complete Works of Gustave Flaubert* was published, with the works in it almost all done by Li Jianwu. In the 1980s and after, more retranslations were done, especially of *Madame Bovary*. Zhou Kexi's retranslation even won a book award in foreign literature for his aesthetic pursuits and the affinity with time.

Jean-Jacques Rousseau (1712—1778), the novelist, was not translated until 1923 when his educational novel *Emile*, or *On Education* was translated by Wei Zhaoji although it was a partial translation from English. In 1929, a partial translation of *Confessions* was first produced by Zhang Jingsheng, who soon churned out a full version. In the same year, another full version was made by Zhang Qiu. In the following years, more and more translations of *Confessions* were done. The translations of these two books have exercised influences on generation after generation of Chinese readers. Ba Jin publicly admitted that he had been affected by Rousseau's *Confessions*.

Prosper Merimee (1803—1870) was first translated by Fan Zhongyun, who published *Carmen* in 1926. Ever since then, the novella had been retranslated five times before the 1980s. Of the re-translations, Fu Lei's was the most popular and had been reprinted many times since its first appearance in 1953. Other works of Mérimée's that had been translated into Chinese included *The Venus of Ille* by Zeng Xubai in 1928 and by Li Liewen in 1948, and the bi-lingual *Selected Short Stories of Prosper Mérimée* by Zheng Yonghui in 1964. The 1980s saw the publication of books: *Selected Fictions of Prosper Mérimée* by Zheng Yonghui in 1980 and that by Wang Yuwei in 1988, and Wang Tuoshan's translation of the novel, *A Chronicle of the Reign of Charles* IX. In 1997, *The Complete Works of Prosper Mérimée* was published.

Stendal (1783—1842) reached the general Chinese readers with *Vanina Vanini*, a collection of short stories translated by Mu Mutian in 1932. Four years later, Li Jianwu brought out *An Anthology of Stendal's Fictions*, containing 6 short stories. In the 1940s, Zhao Ruihong translated his representative work *The Red and the Black* and *Armance* from English. In 1948, Xu Chi produced his translation of *The Charterhouse of Parma* from

French as well as English. Next year, Luo Yujun published her version of *The Red and the Black*, perhaps the most popular one, which was republished numerous times. Stendal's other works were republished or translated and retranslated in the 1980s and after. New translations of *The Red and the Black* kept coming, leading to a heated discussion of retranslation in the mid-1990s.

In 1920, Mao Dun translated Henri Barbusse from an English collection *We Others* and published it in *Oriental*, initiating the translation of this French communist. In the following year, two more stories were translated by Zhongzhi and Wang Songlu respectively. In 1923, Liu Yanling published 4 stories of Barbusse's. Five years later, Zeng Xubai brought his "Funeral March" into Chinese. In 1929, Cheng Shaozong put part of *Lightness* (*Clarté*) into Chinese. Other translations of Barbusse before 1933 included Yao Pengzi's "Hug", Hong Lingfei's "Invincible", Zhu Xiuxia's "Returning Home" (from English), Li Dan's "Their Way" and Zhu Xiangcheng's "A Foreigner". In 1936, a year after his death, Fu Lei translated his "A Primary School Teacher" to honor him. However, the writer was almost forgotten after 1949, and *Under Fire*, for which he is remembered today, has never been rendered into Chinese.

The first translation of Romain Roland (1866—1944) took place in 1926. In this year, Jing Yinyu published his translation of *Jean-Christophe* in *Fictional Monthly*. Two years later, his novella, *Pierre and Luce*, translated by Li Jieren, was published in the same journal. Also in this years, two books, another version of *Pierre and Luce* by Ye Linfeng and *The Game of Love and Death* translated from English by Xia Pingdi and Xu Peiren, were published. In 1929, Mengyin's version of *The Game of Love and Death* was published. In the 1930s, Roland's works began to flood into China. It was in this period that Fu Lei began to translate *Jean-Christophe*. In the 1940s, apart from the translation of new works like *Saint Louis*, some works of his like *The Game of Love and Death* were re-translated or reprinted. In the 1950s, politics entered the Romain Rolland translation: Chen Shi and Huang Qiuyun's *Above the Battle* from English (1950), Xu Yuanchong's *Colas Breugnon* (1958), Qi Fang and Lao Du's *Romain Rolland's Revolutionary Dramas* (1958), Sun Liang's *An Anthology of Romain Rolland* from English (1957). Even so, Fu Lei's *Jean-Christophe* was always a favorite and was reprinted in 1950, 1953 and 1957 by three different publishing houses. In the 1980s and after, Romain Rolland was once again translated, re-translated and reprinted. Despite disputes over his literary achievements, the French writer fared better in China than most of his countrymen, perhaps because "he is to the Chinese taste", as some scholar put it.

8.3.3 Translation of Drama

In 1907, a Chinese version of *La Dame aux Camélias* was staged in Tokyo by the Spring Willow Troupe. That was the first translation of French dramas, but unfortunately, the scripture was lost.

Molière (1622—1673) was first translated into Chinese in 1923 when Gao Zhenchang published *The Miser* in the Commercial Press. In the following year, Zhu Weiji translated another play of his, *Tartuffe*, from English. In 1927, *The School for Wives* was rendered into Chinese by Zeng Pu. The 1930s saw more of Molière's works being translated. *The Impostures of Scapin*, *The Imaginary Invalid*, and *The Misanthrope* were all translated. In 1935, *The Comedies of Molière* were published by Wang Liaoyi (Wang Li). These works were republished or retranslated afterwards. In 1949, Li Jianwu planned to publish a two-volume *Plays of Molière*. Unfortunately, only the first was brought to the public with 8 plays of Molière's: *The Pretentious Young Ladies*, *Don Juan*, *The Physician In Spite Of Himself*, *George Dandin*, *The Miser*, *Monsieur de Pourceaugnac*, *The Middle Class Gentleman* and *The Imaginary Invalid*. In the mid-1950s, nine of Molière's plays translated by Zhao Shaohou etc. were published and republished. In the year of 1959, Zhao published *Comedies of Molière*. Interest in the playwright continued. In 1963, Li Jianwu published *Theatre Choisi*, *or Six Comedies of Molière*, which was reprinted in 1978 when the publishers were very cautious in selecting what to publish even though the Open-door policy was made in this year. In 1981, Zhao Shaohou's *Selected Comedies of Molière* was published. From 1982 to 1983, a four-volume *Comedies of Molière* by Li Jianwu was published, having been the most comprehensive collection so far. Molière wrote more than 30 comedies, most of which had Chinese translations. The translation of him had never stopped ever since he was introduced into China.

Victor Hugo, as a playwright, was introduced into China about 10 years later than he was a novelist. In 1910, Bao Tianxiao and Xu Zhuodai translated his *Angelo* into Chinese, marking the start of the translation of Hugo's plays. In 1916, Zeng Pu turned *Lucretia Borgia* into Chinese. Between 1927 and 1928, he published *Hernani*, *Ruy Blas*, *The Hunckback of Notre-Dame* etc. under the title "Complete Plays of Victor Hugo".

8.4 German Literary Classics

The reservoir of translated German literature was not as large as that of English and Russian, but it did have lasting effects on Chinese readers via works like *The Sorrows of Young Werther*. In the 1950s, 1960s and 1970s, the translation of German literature seemed to go dormant. However, since the 1980s, it had experienced a retaliatory resurgence.

8.4.1 Translation of Poetry

The translation of German poetry started with Wang Tao's translation of Ernst Moritz Arndt's (1769—1860) "Song of the Fatherland" in 1871. But then it stopped till Ma Junwu's translation of "Mignon" by Johann Wolfgang von Goethe (1749—1832). It was said that Ma had translated the song before 1910 and published it in 1914. And it was also in this year that Fu Quan published an anthology of German poems and Guo Moruo embarked on his way of translation with his rendition of "The Elf-King".

In the summer of 1919, Guo Moruo brought out a partial translation of Goethe's long poem, *Faust*. In August, 1920, to ease his economy, he answered an advertisement recruiting translators of *Faust* and finished the first part in the vacation. As the second part was longer and more difficult, he planned to publish the first only. He wrote to the publisher but received no answer. Then part of the draft was destroyed, so he had to wait till 1928 for his translation to be published. The more time-consuming translation of the second was not finished until May, 1947 and was not published until November of this year. Guo's *Faust* was reprinted by three different publishing houses. In December, 1978, it was one of the few foreign literary works that was carefully chosen to be published after the Cultural Revolution.

Before Guo brought out his translation of the second part, Zhou Xuepu published his translation of "Faust" in two volumes in 1935. In the 1980s, Qian Chunqi produced the first new rendition of the long German work. After this, more versions were offered by new translators, like Liang Zongdai (1986), Lu Yuan (1994), and Yang Wuneng (1998).

In the 1920s, Guo also translated Goethe's "May", "Wanderer's Nightsong" and "The Fisherman", which were included in *Selected Poems of Germany* published by the Creation Society. In 1936, he translated "Hermann and Dorothea" but published it in 1942 and republished it in the 1950s.

In 1915, Ma Junwu published some songs from *William Tell* into traditional metrical poems. But the translation of the whole poem, this poetic drama by Friedrich Schiller (1759—1805), was done much later. And interesting enough, it was translated and published by Zhang Weilian and Qian Chunqi respectively in 1956, because it is a poem depicting the Austrians' fight against invasions. Then new publication of the German poet was postponed to 1980 when *Selected Lyrics of Goethe and Schiller* was published. In 1984, Qian Chunqi published *Selected Poems of Friedrich Schiller*. In the 1990s and later, more collections of Schiller were produced.

The translation of Heinrich Heine (1797—1856) was first done in 1914 when "The Grenadiers" was included in Fu Quan's book of German poems. In 1921, Li Zhichang translated his "Love Songs" from English. This initiated the sporadic translation of Heine's poems from 1920s to 1950s. From the 1950s to the end of the Cultural Revolution, Heine fared better than all other German writers, including Goethe. In 1950, Wu Boxiao published *The Silesian Weavers* and a collection of poems, *Baltic Sea*. In the same year, Ai Siqi translated Heine's long poem, *Germany, a Winter's Tale*, maybe because of its stinging attack on reactionary conditions in German. In 1956, Feng Zhi published *Selected Poems of Heinrich Heine*, containing 67 poems of Heine's. In the next year, Qian Chunqi published three anthologies: *Selected Poems*, *New Poems*, and *Romanzero*. Then came Feng Zhi's publication of *The Silesian Weavers*.

After the decision of opening-up policy was made, Heine was also among the first batch of foreign writers to be published. Therefore, Feng Zhi's revision of *Selected Poems of Heinrich Heine* was published in 1978, and Qian Chunqi's new translation of the long satire *Atta Troll, A Midsummer Night's Dream* was published in 1979. In the 1980s and after, interest in Schiller was aroused again and many collections of his poems were published.

Rainer Maria Rilke (1875—1919) was known to Chinese readers chiefly through Feng Zhi, who fell in love with the Austrian poet even since he read the prose poem, "The Song of the Life and Death of the Cornet, Christoph Rilke" in 1926. In April, 1931, he bought *The Complete Works of Rainer Maria Kilke* and began to translate "Letters to a Young Poet" earnestly and published it in *North China Daily*. Next year, he translated and published the famous poem, "The Panther". In November, 1936, the 10th anniversary of Rilke's death, Feng Zhi wrote an article, "Rainer Maria Rilke—Written for the 10 Anniversary of His Death", to which he attached *Selected Poems*. In 1938, he published "Letters to a Young Poet" in a book, indicating there was sporadic translation of Rilke by Bian Zhilin, Liang Zongdai, and Chen Jingrong. In 1943, he translated and published 12 more of Rilke's poems. Then Rilke lapsed into oblivion till the 1980s. In 1986, Zhang Li published his new translation of "Letters to a Young Poet", ushering in a wave of Rilke translation. New translators like Yang Wuneng, Qian Chunqi, and Lu Yuan were engaged in translating Rilke. In September, 1996, Zang Di compiled *Selected Poems of Rainer Maria Kilke*, containing more than 100 poems.

Finally, it should be remembered that from 1914 on, anthologies of German poems kept coming. Apart from the first one of Fu Quan's, Zhang Weilian published *Famous Poems of Germany* by Modern Bookstore 1933. After 1980, anthologies of German poetry emerged one after another.

8.4.2 Translation of Fiction

Zhou Shoujuan's translation of Goethe's "A Tale" in 1917 was an early attempt, if not the first, to introduce German fictions. Compared with the translation of English and Russian fictions, the translation of German novels and short stories was meagre. However, except for, perhaps, Lin Shu and Wang Shouchang's *La Dame aux Camélias*, few created a stir as Guo Moruo's *The Sorrows of Young Werther*, the first novel of the Sturm und Drang movement. When this novel of Goethe's was published in 1922, it achieved an immediate success and had been republished 37 times before the outbreak of the Anti-Japanese War in 1937. This epistolary novel had lasting effects on Chinese readers, some of whom modeled on it and created their own epistolary works.

In face of the Japanese invasion, the translators in the late 1920s started to translate German war novels. Erich Maria Remarque's (1898—1970) *All Quiet on the Western Front* was translated by Hong Shen and Ma Yanxiang in such a context in 1929, and its anti-war tone made it stand out among those "patriotic" novels.

German fictions received little attention afterwards till the 1980s when they experienced a resurgence among Chinese readers. Many novels were translated or published in magazines or in various anthologies. Some long neglected writers and works were introduced to Chinese readers for the first time.

8.4.3 Translation of Drama

Despite some partial translations earlier, the representative work of Friedrich Schiller (1759—1805), *William Tell*, was published in 1925. In the following year, his first play, *The Robbers*, was translated and published by Yang Bingchen. The historical drama

Wallenstein was translated and published by Guo Moruo in 1955. Around the same time, four other plays *Cabal and Love*, *The Maid of Orlean*, *The Robbers*, and *The Bride of Messina* were translated and published either because of praising the fight against foreign invasions or criticizing the tyranny, hypocrisy and cruelty of the ruling class.

The other works of Schiller's had to wait patiently to be translated till 1980s. The translators were no longer baffled by ideological considerations. As a result, more of his plays became accessible to Chinese readers, thanks to such translators as Zhang Weilian, and Qian Chunqi.

Last but not least, Henrik Ibsen (1828—1906) must be mentioned even though he did not fall into the above categories. To talk about foreign playwrights, he was second to none in influence in the late Qing Dynasty and the early Republic of China. On June 18, 1918, *New Youth* even published an Ibsen issue to publicize the Norwegian writer. Works like *A Doll's House*, *An Enemy of the People* and *Little Eyolf* were all translated into Chinese. Among these works, the most influential was *A Doll's House*, whose heroine Nora had aroused great sympathy as well as encouragement from Chinese readers. Articles discussing the play and Nora's rebellion inundated newspapers and magazines at that time. Many girls took Nora as a model and became independent individuals.

Questions for discussion:

1. Why were the translators enthusiastic in rendering foreign fictions in the late Qing Dynasty?

2. What changes were there in the 1920s in translation?

3. Why were some mediocre works published in the 1930s?

4. Are *The Gadfly* and *How the Steel Was Tempered* classics? Why or why not?

References:

国家出版事业管理局版本图书馆,1980. 1949—1979 翻译出版外国古典文学著作目录[M]. 北京:中华书局.

National Publishing Administration Residential Edition Library, 1980. Catalogue of foreign classical literary works in Chinese translation from 1949 to 1979 [M]. Beijing: Zhonghua Book Company.

张璘,2013. 文学传统与文学翻译的互动[M]. 镇江:江苏大学出版社.

Zhang Lin, 2013. The interaction between literary tradition and literary translation [M]. Zhenjiang: Jiangsu University Press.

Chapter 9

Chinese Translation of Western Non-literary Classic Works

Translation can be classified into different categories according to different criteria. It can be generally grouped into literary and non-literary translation. Non-literary works mainly refer to those scientific works of argumentative, explanatory, applied and/or narrative styles, which function as important tools for people to exchange ideas, deal with affairs, solve problems and communicate with one another. Such works are characterized by specific content, fixed writing format, concise language, and proper timeliness in dealing with affairs. The genre of non-literary works can be divided into academic writing, practical writing, scientific research report, graduation thesis, scientific and technological thesis, official documents, business documents, judicial documents, financial documents, etc. Non-literary translation covers a wide range of topics such as politics, economics, philosophy, law, and the like and requires that the translator should not only be proficient in both the source language and the target language, but also be knowledgeable in the area of specialization.

Creative imagination in literary works is one of the fundamental differences between literary and scientific works. The latter is produced by scientists using logical thinking. Both non-literary and literary works are reflections of objective things in terms of the content. The former adopts a more scientific way of writing with full and accurate materials and real time, place, person, cause, process, and result. Non-literary works must also be accurate and reliable when it comes to nature, characteristics, figures, charts, and examples. On the other hand, literary works use a more artistic way of writing, which is based on life but never sticks to real people and things. These features require the translation of non-literary works to reflect the facts with accuracy. It should be corrected if there is any mistake in the texts. Non-literary works and literary works differ greatly in terms of linguistic forms. The language of non-literary works is simple and clear while that of literary works is rhetorical and flowery. Hence, the translation of non-literary works should be simple and clear. Non-literary works differ from literary works in ways of thinking. The former mainly uses logical thinking and objectivity based on facts, statistics, logical judgments, and reasonings while the latter is from imagination with vivid images. Thus, the translation of non-literary works must be logical and coherent in meaning, which must not be contradictory to numerical bases and reasonings. Even the original text should be carefully examined when necessary. Both non-literary and literary works have social value but the former aims to transmit information, focusing on practicalities, while the latter intends to influence, centering on aesthetics. Therefore, the translation of non-literary works should ensure the accuracy of information transmission before considering the beauty of language.

Literary translation of novels, poems, dramas, films, and television shows constitutes the bulk of translation done by publishing houses. However, there is a huge demand for non-literary translation from international institutions, governmental and non-governmental organizations, enterprises, research institutions, etc. Most of them have specialized translation departments. The United Nations, the European Union, and other large international institutions have specialized translation departments and all important documents have to be translated into several official languages. As far as China is concerned, the translation agencies set up throughout Chinese history have been primarily concerned with translating practical matters, whether for administrative purposes or not, such as Chinese texts or foreign works in astronomy, medicine, science and technology. The history of translation in modern China clearly shows that there were far more non-literary translation than literary translation. All government agencies have set up departments of foreign affairs. Translation is also indispensable for multinational companies and large enterprises to carry out transnational production, procurement, and sales. The international exchange of research institutions and non-governmental organizations is also inseparable from translation, and all the translation activities undertaken or outsourced by these institutions are undoubtedly non-literary translation. We can not imagine how many documents of non-literary translation are produced every day in the world, which has far exceeded the number of literary translation. Although non-literary translation has played such a great role in promoting historical progress and social development and accounts for a high proportion in modern translation practice, it seems that non-literary translation has not been given due attention.

9.1 Chinese Translation of Western Classic Works in Politics

The word "politics" evolved from the ancient Greek "city" or "state". "As we see that every city is a society and every society is established for some good purposes, for an apparent good is the spring of all human actions. It is evident that this is the principle upon which they are founded, and this is more especially true of that which has the best possibility for its object, and is itself the most excellent, and comprehends all the rest. Now this is called a city and the society thereof a political society" (Aristotle, 1912). It can be seen that politics is the highest good, so it is also a moral category in essence.

In the Renaissance in Italy, Niccolo Machiavelli (1469—1527) finished his representative work *The Prince* in 1532. This treatise is a summary of political experiments and drastic changes in Florence and even in whole Italy for hundreds of years and of years of Machiavelli's political experience. The book is also a complete exposition of Machiavelli's autocratic monarchy theory as well as the reasons for Italy's long war. *The Prince* initiates a plan to realize the unification of Italy, that is, to establish a strong centralized state. This work is about political theories which lay the foundation for bourgeois politics. It heralds a new era for the development of modern politics and also makes politics independent from philosophy and ethics.

9.1.1 Chinese Translators of Western Classic Works in Politics in the Ming and Qing Dynasties

In the history of Chinese political translation, the second climax of translation did not happen until the end of Ming Dynasty and the beginning of Qing Dynasty. In the late Ming Dynasty, the coastal areas were frequently intruded by Japanese pirates while the northern areas were threatened by Manchu. Some insightful people in the ruling class, together with missionaries with advanced scientific educations, translated and compiled many works of the advanced natural science to enrich the country and strengthen the army. Many enlightened scholars and translators translated a large number of Western books and greatly contributed to the development of China.

During the Opium War from 1840 to 1842, the Qing imperial government suffered repeated defeats. To combat the invaders, Qing Dynasty introduced a large number of

Western books and newspapers to learn from the enemy's strengths. Lin Zexu(林则徐, 1785—1850), born in Fuzhou, was influenced by these innovative ideas. In the period of opium prohibition in Guangzhou, he fought against the British invaders tenaciously. He was not familiar with foreign languages but he was proficient in Manchu language. Lin translated many works in politics including *On China*(《论中国》, *Lun Zhongguo*), *On Tea*(《论茶叶》, *Lun Chaye*), *On Prohititing Opium*(《论禁烟》, *Lun Jinyan*), *On the Use of Military Force*(《论用兵》, *Lun Yongbing*) among others.

Wei Yuan(魏源, 1794—1857), born in Hunan Province, was a famous thinker, historian, writer, and translator in Qing Dynasty. He wrote a large number of books and also translated many political, economic, cultural and artistic works including *Geography of the Maritime Nations*(《海国图志》, *Haiguo Tuzhi*). It is suggested in the book that guns, ships, and other useful civil machinery and industrial products should be made to strengthen the coastal defense and resist the foreign aggression. It is also stated in the book that reforms should be carried out concerning water transportation, salt law systems, tax reductions, and the interests of businessmen. This book had a profound influence on the later bourgeois reformist movement in China and was later circulated in Japan, which had a great impact on Meiji Reform. Both Chen Li and Zhang Zhidong thought highly of this book. Zhang regarded it as the beginning of China's knowledge about Western politics.

Feng Guifen(冯桂芬, 1809—1974), born in Jiangsu Province, was deeply influenced by his teacher Lin Zexu. Feng advocated learning from Western technologies under the influence of the bourgeois ideology and became one of the pioneers of the modern reformist movement in China. He attached great importance to translation and wrote the book *Jiaobinlu Kangyi*(《校邠庐抗议》, *Protest of Jiaobinlu*), which discussed the importance of translation and advanced the idea of systematic reform and improvement. Feng regarded translation as one of the most important government affairs and was the first to propose the establishment of translation office.

Some Westerners also translated a lot of works in politics into Chinese. For example, William A. P. Martin, an American missionary, was a leading "China expert" among foreigners in China in the late Qing Dynasty. He translated Henry Fawcett's *Manual of Political Economy* into *Fuguoce*(《富国策》) in 1886. Around the same time, Joseph Edkins(艾约瑟) put the same book into *Fuguo Yangmince*(《富国养民策》).

Li Fengbao(李凤苞, 1834—1887), born in Jiangsu Province, was proficient in mathematics, astronomy, and politics. He collaborated with American Kreyer in translating many Western political and military works, which played a great role in disseminating the modern Western science and technology and its tactical essentials and made a great contribution to China's territorial and sovereign integrity. Li's translations in the political science and international relations include *Chronology of Four Generations* (《四裔编年表》, *Siyi Biannianbiao*), which is the first book about Western history from 2349 B. C. to 1861. This work arranges the rise and fall of major countries in each era year by year, which corresponds to the Chinese year. Such feature aids those familiar with the national heritage to know the great foreign events easily that happened along the reign of a certain Chinese Dynasty. Li also translated *New Meaning of Land Military Drills*(《陆操新义》, *Lucao Xinyi*), etc.

Ma Jianzhong(马建忠, 1845—1900), born in Jiangsu Province, was proficient in English, French, Latin, and Greek. In 1894, he presented the famous memorial *Nishe Fanyi Shuyuan Yi*(《拟设翻译书院议》, *Proposal of the Establishment of a Translation Academy*) to the Qing government. In the memorial, he posited ideas about good translation, analyzed the situation of foreign languages at that time, and discussed the necessity and significance of establishing an academy of translation. He also expounded on topics like the objectives, source of students, length of schooling, teachers, curricula, rules and regulations, teaching managements, and the books that should be translated, which triggered the clarion call for revitalizing the cause of translation and saving the nation from danger. Such a memorial has become a valuable asset in the history of Chinese translation.

Xu Jianyin (徐建寅, 1845—1901), born in Jiangsu Province, was a modern Chinese translator. He was a patriotic scientist who had great achievements in science and technology in China. He was also a pioneer in spreading Western culture, translating and introducing advanced Western science and technology when the imperialists intensified their aggression against China and the Qing government became increasingly corrupt. Xu Jianyin gradually realized that it was increasingly important to learn from foreigners to strengthen the army and make the country strong. In his early years, he worked in Jiangnan Arsenal with Xu Shou, Li Shanlan(李善兰), Hua Hengfang and other scholars to translate and introduce Western works. In addition to natural science, economics and chemistry, Xu's works of translation were also on Western politics such as *Navy Drills*(《水

师操练》, *Shuishi Caolian*), *Fleet Maneuvering* (《轮船布阵》, *Lunchuan Buzhen*), *A New Book on Military Science* (《兵学新书》, *Bingxue Xinshu*), *Gatling Gun Drill* (《格林炮操法》, *Gelinpao Caofa*), among others. These were about naval drills, ship deployment, military science, etc.

Yan Fu (严复, 1854—1921), born in Fujian Province, was a famous translator, educator, and thinker. During the Westernization period, Qing Dynasty began to set up new schools and sent many students overseas for further study. During this period, a large number of translators were trained. In 1877, Yan Fu was selected as one of the first official students to study in Europe. He went to Britain to study and accepted the political and cultural ideas of the Western bourgeoisie. During his study in Britain from 1877 to 1879, he devoted himself to the study of Western political academic theories, especially Darwin's theory of evolution. Later, Yan translated *Evolution and Ethics* (《天演论》, *Tianyan Lun*) written by British biologist Thomas Henry Huxley. In the course of his translation, Yan not only presented elements of the famous standard of translation, namely, faithfulness, expressiveness, and elegance, but also expounded on the viewpoint of saving the nation from subjugation and striving for survival based on the biological evolution theory of natural selection and survival of the fittest. He opposed both the conservative ideas of the diehards and those of the Westernizers at that time and alerted the people of the whole country to the danger of the motherland, which had a great social impact. The translation *Evolution and Ethics* is a popular pamphlet publicizing Darwin's theory of biological evolution. The first half of the pamphlet is about the theory of evolution and the second half is about the ethics. This work is a thought-provoking political paper, which holds that all things change according to the law of natural selection. Organisms evolve in the process of natural selection. The superior/strong species win over the inferior/weak species. Yan Fu did not translate the book literally but chose to translate part of the introduction and the first half of the book, which was a selective free translation. He warned the people that the nation would be subjugated and exterminated if they did not strive for the self-improvement. However, he was not a pessimist who did nothing. Although China was weak before and after the Opium War, there were still ways to save the country. Situations could be changed through collaborative efforts and competitions. When the country was in a desperate situation, *Evolution and Ethics* called out to the Chinese people to gather their strengths to compete, which had an enlightening influence on Chinese intellectual circles. Kang Youwei (康有为, 1858—1927), the leader of the reformist school, praised Yan Fu for his translation. Yan's translations and thoughts have become an immortal model and milestone in the history of Chinese translation.

Yan Fu returned to China in 1879 and served as a teacher in Beiyang Naval Academy. From the Sino-Japanese War of 1895 to the reform movement of 1898, he became a thinker and propagandist of the movement by translating books, making political comments and running newspapers, propagating the thought of reform, attacking feudal autocracy, advocating scientific democracy and advancing bourgeois reformism. Translation, as an important means of learning from foreigners, was no longer limited to the early works in natural science but also included those in political, economic, legal fields, and other Western social science classics.

From 1901 to 1909, Yan Fu translated more Western masterpieces. In the process, he systematically introduced Western democracy and science as well as Western sociology, politics, economy, philosophy, and natural science to China and publicized the thought of reform. His main works of translation were H. Spencer's *Study of Sociology* (《群学肄言》, *Qunxue Siyan*), Adam Smith's *An Inquiry into the Nature and Causes of the Wealth of Nations* (《原富》, *Yuanfu*), J. S. Mill's *On Liberty* (《群己权界论》, *Qunji Quanjie Lun*), E. Jenks's *A Short History of Politics* (《社会通诠》, *Shehui Tongquan*), J. S. Mill's *A System of Logic* (《穆勒名学》, *Mule Mingxue*), Baron de Montesquieu's *De l'Esprit Des Lois* (《法意》, *Fayi*), W. S. Jevons's *Primer of Logic* (《名学浅说》, *Mingxue Qianshuo*), which totaled more than 1.7 million words with 170,000 additional words for notes. Yan's endeavor was the first systematic introduction of Western social and natural sciences to China. His works of translation were considered as enlightenment reading materials at that time. Yan Fu's goals of translation were to spread the advanced Western ideas and promote the reform for China to be prosperous and strong and for the realization of the dream of saving the country through education. After the revolution of 1911, he became the president of Peking University. He was a great thinker, educator, and translator in China. To reiterate, his works are seen as immortal models and milestones in the history of Chinese translation. His translation principles of faithfulness, expressiveness, and elegance have profoundly and extensively influenced the history of Chinese translation and have become the core of traditional Chinese translation theory.

Kang Youwei, a Cantonese, was a great statesman, thinker, educator, and the representative of bourgeois reformism. In 1879, he experienced the Western capitalist culture in Hong Kong. In 1882, he went to Shanghai to study Western translations. He advocated learning from the West to carry out the reform and save China. In 1895, he, with Wen Tingshi, Chen Chi, and many others, established a translation association in Beijing to discuss China's self-improvement and criticize the diehards' surrender and betrayal. In 1898, Kang organized the national congress in Beijing to publicize the patriotism, mobilize the masses, and expand the influence of the reform and modernization. He founded newspapers and periodicals like *Wanguo Gongbao*(《万国公报》, *Multinational Communique*) and *Zhongwai Jiwen*(《中外纪闻》, *Chronicles of China and Foreign Countries*) which were mostly translations of foreign intelligence and materials. He especially focused on the translation of works in political science, law, and other academic fields.

Liang Qichao(梁启超, 1873—1929) was a bourgeois reformist thinker and patriotic translator. He wrote in his book *Lun Yishu*(《论译书》, *On Translating Books*) that the promotion of Western learning and the translation of Western books were the focus of the reform and ways to save the country. He refuted the conservatives who opposed translation and argued that translation played an important role in the history of Western countries especially in educating their people to promote the development. In his view, the translation of Western books was essential for China to learn from the West and become stronger. He put forward three principles of translation. Firstly, good books should be chosen for translation, especially those great works that have made the West prosperous and strong. These works are in political, legal, historical, educational, agronomic, business, and other relevant fields. Secondly, translation norms should be determined. There are great cultural differences between China and the West so norms are essential to standardize the translation. Thirdly, more translators should be trained. They should not only be proficient in both Western and Chinese languages but also have deep knowledge of the original works. In 1896, Liang created translation columns in the newspaper *Shiwu Bao*(《时务报》, *The Chinese Progress*) to introduce Western newspapers and books. These translation columns gave account of dynamic reports on world issues and published translations of foreign novels. He also wrote and compiled books like *Xixue Shumu Biao* (《西学书目表》, *Western Culture Booklist*) in the same year. In 1897, he established a

Chapter 9 Chinese Translation of Western Non-literary Classic Works

translation company Datong Translation Bureau in Shanghai, aiming to translate books of the political reform from various countries. In 1898, this company became the official translation office of the Qing government. Liang Qichao's ideas of promoting Western learning, translating Western books, and maintaining the political reform emancipated the Chinese people significantly at that critical moment in China.

He translated and introduced Western books such as those on Western bourgeois theory, Marxist works, political novels, and the like. Among these was Bluntschli Johann Caspar's political work *The Theory of State*(《国家论》, *Guojia Lun*), which held that all citizens should regard the patriotism as their first duty. Liang also introduced Marx's theory and was the first Chinese to translate Marx's work. Liang Qichao mentioned two dominant theories in Germany at that time in his article *Jinhualun Gemingzhe Xiede Zhi Xueshuo* (《进化论革命者颉德之学说》, *The Theory of the Evolutionary Revolutionist Kidd*), namely Marx's socialism and Nietzsche's individualism, and further explained in 1902 in *Zada Moubao*(《杂答某报》, *A Reply to a Newspaper*) that socialism would be the most noble and wonderful doctrine in the future. Later, he systematically introduced Spinoza, Rousseau, Montesquieu, Aristotle (384—322 B. C.), Kant, and other Western philosophers and their theories in newspapers like *Qing Yi Bao*(《清议报》, *The China Discussion*) and *Xinmin Congbao*(《新民丛报》, *Sein Min Choong Bou*). In addition, Liang also advocated translating and printing political novels in his article *Yiyin Zhengzhi Xiaoshuo Xu*(《译印政治小说序》, *Preface to the Translated and Printed Political Novels*). He was more focused on translations of political works than those of literary. Thus, translation was an important means of publicizing advanced Western political ideas.

Ma Yifu(马一浮, 1883—1967), born in Zhejiang Province, was a famous scholar, thinker, calligrapher, and translator. He had profound achievements in ancient philosophy, literature, and Buddhism. He was proficient in German, Japanese, French, Latin, and Sanskrit. He once organized a translation society with Ma Junwu, Xie Wuliang, and Shao Liancun and published the first monthly magazine on translation in China *Fanyi Shijie*(《翻译世界》, *World of Translation*), which was a way of introducing Western culture actively. In 1903, Ma went to the United States and read many works of literature, philosophy, and social sciences. He was the first person in China to introduce German and English versions of Marx's *Capital*(《资本论》, *Ziben Lun*), which was an event of great significance in the history of the spread of Marxism in China. Besides, as one of the early representatives of new Confucianism, Ma was known as one of the "three saints of modern times" or "three saints of new Confucianism", and the other two were Liang Shuming and Xiong Shili.

9.1.2 Chinese Translators of Western Classic Works in Politics after the May 4th Movement

May 4th Movement in 1919 was a patriotic political movement. The translation of Marxist works was an important part of the translation activities in that period. Translation studies not only included literary translation but also extended to linguistics, philosophy, psychology, aesthetics, and many other fields. Zhu Zhixin, Li Dazhao, and many other scholars translated part of Marx's *The Communist Manifesto* (《共产党宣言》, *Gongchandang Xuanyan*) from 1906 to 1919. Chen Wangdao's (陈望道, 1891—1977) translation in 1920 was the full version. Marx's second important book was *Capital*, which was not fully and formally translated in China until 1996 by Guo Dali after he had studied and translated Adam Smith's *An Inquiry into the Nature and Causes of the Wealth of Nations* (《国富论》, *Guofu Lun*) and Malthus' *An Essay on the Principle of Population* (《人口论》, *Renkou Lun*), among others. This endeavor laid a solid theoretical foundation for Guo's translation of *Capital*. He proposed in his postscript that translation should be faithful, fluent, and consistent in characteristics with the original. It was his perseverance despite illness that finally completed the translation of this great work of Marx. Guo Dali is a great translator of Marxist works and has established his name in the history of Chinese translation.

Lu Xun (鲁迅, 1881—1936), formerly known as Zhou Zhangshou (周樟寿) and later renamed as Zhou Shuren (周树人), was a great writer, thinker, revolutionist, and translator in China. His translation activities run through his whole life. He challenged the traditional way of translation and caused the revolution of approaches to translation in China. Lu Xun's political view of translation is to enlighten the Chinese people through translation. He conceived the idea of saving China through translation before the May 4th Movement, which was to improve the Chinese people's life, society, and nation by translating the works from the oppressed nations. His translation is a precious wealth in the history of modern Chinese translation and is of great significance to the development of the discipline of translation today.

Zhou Jianren (周建人, 1888—1984), born in Zhejiang Province, was a famous biologist, translator, and one of the pioneers of Women's Liberation Movement. He was also one of the founders of China Association for Promoting Democracy. He was a prolific academic writer and translator. His works of translation were in philosophy, biology, politics, and literature. He also translated Charles Robert Darwin's *The Origin of Species* (《物种起源》, *Wuzhong Qiyuan*) in which Darwin focused on the natural selection and demonstrated the diversity and unity of the species origin and life nature from the aspects of variability, heredity, artificial selection, survival competition and adaptation. These were based on a large amount of research data accumulated in many fields such as paleontology, biogeography, morphology, embryology, and taxonomy for more than 20 years. The book not only ushered a new era in the history of biological development and made the theory of evolution penetrate into all fields of natural science, but also caused a great revolution in the whole human thought. This had a wide and far-reaching impact on the process of world history.

Wu Xianshu (吴献书, 1885—1944) was a famous educator and translator in China. He translated Plato's (427—347 B.C.) *The Republic* (《理想国》, *Lixiang Guo*) in 1929. The book describes the philosophy, politics, art, and education of the slave-owner class from various perspectives. The work takes the form of the quotations from Socrates, analyzes the interrelationship between individual justice and state justice, and points out that only in the republic can justice be truly realized. Plato was born in the period of decline of Athens where there were fierce conflicts between slaves and slave owners. He firmly opposed democracy and strongly advocated that slave owners and nobles should be in power. Plato designed the republic to consolidate the dominant position of the aristocracy of slave owners.

Li Da (李达, 1890—1966) was an outstanding Marxist theorist, propagandist, and educator and one of the main founders and early leaders of the Communist Party of China. Li Da devoted all his life to the research, propaganda, and education of Marxist theory. He made outstanding contributions to the Sinicization of Marxism, which had an important impact on the formation and development of Mao Zedong's philosophical thought. Li Da was also a famous encyclopedic master in the history of Marxism in China and had pioneering achievements in philosophy, economics, politics, history, law, sociology, pedagogy, and many other fields, realizing the overall exploration and comprehensive innovation of Marxist theory. His works of translation cover a wide variety of fields such as historical materialism, Marxist economics, tariff system, jurisprudence, social sciences, agricultural problems, political economics, etc. His political works of translation include *Interpretation of Historical Materialism*(《唯物史观解说》, *Weiwushiguan Jieshuo*), *Critique of Gotha Program*(《德国劳动党纲领栏外批评》, *Deguo Laodongdang Gangling Lanwai Piping*), *Critique of Political Economics*(《政治经济学批评》, *Zhengzhi Jingjixue Piping*), among others. Such works totaled no less than 35 books with more than 2 million words. Li Da emphasized the important role of Marxism, Leninism, and Mao Zedong Thought in translation, especially in the translation of works in social sciences.

Chen Wangdao, born in Zhejiang Province, was a famous linguist, educator, literary theorist, and translator of Marxism and Leninism. He migrated to Japan in his early years. After returning to China in 1919, he actively engaged in the New Culture Movement and the propaganda of Marxism and Leninism. In 1920, he organized China's first Marxism group in Shanghai together with Chen Duxiu and completed the first full Chinese translation of *The Communist Manifesto* in China. This had a great impact on the spread of Marxism in China and also provided ideological and theoretical preparations for the founding of the Communist Party of China. Based on the logic of the capital expansion, Marx expressed his judgment in *The Communist Manifesto*: due to the development of the world market, the bourgeoisie has made the production and the consumption of all countries worldwide. The spiritual products of all ethnic groups have become the public property and the one-sidedness and limitations of ethnic groups have become increasingly impossible. Marx expounded the theory of scientific socialism for the first time in *The Communist Manifesto* and pointed out that the Communist movement had become an irresistible historical trend. Communist groups sprang up all over China after the publication of Chen Wangdao's Chinese translation of *The Communist Manifesto*, which was warmly welcomed by the working class and advanced intellectuals. Since then, this pamphlet with more than 28,000 Chinese characters has become the ideological starting point for the Communist Party of China to build up revolutionary faith. The book played an important role in publicizing Marxism, promoting the development of the revolutionary movement and the establishment of the Communist Party of China. Chen Wangdao's important works of translation also include grammar, logic, aesthetics, rhetoric, and many other fields. His book *Xiucixue Fafan*(《修辞学发凡》, *An Introduction to Rhetoric*) laid the foundation for modern rhetoric, which was regarded as a landmark in rhetorical study

Chapter 9 Chinese Translation of Western Non-literary Classic Works

by later generations.

Hu Shi(胡适, 1891—1962), born in Anhui Province, was a famous thinker, writer, and philosopher in China. In 1910, he went to the United States to study agriculture and to Columbia University to study philosophy and literature. He learned from the pragmatist philosopher Dewey and advocated vernacular and literary revolutions. Hu was a representative of the New Culture Movement and made an important contribution to China's translation. Hu Shi's translation studies not only include linguistic studies and translation strategies, but also political intentions of saving the nation and the people through translation. He believed that it was urgent to translate original foreign works to arouse the patriotic spirit of the people and to resist foreign invasions in view of the domestic and foreign troubles in Chinese society. Hu's translation of Daudet's *The Last Lesson*(《最后一课》, *Zuihou Yike*) was intended to inspire the Chinese people by demonstrating the indomitable patriotic enthusiasm and firm determination of the French people in the French war. Hu Shi's early works of poetry translation also had a clear political inclination such as *The Charge of the Light Brigade*(《六百男儿行》, *Liubai Naner Xing*), *A Soldier's Dream*(《军人梦》, *Junren Meng*), *The Song of the Shirt*(《缝衣歌》, *Fengyi Ge*), *Lord Ullin's Daughter*(《惊涛篇》, *Jingtao Pian*), among others. Such works were all full of patriotic enthusiasm and fighting spirit and described Hu's strong consciousness of political demands and social changes in fighting against the Qing government to save the country. In addition, Hu Shi advocated the translation of Western literary works in vernacular, which was aligned with the purpose of the New Culture Movement and won widespread acclaim and popularity.

Guo Moruo(郭沫若, 1892—1978), born in Sichuan Province, was a modern Chinese writer, historian, archaeologist, and translator. During May 4th Movement, he actively participated in the revolutionary cultural movement against imperialism and feudalism. He was a famous translator in China and translated a lot of works that stunned the translation circles both at home and abroad. In his 60 years of translation, he translated a large number of foreign works in literature, philosophy, art, Marxist theoretical works, etc. Guo Moruo translated many classic works in political economy including Marx's *Critique of Political Economy*(《政治经济学批判》, *Zhengzhi Jingjixue Pipan*), *The German Ideology* (《德意志意识形态》, *Deyizhi Yishi Xingtai*), *Social Organization and Social Revolution*(《社会组织与社会革命》, *Shehui Zhuzhi Yu Shehui*

Geming), etc. In addition, Guo Moruo has translated many works in science, art, and archaeology. The soul of his translation is creativity. Translators are not "parrot celebrities". When translating, translators should immerse themselves into the works and regard translation as a creative task. Guo proposed certain principles for ideal translation: the translator should have a rich knowledge of the language, an in-depth understanding of the original work, a profound study of the author, and the ability to freely manipulate the native language.

Cheng Fangwu(成仿吾, 1897—1984), born in Hunan Province, was a Chinese proletarian revolutionist, an important representative of the New Culture Movement, a proletarian educator, a social scientist, a litterateur, and a great translator of Marxist works. After the May 4th Movement, he engaged in the anti-imperialist, anti-feudal revolutionary activities in Japan and China with Guo Moruo, Yu Dafu, etc. He introduced Mao Zedong's writing principles of "accuracy, clarity, and vividness" into the translation of Marxist works. Besides, Cheng successfully retranslated *Gongchandang Xuanyan* for the fifth time together with Xu Bing and also corrected and translated a lot of Western classic works.

Shen Zhiyuan(沈志远, 1902—1965), born in Zhejiang Province, was a famous Marxist translator. He devoted his life to the study of Marxist-Leninist political economics and philosophy and disseminated Marxism and Leninism as a lifelong pursuit. Shen made outstanding contributions to the field of Marxist economics. He was also a great translator of social sciences. His translations include *Dialectic Materialism and Historical Materialism*(《辩证唯物论与历史唯物论》, *Bianzheng Weiwulun Yu Lishi Weiwulun*), *World Economics and Politics*(《战后世界经济与政治》, *Zhanhou Shijie Jingji Yu Zhengzhi*), *Capitalism*(《资本主义》, *Ziben Zhuyi*), etc. Shen Zhiyuan combined Marxism and Leninism with Chinese practice, which is still of great significance in the construction of the current socialist market economy.

9.1.3 Characteristics of the Translation of Political Works

The main purposes of political documents are to elaborate and explain some viewpoints, theories, and policies so as to achieve the goals of the political propaganda and communication of ideas. Therefore, the language is extremely precise, solemn, accurate, normative, and highly logical. Informal expressions should be avoided. The translation of political documents is highly policy-oriented, theoretical, realistic, and instructive, reflecting national images and speakers' political attitudes. Translation errors can affect readers' correct understanding of the original documents. This can cause confusion in the minds of the readers and bring undue losses to political work. Therefore, faithfulness to the original should be emphasized in translation. Political translation requires not only the faithful transmission of the political connotation of the original text but also the maintenance or close expressions of the original text.

One of the characteristics of political works is the unique preciseness and formality in the selection of words. Translators of political works should have a high sense of political responsibilities and a serious working attitude. Translators should be meticulous and show full respect to the original documents. Besides, the translator should not adopt the mechanical word-for-word translation to avoid obscure interpretations. The translation of political documents should emphasize the principle of unity and flexibility.

Translation of political works often involves a large number of expressions with unique national cultural characteristics. To deal with the cultural transformation of two languages, the translator should not only translate the images of the idioms but also the cultural connotations of the expressions. For example, "安居工程" cannot be translated literally as "Peaceful Living Project" but "Comfortable Housing Project" or "Housing Project for Low-income Urban Residents" instead. Besides, some expressions with national characteristics should be translated flexibly based on the context. For example, 不正之风 can be translated into "unhealthy tendency (in medicine profession)", "(corruption and other) illegal performances", "(correct abuses or) malpractices", etc.

The use of euphemisms is another characteristic of political works. Euphemism is frequently used in political commentaries, not only for politeness but also as a good means for politicians to achieve their goals in diplomacy. Some euphemisms are used to cover up facts or ease social conflicts. For example, "poor nations" is usually replaced by "backward nations". The word "poverty" has more euphemisms such as "need", "underprivileged", and so on. Some expressions are used in the description of war, not out of "politeness" but to "disguise". For example, "civil casualties" is often described as "collateral damage".

Abbreviations are very common in Chinese political commentaries. These are often related to the name of Chinese government agencies and organizations which appear very frequently in the media. The conventional translation of this kind of expressions is to use their abbreviations. For example, CC, CPC, NPC, CPPCC are the abbreviated forms of "Central Committee", "Communist Party of China", "National People's Congress", and "Chinese People's Political Consultative Conference" respectively. Sometimes abbreviations are related to numbers. Therefore, the translator should first understand what the abbreviation actually represents and then use literal translation combined with explanations to make it easy to understand. Explanations are often provided when the abbreviation is used for the first time. For example, "三个代表" can be translated as "Three Represents" which means that our party must always represent the development trend of China's advanced productive forces, the orientation of China's advanced culture, and the fundamental interests of the overwhelming majority of the Chinese people. These abbreviations are usually common government agencies or fixed expressions, which have authoritative translations and cannot be translated blindly so that political misunderstandings among foreign readers could be avoided.

Political works can reflect the political and economic systems of a society as well as social and cultural values. The difficulty of the translation of political works lies in the fact that the target text should not only convey the seriousness and accuracy of the source text but also reflect the characteristics of specific political culture. Good translation of political works is conducive to the communication of different ideologies and values.

Besides, political translation is highly political and sensitive. The translator should pay special attention to its appropriateness. For example, the sentence "中国经济是一个大问题" should be translated as "China's economy is an important question" rather than "China's economy is a big problem". The latter is inappropriate because it seriously distorts the meaning of the original text, as if there is something wrong with China's economy. To ensure the appropriateness of the translation, the translator should pay attention to the context, such as the linguistic style of the original text, etc. The translation of political articles requires translators to have political mind and keep political sensitivity. The translator should carefully weigh the political meaning and influence of the words and have political consciousness.

9.2 Chinese Translation of Western Classic Works in Philosophy

In the overall history of translation, there were some philosophical approaches to translation such as George Steiner's hermeneutic motion, Ezra Pound's energizing of language, Walter Benjamin's "pure" language of translation, and so on. However, hardly any attention has been paid to the translation of the classic works of philosophy. The relationship between philosophy and its translation is considered to be clearly asymmetrical: translators and translation specialists seem to be far more interested in philosophy than philosophers who had explicitly pondered on the conundrums of translation (Pym, 2007). Therefore, the study of Chinese translation of Western classic works of philosophy is an innovative and promising field that is worthy of careful academic explorations.

9.2.1 Chinese Translation of Western Classic Works in Philosophy

The translation of Western works of philosophy can be traced back to the introduction of Christianity into China. It was in the Zhenguan period of Tang Dynasty in 635 that Christianity had been introduced into China for the first time. Bishop Olopen(阿罗本) brought the Bible to Chang'an and was received by Fang Xuanling, the Prime Minister of Tang Dynasty.

At the end of Ming Dynasty in the 17th century, Western works of philosophy were introduced into China by many translators. Xu Guangqi (1562—1633), a native of Shanghai, studied astronomy, mathematics, water conservation, and other fields in Western science and technology under the supervision of Matteo Ricci. Xu was a prolific writer who devoted all his life to the research of science and politics and made important contributions to the cultural exchanges between China and the West in the 17th century. In addition to the translation of many works in natural science, Xu Guangqi also compiled another book of philosophy entitled *On the Soul*(《灵言蠡勺》, *Lingyan Lishao*) as dictated by Italian missionary Francesco Sambiasi. In the book, they followed Aristotle's theory and divided the soul into the soul of plants, the perceptual soul of animals, and the rational soul of humans. Such an idea, in combination with Augustine's theory of the study of soul, was the most beneficial and important knowledge in philosophy and its research purpose was to make people trace their sources and finally worship God to save their souls. The book also integrated Confucianism into the theory of soul to understand all things in the world and promote the rule of the country.

Chinese scholar Li Zhizao(李之藻, 1565—1630) worked with a Jesuit to translate an Aristotelian logic textbook *An Introduction to Aristotle's Dialectics*(《名理探》, *Mingli Tan*) in medieval Europe. Li Zhizao was good at astronomy, arithmetic, geometry, geography, and technology. He translated many Western books together with Western missionaries. He translated *An Introduction to Aristotle's Dialectics* with more than ten volumes. This work introduced Aristotle's logic to the Chinese for the first time. Later, Yan Fu translated *A System of Logic* written by Muller and *Elementary Lessons in Logic* written by William Stanley Jevons. Although the Chinese could immediately notice the similarities between the philosophical thoughts of famous scholars and the logic, such ideas were still different.

Wang Guowei(王国维, 1877—1927) was a famous sinologist, aesthetician, litterateur, and translator in China. He was proficient in Japanese and English and had conducted in-depth research on the philosophy of Kant, Schopenhauer, Nietzsche, and other philosophers. Wang was a prolific writer and translator. His works of translation were about geography, law, Schopenhauer, Nietzsche, psychology, debate, pedagogy, zoology, etc. He made great contributions to the discipline construction of Chinese philosophy. He used the methods of Western philosophy to sort out his pioneering work in Chinese philosophy, which largely determined the embryonic form of Chinese philosophy research in the 20th century. His basic position was obviously influenced by his translation of *Ethics* written by Japanese Yujiro Motora(元良勇次郎) in 1902. Wang Guowei's understanding of Western philosophy at that time far exceeded those that his contemporaries. But his greatest contribution in sorting out Chinese philosophy with the use of ways in Western philosophy was his effort to establish Chinese philosophy as a discipline in modern education. Wang created a paradigm for the 20th-century Chinese ideological circles to further unravel the ancient philosophical tradition. He also interpreted translation from the perspective of philosophy and believed that Western works were characterized by abstraction, classification, and other approaches to analyze and synthesize the tangible and intangible things in the world. In addition, Wang also thought that the translation of ancient philosophical works must be faithful to the original works and one of the difficulties of translation was to find terms equivalent to the original.

More classic works of philosophy were translated into Chinese after May 4th Movement.

Chapter 9　Chinese Translation of Western Non-literary Classic Works

Wu Xianshu translated Plato's *The Republic* which mainly discusses Plato's ideas on the establishment, governance, and justice of the Republic and the theme about the management of the state. Plato was a great philosopher in ancient Greece and one of the greatest philosophers and thinkers in the West. He was born during the decline of Athens. The class struggle between slaves and slave owners became more acute and the power struggle between the democratic group and the aristocratic group of slave owners also began. Plato firmly opposed the democracy and strongly advocated for the slave owner aristocracy to control state power. To consolidate the ruling position of the slave owner aristocracy, he designed the Republic. The cave metaphor and civic thought in the book have long been well-known. Plato was a prolific writer of philosophical works which were mostly translated by Chinese translators such as Yan Qun, Zhu Guangqian, Yang Jiang, Chen Kang, among others. Their translations included *Apology*(《申辩篇》, *Shenbian Pian*), *Crito*(《克里托篇》, *KeliTuo Pian*), *Laches*(《拉凯斯篇》, *Lakaisi Pian*), *Charmides*(《查米德斯篇》, *Chamidesi Pian*), *Hippias Minor*(《小西庇阿斯篇》, *Xiaoxibiasi Pian*), *Ion*(《伊翁篇》, *Yiweng Pian*), *Protagoras*(《普罗泰戈拉篇》, *Puluotaigela Pian*), *Lysis*(《吕西斯篇》, *Lüxisi Pian*), *Cratylus*(《克拉底鲁篇》, *Keladilu Pian*), *Enthudemus*(《游叙弗伦》, *Youxufulun*), *Gorgias*(《高尔吉亚篇》, *Gaoerjiya Pian*), *Hippias Major*(《大西庇阿斯篇》, *Daxibiasi Pian*), *Menexenus*(《美内克索斯篇》, *Meineikesuosi Pian*), *Meno*(《美诺篇》, *Meinuo Pian*), *Symposium*(《会饮篇》, *Huiyin Pian*), *The Republic*(《理想国》, *Lixiang Guo*), *Parmenides*(《巴门尼德篇》, *Bamennide Pian*), *Theaetetus*(《泰阿泰德篇》, *Taiataide Pian*), *Phaedrus*(《斐德罗篇》, *Feideluo Pian*), *Timaeus*(《蒂迈欧篇》, *Dimaiou Pian*), *Critias*(《克里底亚篇》, *Kelidiya Pian*), *Sophist*(《智者篇》, *Zhizhe Pian*), *Statesmen*(《政治家篇》, *Zhengzhijia Pian*), *Philebus*(《菲利布篇》, *Feilibu Pian*), *Laws*(《法律篇》, *Falü Pian*), etc. In 2018, Wang Xiaochao compiled and published the complete works of Plato. Plato's main works are dialogues, most of which were presented by Socrates. However, it is generally believed that the image of Socrates is not completely the real Socrates in history.

Socrates, Plato, and Aristotle are called the "three sages" of Greece. As Plato's student, Aristotle became one of the great Greek philosophers, scientists, and educators in the ancient history of the world. He was an encyclopedic scientist who contributed to almost every subject. He wrote on topics in ethics, metaphysics, psychology, economics, theology, politics, rhetoric, natural science, pedagogy, poetry, customs, and Athenian law. Aristotle's works constructed the first extensive system of Western philosophy including morality, aesthetics, logic and science, politics and metaphysics. Wu Shoupeng had a good command of ancient Greek and was well-known for his translation of Aristotle's works. Wu was often regarded as the first Chinese who translated Aristotle's works. His translations and publications of Aristotle's works were *Metaphysics* (《形而上学》, *Xingershangxue*), *Politics* (《政治学》, *Zhengzhixue*), *On the Soul* (《论灵魂》, *Lun Linghun*), *History of Animals* (《动物志》, *Dongwu Zhi*), etc. Aristotle called metaphysics the "first philosophy", which was theological and studied the divine, and distinguished it from other subjects such as mathematics and natural science. He elaborated his theory of hylomorphism in *Xingershangxue*, concluding that a particular substance is a combination of both matter and form. Aristotle's *Poetics* (《诗学》, *Shixue*) was translated into Chinese by Chen Zhongmei in 1996 and *Physics* (《物理学》, *Wulixue*) was translated into Chinese by Zhang Zhuming in 1982. Miao Litian (1917—2000) had engaged in teaching and research of Western philosophy for more than 50 years. He was a famous historian of Western philosophy, an expert in ancient Greek philosophy, educator, and translator. He compiled and published the complete works of Aristotle in 1993.

In the Middle Ages, the Christian theology was dominant in the field of ideology and scholasticism came into being. Scholasticism refers to the theory that Catholic church used to teach in its established schools. It originated from patristics and uses rational forms, abstract and complicated dialectics to demonstrate the Christian belief and serve the religious theology. Scholasticism advocates religious idealism and is a religious theology that safeguards the system of exploiting the working people. Scholasticism is different from patristics in many ways. The latter serves the slave class while the former serves the feudal ruling class. Patristics publicizes the blind belief and excludes the reason but Scholasticism has produced a theoretical system. Scholasticism is a kind of Christian philosophy theory which is more theoretical and systematic than patristics. Therefore, it is more deceptive. At the end of the 12th century, many of Aristotle's books were introduced to Western Europe and spread widely with the rise of the civil class. The church failed to suppress the heresy and had to change its strategies, allowing to teach Aristotle's philosophy in church schools. Traditional theologians reconciled Aristotelian philosophy with Christian theology by using the negative factors in the philosophy with the aim of consolidating the dominance of religious theology.

One of the theologians was Thomas Aquinas (1225—1274), a theologian of Scholasticism and a master of Christian philosophy. Politically, he was a defender of feudal hierarchy and an advocate of Christian theocracy. He introduced reason into theology and reformed Aristotle's philosophy to replace that of Plato's, which was represented by Augustine as a pillar of Christian theology. Hence, it successfully pushed Christian philosophy to a new heyday and maintained its dominant position in the Middle Ages. The most important representative work of Aquinas was *Summa Theologiae*(《神学大全》, *Shenxue Daquan*). This book, together with the *Bible* and the Pope's orders, was placed on the altar during the Grand Council of Trent in the 16th century, indicating that it was one of the sources of wisdom, reason, inspiration, and various answers. *Summa Theologiae*, which is known as the "Encyclopedia" of Christianity, is comparable to the *Bible* to some degree and is not only a medieval theological work, but also a philosophical work. It was not until 2008 that this book was translated into Chinese and introduced to China. The translators are Liu Junyu, Chen Jiahua, Gao Xudong, Zhou Keqin, Hu Ande, Wang Shoushen, among others. Aquinas' work adopts Aristotle's logic to expound the concepts of God, soul, morality, law, and country, as well as their relationships from the perspectives of philosophical epistemology and ontology.

After the second half of the 14th century, capitalist relations of production sprouted in the feudal society of Western Europe. Production relations in the same context became the shackles and could not adapt to the development of productive forces. The feudal system began to disintegrate and decline. Italy is the region where capitalist relations of production first came into being so it became the birthplace of civil bourgeois renaissance. This rise embraced all aspects of ideological and cultural fields and produced a variety of thoughts including humanism, the renaissance of natural science, and materialist philosophy. Humanism is different from feudal theology and takes man and nature as the object. Domains of this movement are philosophical theory, literature, art, political theory, and ethics, among others. Humanism's essence is bourgeois theory of human nature and humanitarianism. Humanism is not only the bourgeoisie's ideological and cultural movement against feudalism but also their earliest enlightenment movement.

One of the proponents of humanism is Dante Alighieri (1265—1321), an Italian poet in the Middle Ages. He was a pioneer of the European Renaissance and was known as the "father of Italian language". He was not only the greatest poet in Europe but also one of the greatest writers in the world. He was famous for his epic *Divine Comedy*(《神曲》, *Shenqu*) which is divided into three parts with 100 chapters and 14,233 lines. Dante created a new rhyme based on a popular one in folk poetry with the last line of each part rhymed with the word "star". More importantly, *Divine Comedy* was written in Italian slang, which had a great role in solving the problem of Italian literary language. Such feature promoted a unified Italian national language, which made Dante the first national poet of Italy.

Divine Comedy has been translated into many languages and the earliest Chinese translations were Qian Daosun's and Wang Weike's versions. Wang translated *Divine Comedy* based on the Italian original while referring to French, English and other countries' translations. He spent nearly four years translating the book, of which the quality had improved. Besides, he was hardworking, honest, and patriotic and looked down on those people who betrayed their country. He lived a simple life in Jintan and kept writing and translating. In 1951, Hua Luogeng recommended Wang Weike to work as an editor in Beijing Commercial Press. Wang worked so hard that he did not even return to his hometown to visit his relatives during the Spring Festival holiday. Wang Weike translated works of millions of words, greatly contributing to the development of China's culture.

From the end of the 16th century to the beginning of the 18th century, European philosophy witnessed a glorious period. With the rapid development of commerce, trade, handicraft industry and the like, the feathers of the emerging bourgeoisie gradually plumped, making a part of the nobility into a bourgeois "new nobility". They tried their best to break the shackles of the feudal system. The dominant scholasticism at that time did not help but seriously hindered the development of social production and natural science, so they changed the purpose and direction of philosophical research. Francis Bacon, one of the founders of modern philosophy, advanced the slogan that knowledge is power. Descartes also clearly pointed out that practical philosophy should be founded to replace speculative philosophy.

Immanuel Kant was a famous German philosopher and a writer of Latvian descent. He was the founder of German classical philosophy, whose doctrines deeply influenced modern Western philosophy and initiated many schools of thought such as Kantianism. Kant was the last major philosopher of the Enlightenment period and a leading figure in German thought. He reconciled the rationalism of René Descartes with the empiricism of Francis Bacon and was one of the most influential Western thinkers after Socrates, Plato, and Aristotle. Kant graduated from the University of Königsberg and taught at his alma mater from 1755. In 1770, he was appointed as the professor and his study moved into the "post-critical period". From 1781 onwards, he completed three works, *The Critique of Pure Reason*(《纯粹理性批判》, *Chuncui Lixing Pipan*), *The Critique of Practical Reason* (《实践理性批判》, *Shijian Lixing Pipan*), *The Critique of Judgment*(《判断力批判》, *Panduanli Pipan*). This marked the birth of his system of critical philosophy and brought about a philosophical revolution.

Kant wrote extensively throughout his life. A number of his works have been translated into Chinese. *The Critique of Judgment* was translated by Zong Baihua(宗白华, 1897—1986) and published by the Commercial Press in 1964. *The Critique of Pure Reason* was translated by Hu Renyuan and Lan Gongwu and published by the Commercial Press in 1931 and 1982 respectively. *The Critique of Practical Reason* was translated by Zhang Mingding and Guan Wenyun in 1936 and in 1990 respectively. Apart from the retranslation of these three classic works, Deng Xiaomang also translated Kant's *Fundamental Principles of the Metaphysics of Morals*(《道德形而上学原理》, *Daode Xingershangxue Yuanli*). The complete works of Kant were compiled by Li Qiuling and published in the People's University of China Press in 2019.

Zong Baihua, a native of Jiangsu province, also translated Kant's works. He was a famous Chinese philosopher, aesthetician, poet, and translator. He was a pioneer of modern aesthetics in China. Zong Baihua was regarded as the master of aesthetics who integrated Chinese and Western art theories. In addition to his translations of Kant's works, he also translated many Western art treatises and letters of dialogues between artists. His book, *Selected Translations of Western Art Masterpieces*(《西方文化经典选译》, *Xifang Wenhua Jingdian Xuanyi*), was published in 2000, including the painting treatises of Paul Cézanne and Pablo Picasso as well as Rodin's conversations and letters, etc.

Deng Xiaomang is a famous Chinese philosopher, aesthetician, critic, and translator who studied German philosophy, aesthetics, cultural psychology, and the comparison between Chinese and Western cultures. He has been actively engaged in academic criticism and cultural critique and has been very influential in academic and intellectual circles. His representative translations include Kant's series of books as well as those of Husserl, Jonathan Brent, etc. His translation of Kant's books won the First Prize of the Fourth Outstanding Achievements in Humanities and Social Sciences of Chinese Universities by the Ministry of Education.

Another famous German philosopher was Georg Wilhelm Friedrich Hegel (1770—1831), one of the leading figures of German idealist philosophy in the 19th century. His ideas, which marked the culmination of German idealist philosophical movement in the 19th century, had a profound influence on later philosophical schools such as existentialism and Marx's historical materialism.

Hegel was an advanced thinker during the revolutionary preparation of the German bourgeoisie against feudalism in the early 19th century and the most outstanding representative of German classical philosophy. His philosophy reflected the great changes in modern Western society, summarized the achievements of the development of natural science and social knowledge at that time, as well as the progress of philosophical thought in Western Europe. Hegelian philosophy established a huge system integrating dialectical idealism, spiritual phenomenology, logic, natural philosophy, and various sub-branches of spiritual philosophy, particularly philosophies of law, history, and religion, aesthetics, history of philosophy, etc. This played an epoch-making role in applying the dialectical method of thinking in many fields. Hegel's dialectic method was one of the direct theoretical sources of Marxist philosophy. Hegel's philosophical thought had a great influence not only on the development of the national spirit in modern Germany but also on the development of philosophy in the world.

Many of Hegel's philosophical works were translated into Chinese such as *The Philosophy of History* (《历史哲学》, *Lishi Zhexue*), *The Science of Logic* (《小逻辑》, *Xiao Luoji*), translated by Yang Yizhi in 1966; *Aesthetics* (《美学》, *Meixue*), translated by Zhu Guangqian in 1979; *The Phenomenology of Spirit* (《精神现象学》, *Jingshen Xianxiangxue*), translated by He Lin (1902—1992) and Wang Jiuxing in 1979; and *Philosophy of Nature* (《自然哲学》, *Ziran Zhexue*), translated by Liang Xuezhi, among others. These works were published by the Commercial Press.

Zhu Guangqian, a native of Anhui province, was a renowned aesthetician, literary theorist, educator, and translator. He was a patriarch of aesthetics in China's modern era after Wang Guowei. He also put "faith" at the forefront of translation, believing that translation should be faithful to the original text as a whole and to its emotions, ideas, style, sound rhythm, etc. Therefore, translation should be creative not only in appearance but also in spirit, using forms that are pleasing to the people of his country to represent the original text faithfully. His first piece of translation was the Italian aesthetician Croce's *Principles of Aesthetics* (《美学的理论》, *Meixue De Lilun*), which pioneered the translation of Western aesthetic works in China. Subsequently, apart from translating Hegel's three-volume *Meixue*, Zhu also translated *Great Dialogues of Plato* (《柏拉图对话录》, *Bolatu Duihua Lu*) in 1959, the German Lessing's masterpiece on aesthetics *Laocoon* (《拉奥孔》, *Laaokong*), St. Thomas Aquinas' *Summa Theologica* (《神学大全》, *Shenxue Daquan*) (the aesthetic part), Italian *The New Science* (《新科学》, *Xin Kexue*), etc. Zhu Guangqian also proofread translations of Marxist classics and dealt with translation issues from philosophical perspectives, making important contributions to the history of Chinese translation. Zhu also carried out a contrastive study between the East and the West and bridged Western aesthetics and traditional Chinese aesthetics, the old idealist aesthetics and Marxist aesthetics, and modern and contemporary Chinese aesthetics through his profound research since the May 4th Movement. His translation is a bridge between ancient and modern Chinese aesthetics and between Chinese and foreign aesthetics. His seven million words of monographs and translations provide not only an in-depth study of Chinese culture but also an introduction to and commentary on Western aesthetic thought. Zhu Guangqian's works gave him a platform in integrating the East and the West, creating his own aesthetic theory, making pioneering contributions to the teaching and research of aesthetics in China, and enjoying an important place in the history of Chinese literature and aesthetics.

He Lin, born in Sichuan Province, was a famous philosopher, historian, educator, and translator in China. He once studied German classical philosophy in Germany and translated a large number of philosophical works, especially G. W. F. Hegel's works in philosophy, such as *The Phenomenology of Spirit*, among others. He also translated other works related to the study of Hegel like Caird Edward's *Hegel* (《黑格尔》, *Heigeer*), Baruch de Spinoza's *Ethics* (《伦理学》, *Lunlixue*), etc. He Lin was the first person to reveal the essence of translation from a philosophical perspective in China. He believed that translation was a kind of communication between the translator and the source text in a philosophical sense, including understanding, interpretation, comprehension, translation, etc. The relationship between the target text and the source text is the relationship between languages and meanings or between the texts and Taoism, which are inseparable. In other words, the target text and the source text are two linguistic forms of the same meaning, which indicate the importance of "meaning" in translation. He Lin affirmed the practical value of translation for the progress of social civilization, spread of culture, and inspiration of creation. He thought that the significance of translation relies on the Sinicization of Western academic study to enrich and develop rather than bury personality.

Francis Bacon (1561—1626) was an English Renaissance essayist and philosopher whose greatest philosophical contribution lay in constituting a series of principles of materialist empiricism and the formulation of systematic inductive logic. Marx and Engels called him "the first founder of British materialism". Bacon's works were translated by Shui Tiantong, He Xin, Xu Baokui, etc. *Essays*(《论说文集》, *Lunshuo Wenji*) which was translated in 1597 and *New Atlantis*(《新亚特兰蒂斯》, *Xin Yatelandisi*) which was translated in 1627, were among those.

Rene Descartes (1596—1650), a famous French philosopher, mathematician and physicist, was a dualist, rationalist and a pioneer of rationalism and modern materialism in Europe. He was one of the founders of modern Western philosophy. Although there are essential differences between Descartes' philosophy and Bacon's philosophy, they shared the same goal, that is, to replace Aristotle's logic that was distorted in the Middle Ages with a way to obtain really desirable knowledge and to replace speculative philosophy with practical philosophy. Descartes' most famous remark is his "I think, therefore I am".

Meditation on First Philosophy(《第一哲学沉思录》, *Diyi Zhexue Chensi Lu*) is one of Descartes' significant philosophical works, which was translated by Pang Jingren in 1986. In this work, Descartes sought to free people's minds and gain certain knowledge through pure reason through the method of universal doubt. *Principles of Philosophy*(《哲学原理》, *Zhexue Yuanli*) is his another important book, which was translated by Guan Wenyun(关文远, 1904—1973) in 1959. Other works by Descartes have been translated and published by many Chinese translators such as Peng Jixiang, Guan Zhenhu, Wang Taiqing, and so on.

Guan Wenyun, also known as Guan Qitong, born in Shanxi Province, was a famous translator of Western philosophy and a private disciple of Hu Shi. After graduation, Guan was engaged in the translation of Western philosophical works including Bacon's *The New Organon* (《新工具》, *Xin Gongju*), and Hume's *A Treatise of Human Nature* (《人性论》, *Renxing Lun*), among others. Guan Wenyun made great contributions in translating the works of Bacon, Kant, Hume, Descartes, and many other Western philosophers. Guan devoted himself to the research and translation of Western classical philosophy and began to translate Kant and Descartes' works in the 1930s. After the founding of the People's Republic of China, he mainly dedicated himself to the translation of works of Western bourgeois classic writers and those of Marx and Engels. Guan was an outstanding translator with profound knowledge and proficiency in many foreign languages. He had dozens of translated works.

Tang Yue (1891—1987), born in Fujian Province, was a famous Chinese psychologist and translator. He was one of the founders of psychology and made great achievements in the same field and philosophy. But his achievements as a translator were not well-known. Though, Tang Yue introduced a lot of famous Western works of psychology and philosophy to China such as John Stuart Mill's *Utilitarianism* (《功利主义》, *Gonglizhuyi*), etc.

John Stuart Mill (1806—1873) was a famous economist, philosopher, and psychologist in the 19th century. He was a great classical liberal thinker and supported Bentham's utilitarianism. Mill's political economic principle, which combined different theories of the previous generations, made him a master of classical economics. He insisted on capitalism but expressed tolerance and sympathy for Utopian socialism. He also criticized some aspects of the capitalist system and advocated the social improvement. His theory was a comprehensive study in the history of Western economics which also marked the end of classical economics. Mill's works include *A System of Logic* (《逻辑体系》, *Luoji Tixi*), *On Liberty* (《论自由》, *Lun Ziyou*), *Essays on Some Unsettled Questions of Political Economy* (《略论政治经济学的某些有待解决的问题》, *Luelun Zhengzhi Jingjixue De Mouxie Youdai Jiejue De Wenti*), *Considerations on Representative Government* (《代议制政府》, *Daiyizhi Zhengfu*), etc.

Zhang Jin (1927—2013), born in Henan Province, was a famous expert and theorist of translation. He once worked as a translator in the Translation Department of Xinhua News Agency. In 1960, he embarked on work in education, translated and revised foreign works in philosophy and social sciences for the Commercial Press, and continued to study the translation theory and contrastive linguistics. Zhang wrote many works on translation theory and also translated some Western books on philosophy. One of his translations is Bernard Bosanquet's *A History of Aesthetic* (《美学史》, *Meixue Shi*). Zhang Jin formulated a set of Marxist principles on literary translation, which were well-illustrated in his book *Wenxue Fanyi Yuanli*(《文学翻译原理》, *The Principles of Literary Translation*) published in 1987. Based on materialist dialectics, he described ten contradictions and corresponding ten problems in literary translation. The ten contradictions are on the translator's world outlook versus the author's, social versus detail reality, artistic versus life reality, the translator's style versus the author's, the artistic content of the translation versus that of the original work, the language form of the target text versus that of the source text, the language form of the target text versus its artistic content, the natural language versus the identity in the target text, the temporal spirit versus the historical significance of translation, and part contradiction versus whole contradiction. Zhang Jin emphasized that both the science and the art of translation must be guided by translation philosophy and that the ideal translation should be the unity of philosophical translation, scientific translation, and artistic translation. Such an emphasis means that translation theory consists of three parts: the philosophy of translation, the science of translation, and the art of translation. In this way, avoiding the long-standing debate on whether translation is an art or a science is possible while emphasizing on the philosophical characteristics of translation theory. Zhang also advanced a new standard of literary translation: faithfulness, goodness, and beauty, which corresponded to Yan Fu's standard of faithfulness, expressiveness, and elegance. Zhang Jin also stressed on the principle of social benefits that the works of literary translation should serve the political, economic, and cultural progresses of China and the world. The methodology of translation should be the dialectical unity of macro and micro studies which can promote and complement, but cannot be replaced by, each other. Macro research refers to the pure theoretical research of translation while micro research pertains to traditional translation theories. Zhang applied dialectical materialism and historical materialism to the analysis of basic problems in literary translation and constructed a unique, independent, and new system of translation theory.

Until now, the most fruitful achievement of the introduction of Western philosophy to China is the revitalization of the study of Chinese philosophy including Buddhism.

9.2.2 Characteristics of the Translation of Philosophical Works

The translation of philosophical works is different from that of literature or other non-literary works. The main stylistic function of philosophical works is to arouse the readers' reflection. Due to the high generality and abstractness of the language of philosophical literature, if the translator pursues faithfulness to the original text, the language of the translated text will be rigid and obscure. This is even more detrimental to the readers' accurate understanding of the original thought. Therefore, the translator should explore the original ideas thoroughly and choose the target language accurately according to the context.

The language of philosophical works is abstract and obscure, the context is complex, and the meanings of words change with the context. What kind of translation can accurately convey the ideas of the original text and make the translation clear and fluent? Translation is not a mechanical copy or an equivalent replacement of the original. Before translating any philosophical classic or thesis, the translator should study the original carefully and thoroughly and consider the context repeatedly in the process of translation. Therefore, the translation of philosophical works is not a simple replacement of words, let alone a mechanical reproduction of the original ideas.

The translating process is a kind of interpretation and creation, which contains the translator's own understanding of the original. On the basis of striving to be faithful to the original ideas, the translator must break the literal translation. The translator can sometimes break the syntactic structure, adjust the word order, add notes, etc. when necessary, so as to make the target language fluent and easy to understand. The translator can also adopt some strategies like nominalization while translating English philosophical works into Chinese. There is often one predicate verb in an English sentence so nouns are often used to express the words with verb meanings. This is to make the sentence structure compact and logical. In addition, philosophical thought should reflect the experience, facts, and laws of the objective world and focus on the reasoning. The use of nouns can ignore the influence of the subject on the meaning of philosophical literature and highlight its objectivity. For example, "Derrida's basic criticism of Heidegger is that the latter maintained a concern for the metaphysics of presence, even as he was attempting to 'destroy' the tradition" (Pressler, 1984)[325–342]. "Criticism" and "concern" are good examples of nominalization, which can be translated as verbs into Chinese. This sentence can be translated as "德里达对海德格尔的基本批评是后者保持了一种理性的态度关注形而上学的存在，即使他试图'摧毁'传统。".

Another feature of translating philosophical works into Chinese is the transformation of passive voice into active voice. Passive voice appears frequently in philosophical literature. The use of passive voice in philosophical literature is not only to highlight the importance of the action receiver but also to make the context more coherent. De-subjectivity is a trend and characteristic of contemporary philosophy. To express ideas objectively and avoid subjective assumptions, the writer often omits the subject of the action and adopts the form of passive sentences, which can highlight the preciseness and objectivity of philosophical ideology. For example, "Special attention is paid to the relationship between Kant and David Hume whose philosophical investigations, according to Kant's famous quote, first interrupted Kant's dogmatic slumber" (Kant et al., 2004). This sentence can be translated as "特别关注康德与休谟之间的关系，根据康德的名言，休谟的哲学研究首先打断了康德的教条睡眠。". The English passive voice is transformed into Chinese active voice and the noun "attention" is translated as a verb.

Long sentences, complex structures, and strong logic are the prominent linguistic features of philosophical works. Parataxis is typical in Chinese language, which is characterized by less conjunctions and determiners, more short sentences, parallel semantic developments and loose structures. English is quite different from Chinese in thinking mode and syntactic structure. English emphasizes hypotaxis, which is symbolized by long sentences. Generally, the main structure is followed by a number of modifying elements, coordinate elements, appositive elements or inserted elements, and a number of clauses. The structure is complex and rigorous with a strong sense of hierarchy. The language of philosophical literature is highly speculative and logical so its syntactic structure also shows clear logic.

Formal words are preferred in English philosophical works due to the rigorous thinking of philosophers who cannot fully express their unique world outlook and meticulous logical thinking only with the daily vocabulary. For example, "While accounts of epistemic supererogation might be worth exploring for all of these spheres of evaluation, in this paper, our focus will be on theories of Rational Supererogation, accounts that take it that doxastic states can be both rationally permissible and rationally better than other permissible alternatives" (Siscoe, 2022). This is a long sentence with subordinate sentences and appositive and modifying elements, which make the sentence rather formal and logical. Besides, there are also many philosophical terms such as "epistemic", "supererogation", "doxastic", and so on. Since ancient Greece, philosophers have used language to express their thinking about the world. Philosophers' different ideological systems have formed many schools and each school has derived a large number of proper names, terms and the like. When translating these proper names and terms, translators should check more authoritative information to avoid mistranslation. For example, "With these two features in mind, I have elsewhere characterized veritism as epistemic value truth monism" (Pritchard, 2021). "Veritism", "epistemic", and "monism" are all philosophical terms that deserve the translator's careful consideration.

9.3 Chinese Translation of Western Classic Works in Law

As one of the most influential modern thinkers and translators in China, Yan Fu differentiated Chinese "*fa*" from Western "law" in his translation of Montesquieu's *De l'esprit des lois*(《论法的精神》, *Lun Fa De Jingshen*). *Fa*(法) refers to human-made laws, namely, the prohibitions and decrees, while "law" in Western languages can be interpreted as order, rite, rule or *Li*(理), human-made law or *Fa*, and control or *Zhi*(治). Examples of similar difficulties abound in the translation of basic legal concepts across different nations.

Legal translation refers to the translation of texts used in law and legal settings (Cao, 2007). Legal translation can be classified into different categories: 1) legislative texts, such as domestic statutes and subordinate laws, international treaties, and other authorized laws; 2) judicial texts produced in the judicial process; 3) legal scholarly texts produced by academic lawyers or legal scholars; 4) private legal texts, such as contracts, leases, wills, private agreements, witness statements, and other documents used in litigations and legal situations.

9.3.1 The Historical Development of Legal Translation in China

The demand for legal translation is on the rise around the world and the translation of law has an increasingly significant role in the modern globalized world. Legal translation has been developing quickly with the continuous improvement of the legal system in China. The historical development of legal translation in China can be mainly divided into five stages.

The first stage of the translation of law was initiated by Lin Zexu during the Opium Wars. He advocated for and organized the translation of *Law of Nations*(《各国律例》, *Geguo Lüli*) with about two thousand words. As the first legal work in modern China, it plays an important role in promoting the development of modern Chinese law. Legal translation in this period included international laws and laws from different countries, which influenced the emergence of modern Chinese law and jurisprudence. Then, a number of works of legal translation were accomplished in China such as Liang Ting's *Four Descriptions on Foreign Countries*(《海国四说》, *Haiguo Si Shuo*), Wei Yuan's *Geography of the Maritime Nations*(《海国图志》, *Haiguo Tuzhi*), etc. which have laid the foundation for later development of China's legal translation.

The second stage was the development of legal translation during the Westernization Movement(洋务运动). Due to increasing exchanges with foreigners, there was an urgent need for the Qing imperial government to train translators who were fluent in foreign languages. The rise of the Foreign Affairs Movement meant a boom in legal translation. Activities of legal translation were further strengthened by the establishment of some institutes like School of Combined Learning(京师同文馆), Jiangnan Arsenal, Foochow Shipbuilding Institution(福建船政学堂), etc. Many translations of legal documents were introduced to China, as discussed in previous sections. One of the most known representative works in this period was Ding Weiliang's translation of *Elements of International Law: With a Sketch of the History of the Science* written by Henry Wheaton (1785—1848), an American international jurist and diplomat. This was the first complete translation of international law in China and the first official translation of "public law" in the late Qing Dynasty. By the 1880s, this translated work had become an essential book for local officials at China's ports of commerce and those involved in foreign affairs. The introduction of such legal translations made those who were ignorant of public law at that time realize that the Qing Dynasty was by no means the center of the world and that they should learn from the Western legal system.

William A. P. Martin, an American Presbyterian missionary, was fluent in Chinese and had an important role in introducing Western legal works into China. He translated a lot of works of international law into Chinese such as *Elements of International Law*(《万国公法》, *Wanguo Gongfa*), *Achieve Mastery On International Law*(《公法会通》, *Gongfa Huitong*), *Introduction to the Study of International Law*(《公法便览》, *Gongfa*

Chapter 9   Chinese Translation of Western Non-literary Classic Works

Bianlan). He was a leading "China expert" among foreigners in China during the late Qing Dynasty but also a controversial historical figure. He favored overthrowing Qing Dynasty and deposing Empress Dowager Ci Xi.

John Fryer(傅兰雅) was another important translator in this period who translated *International Law*(《公法总论》, *Gongfa Zonglun*), *Commentaries upon International Law* (《各国交涉公法论》, *Geguo Jiaoshe Gongfa Lun*), etc. With the same enthusiasm and dedication as missionaries, he introduced and publicized Western legal and scientific knowledge to the Chinese public and was even called "the priest of preaching science" by missionaries. He hoped that China could prosper through the introduction of Western knowledge in the historical process of importing modern Western scientific and technological knowledge into China. He translated 129 Western books singly or jointly with others, which was the largest number of Western books translated by a foreigner in China.

The third stage was the flourishing period of legal translation. After the Sino-Japanese War and the signing of *Treaty of Shimonoseki*(《马关条约》, *Maguan Tiaoyue*), the political situation in China underwent a great upheaval. The Qing imperial government reflected on and criticized the Foreign Affairs Movement and pressed for reforms and changes in the legal system. Hence, the number of legal translations increased significantly from public law to constitutional and commercial law. The quality of translations was greatly enhanced by the establishment of translation institutes.

Some Western classic works of law were translated into Chinese. For example, Lei Peihong(雷沛鸿) translated *Introduction to Study of Law*(《法学肄言》, *Faxue Yiyan*) written by Pang En(滂恩) from America. Shi Xianmin(施宪民) and Shi Huimin(施惠民) translated *Philosophy of Law*(《法律哲学》, *Falü Zhexue*) written by Roland R. Foulke. Besides, numerous Japanese legal written resources were also translated into Chinese. For example, He Jianmin(何健民) translated *Introduction to the History of Legal Thought*(《法律思想史概说》, *Falü Sixiangshi Gaishuo*) written by Xiaoye Qingyilang(小野清一郎, Seiichiro Ono). Oriental Law Society(东方法学会) translated *An Overview of Civil Law*(《民法要览》, *Minfa Yaolan*) in 1919. *Faxue Tonglun*(《法学通论》) was translated by Gangtian Chaotailang(冈田朝太郎, Asataro Okada). Chen Shixia(陈时夏) translated *On Japanese Criminal Procedure Law*(《日本刑事诉讼法论》, *Riben Xingshi Susongfa Lun*) written by Songshi Zhiyuan(松室致原) in 1913. *Essentials of Japanese Civil Law*(《日本民法要义》, *Riben Minfa Yaoyi*) written by Meiqian Cilang(梅谦次郎) was translated by Meng Sen(孟森), Chen Chengze(陈承泽), Chen Shixia, et al. Later in the 1930s, Hu Changqing(胡长清) translated *Japanese Criminal Law Amendment*(《日本刑法改正案》, *Riben Xingfa Gaizhengan*) written by Gangtian Chaotailang. Ouyang Xi(欧阳溪) translated *Outline of Jurisprudence*(《法理学大纲》, *Falixue Dagang*) written by Hozumi Shigeto(穗积重远, *Suijizhongyuan*).

The fourth stage was a new era of legal translation. In the early years of the founding of P. R. China, the Soviet Union had been a role model for Chinese politics, economy, culture, and law. For example, Yun Bai(允白) translated *Fascist Geopolitics and American Imperialism*(《法西斯地缘政治学与美帝国主义》, *Faxisi Diyuan Zhengzhixue Yu Mei Diguozhuy*) written by Xieming Nuofu(谢明诺夫, А. И. Семёнов) from the Soviet Union in 1950. In 1956, Kang Baotian(康宝田) translated *Limitation of Legal Actions*(《法律行为诉讼时效》, *Falü Xingwei Susong Shixiao*) written by Nuoweiciji(诺维茨基, Nowitzki) from the Soviet Union. There are still Western works of law that have been translated into Chinese. For example, Qian Kexin translated *On Constitution*(《宪法论》, *Xianfa Lun*) written by L. Duguit from France in 1959.

The fifth stage was the translation of law in contemporary China. Huang Liangping(黄良平) and Ding Wenqi(丁文琪) translated *General Theory of Law*(《法的一般理论》, *Fa De Yiban Lilun*) written by C. C. Aleksyev(C. C. 阿列克谢耶夫) from 1988 to 1991. Zhang Qitai(张企泰) translated *The Institutes of Justinian*(《法学总论:法学阶梯》, *Faxue Zonglun Faxue Jieti*) written by Justinian from Rome in 1989. Tang Yue and Su Li(苏力) translated *The Behavior of Law*(《法律的运作行为》, *Falü De Yunzuo Xingwei*) written by Donald J. Black from America in 1994. Su Li also translated *The Problems Of Jurisprudence*(《法理学问题》, *Falixue Wenti*) written by Richard A. Posner from America in 1994. Shen Zongling(沈宗灵) translated Hans Kelsen's *General Theory of Law and State*(《法与国家的一般理论》, *Fa Yu Guojia De Yiban Lilun*) in 1996. Zhang Wenxian(张文显) translated *Concept of Law*(《法律的概念》, *Falü De Gainian*) written by Herbert Lionel Adolphus Hart in 1996.

Not only have Chinese translations of foreign legal works been successful, but also foreign translations of Chinese law have been fruitful. There are countless studies on legal translation. A complete set of legal translation theories and unique practical methods has been basically formulated. At the same time, translation methods have also evolved, from the primitive paper-and-pencil translation to the current computer-assisted translation. This reality brings ever-improving skills and new challenges to the cause of legal translation.

9.3.2 Prerequisites of a Successful Translator of Legal Documents

Some of the most challenging difficulties in legal translation that were confronted by legal translators include the diverse range of linguistic differences, cultural differences, and the like. There are many lexical or terminological features and problems in legal translation causing both linguistic and legal complications. Many legal words in one language do not have ready equivalents in another.

A translator of legal texts must have a good command of linguistic skills and a basic understanding of law. There are three prerequisites for a successful translator of legal documents: he or she must acquire a basic knowledge of the legal systems of both the source language and the target language, be familiar with the relevant terminology, and be competent in the specific legal writing style.

Cao (1996) believes that a good legal translator should possess the proficiency of translational language competence, translational knowledge structures, and translational strategic competence. Translational language competence includes organizational competence and pragmatic competence in the source language and target language. The first consists of grammatical and textual competence while the second covers illocutionary and sociolinguistic competence. Translational knowledge structures include general, specialist, and literary knowledge. General knowledge refers to knowledge about the world including social, cultural, and other areas of knowledge. Specialist knowledge contains technical knowledge in fields such as law, economics, philosophy, politics, science, technology, and so on. Legal knowledge is about propositions of law in a narrow sense and the knowledge of legal culture in a broad sense, including legal systems, legal order, legal institutions, history, and practices and practitioners, etc. (Salmi-Tolonen, 2003). Translational strategic competence embraces the strategic competence that is general to all mental activities, the skills that are demanded during the processing and non-verbal stage of reformulation and the analogy by reasoning, and the psychological mechanisms related to the cognitive and creative aspects of human thought processes.

9.4 Chinese Translation of Other Western Non-literary Classic Works

Apart from the non-literary works discussed above, there are still a lot of other types of non-literary works that remain to be investigated such as those in medical science, physics, mathematics, news reports, business documents, advertising slogans, publicity materials, public signs, enterprise rules and regulations, movie and TV texts, and so on.

9.4.1 Chinese Translators of Other Western Non-literary Classic Works

During the Westernization Movement, John Fryer, an Englishman, interpreted 113 kinds of scientific works. With the great enthusiasm and dedication as a missionary, he introduced and publicized scientific and technological knowledge to the Chinese people. He dedicated his best years to China. He hoped that China could prosper in the historical process of importing modern Western scientific and technological knowledge into China. No foreigner and even few Chinese did more than him at that time. His translations covered a wide range of disciplines including *Acoustics*(《声学》, *Shengxue*), *Illustration of Optics*(《光学图说》, *Guangxue Tushuo*), *Illustration of Hydrology*(《水学图说》, *Shuixue Tushuo*), *Illustration of Thermology*(《热学图说》, *Rexue Tushuo*), *Mine Engineering*(《井矿工程》, *Jingkuang Gongcheng*), *A Guide to Silver Ores*(《银矿指南》, *Yinkuang Zhinan*), etc.

A lot of translators have also made great contributions to the development of Chinese medical science. Yin Duanmo(尹端模) translated *Brief Introduction of Western Medicine*(《西医略论》, *Xiyi Luelun*), *New Theory of Internal Medicine*(《内科新说》, *Neike Xinshuo*), etc. John Glasgow Kerr(嘉约翰) translated *Confucian medicine*(《儒门医学》, *Rumen Yixue*), *On Inflammation*(《炎症论略》, *Yanzheng Lunlue*), etc.

9.4.2 Characteristics of the Translation of Western Non-literary Classic Works

There are some basic requirements for the translation of non-literary works. Firstly, the strategies of translation can be determined according to the information provided by the client. The translator should know the purpose of translation and the readers of the original text, as well as the time, place, occasion, function, so as to determine the strategies of translation. Secondly, the translator should accurately reproduce the objective reality reflected or intended to be reflected in the original text. The following are some guidelines: the translation should be as coherent as the source text; there should be no contradiction in the figures, reasoning, etc.; the language should be accurate to ensure that the meaning is clear without any ambiguity; errors should be corrected if any; any addition or deletion to the original text should not damage the accuracy of the basic information of the original text; and the accuracy of the meaning should be ensured by repeated proofreading. Thirdly, the accuracy of information always comes first. The sentence should conform to the grammatical norms of the target language with common collocations and novel expressions are not suggested. Be simple and clear, avoid wordiness, and never beat around the bush. Fourthly, the language of translation should be standardized and written in plain language. Rhetorical devices such as metaphor, personification, and exaggeration usually need to be translated into basic meanings and boastful texts often need to be rewritten. However, when translating slogans of advertisements, the translator needs to consider both the transmission of information and the aesthetic effects due to the importance of aesthetic functions.

The translator can adopt different strategies to translate non-literary works especially when there are no equivalent expressions in the target language. Firstly, some expressions can be replaced by their superordinates or hyponyms. For example, "楼堂馆所" can be translated as the superordinate "buildings". Secondly, some cultural expressions of the source text can be replaced with those of the target text. For example, "your company" can be translated as "贵公司". Thirdly, neutral words can be used to replace a wide range of similar expressions. For example, such words as "claim" "assert" "argue" can be translated as "认为". Fourthly, transliteration can be used and explanations or notes can be further provided if necessary. Fifthly, perspectives can be shifted and the word order can be adjusted sometimes to facilitate communications. For example, "In his 1776 work, *The Wealth of Nations*, Scottish economist Adam Smith proposed that specialization in production leads to increased output"(苏格兰经济学家亚当·斯密在其1776年所著的《国富论》中认为,专业化生产会引起产出增加。). The terms "specialization in production" is translated as "专业化生产" rather than "生产的专业化" and "increased output" is translated as "产出增加" rather than "增加的产出". Lastly, there are still a lot of other strategies that the translator can adopt in the process of translation such as omission, addition, etc., which can be applied flexibly in the process of non-literary translation.

Most of the common strategies of translation can be applied to the translation of non-literary works, such as literal translation, free translation, amplification, ellipsis, adaptation, substitution, etc. However, different types of non-literary works have different characteristics of translation.

Rhetorical devices such as metaphor, pun, euphemism, etc. are often used in advertisements, news reports, and the like. These devices can be retained if the images and connotations of the ST can be transformed into Chinese in the process of translation to strengthen the expressiveness and aesthetic appeal of the original text. Chinese four-character structure is also suggested sometimes in the process of translation to make the translation fluent.

Many theories such as Halliday's theory of functional stylistics can be of great significance to the translation of public signs. The stylistic function of a text determines the linguistic form of it. The translation that highlights the stylistic function is a good translation. Therefore, the translator should study the original text to fully understand the stylistic function, the communicative purpose, and the prominent stylistic features of it. The translator should be well aware of the cultural differences between the two languages and create a concise and accurate translation of public signs.

There are some similarities between the Chinese and English public signs because the function of social publicity is the common feature of all public signs. The most common features of Chinese and English public signs are to use simple words and make sentences concise, clear, accurate, and easy to understand. Nouns and verbs are frequently used such as "underground"(地铁), "airport"(机场), "mind the step"(小心台阶), and so on. Another is the use of words with a strong affirmative and serious tone such as "No parking"(禁止停车), "No littering"(禁丢垃圾), and so on, to show the function of warning. The basic rule for the translation of public signs is characterized by conciseness, comprehensibility, consistency, etc.

There are still a lot of other translation strategies of non-literary works that remain to be further explored.

Questions for discussion:

1. Could you give a brief account of the four stages of translation of *The Analects of Confucius* in the West?

2. What do you think of the influence of *Tao Te Ching* and *Chuangtse* in the Western countries? Why?

3. Which foreign version of the Four Masterpieces impresses you most? Why?

4. What do you think of the influence of Chinese classical poems on American Imagist poetry?

References:

Aristotle, 1912. Politics: A Treatise on Government[M]. Trans. William Ellis. London & Toronto: J. M. Dent & Sons Ltd.

Cao D, 1996. Towards a model of translation proficiency[J]. Target, 8(2): 325 – 340.

Cao D, 2007. Translating law[M]. Clevedon: Multilingual Matters.

Kant I, 2004. Prolegomena to any future metaphysics[M]. Cambridge: Cambridge University Press.

Pressler C A, 1984. Redoubled: The bridging of Derrida and Heidegger[J]. Human Studies, 7(1): 325 – 342.

Pritchard D, 2021. Veritism and the goal of inquiry[J]. Philosophia, 49(4): 1347 – 1359.

Pym, Anthony, 2007. "Philosophy and Translation", in A Companion to Translation Studies, Piotr Kuhiwczak and Karin Littau (eds), New York: Multilingual Matters Ltd.

Salmi-Tolonen T, 2003. Legal linguistic knowledge and creating and interpreting law in multilingual environments[J]. Brooklyn Journal of International Law, 29: 7.

Siscoe R W, 2022. Rational supererogation and epistemic permissivism[J]. Philosophical Studies, 179(2): 571 – 591.

Chapter 10

The Influence of Translation on Chinese Culture

The questions that are generally accepted as relevant and important enough to be asked in the field of translation studies are very different now from what they were fifty years ago, one of which is the concern about the relation between translation and culture. As what Bassnett and Lefevere argued in *Constructing Cultures: Essays on Literary Translation* (1998), the study of translation is the study of cultural interaction, thus appealing to a "cultural turn" in translation studies. Since the period of the Three Kingdoms (220—280), the translation of Buddhist scriptures and religious documents by foreign missionaries has influenced religions in China, which is also one of the important parts of Chinese culture. In this chapter, we will mainly discuss the influence of translation on Chinese culture from the aspects of language, literature etc. with scholars and students who are interested in the dynamics of translation and Chinese culture.

10.1 Buddhist Translation's Influence on Modern Chinese Literature and Language

Confucianism, Taoism, and Buddhism are the three major philosophical systems of Chinese popular culture. The first two belief systems are native to Chinese culture while Buddhism is from Indian religion. Despite their contradictions, convergence has become the norm in the growth of Chinese cultural thought. As a result, Chinese society has evolved into a structure by combining the three philosophies into one, with Confucianism at the core while Taoism and Buddhism supporting it. Buddhism has permeated into all levels of Chinese society for over 2,000 years, including literature, philosophy, justice, the arts, architecture, and faiths. Thus, Buddhism has been one of the three foundations of orthodox Chinese culture.

Various factors, such as historical, social, and other reasons, may have led to the inclusion of Buddhism into Chinese culture in the process of 2,000 years of contact and communication. The first and most important explanation is that both Confucianism and Buddhism have a liberal mindset. For a culture or thinking to fit into another, both domains must be liberal and tolerant, particularly the receiving one. The following quote from Confucius' *The Analects of Confucius* or *Lunyu* exemplifies Confucianism's open-minded approach: "The gentleman harmonizes (*he*, 和), not simply agrees (*tong*, 同). While the petty individual agrees, he does not harmonize".

The significance of this proverb lies in its message of tolerance and harmony, which is embodied in thought and community. Chinese people esteem peace and unity because of these concepts and thoughts. As Confucius said, "When it comes to the practice of ritual, it is harmonious ease (*he*, 和) that is to be cherished". As also written in *The Doctrine of the Mean* (Hall et al., 1987), "This notion of balance and concentration (*zhong*, 中) is the great source of the universe. Then, unity is the advancement of the proper way (*dadao*, 达道) of the world". Such a liberal and inclusive mentality enables the Chinese people to absorb desirable ideas and customs from other cultures. "Whenever I walk with two other people, I will find a teacher among them", Confucius said. "I want to imitate those that are good and I try to remember what needs to be improved about myself by focusing on those that are evil". "With respect to the rest of the country, the gentleman has no prejudices towards or against others. He only identifies with those he believes to be moral". For over 2,000 years, these theories and thoughts have influenced Chinese people. Buddhism, on the other hand, and its liberality embrace anything fine, as mentioned in the *Anguttaranikaya*'s(《增支部》) *Uttaravipatti Sutta*(《巴利经》). When Sakka(菩萨) asked bhikkhu(比丘) Uttara if his words came from the Buddha, Uttara replied, "Whatever is well said, all that is the Buddha's word." This saying is also found in Kumarajiva's translation of the *Satyasiddhi Sastra* (《成实论》) and the *Mahaprajnaparamita Sastra*(《般若经》), both of them are in Chinese. Because of this mentality, the Buddha urged his lay followers to make sacrifices to local gods who were an integral part of the faith. This way of thinking has had a huge impact on Buddhists and significant ramifications in the spread of Buddhism to other communities. As a result, Buddhism has incorporated into local traditions everywhere it has been spread, rather than causing tensions with them. In China's case, Buddhism becomes Chinese Buddhism with Chinese cultural marks and colors. This is so as Buddhism has embraced many Chinese cultural elements for over 2 millennia.

The second explanation is that Confucianism, Taoism, and Buddhism are Chinese philosophies that have no concept of divine revelation and have no such a notion characterizing open-mindedness. As French sinologist Vincent Goossaert (高万桑, 1969—) wrote in *The Religious Questions in Modern China*(《近代中国的宗教问题》), "they are sects that do not strictly assert reality".

Confucianism, Buddhism, and Taoism within Chinese religion do not function as separate institutions that provide their members with an exclusive way to salvation, as Western concept of religion in the nineteenth-century; rather, the purpose is to transmit traditions of practice and make them available to all, either as individual spiritual techniques or liturgical services to whole communities.

As a result, the three religions' mutual inclusiveness provides the intellectual basis for Buddhism's integration in Chinese culture and thought. From the 4th century onwards, Chinese thinkers like Sun Chuo(孙绰, 314—371) promoted the concept of syncretism among these three belief systems, claiming that the sages Zhou(周公) and Confucius were like the Buddha and the Buddha was like the sages Zhou and Confucius. Buddhism had completely developed in Chinese culture by the 10th century as a result of the efforts of successive Chinese Buddhists and scholars. The three religions complement one another in the holistic cultivation of the person. Buddhism is for the development of the soul, Taoism is for the cultivation of the physical body, and Confucianism is for the governance of the society, according to Chinese scholars of Song Dynasty. Consequently, the three faiths have played significant roles in Chinese culture and society.

The sutras are the guiding principles for Buddhist disciples to practice according to the law. The sutras are the Buddha's understanding of the universe. The universe refers to time and space. The contents covered by the sutras are very complicated and beyond the proficiency of ordinary people. The translators of the sutras are not only translators, but also thinkers, philosophers, educators, Buddhist scholars, and literary scholars. They have the important task of translating the sutras into Chinese. The translation of Buddhist scriptures is very significant in the history of Chinese translation as Kumarajiva. Paramartha, Xuan Zang, and Bukong are known as the "Four Great Masters of Translation". The following is mainly about the influence of Buddhist translation on modern Chinese literature and language.

Chapter 10 The Influence of Translation on Chinese Culture

10.1.1 Buddhist Translation's Influence on Modern Chinese Literature

When Buddhism was introduced to China, many single disciples began to translate the Buddhist scriptures. With such translations, more and more scholars understood the teachings and gradually started to do some researches. Many literary scholars at that time found the Chinese translations of Buddhist scriptures very ethereal and, from then on, Buddhist character biographies gradually became prevalent. All these biographies described the characters' deeds. Although Buddhist culture had been introduced to China for a relatively short time, the literary structure of Buddhist culture, the method of shaping characters' images, and the innovative way of conceptualizing images fully reflected the greatness and richness of Buddhist culture. These attributes greatly helped in exceeding the works on character biographies in that period. It allowed literary creation to excel in the history of ancient China. Buddhism not only had a great influence on the biographies of people in ancient Chinese literature, but also influenced the creation of classical poetry, making it useful for poets. Buddhist culture gradually penetrated into everyone's heart as it spread and developed. It was significant for Buddhist culture to spread its core principles so the world could gradually accepted it and many literati were convinced of its ideas. Poets had an important role in promoting the development of Buddhism as this philosophy inspired them. Ancient Chinese literature and Buddhist culture have been passed on continuously.

Liang Qichao(梁启超, 1873—1929) was the first person in China to speak of the value of Buddhist literature. He defined Buddhist literature rather broadly, believing that all literary works with Buddhist overtones could be called "Buddhist literature". In the chapter "Translated Literature and the Buddhist Canon" of his work *Collection of Buddhist Studies in the Drinking Ice Room*(《饮冰室合集》), he especially emphasized that "the pure literature of our modern times, such as novels and songs, are closely related to the translated literature of the Buddhist canon". For instance, the novel *The Book of the Searching God*(《搜神记》) is very much connected with certain books such as *The Treatise on the Great Sovereign Sutra*(《法苑珠林》). As for *The Water Margin* and *The Dream of Red Mansion*, the style and writing are also deeply influenced by *Avatamsaka Sutra*(《华严经》) and *Nirvana Sutra*(《涅槃经》). Other plays, legends, and long poems since the Song(960—1279), Yuan(1271—1368), and Ming Dynasties(1368—1644) are indirectly affected by the Chinese translation of Buddhist scriptures.

According to Liang, there is a subtle relationship between modern Chinese literature and the Mahayana classics. In brief, there are three influences: first, the expansion of the substance of Chinese language; second, changes in grammar and style; and third, the development of literary interests. The long narrative poems such as *The Southeast Flight of the Peacock*(《孔雀东南飞》) and *Mulan*(《花木兰》) were influenced by the Buddhist classics, which were all very magnificent in their interpretation of moral education. Such dynamics enhanced the Chinese imagination and revolutionized the Chinese writing style. These impacted on short stories and chapter novels after the Song and Yuan Dynasties.

The representative figure who studied the relationship between Buddhism and Chinese literature after Liang Qichao was Hu Shi (胡适, 1891—1962). In his *History of Vernacular Literature*(《白话文学史》), Hu devoted two chapters to Buddhist literature in translation. According to him, the Buddhist scriptures opened up endless new contexts, created many new literary styles, and added countless new materials to the history of Chinese literature. In his view, the importation of Buddhism had three major impacts on Chinese literature. First, the Buddhist masters translated the sutras in a comparatively simple and easy vernacular style, which was easier for Chinese people to understand as it was not embellished. This resulted in the change to a vernacular style of writing. Second, Buddhist literature was the most imaginative and had a great liberating effect on Chinese literature, which lacked imagination. Chinese romantic works such as the novel *The Journey to the West* and the like were products influenced by Indian literary. And third, Indian literature focused on the layout and structure of forms and the importation of Buddhist scriptures contributed directly and indirectly to the emergence and development of new words, novels, and plays. Moreover, the prose of Buddhist scriptures was molded in Madhyamaka(中观哲学) style, which also had an influence on or a relationship with the later literary genres in China.

After Liang Qichao and Hu Shi, Chinese scholars further studied and interpreted the relationship between Buddhist sutras and Chinese literature. Such scholars were Qian Zhongshu(钱钟书, 1910—1998), Chen Yinke(陈寅恪, 1890—1969), Zheng Zhenduo (郑振铎, 1898—1958), Ji Xianlin(季羡林, 1911—2009), Tang Yijie(汤一介, 1927—2014), Jin Kemu(金克木, 1912—2000), Rao Zongyi(饶宗颐, 1917—2018), and Zhou Shaoliang(周绍良, 1917—2005), among others. Among the works on

Buddhist scriptures and Chinese literature in the last fifty years, one of the most representative ones was *A Study of the Relationship between Chinese and Indian Literature* (《中印文学关系研究》) by Pei Puxian(裴普贤). It was published by Commercial Press, Taipei in 1968. This work was followed by two books, *Buddhism and Chinese Literature*(《佛教与中国文学》) and *Buddhism and Chinese Culture*(《佛教与中国文化》), which were edited by Zhang Mantao(张曼涛) and published by Mahayana Press, Taipei in 1978. Seven years later, the mainland scholar Sun Changwu's (孙昌武) *Literature and Buddhism in Tang Dynasty*(《唐代文学与佛教》) was published by Shaanxi People's Publishing House. Zhang Xikun's(张锡坤) *Buddhism and Oriental Art* (《佛教与东方艺术》), published by Jilin Education Press in 1988, deals with the connection between Buddhism and Chinese literature. In the same year, Sun Changwu's *Buddhism and Chinese Literature* was published by Shanghai People's Publishing House, providing a historical account of how Buddhist beliefs and thoughts acted on the literary creations of Chinese literati. There are four aspects: Chinese translations of Buddhist scriptures and their literary value, Buddhism and Chinese literati, Buddhism and Chinese literary creations, and Buddhism and Chinese literary thought. Since then, several monographs on Buddhism and Chinese literature have been published like *The Translation of Buddhist Scriptures and Literary Thought in the Middle Ages*(《佛经传译与中古文学思潮》) by Jiang Shuzhuo(蒋述卓). It was published by Jiangxi People's Publishing House in 1990. This book examines the relationship between Buddhist scripture translation and medieval literary trends from the perspective of the process of Buddhist scripture translation. The work explores the impact of Buddhist scripture translation on the transmutation of medieval literary trends, placing the relationship between the two in the cultural context of the medieval period while providing a solid examination and analysis of some details. In 1993, the Tianjin People's Publishing House published Chen Hong's *Buddhism and Classical Chinese Literature*, a book that describes the influence of Buddhism, mainly from a historical perspective, in four literary genres: poetry, prose, fiction, and drama. The descriptions in these genres are not systematic narratives on the evolution of the sources but rather selections of themes in each genre. In 2001, Wang Li (王立) published the book *Religious Folklore Literature and the Novel Materia*(《宗教民俗文献与小说母题》) and, on the basis of this work, he completed the *Study of Buddhist Sutra Literature and the Ancient Novel Materia*(《佛经文学与古代小说母题比较研

究》). The latter was published by Kunlun Press in 2006. Starting from the Chinese translation of sutra literature, Indian folk tales, and Pali stories of Buddha's life, twenty-one materials and genres were identified in ancient Chinese novels, historical biographies, and wild history notes to correspond to sutra literature. These constitute specific clues of the influence of Indian sutra literature on Chinese narrative literature with the novel as the core. This is specifically divided into the editions on ambient martial arts and illusions, gender and love, animals and human-animal relations, and medical arts and other mystical cults. Hou Chuanwen's (侯传文) *The Literary Interpretation of Buddhist Sutras* (《佛经的文学性解读》), published by China Book Bureau in 2004, is divided into two chapters. The first one focuses on the literary interpretation of some famous Buddhist sutras, analyzing their literary significances and status in the history of literature. The second part revolves around certain literary phenomena in Buddhist scriptures, revealing their literary significances and research value. Yu Xiaohong's (俞晓红) *Study of Buddhism and the Vernacular Novels of the Tang and Five Dynasties* (《佛教与唐五代白话小说研究》) was published by People's Publishing House. This book discusses the relationship between Buddhism and the early Chinese vernacular novels preserved in the Tibetan Scriptures of Mogao Grottoes in Dunhuang, starting from the great influence of Buddhism on Chinese culture. On the basis of a specific examination of the translation of "scriptures", "sutras" and "popular sermons", Yu's work elaborates the formation of these early Chinese vernacular novels and examines the formal system, subject matter, spiritual imagery, and historical significance of the novels. Sun Hongliang's (孙鸿亮) *Narrative Literature of Buddhist Scriptures and the Novels of Tang Dynasty* (《佛经叙事文学与唐代小说研究》), published by the People's Publishing House in 2008, describes the literary properties and value of Buddhist scriptures in the introductory part, gives a concise discussion of the categories and distributions of narrative literature of Buddhist scriptures in the first chapter, studies the dissemination channels of Buddhist scriptures in the second chapter, reveals the influence of Buddhist scriptures on the conceptual and thematic aspects of the novels of Tang Dynasty in the third chapter, and turns to the study of narrative forms in the fourth chapter. Other influential works on Buddhism and Chinese literature are Wu Haiyong's (吴海勇) *A Study of the Narrative Literature of the Buddhist Scriptures Translated into Chinese in the Middle Ages* (《中古汉译佛经叙事文学研究》), Chen Yunji's (陈允吉) *An Essay on Buddhist Tracing in Classical Chinese Literature* (《佛

教中国文学溯论稿》), Pu Hui's(普慧) *Buddhist Literature of the Southern Dynasties* (《南朝佛教与文学》), Ge Xiaoyin's(葛晓音) *Literature and Religion of the Six Dynasties of the Han and Wei Dynasties*(《汉魏六朝文学与宗教》), Ge Zhaoguang's(葛兆光) *Zen Buddhism and Chinese Literature*(《中国宗教与文学论集》), and Gong Xian's(龚贤) *The Buddhist Canon and the Literature of the Southern Dynasties*(《佛典与南朝文学》). Some of the more unique papers in this area in recent years include Xu Jun's *A Study of Pre-Tang Poetry at Dunhuang*, Wang Xiaodun's *A Study of the Art of Vimalakirti at Dunhuang*, He Jianping's *The Golden Corn as Rice in Vimalakirti Literature at Dunhuang*, Quan Yinchu's *A Preliminary Exploration of the Variant Script Novel of Tang Dynasty*, and Wang Zhipeng's *The Art of Creating Traditional Chinese Spoken Language Literature from the Use of Sets of Words in Variant Texts*, which all interpret the relation between Buddhism and Chinese literature from different perspectives.

Buddhism has had a great influence on Chinese literature, especially on popular literature. After the Wei and Jin Dynasties(220—420), Buddhism became closer to the life of the general public. Therefore, all genres of popular literature after the Wei and Jin Dynasties were more or less influenced by Buddhism. In this regard, many scholars have made in-depth discussions, which can be summarized into two aspects: one is the Buddhist literature itself, the so-called "variant literature"; and the other refers to other works of Buddhism-influenced popular literature. The alternate form of storytelling in the form of speech and song provided a genre reference for Chinese popular literature. Many works of popular literature were written in this genre after the Tang and Song Dynasties. The Tang legendary novels were also influenced by the Variant, such as Zhang Zhuo's(张鷟, 660—740) *The Cave of the Traveling Immortals*(《游仙窟》) which was written in alternating prose and rhyme. The Song Dynasty's vernacular novels like the fiction *Popular Stories from Capital Editions*(《京本通俗小说》) and *Qingpingshantang Vernacular Novel* (《清平山堂话本》) and the Ming Dynasty's simulated vernacular novels such as *SanYan* (《三言》) and *ErPai*(《二拍》), short stories generally begining with poems or introducing stories and ending with poems. Ideas to be commented on are often corroborated by references to poetry or ekphrasis, a literary style that is clearly derived from variant texts. Much of the content of Chinese fiction works is somewhat related to Buddhism. In his *Buddhism and Chinese Literature*(《佛教与中国文学》), Zhang Zhongxing(张中行) talks about "the contents of the stories of works, regardless of the genre in which they are expressed, often mention monks, monasteries, cultivation, magical powers, bodhisattvas, luohan, and even yama, hell, ghosts, retribution, etc. Such themes are clearly influenced by Buddhism". In other words, Chinese popular literature has a lot of Buddhist elements in it, even if the story is not Buddhist. For example, the contents of novels such as *The Journey to the West*, *Feng Shen Yan Yi*(《封神演义》), *The Legend of the White Snake*(《白蛇传》), *The Dream of Red Mansion*, and *The Water Margin* are all directly or indirectly related to Buddhism. Among the classical novels, the representative work directly sourced from Buddhist themes is *The Journey to the West*, and the representative work indirectly sourced from Buddhism is the story *Yangxian Goose Cage*(《阳羡书生》). In addition, other scholars have pointed out that Buddhism brought with it the concept of three lives (past life, present life, and future life) and the concepts of cause and effect and reincarnation, as well as the concepts of the three realms and the five paths. These expanded thoughts on time and space and, thus, further broadened the Chinese imagination. Although Chinese translated works were not lacking in imagination, the traditional Chinese thought only had the concept of "this" life. But after Buddhism was introduced to China, people began to think about past life and after life, which made the world of imagination richer and the content of literary works more enriched. The *You Ming Lu*(《幽明录》), the *Ming Xiang Ji*(《冥祥记》), and the *Xu Qi Xie Ji*(《续齐谐记》) were all literary products of the influence of Buddhist scriptures and had a wide impact on the literature of future generations. To encapsulate, the impact of Buddhism on Chinese literature was not limited to the subject of religion as Chinese literary concepts diversified as well. After Buddhism was introduced to China, Chinese culture has adapted to it for a long period of time. Buddhism has taken a form that is compatible with traditional Chinese culture, national psyche, and customs.

Since Western Han Dynasty (202 B. C. —8) when Indian Buddhism arrived in China, this belief system has been influenced by traditional Chinese culture and has been known as Chinese Buddhism. Buddhism later inspired traditional Chinese culture, especially in Chan poetry and painting. These merged with the traditional Chinese art during the Sui and Tang Dynasties (581—907). Sutra translations, on the other hand, have had the biggest impact on Chinese literature. During the Jin and Tang Dynasties, Buddhist texts influenced the development of literature and provided the storyline for later novels such as *The Journey to the West*, *The Romance of the Three Kingdoms*(《三国演

Chapter 10 The Influence of Translation on Chinese Culture

义》), *The Plum Blossoms in a Golden Jar*(《金瓶梅》), and *The Dream of Red Mansion* (Dong, 2005).

Buddhist literature was developed not only to educate people and to be readable because of its beauty of language, but also to depict a carefree life by blending in with nature. Century after century, more and more authors were drawn to produce literary masterpieces with such a style. To sum up, the following are some of Buddhism's contributions to Chinese literature.

1) About 35,000 new words were introduced into Chinese that not only conveyed but also supported new ideas. Some words were used as surnames, given names or location names while certain words reflected the attitudes or views of people about the world. These brought a lot of changes in Chinese literature and culture.

2) In Tang Dynasty, Master Shou wen imitated Sanskrit letters to construct 36 letters of the alphabet. On this basis, Chinese phonetic symbols were later developed.

3) Chinese lexicology, philosophy, epistemology, and analytical reading of ancient texts were inspired by similar Indian elements. The invention of phonetic analysis and four tone accents made poetry reading more enjoyable.

4) The evolution of Chinese grammar was influenced by sutra translations during the Wei, Jin, and Southern and Northern Dynasties(196—589).

5) Popular literature with illustrations became the most favored literature in China.

6) Sutra translations, dialogues between masters and disciples (Koan), and poetry written by enlightened Chan Masters resulted in flourishing poetry and vernacular prose. These two originated from a Buddhist monastery and meditation center, according to Hu Shi, a well-known Chinese literary author.

7) Buddhist lectures coupled with chanting were turned into singing rather than recitation of stories to encourage Buddhism. These revised contents and tales, which were readily accessible to everyone, grew in popularity and became the foundation of Chinese vernacular literature.

8) The Zen Buddhism's theory, which included "no setting up words and letters", "sudden awakening", "clear vision", and "phenomena", was used to scrutinize literature.

9) The Six Patriarch Platform Sutra was one of the nine required books to read for reviving Chinese culture, according to Dr. Qian Mu(钱穆), a famous scholar of traditional Chinese studies.

10) About 1,500 years ago, a group of Chinese monks traveled to India to further their education. Their journeys meant to know in-depth Central Asian, Southeast Asian, and Indian histories and also marked the start of Chinese studying abroad.

Venerable Master Hsing Yun encouraged and localized Humanistic Buddhism by focusing on literary ventures such as the following:

1) Creating a comprehensive and updated Buddhist dictionary, which has been translated into Vietnamese and is available to digital media;

2) Publishing a reinterpretation of the Chinese Buddhist Canon in vernacular;

3) Collecting and writing Master's and Doctoral theses about Buddhist studies;

4) Making Buddhist textbooks available to the public;

5) Compiling a collection of color-illustrated children's storybooks in a variety of languages;

6) Having libraries in branch temples open to the public;

7) Producing Buddhist-themed television programs, films, comics, and dramas;

8) Dividing the lectures and Dharma's sayings into four components that are appreciated and used as guides by common citizens as well as business owners for their workers.

10.1.2 Buddhist Translation's Influence on Modern Chinese Language

Chinese language has been known for its pictographic script and tonal patterns. However, the tenacity of a language is reflected in its ability to adapt to changing circumstances. Chinese language has interacted with different languages, cultures, and religions and yet has managed to retain the flavor of its "special characteristics" (中国特色). One of the major reasons for this is that, despite the rigidity of the language and limitations of its script, Chinese language has been extremely versatile in its vocabulary. It incorporates various words from different languages and eventually adjusts these to suit the conditions of the language. Buddhism has had a deep influence on China not only because of its philosophy but also because of its ability to integrate into the Chinese psyche. This reality is exemplified by the vocabulary of Chinese language, which has adopted not only Buddhist thoughts and concepts but also this belief system's various words to suit the Chinese understanding of the world at large. While the Chinese have adjusted Buddhism to the extent that a new branch called Chinese Buddhism has emerged, the Chinese language could not remain untouched by Buddhist concepts or ideas as many of the words used today

Chapter 10 The Influence of Translation on Chinese Culture

were actually derived from Buddhism, like "立地成佛""大千世界""一刹那""心无挂碍", and so on.

Buddhism has had a huge effect on Chinese language. This is largely attributed to the Chinese translation and introduction of Buddhist scriptures from Sanskrit and other Indic languages. In China, Buddhist scriptures have been translated for over a thousand years and approximately 173 established translators have translated more than 1700 scriptures in more than 7000 Chinese scrolls. There were a lot of differences between Indian and Chinese on both literal meanings and connotations. As a result, Buddhist scripture translators had to invent and add sets of new terms to express Buddhism's complex ideas and principles, because there were no euqivalent words and concepts in Chinese. Such new vocabulary and ideas have eventually become ingrained in the Chinese language and some words have also been used in everyday speech. The text and syntax of medieval Chinese were profoundly influenced by the translation of Buddhist scriptures into Sanskrit and other Indic languages as well as literary genres and rhetorical techniques. The combination of Sanskrit phonetics and Buddhist translation increased Chinese people's knowledge of phonetics in their own words. This sparked a surge in interest in linguistic studies, especially the representation and study of Chinese characters' phonetic value. Consequently, a number of rhyme dictionaries, which are extremely useful for reconstructing the various phases of medieval Chinese phonetic systems, have been compiled.

According to the renowned Chinese linguist Wang Li(王力, 1900—1986), Buddhist terminology has made a significant contribution to Chinese vocabulary. Some of these words have been integrated in the Chinese language and few people are aware that they originated from the Buddhist literature. For example, the word *shijie*(世界) means "world", but the ancient Chinese people used the word *tianxia*(天下) to refer to the same. *Shijie* is derived from the Sanskrit word *loka*, which means "land" or "state of being". Apart from these, Buddhist translators also introduced polysyllabic words such as *puti xin*(菩提心, the mind of enlightenment), *gongde shui*(功德水, meritorious water), *zheng siwei*(正思维, right thought), *bo luo mi duo*(波罗蜜多, *paramita* means perfection), and *fei xiang fei fei xiang*(非想非非想, neither thought nor non-thought).

The arrival of Buddhism and Buddhist literature resulted in new methods for the traditional Chinese linguistic studies, especially phonology analysis and new literary genres. The first Chinese translations of Buddhist texts appeared in the second century

CE. These texts were translated from original sources written in Indo-European languages such as Gandhari, Prakrit languages, Sanskrit, and Pali. In particular, the sources of early translations are often lost (Nattier, 2008). Early translators were often not of Chinese descent and translations were done in teams that included native Chinese speakers. The usefulness of these early translations for comparative linguistic studies is minimal (Zürcher, 1991). In the following periods, a large corpus of Buddhist translation texts grew and the linguistic quality of the translations significantly improved. The highly-educated translators of Buddhist texts developed a writing style that reflected their conventional Chinese education yet attempting to cater to less educated readers. In the linguistic debate, two different approaches in novel syntactic constructs are dominant: 1) Syntactic changes reflect the syntax of the source languages from which the texts were translated; 2) Syntactic inventions are native Chinese developments resulting from changes in the Chinese language.

Following Aldridge, the medieval era was thought to begin in the 1st century B.C., with the beginning of Early Middle Chinese. The Early Medieval period (c. 1st —6th century B.C.) was a critical transitional period for the Chinese language, during which the language's grammar underwent significant changes. These developments had an effect on all facets of Chinese grammar including phonology, morphology, syntax, and lexicon. The foundation of modern Chinese grammar was developed at the end of this century. During the same period, the first translations of Buddhist texts into Chinese were published and many of the linguistic novelties first appeared in written sources. Since many of these developments were limited to translations of Buddhist texts, some scholars attributed them to the influence of the source languages of such texts. Also, it has been suggested that these innovations were diachronic developments within the Chinese language, which were caused by significant changes in the morphology. These changes such as the loss of consonant clusters and the complete loss of a former derivational morphology triggered numerous changes in the Chinese lexicon and syntax. These were thought to have existed in the vernacular language prior to their appearances in Buddhist translation texts.

The travels of Zhang Qian (张骞, c. 164—114 B.C.) to the Western Regions provided the first credible information on China's relations with the Buddhist realm's outskirts. Despite these early encounters, records on Buddhism only appeared later and very rarely in official Chinese documents like the *History of the Later Han Dynasty* (《后汉

书》, *Hou Hanshu*), which was on a history of the Eastern Han period. Buddhism was frequently linked to Daoism in these documents. Even with this clear underrepresentation of Buddhism in official Chinese literature, there were many circumstances which reversed such a situation. The monk Fa Xian had already written his essay on his journey to India and returned at the beginning of the fifth century when the *History of the Later Han Dynasty* was compiled. Similarly, the erudite monk Kumarajiva from Kucha achieved his first partial translation of Buddhist texts into Chinese. Kumarajiva, the son of an Indian Brahmin and a Kuchean princess, was the first of the "four great translators" of Buddhist texts, alongside Paramartha in the sixth century, Xuanzang in the seventh century, and Amoghavajra(不空金刚) in the eighth century. Kumarajiva, like many of his predecessors, did not speak Chinese natively though he learned it during his sixteen years as a prisoner of General Lü Guang(吕光, 337—399). In February 402, Kumarajiva arrived in Chang'an and became the leader of a translation project involving about 800 monks who translated and retranslated Buddhist texts. He is also said to have written some authentic Chinese texts in addition to his translations. He was taught by Buddhayasas, Fotuoyeshe(佛陀耶舍, died 413), another famous translator who was born as the son of a Brahmin in Jìbīn, Kashmir, India. Buddhayasas was trained in epistemology and philosophy, as well as traditional Indian sciences such as grammar and composition, poetry, mathematics, and logic. Dharmaraksa, born in Dunhuang in about 230 of Indian and Scythian parents of Yuezhi (Tochari)(大夏, one of sixteen kingdoms) descent, was the most important Buddhist text translator prior to Kumarajiva. Dharmaraksa's work had been known as the cornerstone of Buddhism in North China. He was well-versed in Confucian teachings. Zhu Fayan accompanied his teacher to the West where he studied the Western Regions' "36 languages" and translated their texts into Chinese. The Parthian Parthamasiris(安世高), a member of the Arsacids royal family who arrived in Luoyang about 148 [possibly during the reign of Emperor Huan(132—168)], was one of the first Buddhist translators. French Sinologist Paul Pelliot(伯希和, 1878—1945) had already mentioned the importance of Iranians and Iranianized people in the spread of Buddhism in China in 1911. "It was possibly he (Parthamasiris) who initiated the systematic translation of Buddhist texts and assembled the first translation team", according to Zürcher (1991). "In this regard, his significance is undeniable: his translations, however crude they may be, mark the beginning of a type of literary practice that, taken as a whole, must be considered as one of Chinese culture's most impressive achievements" (Zürcher, 1991)[279].

The influence of Buddhist texts on Chinese language research and linguistics will be critically evaluated in this section. A few examples will illustrate the invention of the *fanqie*(反切) spelling scheme, which is a watershed moment in the linguistic study of the Chinese phonological system and the significance of Buddhist texts in reconstructing Medieval Chinese pronunciation.

The roots of the *fanqie* scheme, a Chinese spelling system, are unknown. Although it is believed that this system originated from India or was influenced by Indian scholars who came to China in the first century to introduce Buddhism. It has been shown, for example, in Branner, that the *fanqie* system is most likely truly Chinese. The following are the two most compelling points he makes: 1) the existence of fusion words in the Later Archaic period (800—479 B.C.) and 2) the lack of an alphabet or a syllabary scheme to reflect Medieval Chinese phonology in the *fanqie*. One syllable is split into its initial and rhyme in the fanqiè spelling. Both are represented by different characters.

1) The *fanqie*(反切) system

堂 *táng*	dɑŋ	反切:徒郎	dʃɔ	l|aŋ	
蕩 *dàng*	dɑŋ^c	反切:徒朗	dʃɔ	l|aŋ^c	
宕 *dàg* EMC	dɑŋ^h	反切:徒浪	dʃɔ	l|aŋ^h	
鐸 *duò* EMC	dɑk	反切:待各	dʃəj^c	k|ak	

2) Places of articulation

Chún yīn 唇音	'labials'	p,p^h,b,m
Shé yīn 舌音	'linguals'	t,t^h,d,n,tr,tr^h,dr,nr
Chǐ yīn 齿音	'dentals'	ts,ts^h,dz,s,sɦ,tʂ,tʂ^h,(t)ʂɦ,ʂ,ʂɦ
Yá yīn 牙音	'molars'	k,k^h,g,n
Hóu yīn 喉音	'gutturals'	X,Y,j,ʔ

Surprisingly, Buddhist influence did not result in the creation of a phonetic system to reflect the exact reading of Chinese characters or to write foreign names in Chinese. Instead, these were always transcribed using Chinese characters. While not as accurate as an alphabet or a syllabary scheme, these transcriptions provided vital evidence for reconstructing the Chinese dialect spoken by the respective translator. For example,

Chapter 10　The Influence of Translation on Chinese Culture

Coblin classified the dialects used in Kumārajīva's and Buddhayaśas' translation teams as "Old Northwest Chinese". The transcriptions also acted as justifications for determining the source language of the translation document.

　　3) Milè (*mji lək) (Pulleyblank, 1995) 弥勒, Sanskrit: Maitreya, which according to Bailey (1946, 780, cf. Karashima) rather corresponds to the Tocharian 'Maitrāk, Metrak' than to the Snaskrit form);

　　4) Dásà´ājié (MC, nach Karashina: tâsât?âgjät) 怛萨阿竭, Sanskrit: Tathāgata (rúlái 如来); this shows phonological characteristics typical for the Gāndhārī language (Brough 1962 and others, cf. Karashima).

Both examples clearly demonstrate that different source languages underlying the transcription of foreign names into Chinese have to be expected.

As previously mentioned, the first translations of Buddhist texts from Indo-European languages into Chinese coincided with the advent of several developments in the lexicon and grammar of Chinese. The influence of syntactic structures of the IE source languages of these texts was partly due to the developments of Chinese. One of the issues with this method is that determining a direct IE source text or even a source language for early Chinese translation texts is always difficult. Due to the unique climate of the Xinjiang desert, several Chinese Buddhist texts dated from the 4th century CE have been found in good condition in Dunhuang and Turfan (吐鲁番), but this is not the case for early Sanskrit texts. However, since the late nineteenth century, very early records in the Gandhari (古印度陀罗语) language have been found (Salomon, 2007)[159], providing sufficient evidence for the importance of this language in the early years of Buddhist translations in Central Asia. It is still difficult to create a one-to-one relationship between the early source texts and their Chinese translations.

A brief discussion on the disyllabic modal verb *yingdang* (应当, 'should, ought') will serve as a representative example of the many lexico-grammatical shifts in early Middle Chinese Buddhist texts. The two almost synonymous monosyllabic verbs *ying* (应) and *dang* (当) make up this disyllabic verb. All verbs convey deontic modality, that is, the modal principles of duty and need. Since the Han era (202 B. C.—220), the modal functions of the verb *dang* have been recorded. It is frequently expressed in a more indirect way that "something should be done" in suggestions uttered by the speaker with regard to the—frequently unidentified—agent. The duty is founded on statutes, codes, and conventions, and also on circumstances. The modal verb *dang* is clearly part of a class of verbs used in Buddhist literature to express advice and admonishments, in addition to other functions such as expressing future tense.

In Buddhist literature, the number of marked plurals significantly increases. According to Norman (1988)[120], Archaic Chinese is one of the languages that has "a lack of a number of distinctions" for personal pronouns, that is, the nominal objects that are most likely to be marked in this way. This argument is false (Pulleyblank, 1995)[76]. A morphological differentiation between singular and plural personal pronouns was evident in the oldest extant literature, the oracle bone inscriptions. This simple distinction vanished in Late Archaic Chinese: the pronouns of the first group maintained their singular references, while the pronouns with a nasal initial began to be used as general pronouns regardless of number. As a result, there is a distinction in Classical Chinese between general (singular and plural) number and the singular, especially in the first person pronoun (Unger, 1987)[14], that is, the singular and not the plural.

The architecture of the so-called disposal structure is one of those that have been traced to the influence of Buddhist source text languages. From the Early Medieval era onwards, *ba*(把), *jiang*(将), chi(持), and *zhuo*(捉) occur as V1 in a serial verb construction in the disposal structure. Before being the disposal structure in its Modern Mandarin form, the SVC had undergone a series of transformations. This is one of the most widely debated constructions in the linguistic literature. Cao Guangshun and Yu Hsiao-jung (2015) claimed that the construction evolved under the influence of Sanskrit translations to represent its OV word order.

10.2 The Influence of Missionaries' Translation in the Late Ming and Early Qing Dynasties in China

During the late Ming and the early Qing Dynasty (1616—1912), the missionaries' translation activities made quite an impact on many fields in the Chinese society. This part will have an in-depth discussion about such influences.

According to *A History of Translation in China*(《中国翻译简史》) written by Ma Zuyi(马祖毅, 1925—2023), the number of translated religious books is 251 while the number of translated scientific books is 131 (Ma Zuyi et al., 2006)[308]. Books of religion were more than those for science. These works arrived in China with the purpose of bringing the Christian message to the vast empire. The scientific books were brought in to spread the religion. Science was the bait that the missionaries used to guide the natives to the Christian faith. The Jesuits hoped that the Chinese would become interested in the religion. But these missionaries did not expect that this would have aroused the Chinese intellectuals' pursuit for science. The knowledge that the Chinese were interested in were largely on astronomy and mathematics. Therefore, among the scientific books in the 17th century, there were 99 works on both fields, which accounted for the greatest number (Ma Zuyi et al., 2006)[308]. Based on the interests of the Chinese, missionaries selectively brought these books to China. They aimed to attract the Chinese to Catholicism. Actions of the missionaries were governed by their purposes and they just wanted to conceal these by using the scientific knowledge. In fact, their missionary work in China was not as successful as their expectations but the Western science they brought in, indeed, caused a tremendous repercussion in many fields in China. The following part will mention the impacts of missionaries' translation activities on the aspects of ideology, science and technology, Chinese language, and education.

10.2.1 On Ideology

During the late Ming and the early Qing Dynasties, the Chinese feudal ruling class still appraised the Western countries with the eyes of an ethnocentric state. Some people of insight began to realize the importance of science and technology after recognizing the value of Western science and technology in protecting borders and improving military combat effectiveness and the continuous deepening of Sino-Western cultural and scientific and technological exchanges. Such intellectuals paid attention to social practice and analyzed things in a rational way.

The civil strife occurred in China during the end of Ming Dynasty and the beginning of Qing Dynasty. Apart from the brutal rule of the feudal rulers, China had suffered from a natural disaster for a long time, which was an important cause of the unrest. In the face of natural disasters, the feudal rulers did not bother to solve these. They even imposed exorbitant taxes on the people. Under these circumstances, the peasant class had to resist the rulers for their survival. To preserve their shaky regime, the feudal rulers must find ways to alleviate the harm caused by natural disasters. People depended on science and technology to deal with natural disasters to a certain extent. But the development of science and technology was slow locally. In other words, there were no scientific theory and specific social practice. There was no way to really solve the problem. Therefore, the feudal rulers looked out for foreign practices, which promoted exchanges between China and the West. Translating foreign scientific and technological documents was the main tool to understand such possible solutions.

During this period, many Chinese scholars such as Xu Guangqi (1562—1633), Li Zhizao (李之藻, 1565—1630), and Yang Tingyun (杨廷筠, 1557—1627) set good examples in combining theory with practice. *Western Hydro Science* (《泰西水法》) translated by Xu Guangqi and the Italian missionary Sabbathin Ursis (1575—1620) is a document about the Western technology of farmland irrigation and water conservancy. The work mainly introduces the structure and production methods of the Archimedean screw, the usage of reservoir, and the role of hydro science. Based on the current situation of farming in China, Xu Guangqi created farm tools which were suitable for farmlands and improved the efficiency of irrigation. He truly combined theory with practice. During this period, scholars introduced and translated many works in the fields of water conservancy, mathematics, astronomy, geography, and medicine. The missionaries then applied the scientific knowledge in these books to specific practices, which had a positive impact. The effective use of water conservancy knowledge reduced the losses caused by natural disasters such as floods and droughts to a certain extent. The introduction of medicine helped people avoid suffering from certain illnesses. The promotion of astronomical knowledge enhanced the accuracy of weather forecasting. These activities of translating scientific and technological literature improved the living conditions of the people remarkably. In the process of self-help through the introduction of scientific knowledge, people paid more attention to social practice.

In feudal China, the privilege of freely expressing thoughts was mostly for the ruling class, and social customs and learning environment changed with the preferences of the rulers. Matteo Ricci (1552—1610) was able to establish missionary institutions in China because of the support of the Ming emperor. After the death of Matteo Ricci, Western missionary activities were banned once due to the lack of imperial support. It was then difficult for Westerners to promote cultural exchanges. Later, with the help of enlightened scholar-bureaucrats, the missionaries introduced methods for calculating the movement of

Chapter 10 The Influence of Translation on Chinese Culture

celestial bodies through translating books such as *Basic Principles of Geometry*(《圆容较义》) and *Questions and Explanation of Astronomical Phenomena*(《天问略》). These works improved the accuracy of observing astronomical phenomena and the Chinese calendar. "The value of Western learning has been reemphasized" (Xiong Yuezhi, 1994). It revived the social learning atmosphere and further reoriented the way of thinking of people towards a rational way.

China's situation in the late Ming and the early Qing Dynasties was characterized by missionaries practicing the "try to win popular support" principle and translating many natural scientific works to spread their religion. Those scientific works broadened the Chinese horizon in the natural science and social science fields such as astronomy, mathematics, medicine, geography, physics, military, and so on. At the same time, new knowledge also impacted on the traditional Chinese concept of the universe, ideology, and values. Western learning that came into China greatly influenced people's knowledge structure. It led to the change of people's cognition from the visible level of knowledge to the invisible level of consciousness.

During Ming Dynasty, the ruling class exerted huge efforts to further despotically control the ideology and advocate Neo-Confucianism. Therefore, the ruling class played a leading role in the ideology and culture (Yang Wei, 2008)[9]. Regarding Chinese culture, especially Confucianism, the missionaries affirmed the positive value of its ethics in the context of nature and nation. The intellectuals actively brought in Western learning to make the country more prosperous. They supplemented Confucianism in terms of the dominant ideology and traditional value, trying to reestablish the core value of Confucianism. Many enlightened intellectuals accepted Western learning and read the translations. They were truly aware of the powerful influence that Western technology had on Chinese society. They believed that the knowledge in the applied fields of astronomy, military, agricultural production, and irrigation works could help them realize their dreams. The intellectuals began to perfect themselves on the level of ideology and they emphasized on applying learning to strengthen the country. At the same time, they sharply attacked the prevailing impractical academic atmosphere. The Chinese were guided by a large number of Western works in seeking practicality of science and technology and in absorbing and accepting the advantages and valuable knowledge of Western science to enrich themselves. Therefore, they could blend them with Chinese knowledge and establish their own scientific and theoretical system to surpass the Western world.

In the field of mathematics and arithmetic, Europe emphasized on abstract thinking and deduction. Western mathematics stressed on these to further understand its body of knowledge. The study method was also abstract. In other words, Westerners confirmed the truth of the proposition by deduction. *Elements of Geometry*(《几何原本》, *Jihe Yuanben*) written by Euclid (330—275 B. C.) was an epoch-making work which firstly established the deductive system. Before the missionaries brought the principles of Western mathematics to China, the development of mathematics and arithmetic had ups and downs. In the middle period of Ming Dynasty, China was thriving economically. Commercial exchanges and overseas trade were frequent. Mathematics and arithmetic were also well developed. However, since later rulership canceled mathematics and arithmetic subjects and only emphasized the stereotyped writing, people no longer attached importance to mathematics. As observed, the whole mathematical system lacked systematization and symbolization (Yang Wei, 2008)[26].

In astronomy and geography, Europe proved that the earth was round through their navigation. When the missionaries brought the knowledge of astronomy and geography to China, all of these changed the Chinese worldview of round sky and square earth that they had held for thousands of years. The great universal geographic map was a gift for Emperor Wanli when Matteo Ricci was granted an audience. This map had been very popular among people by 1608. It was copied or drawn for more than 12 times. It was also recorded in many books of common knowledge (Yang Wei, 2008)[28]. The Chinese horizon was broadened by this map and the corresponding astronomical knowledge. The world was no longer the round sky and square earth in the universe. And it was revolving in concentric circles. The missionaries showed the world to Chinese. For thousands of years, the heaven had always been the central proposition about the Chinese imperial power, the country, the social order, the ethics, etc. Thanks to Western astronomical knowledge and the precise observation, measurement, and calculation of various scientific instruments, a series of theories emerged. For example, the heliocentric theory of Copernicus (1473—1543) and the celestial bodies motion system and universe structure theory of Ptolemy (90—168) and Tycho (1546—1601) proved the relationship between the earth and the celestial bodies and the fact that the galaxy was composed of the stars (Ge Zhaoguang, 2000). These made the Chinese realize that the dome over their heads was no longer the same as before. Many works about the new worldview were then produced.

In medicine, the heart was the most common and basic category in traditional Chinese philosophical system. The organ played an important role in the domain of Chinese philosophy. People thought that the heart was the organ of thinking, the source of ideas and the root of everything in the world. But Western anatomy was greatly different from the Chinese traditional notions. It demonstrated to the Chinese that the brain, not the heart, was the organ for thinking.

In a word, missionaries' translation activities had a great influence on Chinese ideology in many fields such as mathematics and arithmetic, astronomy, geography and medicine. The Chinese gave importance to social practice and rational thinking.

10.2.2 On Science and Technology

Missionaries' translation activities in the late Ming and the early Qing Dynasties did not make a great impact on the translation theories. However, these missionaries partially spread Western technological and cultural knowledge through their translation activities. These conformed to the ideological trend of practical purposes, which had a great impact on the development of Chinese natural sciences and culture.

In mathematics, the most influential translations were *Jihe Yuanben* (*the Elements of Geometry*), *Tongwen Suanzhi* (《同文算指》, *Epitome Arithmeticae Practicae*), and *Shuli Jingyun* (《数理精蕴》, *Encyclopaedia of Elementary Mathematics*). Western mathematics was different from traditional Chinese mathematics as the former focused on logic and equation. Westerners used abstract symbols to stand for relations, varieties, deductions, and operations of quantities. These formed a rigorous deductive system, which greatly improved the development of Chinese mathematics. For example, the appearance of *Jihe Yuanben* created a precedent in the translation of Western scientific works in the late Ming Dynasty, allowing the Chinese to be exposed to a totally different scientific system—the deductive system. The Euclid geometry and its deductive inference were the newest mode of thinking for the Chinese ideological circles. The publication of the book *On the Revolutions of the Heavenly Spheres* (《天体运行论》, *Tianti Yunxing Lun*) marked the beginning of modern European scientific revolution. The translation of *Elements of Geometry* broke the fettered development of Chinese science. Translation by the foreign missionaries indicated the transition from traditional science to modern science in China (Meng Jie, 2005)[14].

Translation works also greatly influenced the development of astronomy. In the early Ming dynasty, the development of the field was nearly stagnant due to the influence of politics and research methods at that time. But after the reign of Emperor Wanli, astronomy made great strides. The data and calculation methods used in the book *Calendar in the Years of Emperor Chongzhen*(《崇祯历书》, *Chongzhen Lishu*) ensured the accuracy of calendar calculation. Having an accurate calendar to organize specific economic, political, and religious rituals was important to the Mandate of Heaven(天命) of the Chinese emperors, as it could affirm the cosmic order and demonstrate the authority of the ruler over his subjects. By 1580, the Chinese calendar had already been a matter of concern, although its problems were not as bad as the Jesuits had claimed. The European calendars were more accurate. The Ming emperor realized that the missionaries could help the Chinese in correcting the calendar. The translation work brought in many European astronomical achievements and concepts. It was novel for Chinese scholars at that time to read those works. The Jesuits brought advanced astronomical measuring instruments and theories. Matteo Ricci and the other missionaries had introduced some famous universe theories, such as Round-Earth Theory, which promoted the development of astronomy to a higher level. They also introduced a lot of astronomical instruments, such as the armillary sphere, sundial, telescope, star dial, star globe, etc. Their activities enabled Chinese astronomy to undergo the transition from traditional to modern astronomy in the 17th century. Meanwhile, they greatly narrowed the gap between Western and Chinese astronomy.

In geography, the map and geographical knowledge introduced and translated by the missionaries not only showed the Chinese the view of the whole world, but also introduced more accurate mapping methods. Map-making was one of the areas on which the Jesuits had a greater impact. Ming cartographers were knowledgeable about Southeast Asia, the Indian subcontinent, and the Arabian Peninsula after the early Ming voyages headed by Zheng He(郑和, 1371—1433) from 1405 to 1433. The surveying and mapping of China were mainly done by missionaries. These were pioneering works in Chinese history and even in world mapping history.

In agriculture, agricultural translations made great contributions to the spread of Western agricultural technologies. The spread of agricultural technologies mainly concentrated on the irrigation works, the prevention and cure of plant diseases and insect pests and the improvement of agricultural varieties. It also emphasized on agricultural operation and management and the introduction and popularization of chemical fertilizer and agricultural instruments. *Western Hydro Science* was regarded as the framework of modern European engineering. It methodically introduced the Western irrigation system to China for the first time. It made great contributions to the development of Chinese irrigation and water conservation. It contained the Western scientific achievements before the 17th century and included knowledge of physics, geology, etc., which had more scientific value than the previous Chinese technology. In addition, Chinese water conservancy was greatly improved by the new instruments. Machine manufacturing technology and agricultural production were also improved. The *Western Hydro Science* was later collected in Li Zhizao's *Tianxue Chuhan*(《天学初函》, *Natural Science Series by Catholic*). In Ming Dynasty, it was collected in Xu Guangqi's *Nongzheng Quanshu*(《农政全书》, *Comprehensive Agricultural Knowledge before the 17th Century*). With the enlightenment from *Western Hydro Science*, Xu Guangqi comprehensively introduced Western technology about how to build reservoirs in his *Comprehensive Agricultural Knowledge before the 17th Century*, and established Chinese hydraulics. In Qing Dynasty, it was collected in *Siku Quanshu*(《四库全书》, the *Complete Library in the Four Branches of Literature*) (Qiu Longhu, 2010)[24].

In military affairs, rulers of the late Ming and early Qing Dynasties introduced and produced a large number of Western firearms due to the translation of books about these. Those Western guns guaranteed victories one after another, which encouraged people to clearly realize the impracticability of mentalism and to understand the necessity of agriculture, industry, and commerce. This type of technology attracted much attention from people who competed with each other in learning new knowledge and instruments. For example, Wang Zheng(王徵, 1571—1644) and Joannes Terrenz (1576—1630) translated the book *Illustrations and Explanations of Western Machinery*(《远西奇器图说》). It introduced Western mechanical knowledge, which was essential to people's livelihoods and national economy. People began to focus on the science and technologies that made Western countries powerful and prosperous (Yang Wei, 2008)[30-31].

Due to the popularization of Western learning, more Chinese scholars began to conduct researches in science and technology. The trend of concentrating on translation and publication of scientific books came into existence in Chinese publishing history in the

17th century. Although this trend did not last long, the Chinese published many important scientific works during this period, such as *Tiangong Kaiwu*(《天工开物》, *T'ien-kung K'ai-wu*: *Chinese Technology in the Seventeenth Century*), *Bencao Gangmu*(《本草纲目》, *Compendium of Materia Medica*), *Wuli Xiaoshi*(《物理小识》, *The Physical Knowledge*). According to *A History of Translation in China* written by Ma Zuyi, among the scientific books translated by both foreign missionaries and Chinese scholars from 1584 to 1790, there were 109 astronomical and mathematical books, 6 physics books, 3 geological books, 2 military books, and 8 biological and medical books. These scientific books played an important role in the history of Chinese publishing and academia. It had both historic and practical meanings for the publication of China's scientific books and China's development of science and technology.

In Chinese scientific history, it is a great event that missionaries arrived in China and translated many scientific and religious works in the late Ming and early Qing Dynasties. Their translation activities were mainly intended for religious and political purposes. And the spread was mainly among the intellectuals of the upper classes. Although the knowledge missionaries brought in was not the most advanced and integrated scientific theory and its influence was limited, it indeed provided new ideas to the Chinese occlusive academic circle and promoted the development of Chinese science and technology. The development of Chinese science and technology then almost stagnated. Their activities promoted the transformation from traditional science to modern science in China. Chinese science began to blend with the world's sciences. Meanwhile, Western science and technology gradually replaced traditional Chinese science and technology to become the mainstream. It was a new chapter in the history of Chinese modern science and technology.

In a word, missionaries translated many works and brought in knowledge of science and technology, which had a great impact on the fields of mathematics, astronomy, geography, and military. It was a great event in Chinese scientific history and spurred a transformation from traditional science to modern science in China.

10.2.3 On Chinese Language

Language is intrinsically related to the mold of thinking and culture. Words are the most basic and active components of language. In the late Ming and early Qing Dynasties, missionaries, represented by Matteo Ricci, introduced many new terms through translation activities. Such endeavors made a great contribution to the development of the Chinese

Chapter 10 The Influence of Translation on Chinese Culture

language.

As for the word structure, Matteo Ricci created many compound expressions, and these were mostly modifier-head constructions, which enriched the Chinese expressions and created an important word-formation mold. This word-formation mold provided examples for the appearance of new expressions. For example, geographical terms like "the Northern Hemisphere" and "the Southern Hemisphere" provided "the X Hemisphere" modifier-head mold for later generations. The mathematical terms such as "right angle", "acute angle", "obtuse angle", "triangle", and "quadrangle" created in the translation of *Elements of Geometry* provided us with an "X angle" mold, and later, people created the geometrical terms on the basis of it such as "complementary angle", "vertical angle", "supplementary angle", and so on. The terms like "tangent line", "secant line", "meridian line", and "straight line" formed an "X line" modifier-head mold.

In terms of semantics, Matteo Ricci used some old expressions for new meanings and successfully realized the transformation of meanings. The word "geometry" is a good example. When translating *Elements of Geometry*, he turned every term over in his mind. For example, "jihe"(几何, geometry) is an interrogative numeral in the classic Chinese. But, Matteo Ricci used this word as a mathematical term, which refers to the relationship among the shape, size, and location of an object. Nowadays, when "jihe" is mentioned, we know that it is the name of a mathematical subject (Feng Tianyu, 2003[99-100]). On the contrary, people almost forget its meaning in ancient Chinese. Other examples are terms such as "latitude" and "longitude". These terms originally referred to the ordinate and transverse line in weaving, but these are now expanded in meaning and also used as geographical terms.

These professional terms are systematic. For example, when translating *the World Map and the Introduction to Western Astronomy*(《世界地图与西方天文学导论》), Matteo Ricci created terms like "tianqiu"(天球), "diqiu"(地球), "yueqiu"(月球), and so on (Huang Heqing, 2003)[35]. These expressions conform to the naming standard of terms in modern times, so they are still in use and have become common terms in daily life. Moreover, they provided the word-formation mold of "X 球". In addition, he took the relativity and integrity of such terms into account. The emergence of "the South Pole" and "the North Pole" is a good example.

Missionaries simultaneously adopted transliteration and literal translation methods to translate Western terms. For the names of places and people, examples like "Asia" (translated into "亚细亚"), "Europe" (translated into "欧罗巴"), and "Alexander" (translated into "亚历山大") are some of the most typical examples of the transliteration method. In the course of the development of expressions, the creation of terms does not mean that they will naturally exist. Whether these creative terms will become popular or not depends on the degree of acceptance and the rate of utilization. In other words, if the later generations continue their use, they will become popular (Huang Heqing, 2003)[36]. Fortunately, the later missionaries had a similar cultural background to Matteo Ricci and they agreed to use his expressions in their translations. Therefore, those expressions or terms became popular soon, and some of them even spread to Japan.

In a word, missionaries' translation activities had an effect on Chinese language. They formed a modifier-head mold, expanded the meanings of terms, and enriched Chinese expressions.

10.2.4 On Education

After the establishment of the Western capitalist system, a new style of education developed rapidly. The advanced sciences gradually became the mainstream in Western schools. Ming Dynasty promulgated the cultural and educational policies of the eight-part essay to fetter the people's minds. Under such policies, the education in public schools, private schools, and academies in the late Ming and early Qing Dynasties were getting farther and farther away from modern science. Chinese society was still under the feudal influence, so its modernization process gradually fell behind. Under two different cultural environments, the direction of the development of Chinese education and Western education was completely opposite.

The traditional Chinese culture was incompatible with the natural sciences. The intellectuals read The "Four Books" and "Five Classics". "Four Books" are composed of *The Great Learning*(《大学》, *Daxue*), *The Doctrine of the Mean*(《中庸》, *Zhongyong*), *The Analects of Confucius*(《论语》, *Lunyu*), and *The Works of Mencius*(《孟子》, *Mengzi*). "Five Classics" consist of *The Book of Songs*(《诗经》, *Shijing*), *The Book of Documents*(《尚书》, *Shangshu*), *The Book of Changes*(《周易》, *Zhouyi*), *The Book of Rites*(《礼记》, *Liji*), and *The Spring and Autumn Annals*(《春秋》, *Chunqiu*). Intellectuals studied verses, ditties, odes, and songs. They loved lyre-playing, chess, calligraphy, and painting. They did not care about agricultural and industrial production. At the same time, they were not interested in the objective things about the natural world. The knowledge they had had nothing to do with the development of production and science and technology. China and the Western world were in totally different situations. Because of the promotion of the Renaissance, people's minds were no longer constrained by the doctrine. People reaffirmed their value. The economic prosperity and political independence pushed them to explore and change their culture and education. In China, the feudal ethic was stamped on people's minds through receiving traditional education in all schools. The ruling class wanted to use education to control people's minds and consolidate their reign. This traditional mode of education had its advantages and defects. If a person became well-known in the field of philosophy, he might not make efforts to dig into other fields like medicine and mathematics. It led to the fact that very few people were willing to devote to mathematics or medicine. Such subjects were not honored as philosophy, so people who were engaged in mathematics or medicine were not respected. Students would not study these subjects because they would receive no reward or honor. We can clearly understand this from people's keen interests in moral philosophy. A person in this field with a high status confidently thinks that he has reached the summit of happiness (He Gaoji et al., 2001)[25].

Although having the purpose of spreading religious doctrine, missionaries who arrived in China with advanced scientific and technological knowledge and their translation activities changed the country. It allowed Chinese intellectuals to have access to natural science knowledge in addition to their traditional learning. Meanwhile, it set off a reflection on traditional Chinese education and science. Later, new educational thoughts were put forward. Those new thoughts were totally different from traditional ones. The traditional educational contents, methods, notions, and value orientations were deeply influenced by foreign educational thoughts from the Western missionaries. The enlightened intellectuals introduced Western learning, which was a proof of the negation of the so-called "backwardness" of traditional Chinese education. Intellectuals such as Xu Guangqi clearly realized the defects of traditional Chinese education. And he began to understand the value of Western culture, natural science, and technology. They tried to expand the influence of Western learning in China and add science and technology as part of traditional education. A lot of Western scientific knowledge was introduced to China, which laid the foundation for the new subject system of modern Chinese education. It was a shock to traditional Chinese education and teaching. It also provided a reference for the transformation of traditional education systems. The scientific and technological knowledge covered many aspects of science, such as mechanics, geography, astronomy, mathematics, etc. Knowledge greatly influenced the development of modern Chinese education. The different Western learning methods partly transformed the contents of traditional education, which opened a new chapter in the history of Chinese education.

The major way of spreading Western science was translating Western scientific works, and the major translation method was cooperative translation. Translation was done through the cooperation between the Western missionaries and the Chinese scholars. Their translation activities not only gave a shock to the contents of traditional Chinese education but also gave rise to the transformation of teaching methods. These activities also stimulated the emergence of Chinese enlightenment thought in science education. The emphasis on natural science certainly caused adjustments in the methods of teaching. It required people to absorb the essence of both Chinese and overseas science and culture. Scientific experiments, rational thinking, and logical reasoning got attention. And people argued that practice was the criterion of knowledge. Therefore, the emphasis on experiments and practice began to be applied in teaching (especially in teaching natural sciences), and so did the teaching principle of visualization (Tan Chao, 2004)[37]. The book *The Logistics*(《名理探》) introduced Western formal logic in details. This book also showed a new logical thinking system and scientific methodological framework to the Chinese. The translation of *The Logistics* and *Elements of Geometry* was regarded as a milestone, from which China began to introduce Western logical thinking.

Missionaries brought in scientific knowledge, especially the concept of the modern world, through translation. The introduction of scientific knowledge broadened the horizons of the Chinese, which promoted the change of traditional education ideas to some extent. Facing the wave of Western learning, scholars such as Xu Guangqi and Li Zhizao thought that learning from each other could benefit the progress of both parties. As long as it was valuable, it should be used by the Chinese. They applied what they had learned to education practice and pioneered the modernization of Chinese education.

In the early period of Qing Dynasty, the academic circle paid much attention to

Chapter 10 The Influence of Translation on Chinese Culture

Western learning. Chinese intellectuals gradually knew more about Western technology. It was practicable, which captured the minds of the Chinese people. They made efforts to learn Western knowledge and spread it so that China could surpass the Western world by mastering Western technology. The patriots' enthusiasm for introducing Western learning in the late Ming and early Qing Dynasties led to the learning of advanced technology from Europeans.

In a word, the scientific translation of missionaries made contributions to the transformation of traditional Chinese education. They introduced new contents and teaching methods, thus promoting the development of Chinese education. Generally speaking, the translation activities of missionaries in the late Ming and early Qing Dynasties exerted a great influence on Chinese ideology, science and technology, language, and education. They brought in new terms, new theories, and methodologies. They provided new visions and materials for the Chinese to learn and think about their country and the world, and they also promoted the development of scientific and cultural communication between China and the Western countries.

10.3 Relationship between Translation and China's New Culture Movement

In the late Qing Dynasty and the early Republic of China, the Chinese nation was in a period of life and death. Patriots and various social, political, and cultural forces sought ways to save the country. During this period, translation was the main method. *New Youth* was in the forefront of translating foreign works, and a large number of famous writers and translators emerged, such as Yan Fu(严复, 1854—1921), Hu Shi, Lu Xun(鲁迅, 1881—1936), Zhou Zuoren(周作人, 1885—1967), and others.

Translation played an indispensable role in the New Culture Movement. It can even be said that without translation, there could not have been the New Culture Movement. Without translation, Marxism could not have been introduced into China. In this case, translation is not only at the level of language transformation, as people used to know, but also a catalyst for cultural interpretation and change. Similarly, in the spread of Chinese culture and literature, it can also be realized that without translation, Chinese literature and humanistic research cannot go to the world.

10.3.1　Translation and the Rise of China's New Culture Movement

During the New Culture Movement, the translation of foreign works became increasingly popular. At the same time, a large number of writers and scholars began to advocate vernacular literature. During this period, the original text-centered translation strategy became the mainstream of translation practice. Literal translation was affirmed. *New Youth* emphasized faithfulness and literal translation. Faithfulness was the mainstream of translation practice, and literal translation was a good translation standard. Hu Shi, Lu Xun, and Zhou Zuoren all emphasized literal translation, and their translated works also adopted literal translation strategies, emphasizing the respect for the original texts.

During the period of the New Culture Movement, the third climax in the history of Chinese translation transpired. Due to the introduction of Marxist philosophy and the progress of Western learning, more and more Chinese people, especially intellectuals, realized that classical Chinese had greatly hindered the development of Chinese thought. They thought that classical Chinese was not only unable to popularize education and improve the quality of the people but also prevented readers from accepting new ideas. At this point, the Chinese language needed undergoing changes to spread new ideas and concepts.

It is generally believed that the May 4th Movement was the spark that ignited China's New Culture Movement. In fact, as far as the real starting and ending years of the New Culture Movement are concerned, it can be strictly said that the starting time of the New Culture Movement should be earlier. The New Culture Movement can be roughly divided into three stages: the period from 1915 to 1919 was the starting stage, the period from 1919 to 1921 was the second stage, that is, the expansion stage, and the period from 1921 to 1923 was its decline. In the first stage, it was characterized by cultural and knowledge orientations, and its landmark event was the launch of *New Youth* in Shanghai. A large number of foreign literary works and humanistic academic thoughts had been translated into Chinese, which greatly promoted the New Culture Movement. In the second stage, due to the outbreak of the May 4th Movement in 1919, its political and revolutionary orientations became more and more prominent. At the same time, the May 4th movement pushed the New Culture Movement to a new climax. Hu Shi, Chen Duxiu(陈独秀, 1879—1942), Lu Xun, Cai Yuanpei(蔡元培, 1868—1940), Qian Xuantong(钱玄同, 1887—1939),

Li Dazhao(李大钊, 1889—1927), and other intellectual elites from different camps came together and took the lead in launching a large-scale ideological and cultural movement of "anti-tradition, anti-Confucianism, and anti-ancient prose". Its purpose was to make China enter the process of modernization in an all-round way. This made people's eyes turn to the Western countries, thinking that learning the advanced Western science, culture, and technology could save China. In this sense, the role of translation has been greatly promoted. Therefore, a large number of Western social and cultural theories and literary works swarmed into China through translation, which played an important role in the formation of modern Chinese literary classics and the transformation of academic discourse. In particular, it should be pointed out that it was around this time that Marxism was translated in China. Therefore, it can be said that one of the most important events in this period was the establishment of the Communist Party of China in Shanghai in 1921. Due to divergent viewpoints within the New Culture Movement's leadership, the movement eventually fell apart in the third stage. The New Culture Movement has thus become a historical event. It left behind many things worthy of our thinking and research.

At that time, China was in a transition period from an old feudal autocratic country to a new modern democratic country. To promote this transformation, it was not enough to merely rely on the local strength. In this sense, with the help of translation, the pioneers of the New Culture Movement introduced all the new ideas and concepts beneficial to this movement to China. In this way, the New Culture Movement played an important role in making China rapidly transform into a modern democratic country. In this sense, the important role and different forms of translation could be seen clearly. Translators not only translated a large number of academic and literary works into Chinese but also introduced new Western ideas and concepts into China through the leaders and scholars of the New Culture Movement.

Marxism was introduced into China through the New Culture Movement, which certainly foreshadowed the founding of the Communist Party of China and the success of the democratic revolution. According to the life experiences of the leaders and scholars of the New Culture Movement, the importance of translation could be seen. Indeed, those thinkers and humanists were educated either in the West or in Japan. They took the lead in launching the ideological and cultural movement of "anti-tradition, anti-Confucianism, and anti-ancient prose". They tried to achieve the goal of promoting the modernization of

China in an all-around way. If they wanted to introduce advanced Western ideas and cultures, they had to rely on translation, and they were more or less engaged in some translation work or used Chinese to explain Western ideas and theories. Among these, Marxism, as one of the most important theories from the West, would naturally not be ignored by them. They knew that they would get beaten if they were backward, which was illustrated by the continuous oppression and trampling of Western powers in the late Qing Dynasty. In this sense, they made full use of translation to introduce new Western ideas and cultures to China, thus greatly accelerating the process of China's modernization.

It is observable that the introduction of "Mr. De" (德先生, democracy) and "Mr. Sai" (赛先生, science) influenced the development of science and democracy in China throughout the 20th century. Chen Duxiu founded *New Youth*, which specially published some articles introducing or translating the advanced Western thoughts at that time, aiming to enlighten the Chinese people and promote the development of Chinese scientific and humanistic thoughts. It can be said that their efforts laid an important foundation for the introduction and dissemination of Marxism in China. In addition, the New Culture Movement also witnessed the founding of the Communist Party of China in 1921, which led the Chinese people to the victory of the democratic revolution and the establishment of a new socialist P. R. China in 1949. Therefore, translation, as a tool of enlightenment, has indeed played a role in liberating the Chinese people from darkness and ignorance. Without translation, the vast majority of Chinese people might have been living in the darkness of ignorance, while a small number of people with lofty ideals might still be struggling in the dark to pursue the truth about saving the country and the people.

From today's point of view, it can be seen that translation has given birth to the New Culture Movement. Translation has brought a large number of excellent foreign literary works and humanistic academic works into China and enlightened Chinese people's thoughts and concepts. In view of this, our understanding of the importance of translation should not only be based on the level of language conversion but also on the level of cultural interpretation and knowledge dissemination, as well as the level of social change. In short, the role of translation in promoting the new culture movement is undeniable.

The New Culture Movement coincided with the evolution of Chinese modern translation thoughts. The translation activities in the New Culture Movement not only promoted the transformation and development of traditional Chinese translation thoughts but also changed the cultural outlook and humanistic spirit of whole China. In this sense, the translation practice in the period of the New Culture Movement is of great research value. However, from the existing literature, although there are a large number of articles on translation activities during the New Culture Movement, most of them focus on a specific translation theory or practice. Therefore, on the basis of more mature researches in this field, it may be more valuable to make a comparative study of translation activities in this period with other periods, such as the Ming and Qing Dynasties, which can become the focus of the future research.

10.3.2 Yan Fu's Translation Practice

Yan Fu was the first thinker who systematically introduced Western theories to modern China. He played an important role in modern Chinese history. At the same time, he was also the originator of modern Chinese translation. He put forward the criteria for translation: "Xin(信, faithfulness), Da(达, expressiveness), and Ya(雅, elegance)", which have had a great influence on modern Chinese translation practice and theoretical research.

1) Introduction to Yan Fu

Yan Fu was a famous thinker, translator, and scholar in modern China. There are eight major translations of Yan Fu. Six of which are, namely, *Evolution and Ethics*[《天演论》(即《进化论和伦理学》)] of Thomas H. Huxley(托马斯·亨利·赫胥黎, 1825—1895); *The Study of Sociology*(《群学肄言》) by Herbert Spencer(赫伯特·斯宾塞, 1820—1903); *The Wealth of Nations*[《原富》(即《国富论》)] of Adam Smith (亚当·斯密, 1723—1790); *On Liberty and a System of Logic*[《群己权界论》(即《论自由》)] of John Stuart Mill(约翰·斯图亚特·穆勒, 1806—1873); *The Spirit of the Laws*[《法意》(即《论法的精神》)] of Montesquieu(孟德斯鸠, 1689—1755); and *Primer of Logic*(《名学浅说》) of William Stanley Jevons(威廉姆·斯坦利·杰文斯, 1835—1882). Over the past hundred years, his works and translation thoughts have been a hot topic among translators and translation researchers. Generally speaking, his works have won great recognition from many well-known scholars, such as Cai Yuanpei(蔡元培, 1868—1940), Liang Qichao(梁启超, 1873—1929), Wu Rulun(吴汝纶, 1840—1903), Lu Xun(鲁迅, 1881—1936) and Wang Kefei(王克非, 1954—), just to name a few.

In his early years, he studied in Fujian Shipping and Polity School; Foochow Shipbuilding Institution(福州船政学堂), and later in the British Naval Academy, studying advanced mathematics, physics, chemistry, and so on. Yan Fu lived in the time when China became semi-colonial and semi-feudal. Many people with lofty ideals were seeking the road to a powerful country. They believed that the crux of China's backwardness lied in its backward science and technology. In the Opium War and later wars, China was defeated because the foreign ships were strong and the foreign technologies were advanced. In this sense, many people turned their attention to learning the advanced science and technology of the West, and some aspiring young people began to learn advanced Western technology abroad. In 1895, China failed in the Sino-Japanese War in 1894, and the *Treaty of Shimonoseki*(《马关条约》) was signed between China and Japan, which further deepened the degree of China's colonization. Yan Fu realized that if China did not carry out social and ideological changes, it could not survive in the world. Therefore, he joined the Reform Movement. He published an article in the newspaper, advocating the adoption of Western learning and criticizing the feudal autocracy of more than 2,000 years. He decided to translate Western works of philosophy and social sciences. It can be seen that Yan Fu's translation of Western academic works was aimed at promoting changes in Chinese society and people's thinking.

2) The Translation Criteria of Faithfulness, Expressiveness, and Elegance

In the translation standard of faithfulness, expressiveness, and elegance, Yan Fu put faithfulness first. The translation standard of faithfulness is also the first principle followed by the translator in the process of translation. The meaning of "faithfulness" is that the translation should be faithful to the original text, relying on the original, and reflecting the scientific essence and accuracy of the translation. The translation standard of "faithfulness" requires that the translator not borrow from the topic, add too much personal subjectivity, and avoid the mistranslation, omission, and overtranslation. If the translation fails to meet the principle of faithfulness, the criteria of expressiveness and elegance will lose their value and significance. To achieve faithfulness, the translation should be faithful to the meaning of the original text, but not word for word. "Faithfulness" is not to copy the form of the original text but to adjust the original text according to the grammatical form of the target language, so as to make the translation express the meaning of the original text accurately and completely. The translation standard of "faithfulness" analyzed here is different from Lu Xun's principles of "hard translation" and "dead translation". Specifically, the meaning of "faithfulness" means to be faithful to the content, style, and characteristics of the original text. Faithfulness is a principle that must be followed in the process of translation. The translator should convey the ideas and contents expressed in the original text to the readers of the target language completely and accurately, so that they can correctly understand the contents expressed in the original text through the translation.

The translation standard of "expressiveness" proposed by Yan Fu means that the translation should be coherent and intelligible and conform to the thinking and expression habits of the language. In fact, when Yan Fu talked about "expressiveness", he believed that the translator should read the original text carefully and fully. Due to the grammatical differences between the source and the target languages, the translator should adjust the sentence order accordingly. In this sense, the "expressiveness" advocated by Yan Fu only emphasizes that the translator should understand the original text and make corresponding adjustments according to the syntactic rules. Taking the process of translation from English to Chinese as an example, under the translation standard of "expressiveness", the Chinese translation should be smooth and easy to understand, conforming to the thinking and expression habits of Chinese people. "Expressiveness" is based on "faithfulness". At the same time, there is a dialectical unity between these two. As mentioned above, "faithful" translation is faithful to the original text, but not dead translation or hard translation. Therefore, in translation practice, the translator should first comprehensively understand and analyze the original work, master its content, then adjust the sentence structure of it, and finally express it in idiomatic Chinese. In addition, in translation practice, the translator will come into contact with different types of texts. If the translator wants to make the translation smooth and easy to understand, in line with Chinese expression habits, the translator will need to have a certain understanding of the two cultures, including politics, economy, the humanities, customs, law, and history.

The term "elegance" refers to the translated text's literary grace, closeness to the original text's scope and charm, literary beauty, and pursuit of aesthetic values. Yan Fu put the translation standard of "elegance" at the end, which not only shows that translation should seek "elegance" on the basis of "faithfulness and expressiveness", but also shows that "elegance" is a difficult standard in the process of translation. This criterion is more suitable for literary translation. Especially for prose and poetry, the translation pursues the elegance and harmony of the two languages. In addition, it should be noted that elegance refers to the translation according to the style of the original work and cannot blindly pursue the rhetoric of the translation. "Elegance" is the highest translation standard and realm pursued by translators. The translation standard of elegance requires translators to have profound humanistic qualities, literary accumulations, and cultural heritages, as well as rich life experience, emotional experiences, and life associations.

To sum up, Yan Fu's translation standard of "faithfulness, expressiveness, and elegance" is of great significance in the history of Chinese translation. Through the analysis of this standard, we have a comprehensive understanding of it. The translation standard of "faithfulness, expressiveness and elegance" is an organic whole and runs through the whole process of translation. Such a translation standard proposed by Yan Fu has had a great influence on the translation ideas of later generations and has played an indelible role in promoting the progress of China's translation cause. However, with the development and progress of society, our discussion about translation theory should keep pace with the times. It is necessary to make an in-depth and comprehensive interpretation of the theoretical connotation of "faithfulness, expressiveness, and elegance". It is necessary to actively supplement and enrich its theoretical connotation and promote its further development and progress in translation practice so as to contribute to the study of translation theory in China. In this sense, in future translation practice, we should always be strict with our own translation according to the standard of "faithfulness, expressiveness, and elegance". In addition, with the continuous development of translation theory, we should strive to enrich the connotation of this standard and inject new vitality.

3) The Development and Application of "Faithfulness, Expressiveness, and Elegance"

"Faithfulness, expressiveness, and elegance" is a translation standard proposed by Yan Fu based on his own translation experience. Since it was put forward, it has been accepted and respected by numerous scholars. Yu Dafu(郁达夫, 1896—1945) regarded "faithfulness, expressiveness, and elegance" as the "golden rule" in the field of translation. Lin Yutang believed that "faithfulness, expressiveness, and elegance" had rich meanings. Qian Zhongshu, a great translator in modern and contemporary China, was an admirer of Yan Fu's translation standard. Qian Zhongshu expressed his understanding about the translation standard of "faithfulness, expressiveness, and elegance". He believed that the flavor of the original text should be completely preserved in the process of translation. As a great translation theorist and practitioner in the history of Chinese literary translation in the 20th century, Lu Xun was also deeply influenced by Yan Fu's "faithfulness, expressiveness, and elegance". However, Lu Xun's translation theory placed more emphasis on the social function of translation. Lu Xun put great emphasis on literal translation, that is, word-for-word translation. Although Lu Xun emphasized literal translation, he did not oppose both literal and free translation. On the contrary, Lu Xun believed that free translation could be used to some extent in the process of translation. Therefore, Lu Xun's translation theory was also the application and extension of Yan Fu's "faithfulness, expressiveness, and elegance". Fu Lei(傅雷, 1908—1966) was not only a famous translator in China but also an accomplished artist. He believed that the translator should accurately convey the thoughts, feelings, atmosphere, and sentiment of the original text on the basis of "keeping the syntax of the original text" to the maximum extent. In the process of translation, the translator does not stick to the form, but he is more faithful to the original text and more accurately conveys its thoughts, feelings, and purposes.

In a word, translation is an extremely complex activity. Translation is an irreplaceable mode of intercultural communication between two languages. Translation standard is an important criterion to measure the quality of translation and the core issue of translation theory. Translation standards can not only guide translators on how to create translations in practice but also provide a standard for commentators to appreciate and comment on translated works. Whether it is traditional, empirical, literary translation studies or strictly modern linguistics-based translation studies, the issue of translation criteria is an important one. Chinese translation has a long history, and classic translation theories emerged one after another. Every translation theory still has its merits. Different translation purposes have different translation standards. Therefore, translation is a cultural exchange activity. Based on the analysis of specific problems, according to the development of the times and the needs of readers, and guided by different translation theories, we should make translation generally accepted by people in a popular way.

10.3.3 Lu Xun's Translation Practice

As one of the main leaders of China's literary circles, Lu Xun not only inherited and developed the traditional culture of the Chinese nation but also constantly created new literature based on social needs. In addition, he paid more attention to the dissemination of advanced cultural theories from other countries through translation. According to statistics, Lu Xun's works contained as many as five million words, including about 2.9 million words of translation. He hoped to shock the soul of the people through literary and artistic communication so as to fundamentally transform the national character. Therefore, Lu Xun's selection of translation materials reflected his inner motivation. His translation thoughts embodied the social function of translation.

1) Introduction to Lu Xun

The New Culture Movement, which was launched in the early twentieth century, was a modern ideological and cultural campaign among the Chinese intellectuals, arousing a great shock in the fields of politics, economy, culture, literature, and more. Facing the reality of a volatile society, modern Chinese intellectuals made their hard and self-conscious cultural options. In this period, writers regarded learning from foreign literature as the key to China's reform and innovation. A lot of foreign literature was introduced into China during this period, forming the third climax in the history of Chinese translation. Almost all the new literature relied on foreign literature, especially European literature. The literary translation during May Fourth Movement period played an important role in the promotion of modern Chinese literature and the formation of new cultural ideas. Lu Xun, a great translator then, who held a host of penetrating judgments on translation theories, whose discussion was broad and whose views were original in China, promoted the cultural movement and made great contributions to modern Chinese translation theory and Chinese translation history.

From his early twenties, when he went to Japan, to 1936, when he died, Lu Xun attributed half of his life to translation. In 1938, Cai Yuanpei edited *The Complete Works of Lu Xun*(《鲁迅全集》), the first series of twenty volumes, of which all but the second half were Lu Xun's translation. According to Gu Jun(顾钧), Lu Xun translated two hundred and twenty-four pieces of literature, about three hundred thousand Chinese characters, touching upon over one hundred and ten authors from fifteen countries. His translated works include literary and theoretical ones. In all those works, he did not discuss translation at length, but we can clearly see his translation ideas scattered in his own works or the prefaces written for the books of other people. In his whole life, he made many firsts. Lu was the first to advocate strict literal translation in modern China, unintentionally advancing this theory that the literature of Saint Jerome, the father of the *Latin Bible*, could be translated freely while the *Bible* should be literally translated. Lu was the one who translated the most works in modern history, compared to Lin Shu(林纾, 1852—1924), who had the most translated works in recent history. Lu was the first to introduce Polish and Bulgarian literatures into China, and the first to introduce, together with Zhou Zuoren and Mao Dun, the literatures of Finland, Holland, Romania, and many other countries into China. Lu was the first one to bring a group of new Soviet writers into China and to focus on translating collections of short stories of many foreign writers. He was the first one to design and publish a modern translation literature series. Also, Lu was one of the first translators who made translation highly ideological and the first translator who managed to trigger a literature revolution through translation and then launch a social revolution.

Lu Xun made enormous contributions to Chinese translation theory and practice. When probing into those brilliant ideas now, we can get many insights from his translation thoughts, and they are treasures to the construction of translation theories today.

2) Lu Xun's Translation Stages

The process of Lu Xun's translation can be divided into three stages. The first stage was mainly the translation of scientific and philosophical works from 1903 to 1907. At this stage, he mainly chose new Western literary works reflecting science and technology as translation objects. For example, Jules Verne's famous science fiction novel *Travel to the Moon*. In addition, during this period, Lu Xun also translated many Western philosophical thoughts, such as Freud's psychoanalysis, Rousseau and Montesquieu's democracy, Darwin's evolutionism, and Nietzsche's superman philosophy. The second stage was the translation of literary works from 1907 to 1927. Lu Xun's translation materials were mainly literary works from Eastern Europe, Northern Europe, and Japan. The third stage was the translation of revolutionary literary works from 1927 to 1936. This stage was the peak of his translation career. His selection of translation materials in this period mainly focused on revolutionary literature and proletarian literary theory. An example was Fajeyev's *The Rout*.

3) Lu Xun's Translation Thoughts

In the early days, Lu Xun's translation thought was mainly influenced by Lin Shu (1852—1924), Yan Fu, and other scholars and he did not form an independent and complete system of translation thoughts. Since then, influenced by the background of the times and the reality of social development, Lu Xun's translation thought has successively gone through three stages: literary translation, cultural translation, and politicization of translation, with the latter being the mature stage of the translation thought. No matter what stage he was in, Lu Xun regarded translation as a tool and a weapon to serve the needs of social reality. (1) Literary Translation: Lu Xun believed that translation should be subordinated to the needs of the literary revolution. In this sense, translation not only brought new contents to Chinese literature, but also new expressions. He introduced the advanced Western cultures to China to realize the service for the development of Chinese new literature. Lu Xun encouraged Chinese literary creation by means of translation. In the process, he tried to deconstruct and innovate the Chinese literary language by translating foreign literature. In this sense, he made great contributions to the spread of foreign literature and the development of the modern Chinese language. He believed that translation was not so much about the fluency of the language as its ability to contribute to the development of modern Chinese. Lu Xun advocated that translation be used to reflect the new phenomena, ideas, and things in Chinese society. At the same time, he hoped to promote the development of domestic literature by translating foreign literary works. (2) Cultural Translation: Lu Xun was deeply worried about the malpractice of traditional Chinese culture. He thought that the enslavement mindset of people was caused by the backward feudal culture. To change people's thinking, we must first get rid of this backward feudal culture and rebuild China's new culture. Based on this worry and thinking, he believed that translation should not only represent the true intention of the original text, but also meet the needs of the construction of Chinese new culture and the acceptance of the people. Since the New Culture Movement, Lu Xun had been encouraged to translate foreign works selectively. The purpose of translation was to break the shackles of traditional Chinese culture and create a kind of new culture for the Chinese nation. Therefore, in the process of translation, he advocated turning translation into a dynamic cultural interpretation to meet the needs of advanced culture. To sum up, Lu Xun suggested that translators should be faithful to the style of the original text and spread the advanced Western culture in China so as to innovate Chinese cultural thought. In addition, translators should be cautious in choosing translation materials to adapt to the needs of social development and progress and improve spiritual motivations for changing the social reality. (3) Politicization of translation: The change of Lu Xun's translation thought to politicization was the inherent requirement for our nation and country to undertake the mission of saving the nation from subjugation. Specifically, by means of translation, he introduced advanced foreign political theories and cultural thoughts and used them to innovate the old Chinese culture and change the weak national spirit, so as to provide an ideological basis for the realization of social and political changes, which fully reflected the political purpose of Lu Xun's translation work.

4) Lu Xun's Translation Strategies

During the era of serious social crisis and the trend of the New Culture Movement, Lu Xun employed the foreignization translation method and tried to absorb European lexical and syntactical features, transliterations of Western names, Japanese loan words, etc. Under the circumstances, the purpose of his translation was to introduce more useful nourishments to his countrymen. Elegance of language was not the supreme pursuit for him, but the contents of these works were. He translated for the politics and the ideological reasons. He hoped these works could cure the weakness of the nation and refine its characteristics. For him, this method was the best channel to input new thoughts and enrich the expressions of the Chinese language. Not simply Westernized, they also wanted to build a modern indigenous literature, earning the acceptance and esteem of modern writers in Western literature to initiate this new literary tradition. What should be pointed out is that his literal translation is not just word-for-word translation, as he said: "But there are still conditions to this method, namely, to convey the idea by Chinese expressions and to save the original style and show the significance of the language, which refers to elegance and faithfulness".

Moreover, there were not suitable fairy tales for children to read, so he adapted the literal translation of foreign children's literature to promote the creation of children's literature in China. Lu Xun's literal translation served his political agenda: reconstructing Chinese language and culture and initiating humanity, which can be seen in *The Symbol of Depression*(《苦闷的象征》).

The other strategy he would employ was "stiff translation". Though some translations were more elegant and better than his, Lu Xun was confident that he had not deliberately given the distorted translations, and it was just what he expected that "I refuse to add or delete, and that is one reason I have stuck to 'stiff translations'. Of course, there are bound to be better translators who will not give distorted, stiff, or dead translations. When that occurs, my translations will naturally be replaced".

What should be pointed out is that most of his translated works were retranslations from Japanese into Chinese, as he was good at Japanese. According to Lu Xun, retranslation referred to translating from a translated version into a third language. In his opinion, because people in his time knew no more foreign languages than English and Japanese, it would be quite necessary to get access to literature in other languages such as German, French, Spanish, and Russian through retranslation. Once the retranslated version emerged, translation could fall into disuse. However, we could not do so because it was translated directly from the original version. The translated work could not simply be replaced unless it was not as good as the retranslated one. Besides, retranslation also referred to the repeated translation of a certain original work. Since translation could not be done once and for all, retranslation was needed for the improvement of the translated work. Generally speaking, it was used to combat the prevailing tendency toward false translation at that time. In that way, we can approach many other countries' translated literature, whose faithful and more accurate translations are accessible. That is to say, translation strategies serve to transform the national character of the Chinese people and advance the national culture and the Chinese language. And the advocacy and development of Baihua(白话, Chinese vernacular) in 1925 greatly facilitated Lu Xun's foreignizing translation.

At the outbreak of the movement in 1919, Lu Xun translated *The Dream of a Young Man*(《一个青年的梦》). By the time the National Revolution failed in 1927, his translations had shifted to Soviet revolutionary literature and theory. From the historical perspective, we have analyzed Lu Xun's selection of source texts, translation strategies and methods, and his translation purpose under the social and cultural background, from which we get many suggestions and revelations for current translation. Firstly, he endowed translation with such a high position, which is as important as creation and can be used for mind enlightenment and national salvation through translating revealing literature and art. Besides the social function of translation, it can also improve our Chinese language system by introducing exotic expressions and sentence structures. Considering the importance of translation, we should develop studies on translation as an independent discipline, pushing forward Chinese literature and arts.

There should be a thorough reflection on the vernacular Chinese movement since the

May 4th Movement. Hegel once remarked that Chinese writings were far from perfection and would be a great obstacle to scientific development. Even though the view is still somewhat helpful in our days, it is only a superficial judgment, or only one of Hegel's (1770—1831) assumptions unsupported by solid evidence. It is remarkable that Chinese scholars themselves could have been more radical than Western scholars in their antagonisms against traditional Chinese writing and culture. For example, Shen Xue(沈学, 1543—1610) once said that, "When compared with the West, the Chinese seem to be living in the primitive times of Fu Xi. The crudest form of Chinese culture is Chinese writing." In 1892, Lu Zhuangzhang(卢戆章, 1854—1928) said, "Chinese characters may be the most difficult writings in the world." Tan Sitong(谭嗣同, 1865—1898) said that "Chinese characters are pictographic, thus constructing a real obstacle. I propose to adopt alphabetic writing." In the article *Revolution of Chinese Characters*(《汉字革命》), Qian Xuantong(钱玄同, 1887—1939) argued that "to save our country and revive our nationality in the 20th century, the basic solution is to abolish Confucian schools and to eradicate Daoism, while the most basic task is to abolish Chinese characters that record Confucian discourses and Daoist fallacies". Lu Xun also fiercely advocated the Latinization of Chinese writings: "Those square characters are really the best instrument of obscurantism, ... a tuberculous spot where all fatal viruses are latent, inside the body of the working masses who are struggling in poverty. If the disease is not cured, people will perish." He believed that all Chinese people would have no way out if they continued to use Chinese characters. Wu Zhihui(吴稚晖, 1865—1953) also said that, "the primary strategy to save China today is to abolish Chinese writings". There were also many contradictory views then, such as those of Zhang Taiyan(章太炎, 1869—1936), who expressed in his *A Refutation against Replacing Mandarin Chinese with Esperanto*(《驳中国用万国新语说》) that there was no necessary connection between the cultural advancement and the alphabetization of writings because many Latin countries were also far from advance. Zhang's remark was rather weighty but failed in being too general, thus making him incapable of fending off attacks from the full-scale Westernization cult.

If we expect our descendants to inherit the invaluable treasure of traditional culture, courses of classical Chinese studies have to be emphatically endorsed in elementary and high school education, just like Westerners have emphasized the contents of their classical works in their textbooks. Certainly, supplementary courses of vernacular Chinese should also be considered to conform to people's passively cultivated needs of vernacular Chinese today, though the courses must be secondary to classical Chinese in a specific curriculum arrangement. This is because no special teachings are needed for learning vernacular Chinese. Any person who is good at classical Chinese will be almost immediately capable of self-teaching vernacular Chinese.

In nearly one hundred years ever since the May 4th period (1919), with the turbulence of Westernization, the vernacular Chinese movement has greatly promoted cultural jungle-law education. Ever since the era of the Republic of China, the percentage of classical Chinese readings has dwindled in elementary and middle schools' textbooks. Meanwhile, vernacular Chinese has become dominant. Even when many experts and scholars have called for a review of elementary and middle school textbooks and an appropriate percentage of classical Chinese, classical Chinese is still viewed as an adornment to the mainstream vernacular Chinese. The consequence is that at least three or four generations of Chinese in modern China are basically unable to read or have rarely read original materials that have been passed down from ancient China and that have constituted the main body of our cultural vehicle. Being deprived of directly reading one's own traditional texts, a Chinese may at most rely on the limited translations in plain Chinese to explore the vast treasure of traditional culture. That is how an awe-inspiring gap has come into being. People are justifiably complaining that contemporary Chinese intellectuals are no longer as knowledgeable of both Chinese and Western cultures as those intellectuals during the May 4th era. Yet they have failed to realize that such a thorough knowledge of both Chinese and Western cultures should be credited to the complete mastery of traditional culture among these May 4th intellectuals. And the key to such a complete mastery is their proficiency in classical Chinese. Taking Hu Shi, Lu Xun, and Guo Moruo for example, they were the most radical avant-gardes in the vernacular Chinese movement, and their articles are often quoted as exemplary vernacular Chinese in modern Chinese textbooks. Nevertheless, we all know that these people had unexceptionally received classical Chinese education in the old-style private schools or in reformed schools, rather than being educated with vernacular textbooks.

In recent three hundred years, a major cause of China's backwardness in Western-style scientific theories has been the inadequate research of Chinese grammar. The grammatical systematicity is a full implication, nourishment, and training of consecutiveness in human thought. In China, language teaching should be a further step to improve the sensitivity of young people to the sounds, forms, significations, and especially grammatical patterns of our language. With this new temporal-spatial perspective, they will get a better sense of time and space, thus a clearer sense of consecutiveness. Then, the youth may more lucidly express the subtlest and the most wonderful senses and sensibilities within all humans, especially within Chinese people, so as to construct a better way of thinking. Therefore, native language teachings can be regarded as the most pivotal phase in the founding of a solid linguistic base for modern Chinese.

The destiny of economic globalization will inevitably befall this "shrinking" earth village in the 21st century. If globalization signifies a consequent unification of all the world's languages and writings at the same time, isn't it reasonable for us to be much concerned about a possible demise of the Chinese language? According to experts, at least one thousand languages will perish from Earth in the next century. If there was ever a time when only one language was used, a cultural autocracy would probably dominate the world. Therefore, to save, develop, and broadcast Chinese languages and writings is no longer a mere endeavor to salvage other minorities, but also an active pursuit of specific status on the world stage for all the Chinese people. Therefore, it is a great and historical mission for Chinese scholars and educators to disseminate Chinese languages and culture to the world and introduce to the world what modern China is today.

Questions for discussion:

1. According to what you have learned from this chapter, what do you think is the influence of Buddhism on the Chinese language?

2. What are the characteristics of missionaries' translation in the Late Ming and Early Qing Dynasties in China?

3. Why has the Chinese language not adopted an alphabetic writing? During the application of computer technologies, especially the programming languages, the language we use has somewhat become a practical impediment. Is there any possibility for the Chinese language to shift into an alphabetic writing? Why or why not?

References：

冯天瑜,2003. 利玛窦创译西洋术语及其引发的文化论争[J]. 深圳大学学报(人文社会科学版)(3):98-103.

Feng Tianyu, 2003. Matteo Ricci's translation of western terminology and the cultural controversy it provoked[J]. Journal of Shenzhen University (Humanity and Social Science Edition)(3):98-103.

葛兆光,2000. 十七世纪至十九世纪中国的知识、思想与信仰:中国思想史(第二卷)[M]. 上海:复旦大学出版社.

Ge Zhaoguang, 2000. Knowledge, thought, and belief in China from the seventeenth to the nineteenth century: A history of Chinese thought (Volume 2)[M]. Shanghai: Fudan University Press.

黄河清,2003. 利玛窦对汉语的贡献[J]. 语文建设通讯(74):30-37.

Huang Heqing, 2003. Matteo Ricci's contribution to the Chinese language[J]. Language Building Newsletters (74):30-37.

利玛窦,金尼阁,2001. 利玛窦中国札记[M]. 何高济,王遵仲,李申,译. 桂林:广西师范大学出版社.

马祖毅,等,2006. 中国翻译通史[M]. 武汉:湖北教育出版社.

Ma Zuyi, et al., 2006. A history of translation in China[M]. Wuhan: Hubei Education Press.

孟杰,2005. 明末清初耶稣会传教士来华对我国科技发展的影响[J]. 开封教育学院学报(4):13-14.

Meng Jie, 2005. The impact of Jesuit missionaries coming to China in the late Ming and early Qing Dynasties on the development of science and technology in China[J]. Journal of Kaifeng College of Education(4):13-14.

邱龙虎,2010. 试论传教士对农学"东渐西传"的贡献[J]. 农业考古(3):23-25.

Qiu Longhu, 2010. A pilot study on the contribution of missionaries to the "Eastern and Western Spread" of Agronomy[J]. Agricultural Archaeology(3):23-25.

谭超,2004. 明末清初西学的传入及其对中国教育的影响[D]. 重庆:西南师范大学.

Tan Chao, 2004. The introduction of western learning in the late Ming and early Qing Dynasties and its impact on Chinese ducation[D]. Chongqing: Xinan Normal University.

熊月之,1994.西学东渐与晚清社会[M].上海:上海人民出版社.

Xiong Yuezhi,1994. Western learning and late Qing society[M]. Shanghai: Shanghai People's Press.

杨薇,2008.明末西学的传入对士人知识结构和价值观的影响[D].石家庄:河北师范大学.

Yang Wei,2008. The impact of the introduction of western learning at the end of the Ming Dynasty on the intellectual structure and values of the scholars[D]. Shijiazhuang: Hebei Normal University.

Bassnett S, Lefevere A,1998. Constructing cultures: Essays on literary translation[M]. New York: Multilingual Typesetting.

Cao Guangshun, Yu Hsiao-jung, 2015. Language contact and its influence on the development of Chinese syntax [M]//Wang W S Y, Sun Chaofen. The Oxford Handbook of Chinese Linguistics. Oxford: Oxford University Press.

Dong Y, 2005. Buddhism and its contributions to culture [J]. His Lai Journal of Humanistic Buddhism(6):367−380.

Hall D L, Ames R T, 1987. Thinking through Confucius [M]. New York: State University of New York Press.

Nattier Jan, 2008. A guide to the earliest Chinese Buddhist translations. Tokyo: Soka University, The International Research Institute for Advanced Buddhology.

Norman J,1988. Chinese[M]. Cambridge: Cambridge University Press.

Pulleyblank E G,1995. Outline of classical Chinese grammar[M]. Vancouver: UBC Press.

Salomon R,2007. Gāndhārī in the worlds of India, Iran, and Central Asia [J]. Bulletin of the Asia Institute, 21: 179−192.

Unger U,1987. Grammatik des klassischen chinesisch [D]. Münster: [s. n.].

Zürcher E,1991. A new look at the earliest Chinese buddhist texts [A]. Shinohara K, Schopen C. From Benares to Beijing: Essays on Buddhism and Chinese religion. Oakville: Mosaic Press.

Postscript

Writing this textbook has involved the participation and help of my colleagues and professors from other universities. I am lucky to be surrounded by colleagues at Jiangsu University who have much experience in both translation practice and translation studies. My sincere thanks go to my colleagues at Jiangsu University: associate Prof. Dr. Zhang Lin(张璘) for his contribution of Chapters 2, 5 and 8, associate Prof. Zhang Mingquan(张明权) for his contribution of Chapter 6, associate Prof. Dr. Yao Qin(姚琴) for her contribution of Chapter 7, Prof. Dr. Dai Wenjing(戴文静) for her contribution of Chapter 4, associate Prof. Dr. Zhang Weihua(张伟华) for her contribution of Chapter 9, and associate Prof. Feng Ruizhen(冯瑞贞) who collected source materials for Chapter 8 and participated in proofreading the manuscripts. My special thanks go to Prof. Dr. Zeng Jingting(曾景婷), dean of School of Foreign Languages, Jiangsu University of Science and Technology, who contributed Chapter 10.

I am very indebted to professor Wen Jun(文军), a distinguished translator and translation studies scholar at Beihang University, and Dr. Jonathan Evans, a senior lecturer in translation studies at University of Glasgow, for their valuable prefaces. I would also like to thank Mark Ritchie Celcius Cuento Juachon, an English instructor at Jiangsu University, for his participation in proofreading the manuscripts.

Prof. Dr. Li Chongyue(李崇月)
School of Foreign Languages
Jiangsu University
P. R. China